THE AMERICAN WOOL MANUFACTURE

VOLUME I

LONDON : HUMPHREY MILFORD
OXFORD UNIVERSITY PRESS

THE ORIGINAL SCHOLFIELD CARD

The machine is preserved at the plant of the Davis & Furber Machine Company, North Andover, Massachusetts

THE AMERICAN WOOL MANUFACTURE

BY

ARTHUR HARRISON COLE, PH.D.
ASSISTANT PROFESSOR OF ECONOMICS AND TUTOR IN THE DIVISION OF HISTORY, GOVERNMENT, AND ECONOMICS, HARVARD UNIVERSITY

VOLUME I

CAMBRIDGE
HARVARD UNIVERSITY PRESS
1926

PRINTED AT THE UNIVERSITY PRESS
CAMBRIDGE, MASS., U.S.A.

TO

MY WIFE

PREFACE

AMERICAN industrial experience contains few chapters so rich in material illustrative of our whole industrial advance as the development of the domestic wool manufacture. Not only does that development cover an exceptionally long period in our industrial history, going back as it does to the primitive cloth manufacture of the early colonial days, but it has often undergone in heightened force vicissitudes of circumstance which we have come to recognize as characteristic of American industrial progress. The youthful colonial manufacture of wool was the first such manufacture to incur the displeasure and to come under the prohibitive ban of the British government. It soon felt the abnormal boom and subsequent reaction which accompanied and followed intra-imperial friction and war; and with each later war, it went through a similar but more pronounced disturbance. Again, in the difficulty of securing suitable raw material, of attracting a satisfactory labor supply, and of selecting an advantageous line of production, the wool manufacture on the factory basis was handicapped in a special degree. The process of acclimatization was slow and arduous, and not until the third or fourth decade of the last century could it be said to have been accomplished. Then, in later years came the attainment of really large-scale production, — when individual plants for the working of wool equaled or exceeded those of any other textile industry, — and the amalgamation of separate concerns into sizable combinations or consolidations. With all this progress, too, has gone a particularly close relationship between the domestic industry and the tariff, from the time when the manufacture secured marked attention in the early protectionist movement, including a place of distinction in the "Tariff of Abominations," to that when the wool and woolens schedule, Schedule K, was widely regarded as "the keystone of protection." In short, the evolution of the American wool manufacture may be studied as a particularly clear and sometimes even an exaggerated reflection of the entire domestic industrial advance.

But the history of the domestic wool-manufacturing industry contains treasures of its own. For example, it presents a specially interesting and instructive sequence of industrial forms. This sequence has significance to the student of economic history as much by what it lacks as by what it contains, while the differences between the course of advance here and that which foreign wool manufactures followed give additional flavor. Of the stages of industrial development generally recognized, — household, handicraft, domestic or putting-out, and factory, — two played relatively small part in the American development. The handicraft system, for instance, was represented in the colonial period only by specialized weavers, fullers, and worsted-cloth makers and, in the subsequent half-century, only by the proprietors of combined carding-fulling shops and by a few small-scale woolen-cloth manufacturers. The putting-out system also was of little consequence. Indeed, this latter organization of production, so important in English history, can hardly be said to have raised its head in the United States. On the other hand, the household method of operation had a strikingly long and vigorous career. It was to be found, of course, in the earliest colonial settlements, and with the steady westward expansion of the area of settlement it appeared in a continuing repetition of the eastern experience. Improvement of transportation facilities led in time to a decrease in the domain of household production; and this same force, to be sure, had the effect of shortening the period of household manufacture in the western areas. But not until the frontier had disappeared did the last vestiges of this industrial form also vanish. Again, the household method of production melted into the factory system in a series of interesting steps. The fulling mill, ancillary to family manufacture, acquired the newly-imported carding machine; the carding-fulling shop became the nucleus of factory development; the half-formed factory depended upon household workers for certain aid, as in the weaving of factory-made yarns; the youthful mill took commission work from household producers for one, several, or all the processes of manufacture; until finally the factory was able to make its way without such assistance, producing for a distant, impersonal market. Such a course of development is, as far as I know, unique in industrial history.

With respect to a second point the rise of the domestic wool manufacture is particularly noteworthy, — the character of its technological development. The initial equipment of the American production was altogether English. For the colonial times this is, of course, merely what would be expected. But it is interesting to note that despite the British restrictions of later years upon the exportation of machinery, plans of machinery, and upon the emigration of expert workmen, the movement of importation continued. As far as one can ascertain, the English discoveries and inventions were all brought to this country with greater or less promptitude. Then, — a second feature of note, — the American industry starting with this foreign-made outfit went forward independently of any progress abroad until for the woolen branch of the industry it had secured a complement of power-driven, quasi-automatic apparatus which, at least at the time of its evolution, was superior to contemporary foreign equipment. Of special importance was the revolutionary change in carding machinery, the invention of the so-called "American card" or "carde Américaine," which set this woolen production upon a new course of advance. Striking independent progress in the technological field such as the American wool manufacture showed in its earlier days is, I believe, rarely to be found in domestic experience.

But this early woolen advance has not persisted. Indeed, with it the degree and rapidity of technical progress during more recent decades in this branch of the industry, and the technical situation that has confronted the worsted-cloth manufacture throughout its whole career in the United States, present rather sharp contrasts. As for the former, advances have been progressively less significant as the years have gone by, until recently improvement has chiefly taken the form of refinements upon existing mechanisms, coming either from within the domestic industry or from abroad. In the worsted manufacture, — a manufacture which on a factory basis goes back in this country only about seventy-five years,— a complete equipment of well-developed, quasi-automatic machinery was originally borrowed from abroad, and, since its introduction here, it has undergone scarcely any important improvement in type. To be sure, certain apparatus for use in processes auxiliary to the main manufacturing operations have been introduced and, as in the woolen branch, much progress has been made in the perfection of preëxisting machinery. Moreover, with regard to both woolen and worsted machinery, one should note the recent advent of the automatic loom, — a significant exception to the statements just made. Though this mechanism does in fact promise less for the wool-manufacturing industry than a similar machine has already accomplished for the allied cotton-cloth manufacture, and indeed has made little progress in the woolen branch of the former industry, still it must be viewed as a notable improvement. On the whole, however, marked changes and conspicuous advances have been rare during recent decades in the mechanical equipment of either the woolen or worsted manufactures. In short, there appears to be a tendency toward stability in technological form, — observable, I believe, in other industries as well. Progress undoubtedly will come in the future, but seemingly at a generally slower rate. The Industrial Revolution has here about spent its force.

A third and final noteworthy lesson from the present study, — although scores of lesser features might be mentioned, — is that high quality of output and small-scale production are not always so inseparable as has been usually assumed to be the case. The type of fabric first successfully manufactured in domestic factories was of low quality, represented by the satinet and flannel of the thirties. Then, with improvement in technical equipment and manufacturing ability came the enhancement in quality of the domestic output, — the production of cassimeres, fancy cassimeres, worsted coatings, and the like, — until in more recent decades fabrics of highest grade, rivaling the best foreign goods, have been turned out by American mills. In all this development experience has shown that the most effective domestic production has been that of standardized or semi-standardized cloths of not above medium quality proceeding upon a large-scale basis. But the course of operation in the worsted dress-goods production has in recent years demonstrated that fabrics of the finest quality can be turned out in considerable volume by really large concerns. The small mill and quasi-handicraft methods of fabrication are not necessary for the production of truly fine goods. The peculiar conditions of the market for such goods, exceptionally able management of the enterprises, and a particularly high tariff may be all necessary to the particular result. The development may smack of "growing grapes in Scotland." But at least it is a rather novel situation in American or foreign manufacture.

Two further matters alone deserve place among these introductory remarks: a note of warning and a note of thanks. The former refers to the ever-present problem of the protective tariff and its relation to the ensuing study. This history of the wool manufacture is not intended to cover the tariff question in connection with this particular industry, although unavoidably some aspects of that question are touched upon. Whether or not the tariff upon the manufactures of wool is or ever was justified is not a subject upon which I pretend here to give an adequate discussion. Only in so far as the tariff has been an influence, — one among several, — affecting the course of the industry's development am I concerned with the tariff at all. I trust, however, the tariff question in regard to wool manufactures will be envisioned more clearly as a result of my investigations.

As to the second matter, I must here acknowledge that in the several years during which this history has been in intermittent preparation, I have acquired obligations of greater or less degree in many directions. Men in the trade itself, and divers friends in professional life or at the United States Tariff Commission, have all made contributions, some of which they may see reproduced in the ensuing pages. I can express my specific indebtedness in only a few cases. My study of the wool manufacture was auspiciously begun under direction of Professor Frank W. Taussig, progressed rapidly while I was working with Professor Edwin F. Gay, and bears throughout, I fancy, many imprints of their inspired teaching. My colleagues, Professors Homer B. Vanderblue and Richard S. Meriam, were kind enough to read all or practically all of the manuscript and to give me a host of valuable suggestions. Similarly, in the business world, Mr. John P. Wood was most unsparing of his time and energy when he read the galley proof of this study; and his criticisms were always illuminating. To the machine-builders, Davis & Furber Machine Company, Crompton & Knowles Loom Works, and C. G. Sargent's Sons Corporation, I am indebted for many of the illustrations herein presented. And I would not close without expressing my obligation to Miss Ruth Crandall, upon whose helpful assistance I have leaned in the collection of much statistical and other material and in the detailed preparation of these volumes for the press.

ARTHUR H. COLE

CAMBRIDGE,
November, 1925.

CONTENTS

VOLUME I

PART I

THE COLONIAL PERIOD

PART II

THE ERA OF THE SMALL FACTORY

PART III

THE MATURE FACTORY

VOLUME II

PART IV
INDUSTRIAL MATURITY

PART V

APPENDICES

LIST OF ILLUSTRATIONS

VOLUME I

Plates

Figures

VOLUME II

PLATES

FIGURES

THE AMERICAN WOOL MANUFACTURE

VOLUME I

PART I

THE COLONIAL PERIOD

CHAPTER I

THE DOMESTIC PRODUCTION

Introduction

One of the characteristics of the wool manufacture which has differentiated it from the manufacture of most other textile fibers has been its intimate connection, in temperate climates, with economically undeveloped regions. In the period when commercial operations both within and between countries were narrowly confined, the substantially self-dependent families of such primitive communities spun the wool of their own sheep and wove it into cloth. In the remote or economically poor regions of the world similar phenomena may be observed even at the present day, although of course the improved transportation facilities and the eagerness of the industrially advanced countries to exchange manufactured goods for the crude products of the backward areas have narrowly restricted the scope of such household activities.

Now this peculiarity of the wool manufacture in so many parts of the world has been of particular importance in the American development. Primitive conditions occasioned the early appearance of household wool-working in the colonies; and the long-continued movement of settlement was responsible for the persistence of household wool manufacture in some parts of the country for many decades, — until the frontier had disappeared. Moreover, even today, in the most secluded hamlets of the agricultural and lumbering districts, family production with the spinning wheel and handloom may be found, though to be sure this form of production is essentially a relic of bygone days. For the colonial period, however, the characteristic of wool-working above mentioned was of special significance. From the earliest years, even through the Revolution, it played the dominant part in the history of the wool manufacture.

The beginnings of the wool manufacture in this country came with the earliest settlements. Of the Pilgrim Fathers, William White, Robert Cushman, and Richard Masterson are said to have been wool-combers or carders;[1] then, in 1643, some twenty or more families from the cloth-manufacturing section of Yorkshire, England, came to reside in the town of Rowley, in Massachusetts Bay, where they attracted attention by their proficiency in the production of woolen cloths.[2] This settlement in Rowley is also noteworthy in that here for the first time in this country a fulling mill, thereafter the usual complement of the household production, was set up, the gearing having been brought from England.[3] But such details of the commencement in manufacture are of more interest to the antiquarian than to the student of the industry in its larger aspects. We need note merely that the growth of the earlier colonies and the establishment of additional ones were accompanied by the extension of the wool manufacture on the household system and the distribution of fulling mills through the country, even to some extent in the more southerly settlements. The net result was similar for large sections of the country, — a dominant family manufacture. Moreover, the elapse of decades produced little change in the typical situation. Indeed, a close survey of the development in the colonies reveals no marked alteration in conditions within this manufacture between the earlier and the later periods of colonial history. We can proceed at once, therefore, to a description of the methods and types of colonial production as they obtained in the latter years of the colonial era, — the era for which more adequate information is available. We may well fix upon the years around 1760 as the date for analysis, since the typical colonial development was by that time as fully advanced as at a later date, and was as yet undisturbed by influences such as came with the popular opposition to the British tax measures, and with the excitement precursory to the Revolutionary War.

[1] Bishop, *History of American Manufactures*, i, 301. (Hereafter referred to as Bishop.)

[2] Weeden, *Economic and Social History of New England*, p. 177. (Hereafter referred to as Weeden.)

[3] Johnson, *Wonder Working Providence of Zion's Savior in New England*, p. 130.

1. *Wool Supply.*

Sheep were not known to the native American Indians, and the wool used by the English and other colonists came from animals of imported stock. Just what was the breed of these first animals is not definitely known;[1] but whatever their original type, they inevitably deteriorated under the harsh natural conditions and the general neglect of those early days. Usually unprovided with adequate shelter from the rigors of the New England winter, and allowed to breed promiscuously, the sheep yielded a wool which eventually lost all pretense to fineness; nor could improvement through imported stock be secured, for in 1660 the British Parliament forbade the exportation of sheep from England. Down to the time of the Revolution the domestic wool was evidently of indifferent grade, being characterized as "of good strength, in the quality neither fine nor coarse."[2] Comments of contemporaries, in fact, seem rather to stress the poor quality of the colonial fleeces. "The wool of our northern plantations," wrote the Englishman, Douglass, in 1755, "is of as good a staple (length), but coarser than the English wool; and further south in our colonies, the wool becomes coarser . . . as in our sugar islands; therefore the plantations are not capable of rivalling England in fine woollens."[3] Phineas Bond, writing after the Constitution had been adopted, expressed somewhat similar sentiments. "The propagation of sheep" had not been attended with much success, he said, "the climate not being propitious." "What little wool is raised," he added, "is of a very ordinary quality and can only be applied to the coarser manufactures."[4] Even Hamilton was in doubt as to the future of the domestic wool culture. While hoping that the development of the woolen manufacture would stimulate better-

[1] Wright, *Wool Growing and the Tariff* (p. 2), whom I follow quite generally in regard to the wool supply for the industry in every period. (Hereafter referred to as Wright.) The English unimproved sheep seems to have been the one most generally brought over, though the Texel breed probably came to the New Netherlands from the mother country.

[2] Wright, p. 11.

[3] *British Settlements*, ii, 265. Cf. Burnaby, *Travels through North America*, p. 137.

[4] American Historical Association *Reports*, 1896, i, 632.

ment in the flocks of the country, he could see no clear prospect of such advance: "It is yet a problem," he says, "whether our wool be capable of such a degree of improvement as to render it fit for the finer fabrics." [1] However, when the conditions of manufacture in the colonial industry are taken into account, the reasons for this backwardness are apparent. The time was not yet ripe for attention to be drawn to the circumstances of wool production.

Yet, in the meantime, a status of domestic wool-growing such as that just pictured and the practical absence of the importation of wool in the colonial period [2] inevitably placed an important physical limitation upon the character of the wool manufacture. At best, cloths of none but medium to coarse quality could be produced. Yet, as has been said above, the lack of an adequate market restrained improvement of the country's flocks. A vicious circle existed, escape from which was some decades in coming.

As to the quantity of wool, there is conflicting evidence. An Englishman, writing in 1765, made the pessimistic estimate that "all the wool in America is not sufficient to make Stockens for the Inhabitants;" and somewhat later, similar sentiments, perhaps derived indirectly from this man Colden, were expressed by Phineas Bond and by Lord Sheffield.[3] Yet there are no com-

[1] Hamilton's "Report on Manufactures," in Taussig, *State Papers on the Tariff*, p. 99. The eighteenth-century production of wool in England, to be sure, contained no wool comparable with the present-day merino; but if the views of contemporaries are to be accepted, an appreciable, if not a marked, difference in quality existed between the British and the colonial clips.

[2] Winthrop in his *Journal* (p. 323) speaks of the importation of wool in 1643; but the export of wool, as well as of sheep, from England was prohibited after 1660 by the British government.

[3] Colden is quoted in Beer, p. 79. For Bond, see American Historical Association *Reports*, 1896, p. 632, where he doubts if the quantity of wool raised in the country prior to the Revolution was enough to have "supplied the inhabitants of the country with their winter stockings." Lord Sheffield (*Observations*, 1784, p. 25) makes the assertion a bit stronger. Quoting a Mr. Otis, he asserted that there was "not enough wool raised in all America to make each person in it one pair of stockings." The similarity of these various expressions, especially the use of stockings as a standard of measurement, makes one suspicious as to the independence of the three estimates.

plaints in colonial documents of a shortage in supply, at least after the early years of settlement; and the meagerness of importations during this period seems to argue to the same effect. I am inclined to the latter view. It seems very doubtful if the colonial manufacture was restricted in scope by reason of deficient raw material supply. Where the number of sheep existing at the time is known to have been small as in the southern colonies, other influences controlled the situation, dictating not only the meager sheep husbandry but also the procurement of wool-cloth supplies in large measure otherwise than through domestic production.

2. *Technical Equipment.*

The mechanical equipment upon which the colonial wool-workers had to rely for aid in the manufacture of wool cloths naturally reflected the situation in the wool-manufacturing technique of the mother country. No Industrial Revolution had yet wrought havoc with the old, simple methods of production in England, — though by 1760 this Revolution was beginning to exert its powerful influence. The colonial settlers had brought over with them the implements then used in many parts of England in the household production of wool fabrics, or at best those employed by the handicraftsmen in the more extensive wool-working regions of Yorkshire or the West of England. With the exception of the more elaborate fulling mill, these comprised merely a few hand tools. The processes and the technical equipment used in them require examination.

After the wool had been tub-washed and thereby scoured of its dirt and wool-grease as thoroughly as the limited chemistry of the times permitted, it was prepared for the spinning wheel upon hand cards, or, if worsted yarn were desired, upon hand combs. Supplies of both these instruments were imported largely from England throughout the colonial period, although toward the end they began to be manufactured here. Hand cards consisted of small rectangular pieces of leather, backed with board and provided with a handle, through which at regular intervals wires with slightly bent ends had been stuck. The process of carding itself, as with the present carding machines, had for its purpose the straightening and intermixing of the wool fibers. A small quantity of the scoured wool was combed and rubbed between the hand cards until the individual fibers had been laid somewhat parallel and fibers of the various lengths mixed in fairly uniform manner. Such straightening and intermixture promised to give the tensile strength and the homogeneity necessary to the spinning of satisfactory yarn. When the intermixture was deemed by the carder to be sufficient, the movement of one of the hand cards was reversed and the wool cleared from the wires of both cards, condensed in the shape of a loose roll ready for elongation and twisting in the spinning operation.[1]

Hand combs, though also hand tools for working the loose wool, differed materially in construction from these hand cards. They were of somewhat similar form, but were made more largely of metal, were stouter, and were equipped with such heavy and well-tapered wire that the protruding points — fewer in number — resembled spikes rather than pins. The aim and method of use likewise differed. Not only was greater emphasis placed upon the parallelization of the longer fibers, but now the shorter fibers must be removed from the wool and the two products, long and short pieces, separately delivered. To accomplish these ends, one of a pair of combs was secured upon a hook on the wall or held high with one hand; a small quantity of wool was thrust well into its teeth; and the other comb was drawn through this mass of fibers with a repeated downward motion, the whole batch from time to time being replaced on the upper comb and reworked. Finally there remained in the teeth of the upper comb only the longer, paralleled fibers — the "top" — which were carefully removed in a loose form ready for the

[1] Bramwell gives this description of hand-carding: "A card . . . was more like a large brush, and this brush was composed of fine wire bristles, which leaned at a given angle instead of being straight. Two such brushes or cards were used together by the operator, having one in each hand; tufts of wool were placed on them, and by repeatedly stroking one brush against the other, the tufts of wool were straightened and lay amongst the wire bristles, which then required only to be taken carefully away from the card without disturbing the smoothness of the wool." Bramwell, *The Wool-Carders' Vade Mecum*, 1881, p. 130.

spinner; while in the teeth of the working comb clung only the shorter staples — the "noil" — which could then be discarded.[1] Proper manipulation of hand combs required greater strength and skill than that of hand cards. Accordingly, while hand-carding was usually cared for by the women and older children of the family, hand-combing was primarily the province of adult male workers, and, by reason of the skill involved, usually of specialized workers.

The spinning of wool was generally done upon the hand spinning wheel, though the older distaff and spindle were not unknown to the earliest colonists. This operation fell commonly to the charge of the women and older girls of the family, and, though tedious, was a relatively simple affair with relatively simple equipment. The old spinning wheel, still frequently to be seen among relics of the colonial period, consisted essentially of but a spindle, similar to the one which had been used in the earlier distaff and spindle process, made to revolve more evenly and rapidly by means of the cord or band passing around it and over a large wheel that could be turned by hand. The "carding" or "top," according to whether woolen or worsted yarn was being spun, was held in the spinner's left hand and attached to the spindle. By an outward movement of this hand, the slubbing or unformed yarn was elongated to the desired extent. At the same time a stroke of the spinner's other hand set the big wheel in motion and thus caused the spindle to revolve at a more or less rapid rate, as deemed necessary; and by this means the binding twist was put into the yarn. Subsequently, by a change in position of the spinner's left hand, the completed product could be wound upon the spindle.[2]

For weaving, not only was the equipment somewhat more complex, but the strength and skill necessary for its operation were

[1] The terms "top" and "noil" have been retained in the modern worsted terminology, being applied to the corresponding semi-manufactured products of the machine industry. The shorter fibers, or noils, could always be used in the manufacture of woolen yarns.

[2] The wheel with the foot-pedal for driving the spindle, though employed in flax spinning, was not used for spinning wool, presumably because of the greater need of a delicate touch in working the latter.

greater. The loom was a relatively large and heavy apparatus, something of a fixture in the shed or outhouse; and, with the beams, heddles, batten, and shuttle, it was a rather complicated device. Moreover, the colonial looms were usually quite crude affairs, being built frequently by the local carpenter, if they were not indeed the product of the home workbench. Some improvement in the character of the loom, to be sure, seems to have been made during the colonial period, but there was no change in its essential parts. Even the fly shuttle, invented by John Kay of Bury, England, in 1733, was not employed to any considerable extent in this country until after the Revolutionary War.[1] It is narrated, moreover, that even as late as 1793 a manufactory of this device, begun in Philadelphia, was short-lived for want of encouragement and support, and moved to Nova Scotia.[2] The operation of the early machine or implement, however, called for so much energy and skill that usually the labor of men was required. Frequently, too, the situation gave rise to a body of male workers who devoted themselves wholly or chiefly to this task. These men worked at the homes of the customers or in their own shops, weaving up the homespun yarn into cloths of the customers' specifications. Weaving was, accordingly, less exclusively a household operation than were the preceding stages in manufacture.

Woolen cloth produced under such conditions, even though woven by handicraft workers, must have been rather an uneven and surely a rather unsightly fabric. For firmness of texture and for good appearance, much would depend upon the finishing operations. Fortunately for the colonial household industry, and apparently as a result of these very conditions of household production, the essential process of fulling had early come into the hands of men who gave their time and efforts chiefly, if not solely, to this operation.[3] Mention has already been made of the establishment of a fulling mill in Rowley, Massachusetts, in 1643.

[1] Clark, *History of Manufactures in the United States*, 1607–1860, p. 160. (Hereafter referred to as Clark.)

[2] Bishop, i, 333.

[3] Sometimes flour-milling or other power work was combined with cloth fulling in the water-driven mill.

Contesting it in priority was one in Salem.[1] Following these, mills were erected at Roxbury in 1657, Dorchester in 1659, and Watertown in 1662.[2] The erection of mills in the New England colonies thereafter becomes too rapid and widespread to follow closely.[3] In other colonies, the introduction was seemingly not so early, although information concerning this development is not complete. For example, the first mention of one in Virginia relates to 1692, and the first Pennsylvania mill was set up in Darby about 1698. As to total numbers erected in the colonies as a whole, no good estimate is possible. Statistics for a few sections of the country, however, are suggestive. In Philadelphia County, Pennsylvania, twelve were reported in 1760,[4] while Worcester County, Massachusetts, had between thirty and forty in 1793, and Middlesex County, twenty-four in 1796.[5]

The fulling of cloth prior to the introduction or without the employment of the fulling mill was accomplished in a peculiarly inefficient, almost indifferent manner. The most usual among such methods was to soak the fabric thoroughly in warm soapsuds and then beat it with sticks upon a flat surface such as a wooden floor. Another method, in the nature of a pastime similar to a corn-husking bee, was for the family and its guests to draw their chairs into a circle on the kitchen floor about which the soapy cloths were kicked around and around by the bare feet of the company.[6] Seemingly no considerable attention under

[1] Weeden, p. 177.

[2] *Ibid.*, pp. 200, 203.

[3] A partial list for New England is as follows:

1662	and 1686 Watertown.	1687	Newbury, Mass.
1673	Andover.	1689	the Ballards, Mass.
1675	Ipswich.	1693	New London, Conn.
1676	Salem.	1700	Stamford, Conn.
1681	Dedham.	1706	Colchester, Mass.
1682	North Andover.	1707	Guilford, Conn.
1686	East Hartford, Conn.	1709	Dorchester, Mass.
1687	Barnstable, Mass.		

Weeden, pp. 203, 306, 394; and Bagnall, *History of the Textile Industries*, pp. 237, 310.

[4] Bishop, i, 377.

[5] Bishop, i, 420.

[6] S. N. D. North, "The New England Wool Manufacture," in Davis, *New England States*, i, 191–192.

either of these methods was given to the evenness or exact degree in which the fulling or shrinkage took place.

The mechanical fulling carried on in the fulling mills, however, could devote care to the proper treatment of the fabrics. The principles of this machine fulling followed closely those of the hand or household process. The cloth was kept thoroughly wet with soapy water and was subjected to pressure or repeated beatings. The fulling stocks where the operation really occurred consisted of a large wooden box standing on end and with one side partly open. In the upper part of the space within the box were two rollers, and at the bottom was a trough filled with the soapy water. The piece of cloth, tied end to end, was passed between the rollers and was drawn up from the water as, driven by the water-wheel of the mill, these rollers revolved. Originally only the pressure of the rollers seems to have supplied the force given by the sticks or feet in the household process; but later wooden hammers were added, these and the rollers now being both actuated by water power. The rollers, raising the cloth regularly from the trough, squeezed the larger part of the water from the fabric, and by pressure brought about a closer consolidation of the constituent fibers and yarns; and the hammer-strokes falling upon the cloth yet damp aided in the intimate intermeshing of these component parts. The fuller's contribution lay in the knowledge, gained from experience, of the mixture of soap and water — later of fullers' earth as well — that should most advantageously be employed, and of the proper speed and duration of the shrinking operation. He could see to it that the cloth fulled evenly, and as thoroughly as possible without affecting the strength of the fabric. Unquestionably better cloths were secured through the services of a well-conducted fulling mill.[1]

With this highly important operation of fulling, the proprietor of the fulling mill usually combined other finishing operations,—

[1] Another method of fulling is described in Smith, *History of Berkshire County*, i, 471. It was a sort of rubbing process: "the cloth was placed in a long wooden box, a stream of suds was poured in, and the pieces of cloth were pushed forward and back under heavy blocks, which were grooved and made to move alternately over the cloth." This is, as far as I know, a unique method. It had no counterpart in more recent technology.

shearing and sometimes dyeing. Such additional treatment was not considered necessary for all cloths, nor was the practice of various consumers the same for similar fabrics. Frequently, moreover, the dyeing was carried out in the households, especially if the cloth were dyed "in the wool."[1] Proper dyeing, however, is a process calling for considerable knowledge of the dyeing materials and methods and for considerable skill in the handling of the fabrics while in the tub or vat; and both these aptitudes were to be gained in colonial times only as the fruit of long practice. Consequently, all the finer goods were dyed by the fuller, and this operation, as well as that of fulling itself, became largely separated from the household. Again, shearing was a difficult affair. The purpose of this process was to clip evenly the ends of wool fibers which projected from the woven woolen fabric.[2] In the case of face fabrics, such as broadcloths, a much greater number of evenly clipped fiber ends were required than were thrown up by the earlier processes. Shearing was then preceded by a process called napping. Hand cards similar to those used in carding proper were drawn repeatedly over the surface of the cloth, fiber ends being scratched up from the body of the fabric. Shearing itself was accomplished by means of hand shears, — merely large scissors. The cloth was laid out upon a flat table and the shears passed over the surface of the fabric in such a manner that a constant space was maintained between the cutting edge of the shears and the body of the cloth. Obviously this operation demanded peculiar skill. Therefore, it was a process rarely, if ever, found in the household.

3. *Industrial Organization.*

In the foregoing description of manufacturing processes, the features of industrial organization under colonial conditions have

[1] That is, if the wools which went into the making of the fabric were dyed while still in the form of loose fleece. Dyestuffs were peddled about the countryside for use in the household dyeing tubs.

[2] Worsted fabrics did not require shearing. The greater care with which the wool fibers were laid parallel in the preparatory process resulted in a much smoother yarn, and so in a cloth of which the surface was relatively free from protruding fiber ends. To secure an even clearer face, worsted cloths might, and in modern manufacturing practice universally are, also sheared.

in a measure been anticipated. For the woolen-cloth production, the primary factor was the household. Here the wool was scoured, carded, spun, frequently woven, and occasionally fulled. As might be expected, the processes which were customarily confined to members of the household alone were those for which the strength and skill of the women and older children were adequate. Where masculine strength or special dexterity was demanded, the process gravitated to some degree into the hands of special groups of workers. Sufficient consideration has already been given the most numerous and most important variety of specialized workers, the fuller and cloth finisher. Beyond these, the only important group of such workmen connected with woolen-cloth production was that of the weavers. Then, the other, the worsted-cloth branch of the industry, supported the special worsted workers, while in addition there were minor types, some but indirectly connected with the wool manufacture proper, such as the card-makers and comb-makers.

Men who carried on the trade of weaving as a distinct vocation were among the early arrivals in the colonies. Guest states that great numbers of woolen and worsted weavers, who had widely adopted Puritanism, were driven from England by the persecutions of Laud and his followers, and that some of these went to Massachusetts Bay.[1] Other waves of immigration brought representatives of this handicraft, men who had learned the trade in Yorkshire or Suffolk and who continued to follow it in their new homes. William Rix, "a weaver," is mentioned in Boston records as early as 1640.[2] Johnson, writing in 1652, mentions weavers as one group of noteworthy handicraft workers.[3] In Windsor, Connecticut, an inventory of 1669 showed "yarne at the weaver's" and in Virginia, a year earlier, one William Parker is mentioned as owning and operating a loom in York County, receiving much encouragement from the county for his quasi-public service.[4] With the spread of settlement the weaver became

[1] *Cotton Manufacture*, p. 41.
[2] Weeden, p. 213.
[3] *Wonder Working Providence*, p. 209.
[4] Weeden, p. 305; Bruce, *Economic History of Virginia*, ii, 470.

a necessary member of every community. Sometimes, moreover, the business of weaving reached no mean proportions. In 1684 a man at New London, Connecticut, possessed four looms and tackling, besides a silk loom;[1] a Virginia weaver bought a hundred-acre plantation in 1686;[2] and in 1741 Widow Bayley advertised in the *Pennsylvania Gazette* to sell six looms, twisting and warping mills, and several servant weavers.[3] Inasmuch, too, as apprenticeship was frequently followed in this trade, it is apparent that here again, as in the character of implements employed in wool-working, a bit of old Yorkshire had been transplanted practically unmodified to the new country.

These handicraft weavers may further be divided into two general groups. One sort, probably confined to the more populous settlements, maintained a central shop to which his customers brought their yarn to be woven. Widow Bayley's late husband was evidently of this type. Such too would be the case when, as occasionally happened, a fuller set up a weave-shop in conjunction with his mill.[4] The other type was the itinerant weaver. The prosperous farmer who desired a somewhat better grade of fabric than he or members of his family could produce, or families which had no weavers in the household, employed this sort of workman, who traveled the countryside weaving up the season's cloth requirements for his patrons. These latter workers, though infrequently mentioned in colonial records, must have played an increasingly important rôle in the wool manufacture of the times. In certain areas they surely were essential. Thus, in New York, the practice of the later colonial period, it seems, was customarily to requisition the services of such workmen. Gov-

[1] Weeden, p. 305.

[2] Bruce, *Economic History of Virginia*, ii, 470.

[3] Clark, p. 163, note.

[4] William Simmons of Williamsburg, Virginia, a fuller, advertised in 1774: "I advise the Publick, that I have two Looms at Work that weave five Quarter Yard wide Cloth . . . My price for Weaving is one shilling a Yard, Fulling, Dying, Dressing, etc. one shilling more, for common Cloth, but dearer for live Colours. Those persons that dye their Cloth in Grain have it done much cheaper; all mixed Cloths require Nothing more than Fulling and Dressing, which are done at a moderate Price" (*Documentary History of American Industrial Society*, ii, 326).

ernor Moore, writing to the Lords of Trade in 1767 and describing the household system as he saw it on his "last Tour," — where "every house swarms with children, who are set to work as soon as they are able to Spin and Card," — added the following: "As every family is furnished with a Loom, the Itinerant Weavers who travel about the Country, put the finishing hand to the Work."[1] To be sure, these two general types of handicraftsmen merely represent broad classifications. Occasionally a given workman would seem to straddle the two classes, as when a weaver with a town shop went on a country tour during a dull season, or perhaps customarily in the summer months. Such was evidently the case of the Rhode Island workman, spoken of by North, whose operations took him "out among the larger farmers working his trade of weaving, while his wife carried on the business of weaving at home, having a number of apprentices."[2]

In the southern colonies, the form of household production for woolen goods was subject to minor variations, — in so far as wool fabrics were produced at all in the South, — due to the presence of indentured servants and slaves and to the existence of the plantation system. Colonial records in their references to indentured servants who had run away give suggestions as to the number of such people engaged in the cloth manufacture. Weavers are often mentioned, — though of course some allowance must be made for other textile productions, — and sometimes a fuller or "clothier" is sought among the fugitives.[3] There are evidences also of the occasional use of slaves for spinning or weaving. The plantation system, moreover, encouraged the establishment of workshops for cloth production with perhaps two or three workers, though seemingly goods for slaves' garments were about all that was attempted. The account books

[1] *Documentary History of New York*, i, 734.

[2] North, "The New England Wool Manufacture," published in installments in the *Bulletin of the National Association of Wool Manufacturers*, 1899–1900; 1899, p. 125. (Hereafter referred to as North, *Bulletin*.)

[3] A representative case is that of a fugitive who was a "fuller by trade and will brag largely of his knowledge in dyeing cloths of two colors, one side scarlet, the other blue" (New Jersey *Archives*, Newspaper Extracts, v, 552).

for a year or two with respect to a typical workshop of this sort, that of George Washington, are extant, showing that considerable manufacture on behalf of his family was carried through.[1] Even as plantation agriculture was carried on somewhat differently from the manner of northern subsistence farming, so the household system of cloth manufacture was subject to modification in the same environment, — without, however, losing its essential character.[2]

In the worsted trade, the other chief province of the handicraftsman, two types of organization can also be distinguished. In one form, the work had a wholly or almost wholly professional character. Both wool combing and worsted weaving were skilled operations, and apparently not to be undertaken by the unpracticed household workers. Weeden states that he found no mention of worsted combs in either traders' or household inventories;[3] and, considering the minor character of this manufacture, the references to worsted weavers are frequent. Sometimes these two operations of combing and weaving were carried on by one man or under his supervision. The case of John Cornish of Boston may be quoted. When Cornish died in 1695, the appraisal of his estate contained entries of "woosted," "white yarne," two pair of combs, four looms and tackling, and two dye furnaces.[4] In these cases, however, the yarn spinning was not always confined to the shop of the worsted worker. Seemingly, a part of his requirements was usually cared for in his own household, but some of the spinning might be put out on commission. One John Wareing of Salem was loaned money by the town in 1685 "to pay spinners;"[5] and worsted-spinning rates are quoted

[1] These accounts are reprinted in part in *Documentary History of American Industrial Society*, pp. 319–325. They cover the years 1767 and 1768. That the operations of this shop were wholly for the family or plantation's consumption may be gathered from the heading of the second year's accounts: "Spun and Wove in the year 1768 for my own use."

[2] It may be borne in mind that, as intimated above, the household manufacture of woolen cloth was substantially less widespread in the southern than in the northern colonies: see below, pp. 24–26.

[3] Weeden, p. 392.

[4] *Ibid.*, p. 389. He also operated a fulling mill.

[5] Abbott, *Women in Industry*, p. 23.

for Pennsylvania as early as 1698.[1] However, it may be noted that household work of this latter sort was merely supplementary to the handicraftsman's labors — quite different from the situation in the woolen-cloth production.

The other form of worsted manufacture approached more closely that of the primarily household woolen industry. Here the direction of the work was in the hands of the household, and some of the actual manipulation was done by its members. For preparation of the "top," assistance was indeed needed of handicraftsmen, itinerary wool-combers, combing at the home of their patrons. Evidence of this practice is sufficient, though not overabundant. Worsted yarn appears occasionally in the inventories of colonial estates;[2] while a specially clear case pertains to the Hazards of Rhode Island: In 1778 Thomas Hazard in his account book credited one Valentine Ridge with certain sums:[3]

> By combing at my house 40 lbs. of wool
> By combing at thy house 33¾ lbs. of wool.

Seemingly the combed wool in such cases was thereafter spun by the women in the household; and, finally, an itinerant weaver would work the yarn into calimancoes, tammies, or other worsted cloths upon his employer's loom, or at his own shop.[4] Such an organization of production, however, undoubtedly was much less

[1] Thomas, *History of Pennsylvania*, 1698, p. 36. Thomas's reference to women's work in this connection is too entertaining to be omitted. He has been speaking of the exorbitant rates of women's wages, due to the fact that women "are not very numerous." "They have for Spinning either Worsted or Linen, Two Shillings a Pound, and commonly for Knitting a very Course pair of Yarn Stockings, they have half a Crown a Pair; moreover they are usually Marry'd before they are Twenty-Years of Age, and when once in that Noose, are for the most part a little uneasie, and make their Husbands so too, till they procure them a Maid Servant to bear the burden of the Work, as also in some measure to wait on them too."

For other worsted spinning rates, see Abbott, *Women in Industry*, p. 23; Clark, p. 157.

[2] Weeden, pp. 306, 392.

[3] Hazard, *College Tom*, p. 95. However, this phenomenon may have been peculiar to the Revolutionary period.

[4] As early as 1657, a worsted weaver of Boston devised two looms in his will (Weeden, p. 391). Thomas in his *History of West New Jersey*, 1698, speaks of worsted weavers (p. 17) and Clark gives weaving rates for worsted weaving (p. 157). See also Hazard, *College Tom*, pp. 97–103.

common than that in which everything was left to expert artisans. I am inclined to believe it distinctly rare throughout the colonial period.

In sum, then, there was already a difference of industrial form in the two branches of the wool manufacture, woolen and worsted-cloth production. In so far as the worsted-cloth manufacture was prosecuted — and we shall find subsequently that it was quantitatively much inferior to woolen-cloth production — it was more particularly a handicraft affair. Chiefly a town industry, it was dominated by specialized workers. The woolen-cloth manufacture, on the other hand, was primarily a household function. To be sure, at no time except perhaps at the very commencement of a new settlement was there a pure and unqualified household system of production of wool cloths in this country. The professional weaver and the fulling mill appeared early, — whenever a settlement had passed the pioneer stage,— and by 1760 production with such assistance was apparently the commonest form. Still the household system of this modified type was the dominant method. In this branch of the industry, there was no manufacture on a distinctly handicraft system. Moreover, it may be noted that throughout the colonial period forms of production other than household and handicraft were practically unknown. References to a real "putting-out" system of production are so scant as to mark them as distinct exceptions;[1] and not until the disturbances following the Stamp Act

[1] I have found for the woolen manufacture in the pre-Revolutionary period only two references to a system more advanced than the handicraft. Bagnall in his *Textile Industries of the United States* (hereafter referred to as Bagnall) says of Thomas Hazard of South Kingstown, Rhode Island, that "there are indications that he employed handloom weavers as early as 1750 in weaving cloths, linen, woolen, and mixed, for sale in his store" (p. 283). And Clark makes the general statement that "old account books show that merchants gave out flax, cotton, and wool to the country people to spin and weave for them" (p. 163). As will appear later, when the matter of trade in domestic wool fabrics is discussed, the presumption is against any extended development of such systems of production. I am inclined to think that as far as wool manufacture is concerned, production for merchants was for their own needs, details of which not improbably became mixed with the ordinary store accounts.

At the time of the Revolutionary War, woolen spinners working, it seems, upon order became important, at least in certain communities. For example, the towns and accompanying the Revolutionary War did establishments arise that even ventured to call themselves factories. For this woolen branch, then, — which was in fact so predominantly important as really to give character to the whole wool manufacture, — the period until 1760 was unquestionably the era of household production.

4. *Extent and Quality of Colonial Production.*

An exact measurement of the quantity of wool fabrics produced in the colonies at any one time, even in a single colony, is of course impossible from a lack of statistical data; but one may hope to determine roughly the proportion for the country as a whole, which domestic production, based primarily upon the household system, bore to the total consumption; whether this proportion was the same among various sections of the population; whether there was any change in this proportion between the earlier and the later colonial periods; and, finally, what types and qualities of fabric were generally manufactured. In arriving at conclusions upon these points, one must tread warily among the opinions of hostile governors, of colonists who feared to awake opposition of the English government or of English merchants, and of observers who in speaking had in mind only a section of the country.[1]

of East Greenwich, Connecticut, and of Chelmsford, Massachusetts, during the war fixed the price or wage for such work, in the latter case with the specific entries, "Spinning, Woolen warp, taking it home" and "spinning by the week from home" (Weeden, p. 790; Allen, *History of Chelmsford*, pp. 173–174). These rates apparently referred to the labor of women, the rate of "spinning by the week" coming next to and being at about the same figure as "Housework by the week." It may be added that the mention of "woolen warp" suggests the employment of such workers upon the manufacture of warp yarns alone. Warp yarns receive greater strain in the process of weaving, and hence must be somewhat better spun than filling yarns. Yet whatever the frequency with which this phenomenon occurred in the Revolutionary period and whatever the scope of the work, I am inclined to think the occurrence a result of the peculiar conditions of the war years, especially the increased dependence upon household production.

[1] Nearly any view of the extent of colonial manufacture can be argued from individual statements of contemporaries. Occasionally conflicting estimates for the same sections of the country and within a few years of one another in time may be found. Even reports of the Board of Trade, when not prejudiced, were likely to be

The household production of wool cloth will be the starting point in this discussion; and here we may at once take cognizance of certain factors which throughout a long period of our history markedly affected such production. Chief among these factors were the transportation facilities and the style element. Whenever means of transportation were introduced more effective than those which had before existed, domestic or foreign goods produced by more advanced methods penetrated areas which had earlier been dominated by the household manufacture. Better qualities of fabrics were brought into more immediate competition with the household output. Indirectly, too, improved transportation facilities had an important effect. They created or improved the markets for the local products, and thereby increased the purchasing power of the newer communities over alien (non-local) woolen goods. For the colonial period itself, there was at times or in given areas sheer lack of local produce marketable in the cloth-making region, the mother country, by reason chiefly of the high transportation costs. Lacking commodities of relatively high value and small bulk, certain colonies were constrained to go more fully into the manufacture of their own clothing than perhaps otherwise would have been the case,—and under the circumstances of the times such manufacture would take place chiefly in the colonial household. Secondly, wherever the element of fashion developed force, the products of the household loom, at best rough in character, could not withstand the competition of the better made foreign goods,—or, with regard to later periods, the competition of all factory-made goods. And this element of fashion, it may be noted, made appearance whenever any considerable town communities arose. Such successful competition on the part of alien goods was the result in some degree of superior organization of labor, of greater specialization among the workers in wool, and to a large measure of superior machinery.

inaccurate. That such was the case appears from the testimony of Colonel Dunbar, Surveyor-General of his Majesty's Woods, who informed the Board that "it was with the greatest difficulty that they (the officers of the Government) were able to procure true information of the trade and manufactures of New England" (Bishop, i, 341–342).

The conditions of wool-cloth production in the colonies foreshadow these general features that were to characterize the household production throughout its existence in the United States. For example, the area of predominant household manufacture — the area where all or practically all the clothing worn by the people was wrought up in the home — was chiefly the regions where either the difficulties of transportation had play or style did not count. The report to the Board of Trade compiled in 1723 stated: "Those Settlements which are distant from Water Carriage, and are remotely situated in the Woods, have no opportunities of a Market for Grain, and therefore as they do not raise more Corn than is sufficient for their own Use, they have more time to manufacture both Wooll and Flax for the Service of their families, and seem to be under a greater necessity of doing it." [1] Or again, in a more specific case: Governor Hunter of New York, in answer to inquiries in 1715 as to the extent of the use of homespun, wrote back to England that the people of New York and Albany wore no clothing of their own manufacture, but if their Lordships referred to the planters and poorer sorts of country people, the computation (previously sent) had understated rather than exaggerated the situation, although he thought that no homespun was sold in shops.[2] The lack of a "Market for Grain" and for other products of a semi-pioneer community was, I believe, the more important factor. The superior English fabrics would have been used if they could have been purchased, and they were worn where the proceeds of the "three-cornered trade" or other commercial transactions gave purchasing power, or where there were readily marketable products.[3]

[1] *Representation*, p. 20. [2] Lord, *Industrial Experiments*, p. 133.

[3] See below as to southern conditions, pp. 24–26.

The Representation above quoted went on to say with regard to the northern colonies: "We did not find that these People had the same Temptation to go on with those Manufactures (flax and woolen) during the time that the Bounty upon Naval Stores subsisted — for the height of Wages, and the great Price of Labour in general throughout America, make it impracticable for the People there to manufacture Linen Cloth for less than twenty per cent more than it would cost in England, or Woollen Cloth for less than fifty per cent above the Price of that which is exported from hence for Sale" (*Representation*, p. 20). Valueless as these ratios are, the idea behind them is not without merit.

Again, with the growth of the seaport towns, there developed a greater solicitude for fashionable dress than was possible in the earlier days. Such goods came in part from the domestic worsted-cloth makers who carried on their handicraft in these towns, but in larger part fabrics of suitable quality, especially the fancier woolens such as broadcloths, had to come from abroad. A differentiation between "city and country people" was noted in 1758 by Acrelius in writing of New Sweden. The former "procure" their articles of dress "from the merchants' shops," while the latter "make them for themselves, and usually of coarser stuff." [1] The town gentleman in all the colonies probably secured the greater part of his fabrics "from the merchants' shops," that is, he bought imported goods; though in most of the larger centers he soon had the alternative of the worsted-cloth makers who set up their manufacture there. And these gentlemen seem to have displayed a marked prejudice against cloths of family industry. Even in financial straits or despite popular pressure they stuck to their finer fabrics. For instance, in the exciting days of the decade preceding the Revolutionary War, when at times English goods were proscribed by voluntary agreements, the town folk were the people hardest to get into line as far as clothes were concerned.

One may go further, I believe, and draw some distinctions as to the prevalence of household production in the different sections of the country, — at least between the northern and southern colonies. In the former, for instance, the town population by the later days of the colonial period had come to form a somewhat greater proportion — though still really a low proportion — of the total population than was true in the southern area. Shipbuilding, foreign trade, and even minor manufacturing had created a town-dwelling populace, whereas in the colonies lower down the coast the towns were more largely mere transshipment points for the produce of the interior. In so far the northerly plantations would probably be found a less considerable producing region for household fabrics.

[1] Acrelius, "History of New Sweden," in Pennsylvania Historical Society *Memoirs*, xi, 157.

On the other hand, the people living outside these larger centers in the northern colonies, the great majority of the population, utilized their own household productions, it seems, more largely than in the South. Indeed, such people appear to have used their home-made goods almost exclusively. John Bridger, Collector of Customs for New England, reported in 1715 that "country people and planters have entered so far into making their own woolens that not one in forty but wears his own carding, spinning, etc." [1] Governor Moore of New York wrote in 1767: "The Custom of making (these) Coarse Cloths in private families prevails throughout the entire province, and almost in every House a sufficient quantity is manufactured for the use of the family," but, he added, "without the least design of sending any of it to market." [2] Mitchell, in his account of the colonies, published in the same year, estimated of the northern area that "two-thirds or three-fourths of the people are clothed with manufactures of their own making." [3] Such seems to be the consensus of opinion among contemporary observers, although, to be sure, there is an occasional discordant voice, the reason or motive for which is not now discernible.[4]

In the more southerly colonies, however, the situation apparently was somewhat different. There the production of articles such as tobacco and rice, which found a ready sale in English or other foreign markets, gave the inhabitants a greater purchasing power over English wool fabrics. For instance, with regard to Maryland, the earliest seat of the tobacco culture, it was said in 1721: "The Inhabitants wear the like Cloathing, and have the same furniture within their houses with those in this Kingdom (England). The slaves are cloathed in Cottons, Kerseys, flannel,

[1] Lord, *Industrial Experiments in British Colonies*, p. 131.

[2] *Documentary History of New York*, i, 734.

[3] Mitchell, *Present State of Great Britain and her Colonies*, 1767, p. 300, note.

[4] For example, Jonathan Belcher, Governor of Massachusetts, reported in 1731 that "the Country People who used formerly to make most of their Clothing of their own Wooll, do not at present manufacture a Third Part of what is necessary for their own Use, but are generally clothed with English Manufactures;" or Colden's oft-repeated remark made in 1765, that "all the wool in America is not sufficient to make Stockens for the Inhabitants" *Representation of 1733*, p. 12; and Beer, *Commercial Policy*, p. 79).

and coarse linens all imported."[1] Colonel Johnson, Governor of South Carolina, reported a decade later that the manufactures established there which interfered with those of Great Britain were "scarce worth naming," including, as far as woolens were concerned, only "coarse mixed Cloths made of Cotton and Wooll, for the use of their Negroes;"[2] and for Virginia substantially the same story was told.[3] Unquestionably there were regions, such as considerable parts of North Carolina, where household production of wool or cotton and wool fabrics was rather extensively carried on; and on some of the plantations small shops for manufacture with the aid of indentured servants or slaves were established; but the proportion of domestic production to total consumption of wool fabrics was apparently much less than in the colonies north of Maryland, even after allowance for the smaller town population.

The conclusion, then, seems warranted: that only economic pressure induced the colonists to carry on household manufactures of wool, the better cloths of foreign origin normally being preferred. And testimony of both northern and southern commentators gives strength to this view. Lord Cornbury, Governor of New York,— surely one not inclined to make excuses for the colonists,— stated in 1705 that "the want of wherewithall to

[1] *New York Colonial Documents*, v, 606. Beverley in his *History and Present State of Virginia*, London, 1705, makes a more amusing comment on this situation: The Virginians, he said, "have their clothing of all sorts from England, as linen, woollen, and silk, hats and leather. The very furs that their hats are made of perhaps go first from thence. Nay, they are such abominable ill-husbands, that though their country be overrun with wood, yet they have all their wooden ware from England; their cabinets, chairs, tables, stools, chests, boxes, cart-wheels, and all other things, even so much as their bowls and birchen brooms, to the eternal reproach of their laziness" (quoted in Beer, *Commercial Policy*, p. 70).

[2] *Representation of 1733*, p. 15.

[3] *Ibid.*, p. 14: "Some poor People provided themselves with Clothing of a Kind of coarse mixed Cloth made of Wooll and Cotton, and of Linsey-Woolsey, where they were unable to purchase better by their Labour in the Cultivation of Tobacco."

The Commissioners for Trade and Plantations in reporting the fact that in America "the People have fallen into the Manufacture of Woollen and Linen Cloth for the Use of their own families," restricted the area so affected to New England, New York, New Jersey, Pennsylvania, and the County of Somerset in Maryland, i. e., to exclude the southern colonies generally.

make returns for England, sets mens witts to work," leading them to the greater production of domestic goods.[1] Governor Seymour of Maryland in 1708 spoke of "pinching want" putting some men upon family manufacture; and Governor Spotwood of Virginia in 1711 laid the resort to manufacture to "necessity and not inclination."[2] Such conditions, in the light of the general economic situation in northern and southern communities, made for differentiation between the two. At the same time, they presaged a tenacious hold on the domestic manufacture in some parts of the country, at least until commerce and industry were more fully developed.

In neither the northern nor the southern colonies, however, was the extent of domestic production a fixed and constant affair, though the fluctuations were more frequent and more considerable in the South. Minor fluctuations were attributable to irregularities in the less well-organized commerce of the period,—failure of anticipated shipments from England, and the like. To these were added the greater ones caused by failure of cloth supplies during war time or by disaster to an export crop. It will be recalled, too, that war existed during more than a third of the time between 1696 and 1765. In 1695, for example, Governor Nicholson of Virginia wrote to the Lords of Trade: "If ships do not come from England to fetch the tobacco and bring good quantity of linen, woolen, working-tools and other necessaries, it will put the people upon clothing themselves."[3] Again a "great scarcity and dearness of (woolen) goods" was reported in 1706, during which such fabrics sold at 200 per cent advance. And this scarcity, it was said, forced the people to set up "a very considerable manufactury . . . for Stuffs, Kerseys, Linsey Woolseys, Flannels, Buttons, etc."[4] Failure of the regular convoy in 1707 caused scarcity of clothing and other goods in Maryland;[5] in

[1] *Documentary History of New York*, i, 711. Part of this message to the Board of Trade was the well-known sentiment: "I hope I may be pardoned if I declare my opinion to be that all these Colloneys are but twigs belonging to the main tree (England)," etc.

[2] Dickerson, *American Colonial Government*, p. 305.

[3] *Calendar of British State Papers, Colonial*, xiv, 509.

[4] Smith, *Memoirs of Wool*, ii, 158.

[5] Dickerson, *American Colonial Government*, p. 305.

1711 an overproduction of tobacco in Virginia, and in 1743 an overstock of rice in South Carolina made difficulties.[1] It is doubtful, however, if such events influenced materially the situation in the colonies. After the several colonies had been founded a few years, the land tested out, and the course of commerce well laid, there was apparently little change prior to 1760 in the degree to which domestic goods were produced and worn. With the increase in size of the seaports, there was some extension of the market for the finer, imported fabrics, but the rate of such growth was of course very gradual. Even long after national independence had been secured, we were preponderantly an agricultural people, and until internal commerce was well developed, the farms continued the source of considerable household wool-cloth production.

The range in types among woolen goods produced in the colonies was not great. Chief among such products was that called "homespun." This was an all-wool fabric, well fulled, worn without artificial coloring or piece-dyed, and more rarely dyed in the wool, but ever distinctly rough in character. As the name implies, this was strictly a household product. A somewhat similar cloth was "linsey-woolsey," differing particularly in that the warp or longitudinal threads were spun of flax. It was an extraordinarily durable fabric, lasting for years. Probably, too, somewhat greater pains were taken in its manufacture. On account of one or both of these factors, linsey-woolsey was generally valued at about twice homespun. These two fabrics far exceeded all others in importance. For example, none others are mentioned by Governor Moore in his description of the wool manufacture in New York in 1767: "There is a general manu-

[1] Virginia Historical Society, *Collections*, i, 72–74; Macpherson, *Annals of Commerce*, iii, 260.

Another colonial phenomenon, seemingly connected with the periods of cloth shortage, is that of the "spinning craze," as the contemporaries denominated it. The first "craze" of any note occurred in 1721. At the fourth anniversary of the Boston Society for Promoting Industry and Frugality, three hundred "young female spinsters" worked at their wheels on Boston Common, where weavers with their looms also attended. A few years later, 1753–1754, there was another "spinning craze," during which Charlestown, Massachusetts, voted to turn its old town-house into a spinning school. (Weeden, p. 680; Tryon, *Household Manufactures*, p. 86.)

factory of woolen carried on here, and consists of two sorts, the first a coarse cloth entirely woolen three quarters of a yard wide; and another stuff which they call linsey-woolsey."[1] In the South, a cloth made of cotton and wool mixed, which apparently had no specific name, was of some importance. It was used by the poorer sorts of people, and was given to the slaves. Outside of these goods, others are but infrequently mentioned; kersey and flannel are the only ones worth noting. The production of such a luxurious fabric as broadcloth was rarely attempted. I have found no mention of its manufacture prior to 1760. About that time, however, one Martin Read, a weaver located in Rhode Island, was weaving up broadcloth for people of his clientèle. For example, records show that in 1766 he wove for one customer fifty-seven yards of this fabric at a price of £34. 4s.[2] Presumably other professional weavers were turning out similar goods from time to time. But the time was not ripe for any large domestic production of so fine a fabric: in 1767 some Yorkshire weavers who had recently come from England in the hopes of setting up such a manufacture in America soon found the conditions unfavorable.[3] For many years no considerable amount of broadcloth was produced in this country.

[1] *Documentary History of New York*, i, 734.

[2] North, *Bulletin*, 1899, p. 125; quoting from Mrs. Earle's *Narragansett Days*.

[3] "Report of Gov. Moore to the Board of Trade," January, 1767; quoted in Bishop, i, 371.

The adventures of the Yorkshire weavers may have had connection with the scheme for wool manufacturing reported in the *Connecticut Courant* for October 29, 1764. This report outlines the most ambitious project for the production of wool cloth that I have found in colonial material. Though its ultimate fate is uncertain, the announcement in the *Courant* is exceedingly interesting:

"Dispatch from Boston, October 8. There seems to be a disposition in many of the inhabitants of this and the neighboring governments to cloath themselves with their own manufacture. — At Hampstead, on Long Island, in the Province of N. York, a company of gentlemen have set up a new woollen manufactory, and having given notice to gentlemen shopkeepers and others, of any of the provinces, that by sending proper patterns of any colour, they may be supplied with broadcloths, equal in fineness, colour, and goodness, and cheaper than any imported, the proprietors give good encouragement to any persons who are any way vested in the woollen manufactory, such as wool combers, weavers, clothiers, shearers, dyers, spinners, carders, or understand any branch of the broad-cloth, blanket, or stroud manufactory."

One feature about the colonial woolen-cloth manufacture deserves special notice, the utilization of cotton and linen in conjunction with the wool fiber. This was, as far as I can ascertain, a new departure. Neither in England nor on the Continent was there such a fabric as linsey-woolsey, nor was there an intermixture of the wool and cotton fibers for the formation of a yarn.[1] Apparently these American practices were the result of the peculiar colonial environment: the need of a stout fabric, and at least for some parts of the country the need of one with a lower heat resistance than all-wool cloth; the growth of wool and flax or wool and cotton in close proximity to one another; and the freedom from guild regulations or the habituations of long-continued commerce. Left to itself and given a variety of raw materials, the American wool manufacture developed cloths which satisfied the particular needs of the community.

Carried on in a more highly organized system, the colonial worsted manufacture correspondingly yielded a greater diversity of products. Moreover, inasmuch as the trade was in the hands of professionals to a considerable degree, men who frequently had practiced the manufacture in the mother country, the cloths not uncommonly were copies of English goods. Among these may be mentioned serge, calimanco, druggets, crapes, camblets,—perhaps all to be included under the general term of stuff-goods. The only worsted fabric which appears to have been of American origin is that called "tammies," a light cloth used for dresses. Little is known of this fabric, especially as to how it differed from the other worsted cloths. These others, including serge, were somewhat of the character of the present English "stuffs," the dress-goods and linings made so extensively in the Bradford (England) district. Like the latter, they were rather stiff and glossy, but they were probably heavier than the modern stuffs.

[1] This type of mixed yarn has until recently been called merino. Despite the fact that this appellation was common in the trade, the Federal Trade Commission has latterly (1922) ruled that "merino" is a term of deception, misleading prospective purchasers of goods so named into believing the fabric is made of wool from the merino sheep. Accordingly practice in the trade is now upset. However, since no new description of this type of mixed yarn can be said to have become general, I shall use the old term throughout this study.

Finally, we should note that the worsted fabrics made in this country during the colonial era seemingly approached more closely than the woolen ones the standard of English cloths. Lord Cornbury stated as early as 1705: "I myself have seen Serge made upon Long Island that any man may wear"[1] — probably a substantial exaggeration, but suggesting that this coarse worsted cloth was produced not without skill.

In general it may be said that the domestic wool manufacture was primarily by and for the household. It was carried on chiefly in the home and turned out fabrics which, while perhaps not stylish, were distinctly serviceable, as homely things should be; and the manufacture was sufficiently extensive through the northern colonies to cover the requirements of the larger proportion of the population, the people who lived outside the larger towns. The southern communities were less dependent upon the domestic production, but they possessed some household activity, especially among the back settlements and the "poorer sort of housekeepers."[2] As yet the domestic market was too restricted and uncertain to encourage the development of manufacture upon a more elaborate basis than the part-household and part-handicraft system of the colonial era.

5. *Colonial Trade in Wool Manufactures.*

The extent to which domestic manufactures of wool entered into colonial and into intercolonial commerce is on the face of the evidence a rather uncertain matter. On the one hand, there are data of individual cases where homespun or other wool products were sold or traded within or between colonies; and on the other, emphatic statements from contemporaries that such events never occurred.

On the first side of the question may be instanced the report of Armstrong, Collector of Customs for New England, in 1720, that the wool manufacture had been "brought to such perfection that thousands of pounds' worth of stuffs and druggets (worsted

[1] *Documentary History of New York*, i, 711.

[2] Governor Spotwood of Virginia in Virginia Historical Society *Collections*, i, 72.

fabrics) were sold in Boston shops."[1] Or one may note the advertisement of a fair at Burlington, New Jersey (1764), inviting the colonists to bring "all kinds of linen and woolen manufactures of this and neighboring colonies" for sale.[2] Again, the report of the Council for Trade and Plantations to the Queen in 1702 made mention of the fact that the northern colonies "do not only cloath themselves with woollen goods, but furnish the same commodity to the more Southern Plantations, notwithstanding the prohibition" in the Woolens Act of 1699.[3] In 1756 it was recorded that a shipment of two hundred homespun jackets was made from Boston to Albany;[4] and Germantown worsteds and stockings formed part of the merchandise sent southward from Philadelphia, an early distributing center.[5] But perhaps the most suggestive fact is the duty of ten per cent ad valorem imposed in 1699 by New York upon "all woolen manufactures made in our neighbor-

[1] Quoted from Board of Trade papers in Lord, *Industrial Experiments*, p. 136. Weeden mentions that in 1747–1748 "white and striped" homespun appear in merchants' stocks in Boston (p. 679). Cf. also Mitchell, *Present State of Great Britain and her Colonies*, 1767, p. 300, note.

Note might also be made of the entries in an old account book of a Boston storekeeper (now in the Boston Public Library) covering the years 1685–1689, which credited several persons with cloth, almost all worsted, that had evidently been accepted in lieu of cash. (This account book is quoted in Abbott, *Women in Industry*, p. 24.) The number of entries is not over a dozen in the four years, and the greatest quantity credited to a single individual was sixty-two yards, all serge. See also Bagnall, *Textile Industries of the United States*, p. 283, referring to Thomas Hazard's putting-out of weaving (see above, p. 19, note 1), which may be an occurrence of the same sort as the above. There is further evidence of prices of colonial wool manufactures (e. g., cf. Clark, p. 140), but the great majority of such quotations are from probate records.

[2] New Jersey *Archives*, Newspaper Extracts, v, 439. Cf. also Bishop, i, 315.

[3] *Calendar of British State Papers, Colonial*, xx, 695. The Woolens Act is described below (see pp. 40–44). In brief it prohibited all export and intercolonial trade in wool and wool products. This account goes on to state: "We have been particularly informed by persons employed by us to make enquiries, that as good druggets are made in those countries as any in England, and sold there for 4s. and 4s. 6d. per yard."

[4] Weeden, p. 679.

[5] Clark, p. 117; quoting Weeden, ii, 590, and others. In Maryland Historical Society, *Publications* (No. 4, p. 56), it is stated that goods sent from Fredericktown to Georgia included fine woolen goods, though these were imported in all probability.

ing colonies which shall be imported into the Province and Dependency."[1]

Contrariwise, Governor Hunter of New York stated in 1715 that it did not consist with his knowledge that "ever any homespun was sold in the shops."[2] Governor Tryon of North Carolina similarly asserted: "I have not heard of a piece of woolen or linnen cloth being ever sold that was the manufacture of this province."[3] Finally, among other similar statements may be noted the most astonishing one, made by the Commissioners of Trade and Plantations who in 1702 had reported the shipment to the southern plantations of cloth made in New England and other northern colonies: they assert in 1728, with reference to all the provinces north of Maryland, "We could not learn that (the people) have ever manufactured any (Woollen or Linen Cloth) for Sale in any of the Colonies, except in a small Indian Town in Pennsylvania, where some Palatines have of late years settled."[4]

An appreciation of the character and circumstances of the domestic wool-manufacturing industry enables one to make a partial resolution of these apparent contradictions. The earlier report of the Commissioners reporting intercolonial traffic in woolens coincided with Queen Anne's War, and may well have been a temporary phenomenon.[5] Again, worsteds, the product of the specialized handicraftsmen, are the goods that, quite disproportionate to the relative size of worsted-cloth production in the colonies, are more particularly mentioned in the provincial commerce. Nor is there anything surprising in the possibility that storekeepers accepted worsted cloth in exchange for other com-

[1] *New York Colonial Laws*, i, 404.

However, this phrase in the law regulating customs was dropped two years later when an act otherwise substantially the same was passed. Possibly a tax on woolen goods from the "neighboring colonies" was not worth the trouble of collection.

[2] *Documentary History of New York*, i, 714. Cf. also p. 722.

[3] *Colonial Records of North Carolina*, vii, 429.

[4] *Representation of 1733*, p. 19.

[5] It may be noted that the date of Armstrong's allegation concerning the "thousands of pounds' worth of stuffs and druggets" (1720) is also the date of a temporary shortage of supplies in Maryland (Lord, *Industrial Experiments*, p. 137), and just precedes the first "spinning craze" in Boston, 1721 (Tryon, *Household Manufactures*, p. 86).

modities, or that an occasional bale of worsted manufactures was shipped southward. When these two groups of cases have been eliminated, the number of instances that probably occurred where real homespun woolens were "sold in the shops" or at fairs, become so few that they may well be put down as mere exceptions to the general statement that such fabrics were not produced for sale. Goods might be exchanged locally between households when one was made up of more men than women — and so had a deficiency of output — and another was composed chiefly of women, thereby having a surplus capacity of manufacture. But in view of the quality of the household productions,[1] and of the availability of worsteds and imported woolens in the seaport towns and in the larger sections of the southern plantations, a considerable trade in the predominant household manufactures would appear most unlikely. It seems to me more probable that local or intercolonial commerce in such goods was a negligible feature of the colonial period.

[1] Mitchell says: "Two-thirds or three-quarters of the people are clothed with manufactures of their own making. . . . They make them for their own use, and as these are so much better than what are made for sale, it is an inducement for every one almost to make them" (*Present State of Great Britain and her Colonies*, 1767, p. 300, note).

CHAPTER II

GOVERNMENTAL POLICY

Introduction

The period during which the wool manufacture was begun in the colonies was one in which governmental interference in industry, and governmental encouragement and control of industry, were commonly believed to be beneficial and even necessary. Accordingly, one is not surprised to find both colonial and British legislatures attempting to stimulate or check the development of the wool-cloth manufacture as their interests dictated, or at least as they thought their interests dictated. To trace the course of these governmental policies and to assess the real effects thereof upon the industry are the purposes of this chapter.

1. *Colonial Encouragement.*

The difficulties in inaugurating the wool manufacture, and the irregularities of cloth supplies, were the forces which led localities and colonies from time to time to grant various inducements for the benefit of the industry, or to institute various regulations for the control of the trade. Two broad types of action may here be distinguished, — the more specific sort in which the end sought was the inauguration of a particular development or change, and the broader type when by bounties or general regulations improvement in the welfare of the whole industry was desired.

The more specific type of encouragement was offered in the form of grants of land or of special privilege contingent upon or in return for certain services to be rendered the wool manufacture. Such enactments were confined largely to the period before 1700, to the period of beginnings within the industry. For example, the town of Chelmsford, Massachusetts, in 1656 secured its first professional weaver by admitting him as an inhabitant and allotting him thirty acres of land "provided he set up his trade of weaving and perform the town's work." [1] The General Court of Connecticut in 1686 granted Francis Thrasher and his servant "freedom from training and work at highways" so long as they carried on their trade of making cloth and serge.[2] Massachusetts allotted as much as three hundred acres of land to William Hubblefield of Boston "in consideration of his good services in promoting and instructing many persons in the trade and mystery of cloth-making." [3] Then, of somewhat wider scope were enactments like that of Virginia in 1693 which gave to fullers who owned land on one side of a stream, the right to have an acre on the other side condemned for the convenience of carrying on the work of their mills; [4] and that of Rhode Island as late as 1751, which exempted "clothiers, fullers, weavers, and artificers" from taxes and public service for seven years.[5]

The more general sort of provincial aid dated from the period 1640–1650. In Massachusetts a bounty measure was voted by the General Court in 1640: 3d. in a shilling were to be given during a period of three years for every yard of linen, woolen, or cotton cloth, provided, in the case of the two former, they were spun and woven of "wool or linen grown here." This was but temporary, being repealed in seven months as "too burthensome to the country." [6] Other acts followed: one forbidding the export and attempting to check the slaughter of sheep, as the colony was "in great straits in respect to clothing" (1654),[7] and a broader act two years later which aimed to compel greater household manufacture, as well as to make conditions more favorable for the pasturing and improvement

[1] Bishop, i, 312.
[2] Connecticut *Public Records*, iii, 196; quoted in Clark, p. 46.
[3] Massachusetts *Archives*, lix, 234–236; quoted in Clark, p. 40.
[4] Bruce, *Economic History of Virginia*, ii, 464.
[5] Rhode Island, *Acts and Resolves*, April, 1751, 80–81; quoted in Clark, p. 46.
[6] Weeden, p. 170.
[7] Wright, p. 3; quoting from the *Records of the Massachusetts Bay Company*, iii, 355–356.

of sheep.[1] Subsequently, in 1675, the exportation of wool was forbidden.[2]

Other colonies found it necessary or thought it advantageous to enact similar statutes. Maryland granted a bounty of ten pounds of tobacco for every yard of woolen cloth produced in the colony;[3] and in 1663 forbade the export of wool.[4] Rhode Island as late as 1751 granted a bounty on cloth manufactured of wool, equal to one-third the appraised value thereof.[5] But most elaborate of all was the series of enactments passed by Virginia extending from 1656 to 1705, and covering prohibitions of exportations for both sheep and wool, bounties on cloth manufactured, and the compulsory erection and maintenance of a weaving shop in each county.[6]

[1] The General Court urged the selectmen of every town to encourage women, boys, and girls in spinning and weaving; every family was to be assessed for one or more spinners, or for a fractional part, and that "every one thus assessed do after this present year 1656 spin for thirty weeks every yeare, a pound per week, of lining, cotton, or woolen and so proportionably for halfe or quarter spinners under the penalty of 12d. for every pound Short;" and for the increase of raw material, the commons were to be devoted to sheep, rams were to be inspected, and hemp and flax seed saved and sown (Weeden, p. 198. For text, cf. Bishop, i, 311–312). Weeden says this law had little effect beyond to make spinners at home (p. 304); but how considerable was this increase is unknown. It probably was not large, since the law could not have been strictly enforced.

[2] Bishop, i, 311.

[3] Maryland *Archives*, "Proceedings of Assembly," vii, 325; quoted in Clark, p. 34.

[4] *Calendar of British State Papers, Colonial*, v, 163.

[5] Rhode Island, *Public Records*, v, 318; quoted in Clark, p. 35. This law was repealed in three months' time since "it may draw the displeasure of Great Britain upon us, as it will interfere with their most favorite manufactury" (p. 319).

[6] The series of laws are of sufficient moment to be briefly listed:

1656 Northampton County, across the Bay, was given authority to promote and govern its own manufactures, among which the woolen industry was of some importance (Wise, *Early History of the Eastern Shore of Virginia*, p. 303).

1657 Export of sheep prohibited (Bishop, i, 321).

1659 Export of wool prohibited (Bruce, *Economic History of Virginia*, ii, 461).

1662 Bounties of five pounds of tobacco for every yard of woolen cloth made in the Province, as well as a lesser one for linen cloth and for the preparation of flax and hemp; of ten pounds for every good hat made of wool or fur, and for every dozen pair of woolen or worsted stockings (Bishop, i, 320).

Obviously there was no regularity of form and no continuity of policy with respect to special encouragement of the wool manufacture. Nor in the diverse and varying conditions of the several colonies could one expect uniformity or continuity. Again, the encouragements extended apparently had little or no influence upon the industry's development, except perhaps in a very local or temporary way. Stronger forces than bounties or restrictions upon trade held the manufacture in its grip, and really directed the course of its growth. However, these cases of direct public aid given to the wool manufacture do have a particular significance to one who is surveying the whole development of the industry, by reason of their relation to subsequent national policy. Public encouragement to the wool-manufacturing industry is not a product of the nineteenth century. It dates back almost to the first attempt at such manufacture in this country; and, as will appear later, the line of descent from these early grants of land or of exemption from taxation is direct to the more recent grants of special protection.

1666 The General Assembly ordered the court of each county to set up a loom and employ a weaver at it, under penalty of 2,000 pounds of tobacco (Bruce, ii, 461). Repealed in 1684 (Bishop, i, 321).

1668 Children of indigent parents were to be instructed to spin and weave, among other trades (Bruce, ii, 461).

1671 Prohibition on the exportation of wool repealed; but it was re-enacted in 1682 (Bruce, ii, 462).

1682 At the instance of Lord Culpeper, the bounty law was revived: six pounds of tobacco was to be paid for every yard of woolen, linsey-woolsey, or linen cloth, which must be made from materials grown by the person who manufactured it. Also bounties were given on fur or woolen hats (ten pounds each), and for each dozen pair of worsted hose for men and women (twelve pounds). Bruce thinks the results of this act were good, as in the year there were presented to the county court of Middlesex productions of 14, 34, 45, 55, 61, and even 95 yards of woolen cloth by different men. Records of other counties are lost (Bruce, ii, 463). In 1684, this measure was repealed, because it was too heavy a burden on the public, and there was no longer need of encouragement.

1686 This law was revived, and was continued until 1694 (Bruce, ii, 464).

1693 A bonus of two acres of land, as already noted, was granted to each fulling mill erected (Bruce, ii, 464).

1705 In the famous Act of Ports, a duty of 6d. a pound was placed upon the export of wool (Bruce, ii, 561).

2. *British Interference.*

The policy of the British government toward the wool manufacture in the colonies had its origin, as has already been intimated, in the Mercantilist thought of the seventeenth century. Among the various phases of this thought was a well-elaborated colonial policy which conceived of the mother country and her offspring as being mutually dependent, — rather more than in Lord Cornbury's concept that "all Colloneys . . . are but twigs of the main tree," for the homeland was to be the complement of the plantations. The mother country was to work up the raw materials supplied by the colonies, and the colonies to consume the manufactures produced by the mother country. With this theory of colonial position and responsibilities in mind, the people and government of England would be bound to view with apprehension the possibility of a competitive woolen industry arising in their American possessions.

As it happened, the wool manufacture was, in fact, the first among various colonial attempts at industrial activity to attract the attention of the home authorities — at least, it was the first manufacture to be restricted.[1] Why the modest colonial wool manufacture that I have sketched above should have raised apprehension in England, may well seem puzzling, — especially at the early date when regulatory action was in fact taken, at the close of the seventeenth century. Several reasons or possible explanations may be suggested. Unquestionably there had been a development of household woolen production in many of the colonies, assisted by the operations of handicraft weavers and by the employment of fulling mills. This provincial manufacture, regarded by the colonists as a mere necessity under the economic conditions, might well be considered by Englishmen to work a diminution of the market for English fabrics. In point of fact, the colonial market for such goods may not have expanded during the preceding half-century or so, proportionately with the

[1] The hat manufacture was not prohibited until 1733, and iron-working was not restricted until 1750; and it should be noted that these with the wool manufacture were the only ones attacked by British legislation.

increase in settlement. We do not know whether or not this in truth was so. Furthermore, exaggerated accounts of the colonial manufacture had apparently reached England. Macpherson reports that complaints were made of the exportation of wool and wool manufactures from "our North-American plantations . . . to foreign markets formerly supplied by England." [1] The facts were that a negligible shipment of wool from the hard-pressed northern colonies did occur — Nantucket is the only place specifically mentioned [2] — but I have found no evidence at all implying an exportation of wool manufactures. Yet not only the more widespread woolen industry, but the frail and hesitant worsted production was a source of perturbation to Englishmen.[3] Then, the fancied threat of the colonial wool-manufacturing industry made a greater impression upon those interested in the English manufacture because English exports of wool fabrics had during the seventeenth century been suffering increasingly severe competition from the expanding continental industries, and in the latter part of the period from the manufactures exported out of Ireland.[4] Such a situation as this easily stirred the British government to action, since of all the English industries the wool manufacture was the "most favorite." [5] Indeed, during the period of the seventeenth and eighteenth centuries, wool-manufacturing was in England popularly considered the backbone of the country's strength, the source of her greatness. Hence any threat or possible misfortune to that enterprise was to be warded off by the most effective measures available. Thus, then, the

[1] Macpherson, *Annals of Commerce*, ii, 705.

[2] Douglass, *British Settlements*, 1755, ii, 182, note: "Some years since . . . some (wool) was shipped from Nantucket to France, very small quantities."

[3] James in his *History of the* (English) *Worsted Manufacture* says of this period: "From the jealousy . . . exhibited of the worsted manufacturers of our Plantations, it is evident that the weavers who in the time of Charles I were forced from their homes to find refuge in New England, and other parts of America, had prospered, and so far advanced in their occupations as by just retribution to be competitors with us in the markets of the Continent" (p. 177).

[4] James, *op. cit.*, pp. 175–176.

[5] See above, p. 36, note 5.

The wool-sack of the House of Lords typifies the elevated esteem in which this manufacture was then held.

prevailing colonial theory, seconded by material and nationalistic interest in the most precious British industry, called for legislation which would curb the advancing colonial interest in wool.

The first step in this direction came in 1683 when the British Commissioners of the Customs disallowed the two laws passed by Virginia in the preceding year, which prohibited the exportation of wool from the colony and granted bounties upon the manufacture of woolen and linen cloth and some other woolen products.[1] The disapproval or veto of these laws was based on the ground that they conflicted with the spirit of the Navigation Laws.[2] The Virginia government, however, paid little attention to this decision, continuing to carry out her laws, and to give bounties for ten years longer.

Then, at the close of the century, came the second step in the development of the government's policy. Without preliminary investigation and apparently without serious consideration, as far as the colonies are concerned, Parliament passed the so-called Woolens Act of 1699, which proposed a new departure in the mother country's attitude toward the provincial wool manufacture. Passage of the act was made possible, it seems, merely by the circumstance that in the main the law conformed with the prevalent opinion as to the proper function and position of a colony, that the precious wool manufacture of the country was somehow concerned, and that a convenient opportunity arose for enacting this piece of legislation. Consideration apparently was not given to the facts: that, on the one hand, a portion of the act was actually prejudicial to England's real interest with respect to the colonies; while, on the other hand, the law was chiefly unnecessary and could not but be irritating to the oversea subjects of the Crown.

The text of the act is seemingly of sweeping character, and by

[1] See above, p. 36, note 6.

[2] The relation of these Virginian laws to the Navigation Laws was discussed in full in the veto, and ranged from the contention that they lessened the dependence of the colonial population upon England to that, that they advanced the cost of tobacco to the English consumer by raising the charges of navigation — seemingly, through the diminution of the return cargo (Bruce, ii, 464).

reason of the law's importance it will be given in full, in so far as it relates to the colonies:[1]

XIX. And for the more effectual Encouragement of the Woollen Manufactures of this Kingdom, be it further enacted by the Authority aforesaid, That from and after the first Day of December in the Year of Our Lord One Thousand Six Hundred and Ninety-Nine, no Wooll, Woollfells, Shortlings, Mortlings, Wooll-flocks, Worsted, Bay, or Woollen Yarn, Cloth, Serge, Bays, Kerseys, Says, Frizes, Druggets, Cloth-Serges, Shalloons, or any other Drapery Stuffs or Woollen Manufactures whatsoever, made or mixed with Wooll or Wooll-flocks, being of the Product or Manufacture of any of the English Plantations in America, shall be loaden or laid on board in any Ship or Vessel, in any Place or Parts within any of the said English Plantations, upon any Pretense whatsoever; as likewise, that no such Wooll, Woollfells, (or other goods afore-mentioned) . . . shall be loaden upon any Horse, Cart, or other Carriage, to the Intent and Purpose to be exported, transported, carried or conveyed out of the said English Plantations to any other of the said Plantations, or to any other Place whatsoever; . . . and all Governors or Commanders in Chief of the said respective Plantations, as also all Officers employed in the Customs, or other Branches of his Majesty's Revenue there, are hereby authorized, charged, and required to take effectual Care, that the true Intent and Meaning of this Act, so far forth as it relates to the said respective Plantations, be duly put in Execution.

Curiously enough, there has been some dispute as to the "true Intent and Meaning" of this legislation. Weeden seems to have been responsible for the original misunderstanding. He misread the law as prohibiting not merely export or intercolonial trade but even trade within a given colony, or, as he puts it, as "forbidding the transport of wool or woolens, by horse or cart, away from the New England husbandman's door."[2] Other writers apparently have followed his interpretation.[3] However, a careful reading of the paragraph quoted above would show the excessive breadth that he gave to the law. An examination of the conditions under which the legislation was passed, and of the interpretation given it by contemporaries, sweeps away all support to the foregoing view.

The paragraph already given was attached at the end of a law relating to the Irish wool manufacture, the intent of which was

[1] *10 and 11 William III*, ch. 10, art. xix.

[2] Weeden, i, 388, 393.

[3] Rabbeno, *American Commercial Policy*, p. 19; Bancroft, *History of the United States*, iii, 106; Beer, *Commercial Policy of England toward the American Colonies*, p. 77; Busching, *England und seinen Kolonien*, p. 32.

explicitly to check the competition of Irish woolens with the English upon the continental markets. There is no trace of a purpose to prevent Irish production for Irish needs. Even the enforcement machinery set up by these leading sections of the act, including patrolling squadrons off the Irish coast, indicates that exportation from that island, not local manufacture, was the action at which objection was leveled. As for the portion of the act pertaining to the colonies, the similarity of phraseology in this portion would itself suggest a probable similarity of interpretation. So, too, would the manner with which application of restrictions, — aimed in the first instance at a far different situation in Ireland, — was made to colonial activity. The representation of the Commissioners for Trade and Plantations to the House of Commons, recommending the bill, gives the impression that application of similar legislation to the colonies was an afterthought. This recommendation reads that, since the northern colonies, especially New England, had improved themselves in woolen manufactures, "which, in its proportion, is as prejudicial to this Kingdom, as working of those Manufactures in Ireland," it is accordingly suggested that "upon Occasion, the like Prohibitions be made with relation to" those northern colonies as to Ireland.[1] That Parliament was actuated by a similar thought is indicated by the position in the law of the clause relating to the colonies, — the nineteenth paragraph of an act otherwise concerned with the Irish problem. Consequently, whether we depend upon a careful reading of this nineteenth paragraph itself or view the paragraph in its logical and historical setting, we can arrive at but one tenable interpretation of that legislation: that Parliament intended to prevent merely the exportation of wool and wool manufactures, not the movement within the several colonies. To be sure, intercolonial trade was prohibited, since the several colonies were considered as distinct units. But there was no restraint such as suggested by Weeden, that no wool nor woolens could leave the premises of the local producer.[2]

[1] *Calendar of British State Papers, Colonial*, xvii, 17.

[2] Some aspects of this legislation too detailed for the general discussion may be found in Appendix A.

For evidence outside the act itself, one may turn to the Representation, already mentioned, of the Commissioners for Trade and Plantations to the House of Commons. Speaking of commodities in general, though presumably having the wool manufacture chiefly in mind, the Commissioners excepted from the harmful activities of the colonists the production of "so much as should be wanting for their own Sustenance, and Supply of Provisions to their Neighbors." [1] Then, various writers, as, for example, Sir William Keith in 1728 and John Adams in 1783, speak of the prohibition upon "export" or upon "water-borne" traffic in wool; but never of interference with local trade.[2] Nor have I found a single statement of a contemporary giving the view held by Weeden and others. The act, then, merely imposed a prohibition of export or intercolonial shipment upon an industry which was as yet in the earliest stages of development, — on its face quite a harmless and useless proceeding. The reason for it, already intimated, is probably that expressed in the recommendation of the Committee reporting the bill to the House of Commons: "That Care be taken to prevent the Setting up of the Woollen Manufacture in the English Plantations in America." [3]

If the act itself was harmless, the difficulties of administration rendered the legislation still more innocuous. Unlike the portions of the legislation respecting the Irish industry, the paragraph pertaining to the colonial manufacture provided for no special means of enforcement, merely the Crown's ordinary administrative officers in America. Such officers, few in number and subject in greater or less degree to local influences, were powerless to provide effective execution. For example, since the act forbade the placing of wool or woolen goods "on board any Ship or Vessel . . . upon any Pretense whatsoever," an attempt was made to prevent the shipment to coastal towns of wool grown upon Nantucket and other outlying islands where, by reason of the protection from wolves, wool-growing had early prospered. Of this matter the Surveyor of Cus-

[1] *Journal of the House of Commons*, xii, 427.

[2] New Jersey *Archives*, 1st Series, v, 203; Callender, *Economic History of the United States*, p. 199. Cf. also Griffith, *Sketches of the Early History of Maryland*, 1821, p. 39; and Smith, *Memoirs of Wool*, ii, 264, note.

[3] *Journal of the House of Commons*, xii, 532.

toms in New England wrote in 1704: "Since the wool act, we have used our endeavor to prevent the carrying of wool from the islands to the main, but I do not think it possible wholly to prevent it, for some of the islands lie very near — within a half or a quarter of a mile of the main. The country is large and the officers so few, that it may be carried in boats and canoes, in the night, from one place to another, notwithstanding all that the officers can do." [1] Moreover, attention has already been directed to the occasional trade in wool fabrics between colonies.[2] It may be noted further that the attitude subsequently assumed by the Board of Trade with respect to the colonial wool manufacture was not one likely to lead to a vigorous enforcement of this particular law.[3]

After the passage of the Woolens Act, the further activity of Parliament itself was confined to the enactment of two minor laws supplementary to the act of 1699. With the apparent intent of closing every loophole for possible evasion of the Woolens Act, it was provided in the year following the enactment of that act, that no mariner nor passenger upon a vessel should purchase in the colonies more than forty shillings' worth of woolen goods.[4] Again, to give greater facility to the trade in woolen cloths from England to the plantations, a further act of this same year 1700 abolished the export duties which previously had been in force upon such fabrics leaving England.[5] The close proximity of these several acts and the subsequent inaction of Parliament [6] suggest that after a momentary alarm over "the Setting up of the Woollen Manufacture in the English Plantations in America," interest in the subject flagged; and, as has already appeared, nothing occurred in the

[1] Lord, *Industrial Experiments*, p. 129. It will be recalled that charges had been made of the exportation of wool from Nantucket to France, and hence enforcement of the new law was presumably directed with some special attention to this point.

[2] See above, pp. 30–33.

[3] See below, pp. 45–46.

[4] *11 and 12 William III*, ch. 13.

[5] *11 and 12 William III*, ch. 20.

[6] It may be noted that certain laws, the extension of which to the colonies might have been hurtful, were not so extended: *5 George I*, ch. 27, 1719, which forbade the transporting or seducing of artificers to settle abroad; *23 George II*, ch. 13, 1750, which prohibited the exportation of tools and utensils employed in the woolen and silk trades; while *14 George III*, ch. 71, 1774, which laid a similar prohibition upon the export of tools or utensils used in the cotton and linen industries, contained a special provision excepting wool cards shipped to North America.

course of the colonial wool manufacture during the later years of the colonial period really to reawaken apprehension concerning that manufacture.

The interference of the home government was, accordingly, confined thereafter to the operations of the Board of Trade, acting usually through the colonial governors or other administrative officers. As has just been suggested, the attitude of the Board of Trade toward the colonial wool manufacture was not oppressive. For instance, in 1706, certain London merchants petitioned that the planters be compelled to clothe their white, black, and Indian slaves or servants in woolen cloths of English production; but the Board would not endorse such a move, and pointed out its impracticality.[1] Or again, when a complete prohibition of woolen manufacture in the colonies was asked for, the Board did not favor the measure, since then, as it said, the poor could not clothe themselves, — though, on the other hand, it was willing to forbid the exposing for sale of colonial-made fabrics.[2] Apparently, too, the Board apprehended the peculiar economic situation of the northern colonies, the chief offenders against the dictates of the Mercantilist spirit in England's colonial policy. In 1717, the Board spoke of these districts as being "under the necessity of applying themselves" to the woolen, linen, and other manufactures; and, in 1721, even more pointedly, it said that presumably "necessity and not choice has put them to erecting manufactures." [3]

Wherefore, the Board and through it the government confined themselves to a negative policy, or perhaps better a policy of diversion. It was their purpose — strictly in keeping with the Mercantilistic thought of the times — to encourage the colonies "to supply us with such commodities as we are necessitated to purchase from

[1] Lord, *Industrial Experiments*, p. 130. Joshua Gee, writing in 1747, proposed that all sale of woolen goods be forbidden in the colonies, private sales as well as those at any market or fair; that negroes be prohibited from combing or spinning wool, or from weaving woolen or linen cloth; and that all weavers be licensed by the colonial governors, so that industries might be watched and encouraged or discouraged according "to their wants, or the danger of their too much interfering with us" (*Trade and Navigation of Great Britain Considered*, pp. 142–144).

[2] *Representation of the Board*, 1728; quoted in Dickerson, *American Colonial Government*, p. 310, note.

[3] Dickerson, p. 309.

foreigners with our money."[1] More specifically, and in the Board's own words, "we humbly propose that these people particularly in New England and New York should be diverted from that undertaking (the manufacture of woolen cloth) by being encouraged in the production of naval stores, since in return of such stores, they would take off considerable quantities of woolen manufactures from hence, which would be a double advantage to this Kingdom."[2] By reason of the primary importance to England of her navy and merchant marine, of the consequent objections to drawing naval supplies from foreign nations, and of the gradual failure of the Baltic sources, the direct benefits to be secured from a large American production of pitch, resin, masts, timber, and the like were fully as important as the indirect benefit.[3] By bounties, by the exhortation and personal influence of colonial governors, and by other measures, diversion of the colonists to this field of productive activity was sought. Under what difficulties this propaganda proceeded, and with what effect upon the supply of naval stores, it is not our province to inquire;[4] but as regards the wool manufacture, it appears that little or no change resulted. The domestic wool-cloth production had too firm a root, and was too expressive of the economic conditions of the times. Accordingly, as has already been indicated, it continued to play the predominant part in the supply of woolen cloths of the colonies.[5]

[1] New Jersey *Archives*, 1st Series, v, 309.

[2] Dickerson, p. 309.

[3] Sometimes other products, such as salt, potash, wines, and even silk were also encouraged; but the main stress was laid on naval stores. The source of such stores was naturally the outlying districts for the most part, the regions most likely to set upon cloth manufacture. The New England colonies, North Carolina, and to a lesser extent the other colonies, were affected.

[4] See particularly Lord, *Industrial Experiments*, pp. 56–124.

[5] The Board of Trade also maintained a general supervision over the development of colonial industries, particularly the wool manufacture. To this end "certain general Queries" were sent to the several governors in America, of which several related to trade and manufactures, beginning in 1719 and being repeated "as often as necessity required," or "from Time to Time," until 1733–1734. Again in 1766, at the commencement of the pre-Revolutionary unrest, the Board sent out a circular requiring "a particular and exact account of the several Manufactures which have been set up and carried on since 1734," and that an annual report be made thereafter. Incidentally it may be noted that much of our data upon the state of the industries during this period are derived from answers to these demands.

Taken as a whole, the interference of the British government was of negligible importance in checking or modifying the general development of the woolen industry in the colonies, and in that respect corresponds roughly with the more modern view of the economic effects upon the American "plantations" of the early British colonial policy. Far from regarding manufacture similar to that of Englishmen as "a sort of forgery, punishable, like an imitation of the British coin," [1] the government in this case seemed content merely to remove all threat to England's export trade, allowing the domestic production to proceed as it would. Under conditions of a greatly expanded colonial development, to be sure, there lay in the encircling bonds of the Woolens Act, if well enforced, a possibility of serious conflict between the mother country and her children, especially in the prohibition of intercolonial traffic in wool or wool products; but, as our survey of the actual situation in the colonial industry would suggest, the conflict never became imminent during the whole period of political dependence.[2]

[1] Bancroft, *History of the United States*, ii, 520.

[2] The experience of the American wool-manufacturing industry may perhaps be contrasted with that of the Irish industry with which it was linked in the Woolens Act. While the former proceeded without appreciable alteration, the latter was virtually set back a century in development, the organization permitting an export trade being practically stamped out within a few years.

CHAPTER III

IMPORTATIONS

A KNOWLEDGE of the conditions of colonial domestic production, — its quality, and the area and magnitude of its operations, — suggests, by process of inference, the nature of the import movement of wool products. It is obvious, for example, that no considerable trade in semi-manufactured goods, such as tops and yarns, was possible. In fact, no reference to such importations appears in colonial records. Again, it is evident that by reason of wars and misadventures in the colonial export trade the course of importations would be largely irregular, probably more irregular than in later times. Another feature of the period, making for a simplification of the import trade, was the prohibition of shipment to British colonies of cloths other than the product of the mother country.[1]

It has become apparent in the foregoing discussion that the market for imported fabrics was relatively circumscribed. Probably it was true, as one writer remarked, that the colonists' "delight was to wear English manufactures;" [2] but disability frequently interfered with the satisfaction of their desires. The use of English cloths in the regions which lay away from the coast, or lacked easy transportation facilities, or possessed few acceptable export commodities, was undoubtedly small indeed. Such were the interior communities of the New England colonies, and to some extent those of the middle and southern provinces. The remaining area, that which might offer a market for English woolens, included chiefly the northern towns and commercial centers, and a considerable portion of the planter colonies: Maryland, Virginia, and South Carolina. Of the more northerly communities, much has already been said as to their economic position. It

[1] Douglass, *British Settlements*, 1755, ii, 266, note.

[2] "Letter to member of Parliament, 1720," quoted by Lord, *Industrial Experiments*, p. 126.

will, therefore, suffice to add the statement of Joshua Gee, who, speaking apparently of the provinces in general, said in 1747: that "New England and the northern colonies have not commodities and products enough to send us in return for purchasing their necessary clothing, etc., but are under very great difficulties." [1] Yet in the towns there existed a demand,—moderate in volume, to be sure,—for well-finished wool fabrics. Such cloths, it has already appeared, were not forthcoming from the domestic household manufacture. Probably on the score of quality this demand could not have been satisfied by household products. Accordingly, reliance upon foreign goods was found here to be necessary, in so far as the local handicraftsmen did not meet the requirements either in quantity or quality. Probably, too, such reliance was frequently a profitable affair. Bennett, the historian, in reference to "almost all sorts of English goods, but more especially clothing for men, women, and children," states that "workmen's wages are so high in this part of the World, that they (the people) find it cheaper to import them from London." [2] Again, it was estimated by British authorities that in America high wages made it cost 20 per cent more to manufacture linen, and 50 per cent more to produce woolen cloths than in England.[3]

Of the plantation colonies, evidence is abundant as to the extent of their dependence upon England. Beverley wrote in 1705 of the Virginians that "they have their clothing of all sorts from England, as linen, woollen and silk, hats and leather." [4] The inhabitants of Maryland were said a few years later "to wear the like Cloathing and have the same furniture within their houses with those in this Kingdom (England). The slaves are cloathed with Cottons, Kerseys, flannel, and coarse linens, all imported." [5]

[1] *Trade and Navigation of Great Britain Considered*, p. 171.

[2] *Proceedings* of the Massachusetts Historical Society, 1860–1862, p. 111 (quoted in Beer, *Commercial Policy of England*, p. 80).

[3] "Report of the Board of Trade, 1728," in New Jersey *Archives*, v, 208–209. The references to "workmen's wages" or "wages" indicate quite conclusively that the writers were thinking of the town conditions. In the colonial period a wage-earning class outside the towns may be said to have been practically nonexistent.

[4] Quoted in Beer, p. 70.

[5] *New York Colonial Documents*, v, 606.

Imports of wool cloths into South Carolina in 1761 were recorded as including "finest broadcloth down to negro cloth . . . blankets, flannels, and woolen stockings." [1] Apparently, then, right up to the disturbances which heralded the Revolutionary War, the southern colonies continued to secure a large portion of their requirements for wool cloth from England.

That the American market for such British goods was not larger may be in part attributed to the natural disadvantages, or a combination of natural and artificial disadvantages, attending the importation from the mother country. The freight charges of that period were without doubt peculiarly heavy, judged by modern standards. For example, we know that as late as 1775 the average charges covering land-carriage, insurance, and commissions, for goods shipped from the north of England to America through London were 32 per cent of their value, exclusive of ocean freight.[2] In consequence, perhaps, one should not be surprised to find that in 1685 English worsted serge sold in Connecticut at an advance of over 100 per cent upon its London cost,[3] and that at other times (1706 and 1709) figures of 150 and 200 per cent were reported.[4] But, apparently, at times and in certain places, prices were increased somewhat higher than necessary to cover minimum costs. It is interesting, for example, to find in Maryland that early in the eighteenth century "the trader (or merchant) gets as much for his goods as he can in tobacco, having always the whip-hand of the planters' necessity for cloths and tools," [5] — a foreshadowing of that evil debt relation which was to be the lot of the southern plantation-owner in so many later

[1] *Historical Collections of South Carolina* (Carroll's), ii, 229. Cf. also letter of a Georgia planter ordering negro cloths in London: Georgia Historical Society, *Collections*, vi, 15–17. Furthermore, see Joshua Gee's statement: "the Tobacco Plantations take from England their Cloathing, Household Goods, Iron Manufactures . . . and almost everything else that may be called the Manufacture of England" (*Trade and Navigation of Great Britain Considered*, 3rd Edition, 1731, pp. 20–21).

[2] Clark, p. 148, quoting from "British Transcripts in Library of Congress." For more modern figures, see *Review of Economic Statistics*, July, 1919.

[3] *Connecticut Public Records*, iii, 185, note.

[4] Bishop, i, 330; *Documents relative to New York Colonial History*, v, 460; Dickerson, *American Colonial Government*, p. 304, note.

[5] *Archives of Maryland*, xxv, 604.

decades. In sum, then, with astounding enhancements in price due to natural or other causes, it is easily comprehensible that the colonial market would be likely to be relatively small, and that the domestic household production of woolens supplemented by the partially or wholly handicraft manufacture of worsteds would supply the great bulk of colonial needs.

In correspondence with the chief characteristics of the colonial market, the qualities of cloth imported were principally of two types, the better qualities of fabrics for the upper classes of the northern towns and for the planters, and the cheap grades for the poorer elements of the towns — in so far as they did not keep up a partially sufficient household manufacture — and for the planters' slaves. Broadcloth, a standard English fabric of a superior variety and as yet not made in the colonies, was an important article in the trade. Likewise important were worsteds, — shalloons, calimancoes, camblets, and the like. In the second quality-group were duffells, friezes, coarse kerseys and negro cloths. The medium qualities of fabrics doubtless were not wholly neglected. Apparently flannel and blankets were frequently brought in. Presumably their sale was pretty closely confined to the towns, — this being especially true of flannels of which there was a substantial household production in the country areas. Blankets may have commanded a somewhat wider distribution, since most of the country looms were narrow affairs and could not weave up the farmers' needs for this article. Yet here I am inclined to think substitutes in the form of feather beds, comforters, and the like would restrict the domestic sales of imported blankets. On the whole, medium-grade fabrics seem not to have been significant factors in the import trade. To be sure, just what the proportions among these various qualities of fabrics were around 1760, it is impossible to determine. My own impression is that the groups first mentioned, the superior and the specially cheap, considerably surpassed the medium quality in importance.[1]

[1] Some idea of the differences in quality may be obtained by an examination of prices, though information upon prices is meager. Bishop (i, 344) gives the qualities of cloths imported as broad and narrow fabrics between 6s. and 12s. a yard, and

Data regarding the volume of the import trade in wool fabrics, though fragmentary in character, indicate clearly the rapid increase of that commerce. For the seventeenth century the references are of course only casual and in rough terms, as when in 1657 John Hull of Boston noted in his diary that three ships had arrived from London with clothing.[1] Information concerning this period suggests that for most of the colonies no organized and regular trade had been established. By 1721, however, the movement had reached fair proportions. Statistics covering the export of wool cloth and other commodities from England, the first orderly figures for that traffic, show that the value of wool fabrics shipped from the mother country had attained £147,000. Beside this figure the value of other British-made textiles sent from England, £30,000, appears diminutive. Indeed, of all textiles, foreign or British, exported from England, these British wool manufactures formed more than half on the basis of value. Moreover, they amounted to a third of the whole export trade from Great Britain to the provinces.[2] At approximately the same time (1728), Sir William Keith, former governor of Pennsylvania, represented that the colonies "took off and consumed" a sixth of the wool manufacture of the mother country.[3]

Not until the years just preceding the Revolutionary War were further statistics gathered as to the British trade in wool fabrics. At that time, for the years 1772 to 1774, the average annual ex-

duffells and friezes from 3s. 6d. to 6s. a yard. Broadcloth is elsewhere (Clark, p. 140) said to have retailed throughout the colonial period at about $2 to $3 per yard; serges, an inferior worsted fabric, in the seventeenth century at 70 cents to $1.10 a yard; and kerseys, in Philadelphia, between 1721 and 1731 at 50 to 60 cents a yard. On the other hand, Weeden (Appendix) gives the value of colonial plain cloth in 1713 at 1s. 3d. a yard, and of drugget at 12d. Linsey-woolsey, a staple domestic fabric, was valued in probate records at only 15 cents a yard in 1690 (Clark, p. 141).

Joshua Gee makes an interesting comment upon the character of the wool fabrics exported to the northern colonies: "Any ordinary sort sells with them, and when they are grown out of fashion with us, they are new fashioned enough there; and therefore those places are the great markets we have to dispose of such goods" (*Trade and Navigation of Great Britain Considered*, p. 171).

[1] Weeden, p. 159.

[2] Dickerson, *American Colonial Government*, p. 302.

[3] Bishop, i, 338.

portation of such goods amounted to approximately £775,000.[1] Such a startling increase over the figure for 1721, over 500 per cent, would at first thought seem to indicate an encroachment of the imported fabrics upon the area previously dominated by the colonial household system. However, the growth of population during this half century was also astounding, amounting to 400 to 450 per cent.[2] The general level of English prices moved upward during this period, and presumably the prices of wool fabrics shipped to the colonies followed along. Accordingly, the increase in colonial per capita consumption could not have been considerable. If, nevertheless, some moderate enhancement in per capita consumption did occur, it was probably of limited influence. Consumption in the towns and on the larger plantations would be chiefly affected; and, indeed, as lines of profitable commerce were opened up and as trade in tobacco and rice developed, such local increase of consumption is wholly credible.[3] At most, then, this enhancement in total volume of imported fabrics between 1721 and 1772–1774 occasioned, it seems, merely a diminution in the household production within or close by the towns, with perhaps some increase of consumption in the South as the plantation system became more widely established.

The statistics for 1772–1774 are of further interest in showing the relative proportions of the trade taken by the several sections of the country. New England, despite an early settlement, a considerable increase of population, and a wide-flung commerce, was able to take but little over a quarter (27 per cent) of the total. The middle colonies of New York and Pennsylvania took half as

[1] Macpherson, *Annals of Commerce*, iii, 602. These statistics are as follows:

	1772	1773	1774	1775	1776
New England	£284,553	£147,717	£168,815	£8,382	£15,657
New York and Pennsylvania . .	344,934	211,617	346,752	555	. . .
Maryland, Virginia, Carolina, Georgia	296,155	189,695	239,900	40,831	. . . .
Total	£925,642	£549,029	£755,467	£49,768	£15,657

[2] Clark, pp. 102–103. From a population of roughly half a million in 1720, the country is supposed to have increased to over two and a quarter million whites and half a million negroes by 1775.

[3] Clark (p. 110) reaches the conclusion that "not improbably the per capita consumption (of imported wool fabrics) rose somewhat" in the half century after 1720.

much again (40.5 per cent), explicable both on the ground of a sizable town population and on the facilities within these colonies for an appreciable internal trade up the rivers. Thus, for example, it was reported that the people of Albany were clothed wholly in imported fabrics.[1] The southern colonies, finally, took nearly a third of the whole importation (32.5 per cent), a large proportion in view of the late development in some sections, and of the lower value per unit of quantity for much of the cloth consumed in the South. However, such a share for the southern area is not an unexpected phenomenon when the features of the domestic manufacture are understood.

It may be added with respect to these figures for 1772–1774 that at that time the exportation to the colonies formed approximately a sixth (in the single year 1772 a fifth) of the total British export trade in wool goods.[2] James states with regard to this later colonial period that "after the home trade, probably the most beneficial in every respect was the export of woolen and worsted fabrics to our American plantations."[3] Under these circumstances it is not to be wondered at that the British officials kept reasonably close watch of the American wool manufacture, or again that in the retaliatory measures favored by the colonies at the time of the Stamp Act and later disturbances, a self-sufficiency in wool fabrics was advocated.

With respect to the import trade in general, there remains only to note the organization of that movement. Upon this point Joshua Gee throws some light. He remarks that wool goods "are generally sent (to America) at the risk of the shop-keepers and traders of England, who are the great exporters, and not the inhabitants of the colonies, as some have imagined." The local representatives of the English exporters are said to be "young merchants who have not stocks of their own; and therefore all our plantations are filled with such who receive the consignments of their friends from hence; and when they have got a sufficient

[1] Lord, *Industrial Experiments*, p. 133.

[2] Inasmuch as Sir William Keith's somewhat similar estimate for 1728 (one-sixth of England's wool-cloth production going to the colonies) was only a rough figure, no comparison with the above is attempted.

[3] *History of Worsted Manufacture in England*, p. 186.

stock to trade with, they generally return home and other young men take their place." [1] Within the country, the goods were probably sold in large measure through individual negotiations of the importers and the local merchants, but the auction method was also sometimes employed.[2] The latter system, offering a quick and cheap manner of selling goods which were likely to arrive in large quantities, was destined to play an increasing part in the American distributive organization for imported fabrics.

[1] *Trade and Commerce of Great Britain Considered*, pp. 171–172. He continued quaintly: "so that the continual motion and intercourse our people have into the colonies, may be compared to the bees of a hive, which go out empty, and come back again loaded."

[2] Examples may be drawn from most colonial newspapers. For example, in the *Boston Gazette* of January 11, 1768, appears the advertisement: "To be sold by Benjamin Church at his usual Place of Sale on Thursday evening next a Great Variety of valuable Articles, viz. Broad Cloths, Kerseys, Ranteens, Camblets," etc. See again New Jersey *Archives*, Newspaper Extracts, v, 468, a quotation from the *Pennsylvania Gazette* of January 3, 1765, "To be sold by Public Vendue . . . an assortment of goods . . . (including) broadcloths, coatings, shalloons, flannels . . . worsted stockings."

Conclusion of Part I.

The distinctly colonial period of wool manufacture drew to a close about 1760. The disturbances accompanying the Stamp Act and other British tax measures, and the unsettled condition of commerce which was occasioned by the Revolutionary War, and later by the Franco-British warfare, ushered in a new era. There was, of course, no sharp break with the preceding development, — industrial history shows few sudden changes. In many ways a noteworthy feature of these later decades was to be the maintenance of the organization in wool manufacture which had characterized the colonial system, — the household production. Certain underlying conditions, indeed, were for many years antagonistic to any real transformation of the industry. The wool supply was too poor in quality for the manufacture of cloths which could compete in the open market with English fabrics, and the growing of wool had as yet not reached the commercial stage. Again, technical advance had not really begun. Practically none of the improvements in apparatus which were the concomitants of the Industrial Revolution in England had reached America as yet, nor had an independent evolution appeared. But chiefly no market for domestic fabrics existed sufficiently large in scope to encourage the expansion of operations in the local industry. The market for "boughten" cloth was narrow in 1760, and the trade therein small. Again, the existing market was so situated that English fabrics could be readily introduced, and was at the time firmly wedded to the (as yet) superior cloths derived through importation. Thus a vicious circle was created: cloths inferior to the English would not find favor in the restricted and prejudiced domestic market, and yet neither the quality of the domestic wool nor the status of the local technique was conducive to the production of competitive fabrics. The industry, then, had perforce to undergo a transitional period during which conditions conducive to factory operations could be attained.

PART II

THE ERA OF THE SMALL FACTORY

INTRODUCTION

In the transitional period which succeeded the simpler colonial era, the essential feature was the appearance and development of the factory. Nothing in nature approaching a factory had existed in the earlier times. The highest industrial form was that of the workshop, either of the southern plantation or of the handicraft worsted worker in the towns. By the third decade of the nineteenth century, however, the factory had become the characteristic type of industrial organization in the American wool manufacture. It had not, indeed, prevailed over the whole production of wool fabrics. The household method of manufacture had a strong root and was specially adapted to certain economic conditions, — economic conditions which, in the westward settlement of the United States, came to be repeated over and over again. Moreover, the representative factory was a distinctly small affair. Yet in the eastern communities, which in most industrial matters set the pace for the rest of the country, the factory of this limited sort had become the typical form of organization by 1830, — in some respects the dominant form. The older method of manufacture might in some localities and sections of the country still retain its earlier strength; in others its power might yet increase for a time; but its decline and ultimate disappearance could be forecast. The young, factory form of manufacture had proved itself. For this reason, the steady progress of development in the industry may be broken arbitrarily at this date, approximately 1830, in order that we may inquire more fully into the status of the manufacture at that time, even as similarly we fixed upon 1760 as a convenient date for examining the typical colonial method of production.

At first thought a jump of seventy years may seem unreasonable. Only ninety years have elapsed between 1830 and the present time, and these years, as will appear, have been divided into two further periods. Yet a closer examination of the decades following 1760 gives justification for this long leap. Of special influence in prolonging the formative period was the number of false starts which attended the commencement of the more advanced manufacture. A survey of this whole period if hastily made might well suggest to the observer that there was an uninterrupted evolution throughout its course, — from the time when operations on something more than a household or handicraft system were first attempted to the acquisition of the complete and intrenched factory form. Such, however, would be wide of the truth. For example, after a few years of progress, including even the space of the Revolutionary War, there was a reaction which left the industry at a point not far from that at which it had started. Probably experience thus dearly bought with the failures of early establishments and the disappointment of high hopes was necessary and on the whole advantageous; and to be sure each new venture was initiated under more promising auspices. But equally important in prolonging this formative period was the time required for securing the firm foundation upon which further and more definite advance might be assured. Only with aggravating slowness, step by step, could the preparation be accomplished, — in improvement of wool supply, in betterment of technical equipment, and the like. Yet only when the preparation was relatively complete could the young factory be pushed forward with confidence in its success and with any considerable vigor.

CHAPTER IV

EARLY ATTEMPTS AT FACTORY PRODUCTION

INITIATED by the agitation which centered around the Stamp Act, there came a series of popular demonstrations, extending over the next half century, in favor of domestic manufactures, in which demand for a larger domestic production of wool fabrics always played a prominent part. In a considerable measure these demonstrations worked themselves out in mere effervescence, but they were not without real influence upon the course of development, at least in the wool manufacture. Particularly they seem to have awakened in various individuals a zeal for a more effective domestic production, which persisted after the popular excitement had died down and which brought important contributions to the advance of the industry.

The events of the first movement, that evoked by the Stamp Act, may be taken as typical of those which followed. In this instance, feeling perhaps ran exceptionally high by reason of the novelty of the situation. Merchants agreed not to import British wool fabrics, orders previously given were canceled, and with some exceptions, of course, the people, rich as well as poor, dressed in homespun, and to conserve the wool supply vowed to eat no lamb.[1] In 1766 the Daughters of Liberty at Providence held all-day sessions in spinning. Premiums were offered by voluntary societies to encourage the growth of raw materials.[2] In Massachusetts, in 1768, several of his Majesty's Council and many members of the House of Representatives as well as a num-

[1] Weeden, p. 719. The forebodings of trouble are quaintly expressed in a Boston dispatch to the *Connecticut Courant*, October 29, 1764: "It is fear'd by many who wish well to Great Britain, that the new A——t of P———t will greatly distress, if not totally ruin some of HER own manufactures. — It is thought that by means of this A——t, less of her woollen cloths, to the amount of some thousands sterling, will be purchased in this cold climate the insuing winter."

[2] Weeden, p. 732.

ber of the Clergy were reported to have appeared "completely cloathed in the Manufacture of this Country." [1] At Commencement in 1769 the president and graduating class at the Rhode Island College were clad in homespun, an example which was followed at Harvard the succeeding year.[2] And apparently such enthusiasm was not without its effect upon the general public.

Unquestionably there was an outburst of domestic production unlike anything that had gone before. East Hartford, Connecticut, was reported to be weaving 17,000 yards of cloth annually.[3] The borough of Elizabeth, New Jersey, produced "upwards of 100,000 yards of linen and woolen cloth" during 1769.[4] Merchants began to carry and advertise domestic woolens, such goods were sold at auction, and markets for their sale were established.[5] The manufacture of broadcloth was attempted for the first time.[6] But, more important for our purpose, enterprises partaking of the nature of factories were attempted. Of two of them no detailed data are available: those at Brookfield, Massachusetts, and in Somerset County, Maryland.[7] We know more of William Molineaux's establishment in Boston. It started in as a Spinning School in 1769, aided by public contribution. Within a year's time, in a petition to the Legislature, he asserted that he had already "learned" at least three hundred children and women to spin "in the most compleat manner." Thereafter he added warping and twisting mills, looms (by the terms of his lease he was to keep ten looms constantly busy weaving worsteds), and some finishing and dyeing apparatus.[8] Just what he produced,

[1] *Boston Gazette*, January 11, 1768.

[2] Weeden, p. 732, and *Census of 1860*, iii, p. xxix.

[3] *Massachusetts Gazette*, January 14, 1768.

[4] New Jersey *Archives*, Newspaper Extracts, viii, 195.

[5] Contemporary newspapers, e. g., *Boston Gazette*, September 19, 1768; Enoch Brown "Informs those Persons who are desirous of Promoting our Own Manufactures as well as serving themselves: That he takes in all Sorts of Country-made Cloths at his Store on Boston Neck, either on Commissions, or in Exchange for any kind of West-India Goods at a reasonable Rate." Also, Weeden, p. 732; Scharf and Westcott, *History of Philadelphia*, iii, 2227.

[6] *Census of 1860*, iii, pp. xxviii, xxxix; Hazard, *College Tom*, p. 101; New Jersey *Archives*, xxvi, 157; Bishop, i, 377.

[7] Warden, *Account of the United States*, 1819, ii, 161.

[8] Bagnall, pp. 42, 47, 48; Bishop, i, 375–376; Clark, pp. 189–190.

and particularly whether or not this was more than an expanded workshop of a worsted handicraftsman, are questions it is impossible to answer definitively. But Clark is right in that it was the nearest approach to a textile factory of which we have any real knowledge before the Revolutionary War.[1]

In a manner somewhat similar to the above, the outburst of popular feeling which ushered in the Revolutionary War led not only to a signed agreement among Philadelphia butchers not to slaughter sheep and to like demonstrations of zeal for domestic industries,[2] but also to the organization in that city of "The United Company for Promoting American Manufactures." The spinning was given out to household workers for the most part, although a spinning jenny of twenty-four spindles is reported as part of the concern's equipment at one time. Later, when in 1787 the Company was revived, it possessed four jennies carrying a total of two hundred and twenty-four spindles, a carding machine, and twenty-six looms. However, one cannot ascertain just how large a part the spinning and weaving of wool played in this establishment, or how much of this equipment was woolen machinery. In common with many of the early textile enterprises, the United Company did not tie itself to any one material. Cotton, flax, and wool were all employed, and seemingly the former two bulked largest. At one time during the war, Samuel Wetherill, Jr., who seems to have been a leading spirit in the endeavor and to have somehow secured control of the establishment, contracted with the government to supply woolen cloth, though it is not definitely known that any of this cloth was actually delivered; and again in 1782 he advertised everlastings and coatings among the fabrics, chiefly linen, which were for sale at his "manufactory." In the resuscitated company of 1787, the principal products were surely cotton and linen fabrics. While, then, one should presumably designate this concern as an immature factory, he is

[1] Clark, p. 190. Apparently the enterprise was continued until the death of the promoter in 1774. See *Massachusetts Gazette*, December 16, 1774: advertisement of the sale "by Public Vendue at the Province Manufacturing House" of all the looms, warping, twisting and other machines, "Dying Presses, etc." belonging to the estate of William Molineaux.

[2] Bishop, i, 381.

doubtful whether to call it an immature woolen factory. Moreover, with the mixture of textile materials and the paucity of definite information, one can learn from this episode little of a detailed character as to the state of the organized wool manufacture at that time.[1]

Beyond this establishment, in part the fruition of patriotic zeal, there was no enterprise of note. A subsidy of £300 toward the erection of a factory was given to Edward Parker of Cecil County, Maryland, by the state legislature; but nothing more is known of his endeavor.[2] In addition, there were several small establishments in Virginia and Maryland, such as that of Charles Carroll of Carrollton and that of Robert Carter of Aires, Virginia. Apparently, however, these were only enlarged plantation workshops, where negroes, even up to the number of thirty, worked under the supervision of experienced white artisans.[3] The times, then, were not ripe for factory production on any considerable scale.[4]

The first purely wool-manufacturing concern founded on a strictly business basis, and the first in which power machinery was employed,[5] as well as the first wool-working enterprise of which any considerable data are available, was one launched at Hartford, Connecticut, in 1788. The initial capital for the enterprise consisted of £1250, in part raised by means of a subscription paper circulated in Hartford and neighboring towns. Later a capital of £2800 was reported. To these private efforts was added the patronage of the state. With particular regard for this Hartford venture, all buildings used as woolen factories were

[1] For data concerning this enterprise, see Bishop, i, 387–388; Scharf and Westcott, *op. cit.*, iii, 2314; Bagnall, pp. 63–64, 71; Clark, pp. 183, 190, 226.

[2] Johnston, *History of Cecil County*, p. 324.

[3] *Documentary History of American Industrial Society*, ii, 274, 314–316, 326–327.

[4] Cases of the employment of household workers in the putting-out of spinning and weaving — cases which are encountered but rarely in American experience — are referred to below, pp. 192, 224–225.

[5] Bishop (i, 376) thinks there was some sort of power machinery in the Molineaux factory of 1769, since "two boys only" were stated to wind and twist yarn for fifty looms. It is problematical what sort of machine was referred to, and whether it applied to cotton, woolen, or linen yarn. Perhaps it was a cop-building machine, which could be worked by a foot-treddle.

exempted from taxation for five years and all workmen therein from payment of the poll tax for two years. Furthermore, a bounty of one penny per pound was given for all yarn spun in the factory at Hartford before June 1, 1789. This, however, did not suffice to put the concern on its feet. Other appeals for aid followed; and in response, a lottery of £1000 was granted (1790), the avowed purpose of which was to provide funds for the purchase of machinery. This device actually yielded nearly twice that amount. Then to these pecuniary aids should be joined the interest taken in the enterprise by public men: Washington visited the establishment during his eastern tour, inspected it, and ordered cloth; Hamilton commended it in his Report on Manufactures as a "precious embryo;" and it is probable that it attracted much attention from other patriots of the time.[1] Though it was announced in 1792 that "this manufacture, after struggling with every obstacle, begins to flourish, and bids fair to be advantageous to the proprietors as well as to the public," the hoped-for success was in fact never attained.[2]

The difficulties in launching the enterprise are narrated in the petitions to the Legislature for assistance, — difficulties in getting machinery and suitable buildings, in finding proper materials, and in securing skilled labor or expert supervision. The machines had to be purchased in the country, as England forbade the exportation of wool-working machinery; and for the first year or two these mechanisms comprised, it appears, only such apparatus as might have been found in any of the establishments

[1] As regards Hamilton, see Taussig, *State Papers and Speeches on the Tariff*, p. 99. Hamilton's optimistic account should be given: "A promising essay towards the fabrication of cloths, cassimeres, and other woolen goods, is going on at Hartford, in Connecticut. Specimens of the different kinds which are made, in the possession of the secretary, evince that these fabrics have attained a very considerable degree of perfection. Their quality certainly surpasses anything that could have been looked for in so short a time and under so great disadvantages, and conspires with the scantiness of the means which have been at the command of the directors to form the eulogium of that public spirit, perseverance and judgment which have been able to accomplish so much" (p. 98).

[2] Davis, *Essays in the Earlier History of American Corporations*, ii, 267. Other accounts of the Hartford enterprise are to be found in Bagnall, p. 101, *seq.*, and North, *Bulletin*, 1899, pp. 139–147.

already considered, such as looms, a fulling mill, and some finishing machinery. According to Washington, the spinning in 1792 was done wholly "by the country people, who are paid by the cut," —presumably the spinning of both woolen and worsted yarns; and the machinery which it was proposed to buy from the receipts of the lottery was said to be "Spinning, Carding, and Scribbling Machines, to expedite the labor and reduce that (preparatory) part of the business."

Thereafter came a change of such importance as to justify the designation of this establishment as the first complete manufactory in the American industry devoted solely to wool: power-driven machines other than the old fulling mill were introduced, and the yarn spinning was brought within the factory walls. In 1795, when the concern sold out its equipment, the machinery included two carding machines, a spinning jenny, and a twisting machine, besides eight looms, etc. Of the spinning jenny, we know little: it was procured during the last year or two of the company's existence, was undoubtedly worked by hand, and probably was an adaptation of the jennies for cotton spinning, of which the earliest mentioned is one brought from England in 1775.[1] The carding machines were described by Henry Wansey, an English clothier, who visited the plant in 1794: "I saw two carding-engines, working by water, of a very inferior construction. Two large center cylinders in each, with two doffers, and only two working cylinders, of the breadth of bare sixteen inches, said to be invented by some person there." The performance was equally unsatisfactory, "the wool not being half worked;" and accordingly "the spinning (then done on spinning wheels) was very bad."[2] In addition, as already suggested, there was the difficulty of securing skilled labor and expert supervision. Men acquainted with the production of the finer woolen fabrics ob-

[1] This first spinning jenny was said to be suitable for spinning either wool or cotton (North, *Bulletin*, 1901, p. 256, quoting the *Philadelphia Magazine*); but it is doubtful if it was used for the former in the United Company above described, particularly because the Hartford concern was so slow in adopting it. On the other hand, jennies were early employed in the cotton industry, though soon superseded by other machines (Clark, pp. 191–192, 424–425).

[2] Bagnall, p. 107.

viously must have been scarce indeed in the country. In this regard Wansey stated: "None of the partners understands anything about (the manufacture), and all depends on an Englishman who is a sorter of wool." In a concern of such limited size skilled workmen were perhaps not so necessary as in later factories. For expert supervision, however, there undoubtedly was need. Yet if one discounts the statements of this experienced foreigner, as probably he should, it is evident that technical difficulties were great. Effective production could not be expected.

A second major obstacle in the way of successful manufacture was the difficulty in securing a satisfactory supply of raw material. Most of the wool must have come from domestic sources, but as yet there had come no substantial improvement in the quality of domestic sheep above the condition which obtained in latter days of the colonial period. Indeed, possibly the general character of the American clip had worsened in the interim. The mill seems to have procured some wool from Georgia, — at least so Wansey was told. This was "very fine wool," he remarked, "but it was in bad condition." [1] Even the company itself could praise the domestic fiber but faintly. Wool of this country, the proprietors said, when properly sorted, will make cloths "equal to British Seconds," presumably English second-best goods.[2] In the end, effort was made to get suitable foreign wool, and four thousand pounds at least were imported from Spain.[3] With suitable fiber so hard to secure, inevitably the price ruled high; and thus the power of the mill to compete with foreign-made cloths was the further lowered. But, more serious still, it is not improbable that the factory just could not find a sufficient quantity of wool in quality proper for the manufacture of cloths which would compare favorably with the imported goods.[4]

[1] Bagnall, p. 107.

[2] *Ibid.*, pp. 104–105; quoting a memorial to the legislature.

[3] *Bulletin*, 1899, p. 142.

[4] Of course foreign-grown wools might in time have been secured in adequate volume to satisfy the needs of the concern. Just what difficulties such a scheme would meet, we cannot now gauge. At best, however, dependence on foreign supplies would make a less favorable basis for the development of factory production on any considerable scale than the existence of adequate domestic supply.

Finally, on the side of quality in production the enterprise also was handicapped. The existing market for "boughten" cloth was narrow by reason of the persisting large household production of wool fabrics, and, being largely limited to the towns, it demanded for the most part fabrics of relatively high grade, — fabrics such as were available by importation. Accordingly we find the establishment engaged on goods generally of the finer qualities: superior woolens such as broadcloths and cassimeres. Inferior fabrics, e. g., coatings and "everlastings," were also manufactured; but the proportion between the finer and poorer grades of goods may perhaps be judged from the statement of Wansey, who found in the weave-shop two looms employed upon broadcloth, two upon cassimeres with worsted warps, and only one upon narrow or "ferret" cloth.[1] A young factory, however, could not hope to produce fine goods at once; and even the testimony of contemporaries favorably disposed to this Hartford enterprise is evidence that the production of the new mill fell short of the standard desired by the market. Washington was lukewarm. He wrote of the broadcloths that they "are not of the first quality as yet, but they are good." And Hamilton, although trying to speak as appreciatively as he could of the "essay," hesitated before a full commendation of its products.[2] Moreover, the ineffectiveness of the Hartford goods in competition with imported fabrics gives further suggestion in this matter.

The disposition of the cloth produced seems to have been in the hands of local storekeepers and sometimes of merchants in New York to whom the cloth was consigned.[3] But seemingly neither means was of much avail, and the stock of goods piled up

[1] An advertisement of 1789 gives a list of the goods produced, but conveys nothing as to respective quantities of each: "fine, middling, and coarse, Broad, and narrow Cloths, Serges, Coating, Baizes, etc." (Bagnall, p. 103). Some cloths, it is asserted, were sold for as much as five dollars a yard (Bishop, i, 418).

[2] See p. 65 above, note 1.

[3] Henry Wansey speaks of a storekeeper, Elisha Colt, who was interested in the enterprise, as having twenty or thirty pieces on hand. The latter, he says, sold the cloths, although of inferior quality, "at about the same price, I found, as our English goods when delivered into the stores there" (Bagnall, p. 107). A quantity of goods was sent to Nathaniel Hazard, a merchant of New York, in 1789 (*ibid.*, p. 101).

in the storehouse. Various schemes were employed to get rid of it: the prizes of the lottery granted by the state, it seems, were paid in cloth; auctions — to be sure, not an unusual method of sale with respect to imported goods — were resorted to in 1792 and 1793, the first to get ready money; and finally in 1794 the one and only dividend ever paid by the company was announced, a 50 per cent dividend on the original shares, paid in cloth! And even then there were one hundred and forty pieces of finished goods on hand when the business was sold.

The end came in 1795, after seven years of trials, when the equipment was put on the auction-block. It was purchased, perhaps bought in, by Colonel Wadsworth, one of the original promoters, who carried on the business for a couple of years, and then closed down the whole factory.

After the Hartford attempt, only three others, all located in Massachusetts, require attention in the present connection: "factories" established at Stockbridge in 1789, one at Watertown in 1790,[1] and a third at Ipswich two years later. Of these, information is available only with respect to the last. This concern, called the "Massachusetts Woollen Manufactory," was promoted by John Manning, a physician; received encouragement from the state and town; and for a few years (until it was converted to the working of cotton) produced broadcloths, blankets, and flannels. The establishment was not so well organized as that at Hartford. The carding, spinning, and weaving were all done by hand, and in part perhaps at the homes of the workers. The manufacture of wool fabrics under such disadvantages was probably bound to be unsuccessful.[2]

Such, then, was the history of the first endeavors to bring the wool manufacture from the home or workshop and organize it on a more extensive basis. It is a history of failures, but to the investigator the reasons for the failures, as far as one can ascertain them, are particularly instructive. It was quite clear that

[1] Bishop, i, 420.

[2] Bagnall, pp. 195–196. This venture was noteworthy in at least one respect: when Dr. Manning began the manufacture, he proposed to utilize the power of the wind, — possibly, as Bagnall says, a unique case in textile history.

American woolens of the qualities that could then be turned out, could not hope to compete with imported goods. Timothy Dwight expressed this view in 1796: "While population is so thin, and labour so high, as in this country, there is reason to fear that extensive manufactories (of woolens) will rarely be profitable."[1] The failure of a company, such as the Hartford enterprise, to sell its products was but the natural result of existing conditions. Chief among these unfavorable circumstances were the narrowness and peculiar character of the domestic market, which, being limited largely to the towns and to the superior grades of fabrics, not only made the competition of British goods especially severe, but called for a higher quality of domestic product than the conditions of wool supply, technical equipment, and manufacturing skill in the American industry rendered possible.[2] But remedies were not beyond hope. Dwight himself recognized that important gains might be derived "from the several kinds of machinery by which labour is abridged." Furthermore, a widening of the American market, the acquisition of a better and more dependable wool supply, and the accumulation of experience in the art of wool manufacture would add important stimulus and strength to the infant industry.

Already its chief rival, the British industry, had secured the advantage upon all these points. To the large British wool production was added the Spanish and other Continental stocks, the purchase of which was the readier by virtue of the world-wide demand for England's manufactures. Then, British genius had contributed various "labor-abridging" inventions, notably a good carding machine and the spinning jenny. These had not been universally adopted in England, but in the growing Yorkshire

[1] *Travels*, i, 443.

[2] Better trained operatives and more competent supervision would both be needed in the effective operation of the domestic industry, particularly with respect to these goods of higher quality where the element of "finish," always difficult to impart properly, played an important rôle. A lesser, and not wholly independent factor, is that of capital. This appears, for example, in the fact that the Hartford mill purchased at least some foreign wool because it could get it on credit instead of the local staple for which cash was needed (Clark, p. 366). However, presumably an effective and otherwise successful manufacture would have attracted or accumulated capital.

manufacture, where they could be utilized without change in the prevailing form of the production, — that of independent clothier, — they had given additional competitive power. Finally, the century-old practice in wool-working had given the British manufacture a skill in the fabrication of cloths which, in consequence of the localization of the industry, the permanence of the population, and the stable occupational habits of the people, was passed on from generation to generation of wool workers.

Surprisingly enough, the American industry by approximately 1830 had acquired a position not much, if at all, inferior in competitive strength to the British manufacture, at least in so far as the common run of fabrics is concerned. How was this change effected? By virtue of improvement in what factors? These are questions to which obviously no ready answer may be given. Some attempt at reply, however, will be made in the succeeding chapters.

CHAPTER V

IMPROVEMENT OF THE WOOL SUPPLY

THE changes in the character of the raw material supply are of an outstanding importance when considering the development of the American wool-manufacturing industry. A detailed inquiry into the history of wool-growing within the United States, to be sure, would be out of place here,[1] but sufficient discussion must be brought within this survey to show the interactions between the two industries of wool-growing and wool-manufacturing,—the effect upon the wool-growing side of the needs or aspirations of the manufacturing end, and contrariwise the influence of the supply of raw materials in encompassing and so to a degree determining indirectly the character of the wool-cloth production. Incidentally, one method will be indicated whereby a break was secured in the vicious circle which, it is suggested above, existed in colonial times between the quality of domestic wool clip and that of domestic wool manufacture.[2]

The dependence of the wool manufacture upon the raw material, and the difficulties of successful fabric production for domestic markets without improvement of the local wool supply, were perceived by contemporary observers. The first circular sent out by the New York Society for the Promotion of Useful Arts contained the query: "Can you suggest any plan of improving our wool so as to render it more fit for superfine fabrics?" and Hamilton in his celebrated Report suggested the high expediency of "raising and improving the breed of sheep at home" as "the most efficacious aid" to the manufacturing

[1] See Wright, *Wool-Growing and the Tariff*, pp. 12–16, 22–31, which will form the basis of this review, although Randall's *Fine Wool Sheep Husbandry*, and the *Special Report on the Sheep Industry* (Carman), 1892, also contain accounts of the period.

[2] See above, p. 56.

industry.[1] To these ends efforts had been made long before the first considerable importations of improved breeds actually occurred. These efforts exemplify particularly that patriotic movement for self-sufficient cloth production to which some reference has already been made.[2] Indeed, the events of the period prior to the Embargo of 1807 that are concerned with betterment of the domestic wool supply are, I believe, to be interpreted as the expressions of that spirit, rather than as the result of the action of economic forces. As early as 1785 the South Carolina Agricultural Society offered a premium for the first full-blooded merino — the highly improved Spanish breed — that was introduced into the state, and Massachusetts soon did likewise.[3] Again, the New York Society already mentioned caused "Instructions" to be printed for the attention of captains of vessels sailing to foreign lands. These instructions, which were "to be stuck up in their respective cabbins," made special

[1] *Transactions* of this Society, i, xiv; Taussig, *State Papers on the Tariff*, p. 99. The Hartford company also urged an improvement in sheep breeding (North, *Bulletin*, 1899, p. 141).

[2] See above, pp. 61–64. Other evidences of this spirit are numerous. In the period of the Confederation, several of the States, e. g., Massachusetts, Rhode Island, and Pennsylvania, had enacted tariffs of a protectionist trend and, in the first case, avowedly for protection (Hill, *First Stages of the Tariff Policy*, pp. 75–90; Giesecke, *American Commercial Legislation before 1789*, pp. 131–134). The Massachusetts General Court appointed a joint committee "to view any new invented machines that are making within this commonwealth, for the purpose of manufacturing sheep's and cotton wool, and report what measures are proper for the legislature to take to encourage the same" (Taft, *Some Notes on the Introduction of the Woolen Manufacture into the United States*, p. 3; hereafter referred to as Taft, *Notes*). Connecticut exempted all woolen factories from taxation for a period of years, and their workers from the poll tax (Bagnall, p. 100). Finally, voluntary associations for the furtherance of domestic manufactures were organized, in Philadelphia in 1787, which revived the short-lived "Company" of 1775, in Germantown in 1790 (Scharf and Westcott, *op. cit.*, iii, 2314), and in New York in 1791, the one whose *Transactions* have already been quoted.

[3] Wright, p. 11; *Bulletin of the National Association of Wool Manufacturers* (hereafter referred to as *Bulletin*), 1905, p. 224.

The Spanish merino, it may be noted, was a breed improved by the Moors during their occupation of Spain, and preserved by their subsequent conquerors. In the latter part of the eighteenth century the exportation of these animals was prohibited, in an endeavor of Spain to maintain a monopoly of this superior sheep. Hence the special efforts on the part of the American societies to secure specimens.

note of sheep: "particularly if you should be able to obtain the sheep of Spain or Barbary, which are amongst the most valuable, even though they should not appear to you superior to those of this country."[1] Thus the spirit of improvement was abroad.

The earlier importations of the much coveted merino bear out this contention of zealous patriotism. The first sheep to arrive — barring two which were sent in 1793 to Cambridge, Massachusetts, and which the owner, in his ignorance of their value, "simply ate up"[2] — was the full-blooded ram Don Pedro, brought over by Messrs. Du Pont de Nemours and Delessert in 1801. Their purpose seems to have been altruistic, both negatively, in that they were not as yet interested in the wool manufacture, and positively, in that they soon afterwards offered gratis to neighboring farmers the use of this animal for stud purposes.[3] The next groups to come were those which in the following year were brought in by Robert Livingston and David Humphreys, men who undoubtedly were moved by whole-hearted desire to serve the country. The former had been active in the New York Society above referred to, and later, as he writes in his *Essay on Sheep*, his ambition had led him to render himself yet "more extensively useful, by suggesting and enforcing such improvements in agriculture as might add to the wealth of individuals, and, by forming the basis of manufactures, to the independence of our country."[4] Humphreys gave a similar explanation of his interest in this project: in brief, that he was "convinced that this race of sheep . . . might be introduced with great benefit to our country."[5] By their efforts, the former was able to secure two

[1] *Transactions* of the New York Society, i, 96. The latter clause was evoked because of the fact that in improving the fleece of the merino the carcass had been sacrificed to a degree. They were, and still are, small animals as compared, for example, with the English "mutton" breeds, where in the main the object of the improvement had been in the opposite direction.

[2] Randall, p. 30.

[3] Bishop, ii, 87.

[4] *Essay on Sheep*, 1809 ed., p. 6.

[5] Letter (on importation of sheep) for which he was given a gold medal by the Massachusetts Society for Promoting Agriculture; reproduced in *Bulletin*, 1905, p. 245.

E. I. DU PONT DE NEMOURS

Who became interested in fine-wool culture and in wool manufacture during the early years of the nineteenth century

CAPTAIN NATHANIEL STEVENS

One of the first flannel manufacturers of the country and the founder of a family of wool manufacturers

pair from the French flock at Rambouillet, a flock originated by gifts of sheep from the Spanish to the French king; while the latter made the first large importation, twenty-one rams and seventy-five ewes, bringing them direct from Spain after English invasion of that country had made exportation possible.[1] These were the main arrivals before the Embargo was imposed, although two or three additional pair actually entered, the purpose of whose owners is not clear.

Immediate reformation of the American wool supply was, however, by no means forthcoming. For example, Livingston, returning in 1805 to the United States after a protracted stay abroad, was chagrined to find that the efforts of Du Pont, Humphreys, and himself had brought so little result.[2] But the obstacles were various: beside the normal conservatism of the farmer, there was a further dislike for these sheep in particular by reason of their small size and of the poor quality of their flesh for food; while, above all, the economic motive was lacking, "a vital impulse," as Humphreys phrased it. There had first to be a demand for the finer wool from a growing wool manufacture so situated as to be able to supply the domestic market for the finer fabrics. An inkling of this necessity may have come to these early propagandists of the merino breeds, since Humphreys in 1806, followed by Livingston and Du Pont, began the manufacture of fine woolen cloths.[3] The superiority of this new wool, to be sure, may have been appreciated and sometimes employed by the small-scale manufacturers of those early years,—of whom something will be said later. But it took the suddenly opened opportunity created by the Embargo and Non-Intercourse laws, particularly the reduction of competition in the domestic woolen-goods market, to bring forth a strong economic motive or "vital impulse" for the use of fine wool.

The movement of prices for merino wool during these troubled years of commercial hostilities reflects the altered condition of demand. During 1807 wool of this quality rose to a dollar a pound.[4] By 1809 it was stated to be double that amount, while

[1] Wright, pp. 14–15.

[2] *Ibid.*, p. 15.

[3] Randall, *Fine Wool Sheep Husbandry*, p. 44.

[4] *Ibid.*, p. 45.

the value of the wool from the "good common sheep" was given as but fifty cents per pound.[1] In sympathy with this course of merino wool prices, the value of the animals began to soar. A "merino mania" set in, during which speculation ran riot and as much as a thousand and fifteen hundred dollars were given for full-blooded rams.[2] As yet, however, there did not exist a sufficiently broad and firm demand for the finer staple to warrant such extreme prices for merino wool, or for the fine-wooled animals. A collapse in prices was inevitable; but in part this collapse was brought about through an increase in the supply of merino sheep. William Jarvis, American Consul to Portugal, seized the opportunity offered by the current political convulsions in Spain and by the lifting of the American embargo, to ship some four thousand sheep to the United States. The shipments were begun in 1810. The animals were distributed "to every state which (Jarvis thought) would be likely to profit by the acquisition," being sent to various ports from Wiscasset, Maine, to Norfolk, Virginia.[3] Other large importations followed, apparently now impelled by a commercial motive, until by the latter part of 1811, probably over twenty-five thousand merino sheep had been secured.[4]

[1] Livingston, *Essay on Sheep*, p. 141.

[2] Randall, *Fine Wool Sheep Husbandry*, p. 45; Westcott, *History of Philadelphia*, ch. 785; Capron, *Bulletin*, 1881, p. 128; *Census of 1860*, iii, p. xxix.

Elkanah Watson, who was influential in spreading the culture of merino sheep, writes of the "astonishing inflation," giving a personal experience: "I purchased a beautiful buck of the Chancellor (Livingston), at $175, for which I repeatedly refused one thousand dollars, and afterwards sold him for twelve dollars" (*Memoirs*, p. 343). Westcott (*History of Philadelphia*, ch. 785) quotes largely from a pamphlet of certain cautious writers who as early as 1810 inveighed against the speculation which was going on in merino sheep. The title of their publication was: "An Antidote to the Merino Mania now progressing through the United States, or the Value of the Merino Breed placed upon a Proper Basis. 'Look before you leap.'" The substance of their criticism was that merino wool was of no great value unless the wool-manufacturing industry proved capable of withstanding foreign competition.

[3] Benton and Barry, *Statistical View*, 1837, p. 130.

[4] Carman, pp. 193–197. The following is an interesting commentary on the whole movement:

When first Merino's bless'd our land
Thro' Humphrey's patriotic hand,
Methought I'd be a patriot too
And buy a ram Merino true;

The acquisition of so considerable a number of pure-blooded merinos laid the basis for a substantial production of fine stapled wool, rendered more firm and beneficial by the general dispersion of these animals through the country. As a result of governmental assistance and of the formation of agricultural societies, hardly a section of the northern and middle states (and including Virginia) was unaffected, the tide reaching the West, Ohio and Kentucky, by 1810 and extending there with much rapidity.[1]

Since the stimulation of interest in the merino sheep after about 1807 was primarily the result of the altered conditions in the wool manufacture, the relation between the distribution of these animals and the location of many early factories is significant, and is pertinent to the present discussion. For example, Du Pont, who had from the first fostered the establishment of the merino breed in Delaware and who was said in 1812 to have "perhaps the largest and best" flock of sheep in America, erected three wool-manufacturing plants himself. Apparently as a result of this and similar events, twenty-one farmers in the neighborhood of Wilmington were reported in 1814 to have over two-thirds full or grade merino among their 4300 sheep.[2] The Harmony Society in Pennsylvania raised merino sheep and established the manufacture of broadcloth.[3] In Windham County, Connecticut, in Dutchess County and near Oriskany, New York, and around

One hundred eagles was the price,
I paid the shiners in a trice;
I'll risque my fame and fortune too,
Quoth I, on what a ram can do.
Scarce did my hobby 'gin to thrive,
'Ere thousand Spanish rams arrive,
And what I dream'd not of before,
My *ram* turned out to be a *bore*.

Quoted from the *Hampshire Federalist*, by *American Watchman* (Wilmington, Delaware), November 3, 1810.

[1] Wright, pp. 25–30; Goodwin, *American Historical Review*, xii, 770. The further history of the merino sheep in the United States cannot here be traced in detail. In general one may note, however, that not until the more recent decades has there been scarcity of fine wool in the country sufficient to affect materially the development of the wool manufacture.

[2] North, *Bulletin*, 1900, p. 41; Niles, i, 390. "Grade merino" is a term used to imply a mixture of merino blood and that of common or unimproved sheep.

[3] Bishop, ii, 105.

Steubenville, Ohio, wool improvement and factory development went hand in hand, the proprietors of the Steubenville factory themselves having a large flock.[1] In Massachusetts, Derby of Salem, a prominent merchant-shipper, imported 1100 merinos in 1811 and two years later set up the manufacture of fine cloths.[2] Again, in Berkshire County, the early and sustained interest in the wool manufacture, supplemented by the activity of Elkanah Watson in introducing the improved sheep culture, created a marked correlation between the two industries, and in 1815, of the sheep owned within a mile of Pittsfield, approximately 8500 in number, only 852 were of the common breed.[3]

Attempts at improvement in quality of wool production, however, were not exclusively concerned with the merino development. Other breeds of sheep, quite different from the merino, were also introduced into the United States during the early years of the century, — the long-wooled English varieties, which during the preceding century had been improved by Bakewell, the Culleys, and others in England. Of these Washington had one of the finest flocks in the country; and after his death and under the care of Mr. Custis, the Arlington long-wool sheep, which were partly of the Bakewell variety, became famous throughout the country.[4] Occasionally, too, sheep of the English breeds were smuggled into the country despite the British prohibition of ex-

[1] Larned, *History of Windham County*, ii, 427; Bishop, ii, 195; Capron, *Bulletin*, 1881, p. 127; *Columbia Gazette* (Utica, New York), May 28, 1811.

[2] Bishop, ii, 195.

[3] *Pittsfield Sun*, June 15, 1815.

In other instances, manufacturers made a direct appeal to farmers to increase their fine-wool production. For example, the Housatonic Woolen Factory, located at Pittsfield, Massachusetts, offered to receive wool in payment of merino rams which the proprietors had for sale, and fixed prices for its receipt, ranging from $2 a pound for full-blood, $1 a pound for half-blood, to 50 cents for common wool (*Pittsfield Sun*, date lost). In another case, a Wilmington (Delaware) concern offered merino rams at a low rental per season, agreeing to buy all the wool produced from crosses of these animals on common sheep at double the price of common wool, whatever it might be, provided the farmer in turn agreed to turn over to them all his grade wool (*American Watchman*, July 28, 1813). Arthur W. Magill, the leading spirit in the Middletown (Connecticut) Woolen Factory advertised merino bucks to rent (*Middlesex Gazette*, September 12, 1811).

[4] Wright, p. 10; Livingston, *Essay on Sheep*, 1809, p. 147.

port,[1] and sales thereof are sometimes reported.[2] Finally, Mease, writing in 1813, stated that though the *Census of 1810* had taken no account of the "invaluable new Leicester or Bakewell sheep," they were spreading rapidly through the middle states, New Jersey, Pennsylvania, and New York.[3] The introduction of such breeds, however, was not of immediate value to the wool manufacture. While the wool was usable in coarse cloths and blankets, sometimes apparently "chopped" to render it more easily workable, it was best adapted to the worsted branch of the industry, which, as will shortly appear, had slight importance in the United States for many years. The animals, nevertheless, did probably prove of service for crossing purposes. The breeding of a long-wool ram with a merino ewe gave issue which possessed some of the characteristics of each parent, a somewhat better carcass than the merino animal and somewhat finer wool than the English type. For this purpose, English breeds were much more valuable than the common sheep of the country. In subsequent years, furthermore, with the rise of the trade in mutton and the later development of the worsted manufacture, crossbred sheep of this sort, the typical "crossbreds" of this country, became of exceptional utility. No variety of sheep has quite so well satisfied the requirements of the small sheepman on the one hand — he has usually been a farmer carrying a small flock incidentally to arable cultivation — and the packer and wool manufacturer on the other hand.

But concerning this whole matter of the introduction of new breeds of sheep, a word of caution is necessary. It is an aspect of wool production that may be too heavily stressed. The quality of the domestic wool supply was not immediately revolutionized by the introduction of the improved types. While during the first important period of factory development, in the "hot-house" period of embargo and war, the supply of fine wool played a particularly important part in the domestic wool manufacture, such

[1] *Pittsfield Sun*, September 12, 1807; Bishop, ii, 119.

[2] *Pittsfield Sun*, August 28, 1809; January 24, 1810; Bishop, ii, 136, note.

[3] Mease, *Archives of Useful Knowledge*, iii, 125.

wool really formed a very small part of the total domestic clip.[1] Moreover, with the collapse of the "merino mania," and with the post-war depression in the wool manufacture, which was especially disastrous to the production of fine fabrics, the reaction against the merino breed was severe. Some of the fine-wooled sheep were slaughtered, various excellent flocks were scattered, and other flocks suffered from neglect. The spirit of improvement, to be sure, was not altogether dissipated. In 1818, the secretary of the Massachusetts Society for Promoting Agriculture ventured to speak in favor of preserving the breed, though in tones of abject apology: "Shall we dare to mention the merino sheep? . . . May we not take the liberty to plead the cause of this offending race of animals?"[2] And gradually calmer counsels gained ground. The merino mania, it was said, had "had its day and injured many; but it is not likely that we shall have a return of it. We shall go on regularly."[3] Then, as the wool-manufacturing industry improved in stability during the twenties, aided in part by the rising tariff duties, the conditions in the wool-growing end similarly became stabilized. Indeed, with that perversity which characterized the early history of our agriculture, another fine-wool mania soon set in; not in merino — that was impossible — but in the Saxony sheep.

The Saxony was a sheep descended from the original Spanish merino. Animals of the latter breed were imported into Germany about 1765, coming largely as the gift to the Elector of Saxony from the King of Spain. There they were bred with special care. All efforts were directed to the attainment of the finest possible staple, although in the breeding to this end other qualities such as size, flesh, and reproductive powers suffered. The fleece, in consequence, averaged a pound or so less than the Spanish full-blood, but being of finer quality brought more in

[1] Wright, p. 26. He also has given considerable space to the early movement of importations, and adds: "Greater attention is devoted to it (fine wool) because it was largely from this side that there came the first and most effective stimulus to improve the country's flocks."

[2] *Massachusetts Agricultural Depository and Journal*, v, 230–235; quoted in Wright, p. 61.

[3] Niles, xx, 85.

the market. Seeing only the latter, the farmers took up the novelty, although not carried away to the same degree as in the earlier merino movement. The increase in American wool manufacture, and especially the continued interest, almost obsession, of the domestic manufacturer for the production of the finer fabrics, gave sufficient economic stimulus to the speculation.[1]

The first importation, suggestively enough, is said to have been made by a manufacturer of fine woolens, Colonel James Shepherd, of Northampton, Massachusetts.[2] Introduction in volume began in 1824, and reached its height two years later, when some two thousand sheep were brought in. Sold initially at extravagant prices, but experiencing a considerable fall in value after the increased acquisitions, they followed the course of their predecessors in favor. In this case, moreover, the advent of a commercial reaction in 1826 assisted in the decline. But the spread of this breed at best was not so rapid as had been that of the merinos, nor on account also of the fewer numbers was its influence so great.[3] Still the Saxony made a minor contribution to the improvement of our wool.

By 1830, the wool production of the country had, as regards quality, apparently settled down to an intermediate position. The finest grades of wool, full-blood merino, were not, it appears, produced on any large scale. Thus in examinations made in 1829 around Pittsfield, Massachusetts, and in Dutchess County, New York, to locate wool suitable for the finest of fabrics, — "pick-lock wool," — only one pound in seven hundred, and

[1] John L. Hayes, the leading spirit and first secretary of the National Association of Wool Manufacturers, gave the following account of the introduction of the Saxony sheep: "In 1824 a new impulse was given to our wool-manufacture through legislative influences. Factories on a large scale were established for making broadcloths. The fashion of the times required cloths of great firmness, such as were made in England and France from wools of German Electoral sheep-husbandry, which was then at the height of its prosperity. The necessities of the broadcloth-manufacture required a finer wool than was supplied by the Spanish Merinos, as they then were commonly called. Saxon, or electoral Merinos were imported in large numbers" (*Report on Group IX at International Exhibition of 1876*, v, 29).

[2] *Transactions* of the New York State Agricultural Society, i, 313.

[3] Importations during the first five years of the movement have been estimated at about 3300 animals (Randall, *Fine Wool Sheep Husbandry*, pp. 52–54).

one in two hundred, respectively, were found.[1] Imports of wool indicate the same situation: there were substantial purchases of the staple from the fine-wool countries such as Spain and Germany.[2] Again, the bulk of the domestic wool production still consisted of the fleeces from the so-called common sheep, especially in the regions unaffected by the rising factory system. The fleece of such sheep served well enough in household manufacture. But the introduction of the merino and Saxony sheep had not been without effect. In certain sections of the country, notably Washington County, New York, Vermont in general, West Virginia, and around Steubenville, Ohio, flocks of superior grade are known to have existed.[3] There, and probably elsewhere, the sheep were presumably of blooded quality, i. e., the common breed improved by a mixture of the pure blood from the imported stock. The wool manufacturers, moreover, following the early precedents, frequently kept their own flocks. Dickinson, the Steubenville proprietor, had the largest: he owned three or four thousand sheep himself, and his partner as many more.[4] Unquestionably, then, wool production by 1830 had made an important advance over the conditions of the colonial period or those in 1800. No longer was the wool manufacture heavily handicapped, as in the days of the Hartford "adventure," by the lack of fairly satisfactory raw material. From the fine and "grade" domestic flocks, supplemented by importations, the manufacturer was able to secure a stock of wool which did not compare hopelessly with the supplies available to foreign producers.

The further outstanding feature of the wool-growing industry during this period, the transference from what might be called a

[1] Niles, xxxvii, 97. This test was probably for full-blooded merino or Saxony wool.

[2] Wright, pp. 67–72. There was also an importation of coarse wool, from Turkey, South America, and elsewhere, which did not compete with even the common wool of this country, and which found employment in the production of negro cloth, coarse blankets, carpets, and the like.

[3] Wright, pp. 70–71. Washington and Lawrence counties in Pennsylvania might also be mentioned.

[4] *State Papers, Finance*, 1828, v, 794, 796, 797, 798, 799, 801 (Dickinson), 806. Also, Lippincott, *Manufactures in the Ohio Valley*, p. 93.

casual to a commercial basis, is of special interest in this study by reason of the development of marketing agencies intermediary between grower and manufacturer. Previously, it seems, the trade had been wholly unorganized, depending upon the personal contact of the two parties. The Hartford factory had apparently felt itself restricted to local wool supplies, in so far as foreign wool was not attainable; and, in the Byfield establishment of 1793,—to be described shortly,—John Scholfield went about the country buying wool.[1] With the higher development of the wool manufacture, there was the beginning of a new era, although, to be sure, the earlier system, or lack of system, did not wholly pass away for many years. The country storekeepers, who in the colonial period had traded somewhat in wool, now seemingly expanded their operations; and sometimes men in other lines took up the business as an incidental source of gain,—as, for example, Taylor & Peck of Pittsfield sometime before 1812, men who were primarily cabinet-makers.[2] Then still other agencies arose. The various Societies for the Encouragement of Domestic Manufactures seem to have done some dealing in wool as well as in the finished goods.[3] And soon thereafter, as we shall see to have been the development in the case of cloth marketing, strictly commercial establishments soon followed in the footsteps of these patriotic institutions. For instance, a wool warehouse was set up in Boston by 1814. Here advances were made on wool deposited and sales were made on commission.[4] Other such intermediaries undoubtedly sprang up, trading wholly or principally in this material. The increased domestic commerce in wool is evidence of this development. Niles reported in 1825 that "wool in large quantities is now brought from the west," since it bore

[1] Clark, p. 366; Taft, *Notes*, p. 15.

[2] *Pittsfield Sun*, June 13, 1812.

[3] E. g., Philadelphia Society, Bishop, ii, 118.

These societies were founded: Massachusetts, 1792; New York, 1798; Philadelphia, 1805; and Baltimore, 1809.

[4] *Massachusetts Spy*, July 20, 1814. The advertisement continues: "To the manufacturer of Wool, and the proprietor of flocks, the advantage of this establishment will be manifest. . . . To the purchaser . . . the most favorable selections, and to the seller . . . the ready sale for his fleeces, on as good terms as the market will afford."

the cost of transportation better than most other commodities that could be produced beyond the mountains.[1] In 1828 the proprietors of the Steubenville (Ohio) factory were collecting wool from the surrounding country for shipment east, and another house of the same place was said to have sent to Boston 150,000 pounds in a single year.[2] Massachusetts, the rising wool-manufacturing state, was estimated at the time to grow not over a third of its requirements, and generally the manufacturers who testified in the inquiry of 1828, with the exception of those in New York, spoke of the deficiency of local supplies.[3] The woolen mill still dealt largely with the individual farmers in the surrounding country, sometimes offering cloth in exchange for wool; but a distinct organization for the marketing of wool was surely growing.

Of less general import to the present discussion than the factors of quality in production and methods of marketing is that of quantity in the annual wool clip. It happens, too, that the changes in quantity of domestic wool production were less striking during the period under review than were the changes in those other aspects. The annual clip increased considerably, of course, between 1760 and 1830, although one cannot even estimate by what measure. We know only that between 1810 and 1830 the increase was something like 100 per cent.[4] But such an enlargement of the national production one would expect, with the advance in population and with the enhancement in domestic prosperity. It is probable, too, that whether the factory had come or not, an increase of not dissimilar proportions might well have occurred. The factory in considerable degree merely seized

[1] Niles, xxix, 166.

[2] *State Papers, Finance*, v, 801; Niles, xxxiii, 155.

[3] *State Papers, Finance*, v, 794, 796, 799, 805, 807. Exceptions in New York, *ibid.*, pp. 793, 797, 802. Sundry considerable sales of domestic wool in eastern centers are spoken of by Niles. For example (xviii, 464), a wagon, drawn by seven horses and containing three tons of wool, was passed on its way from New Hampshire to Danvers, Massachusetts. See also Niles, xxx, 20; xxxii, 359; *State Papers, Finance*, v, 805.

[4] Wright, pp. 27, 75.

In the decades just prior to 1830 there was also a substantial increase in the volume of raw-wool imports (Wright, pp. 30, note, and 65–73).

upon sections of the domestic wool-cloth market which had heretofore been dominated by the household production, or which, barring the existence of the factory, would have fallen under the sway of the household system.

In summary, then, it may be said that, by 1830, the domestic wool supply, which had grown with somewhat the same pace as that of the country's expansion, had received an appreciable improvement in quality through the introduction of foreign breeds of sheep and their important though faltering culture. By this means and by the growth of a larger wool-import trade, the wool manufacture had been freed from dependence upon the unimproved staple of the common-wool sheep, so distinctly inferior to the raw materials available to foreign wool-manufacturing industries. Likewise, there had been a beginning of country-wide dealings in wool through an organization of increasing virility, which in diverse ways promised additional strength to the manufacturing end of the industry. Not only did these improved facilities proffer a wider choice of staple to the manufacturing enterprise, but they came to relieve it of a considerable financial burden [1] and particularly of the duty, arduous to an industrial concern, of searching out its raw material.[2]

[1] Bond (*Report on Wool and Manufactures of Wool*, 1887, p. lviii), gives an account, probably exaggerated, of the frequent mortgaging of mills and machinery in the recovery of the wool manufacture after 1829, in order to procure wool. But undoubtedly the investment of capital in the year's supply of raw material was much heavier under the old than under the rising system.

[2] The above account of the evolution of wool dealing in this country puts the beginnings somewhat earlier than does Wright, who, following Bond (*op. cit.*), states that "the buying and selling of wool did not become a distinct branch of trade until about 1830," and that "up to 1825, or thereabouts, manufacturers bought most of their wool direct from the farmers" (Wright, p. 74). However, Shaw, in his *Wool Trade of the United States* (p. 29), puts the "birth" of the independent trade in the decade of the twenties; and the evidence appears to point to a commencement really somewhat earlier still.

CHAPTER VI

ADVANCE IN TECHNICAL EQUIPMENT

Two outstanding facts impress the investigator who dips into the technological history of the wool manufacture during the period ending approximately 1830: first, that starting with an assortment of apparatus composed chiefly of hand tools (barring the old fulling mill), the industry had by the end of that time acquired a technical equipment nearly all of which was in the modern form; and secondly, that this period marks the heyday of American invention with respect to machines for this industry.[1] The Hartford factory, it will be recalled, possessed at the conclusion of its brief career only carding machines, small in diameter and of unsatisfactory performance; one spinning jenny, a hand-operated mechanism of unknown value; hand looms, and probably hand tools for the finishing operations, except the fulling. Probably, also, the greater part of the yarn preparation, including both carding and spinning, was done in the households of the surrounding country throughout the unhappy life of this enterprise. Within forty years, improvements, chiefly of American origin, had given a new significance to the power-driven carding machine borrowed from England; had made the spinning operation quasi-automatic by a development unknown abroad; had harnessed the loom to power, for the most part independently of foreign advance; and had largely removed hand processes from the cloth-finishing operations through the invention of machines so valuable that they were frequently copied by other nations in subsequent years. This portion of our history, then, deserves particular attention; and perhaps more than in other periods of

[1] These statements are really limited to the woolen branch of the industry. This was practically the only section of wool-cloth manufacture carried on in the country at about 1830, the worsted branch being of negligible proportions.

our discussion it necessitates a considerable amount of comparison with developments in foreign countries.[1]

1. *The Carding Machine.*

The power-driven carding machine, which came ultimately to replace the hand cards of the old household system, was wholly an English development. Contributions to it covered particularly the period from 1748 to approximately 1790, and among the names of inventors who deserve special note are Daniel Bourne, Richard Arkwright, and James Hargreaves.[2] As these names suggest to the student of the Industrial Revolution, the machine was originally intended for the cotton industry, where indeed a sort of carding machine has always since then been used; but some time elapsed before it was adapted to the wool manufacture.[3] It was not until the last decade in the eighteenth century that this machine was coming into anywhere near general use in the British wool-manufacturing industry.[4]

[1] It is impracticable, and probably would be unprofitable, to attempt examination into the source of every machine used in the wool manufacture. I have accordingly restricted attention almost entirely to machinery involved in the chief processes — carding, spinning, weaving, and finishing. (For a description of modern wool-manufacturing processes, see Appendix C.)

A minor feature would be that of pickers or willows, machines for opening up the matted locks of wool as they come from the scouring process. It has been claimed (Clark, p. 422) that these were New England inventions; but as early as 1806 Arthur Scholfield was building pickers at Pittsfield (Taft, *Notes*, p. 29); a similar machine called a "twilly" is stated to have been "in general use" in the West of England in 1810, having replaced an early apparatus called a "devil" (*Philadelphia Aurora*, September 7, 1810); and a machine for opening, tended by a boy and doing the work of forty persons, is said to have been exhibited at the French Exposition of 1806 (Alcan's *Traité du Travail des Laines*, reviewed in *Bulletin*, 1870–1871, p. 415). See also Cunningham, *Growth of English Industry and Commerce*, p. 650.

[2] Bramwell, *The Wool-Carders' Vade Mecum*, pp. 132–135, 376–380, gives as full an account as any of this development. Arkwright's and Hargreaves' contributions were the idea of workers and strippers and the doffer comb for the former, and the "fancy" for the latter. However, John Lees claimed that he invented the feed for cards which Arkwright used, and Hargreaves insisted that he originated the idea of the doffer comb covered by Arkwright's patent (p. 378).

[3] Probably the same, or nearly the same, machine was at first employed in both industries, though subsequent developments have carried the machines for the two manufactures quite widely apart in structure.

[4] Cunningham, *Growth of English Industry and Commerce*, pp. 650–651.

Its introduction into the United States has been particularly associated with the family of Scholfield.[1] In March, 1793, John and Arthur Scholfield left their home in Saddleworth, Yorkshire, accompanied by John's wife, his six children, and one John Shaw, a spinner and weaver, and sailed from Liverpool for America, landing in Boston a month or so later.[2] Upon arrival, the Scholfields sought out Mr. Jedediah Morse, author of *Morse's Geography and Gazetteer* and a man of some influence at the time, and introduced themselves as manufacturers well versed in the method of manufacturing woolen goods most approved in England. While awaiting Mr. Morse's kindly efforts in their behalf, they located temporarily in Charlestown, and at once began the production of woolen goods, building for that purpose a spinning jenny of forty spindles and a hand loom, upon which, with the aid of Shaw, they manufactured black and mixed broadcloth. But this was mere "pot-boiling," as it were.

Through Mr. Morse's good offices, the two brothers went later in 1793 to Newburyport, where they met people of influence who were inquisitive about the wool manufacture. For them the Scholfields built a carding machine, — the first specimen of the machine which the Scholfields were to be so influential in making an intimate part of the equipment in the American wool manufacture. Though twenty-four inches broad,—as compared with the sixteen-inch machine of the Hartford adventure,—it had but

[1] Mr. Royal C. Taft, in his valuable contribution to textile history, *Some Notes on the Introduction of the Woolen Manufacture into the United States*, 1882, has taken a special interest in tracing the experience of these men. I have used his account freely.

[2] The *Census of 1860* (iii, p. xxix) stated that "Arthur Scholfield and other English operatives . . . emigrated in company with Samuel Slater." It is picturesque to think of these men who, with Arthur's brother John, were to play such important parts in the history of American textiles, as coming over in the same bottom; but Mr. Taft has pricked the bubble.

Incidentally it may be noted that the Scholfields and Shaws were or came to be common names in the Yorkshire woolen trade. Dodd (*Textile Manufactures of Great Britain*, 1851, p. 124) gives eleven Scholfields and eleven Shaws as independent manufacturers of woolen cloth in Saddleworth, the large number being due to the Yorkshire practice under the domestic system of each father bringing up his sons in the business.

a single cylinder, and appears a pygmy beside modern cards.[1] However, it was a machine of great potentialities.

Having demonstrated the practicality of the machine by operation in "Lord" Timothy Dexter's barn, the Scholfields were engaged by a hastily organized company called the "Newbury-Port Woolen Manufactory" to superintend the erection of machinery and later the manufacture of woolen cloth in a mill which was constructed in the neighboring parish of Byfield.[2] In this plant they placed the original single-cylinder machine, and two double-cylinder machines which they had built in Newburyport after the approved pattern of the former; and the three machines were harnessed to water power. The factory presumably contained a full complement of woolen machinery, including probably the spinning jenny and hand loom that the Scholfields had erected in Charlestown. Of these, only the carding and fulling machines were power-driven.

But the enterprise, however improved its technical equipment over its predecessors, was not a success financially. Broadcloths and flannel are said to have been its chief products. These were to be sold at the store of the principal stockholder in the enterprise, William Bartlett of Newburyport; but despite all efforts of the promoters the goods refused to move with sufficient rapidity. As early as 1795 a petition for aid was sent to the Massachusetts legislature, and repeated in 1797. A small revenue was derived from charging admission to the strangers who came out of curiosity to view the new phenomenon, a factory. Goods on hand were sold at "public vendue," and funds were borrowed to pay the workmen. Struggling against such adversities, the business dragged on for a decade, until in 1803 it was sold to an Englishman and converted into a cotton mill.[3]

The importance of the Scholfields, however, is not dependent upon the success or failure of a single industrial establishment.

[1] What is claimed to be the original machine, and presumably the real one, is preserved at the Davis & Furber Machine Company, North Andover, Massachusetts.

[2] Among the stockholders was the eminent jurist, Theophilus Parsons.

[3] Davis (*Essays in the Earlier History of Corporations*, ii, 277) gives the best account on the financial side.

Their more significant rôle in the history of the American wool manufacture relates to the dissemination of the carding machine. The assertion has been made, it is true, that John and Arthur Scholfield were the very first to bring to the United States a carding machine of the improved model;[1] but of this there is some doubt. One Samuel Mayall, for example, who was also an Englishman, is said to have set up a carding machine on Bunker Hill sometime in 1788 or 1789, shortly after his arrival in Boston. The machine, it is narrated, was operated with horse power, and was one of two machines which Mayall succeeded in smuggling out of England. Later he went to Gray, Maine, where about 1791 he conducted a shop for wool-carding and cloth-dressing, also manufacturing cloth on a small scale.[2] Again, Phineas Bond asserted in 1790 that "carding machines from the English models are in great use and well made in Massachusetts Bay and in other parts of New England,"—a statement which must, it seems to me, refer to cotton cards, although Bond does not limit it so;[3] while in Philadelphia a couple of years later (1793–1794) carding machines specifically mentioned as intended for wool-working are reported to have been constructed.[4] To be sure, the evidence concerning these cases is not so good as that of the Scholfield development, either upon exact dates or upon the true character of the machine; and possibly the Scholfields may be credited with the primary introduction of the improved carding apparatus.

But the real claim of the Scholfield family to special recognition, it appears to me, rests on what seems a broader and more substantial basis than primacy of introduction alone. The other

[1] Taft, *Notes*, p. 14.

[2] North, *Bulletin*, 1899, pp. 215–216. The source of North's information was a letter from Mayall's son written in 1889.

There is mention of a machine earlier than the Hartford episode: see Bagnall, p. 238. This was probably an unimproved apparatus.

[3] American Historical Association *Reports*, 1896, i, 651. Cotton carding machines were of different construction than the wool cards, although quite similar in function. They were introduced earlier than wool cards: see Bagnall, pp. 186, 272; *Pennsylvania Magazine of History*, viii, 378; Davis, *Essays in the Earlier History of Corporations*, i, 471.

[4] *Essay on the Manufacturing Interest of the United States* (1804), p. 27. As to Hartford machine, see above, p. 66.

instances apparently were isolated affairs; the most that one can say of them is that they occurred; they did not affect the general course of the industry. Not so with the Scholfields. Like Slater, the father of the American cotton industry, the Scholfield family exercised a widespread influence, making up in their number what any single one of them lacked in signal business success as compared with the pioneer of the cotton manufacture.

Dissemination by the Scholfields of knowledge concerning the improved carding machine was a result of the family's dispersion through New England within a comparatively few years. Let us trace the course of these peregrinations. John Scholfield, in one of his wool-purchasing trips for the Byfield factory, became interested in a water-power site at Montville, Connecticut; and there the Scholfields went in 1799, after selling out their interest in the Byfield concern. In 1801 Arthur parted from his brother and moved to Pittsfield, Massachusetts; while John, after staying in Montville until 1806, sold out and purchased a mill-site at Stonington, Connecticut.[1] Subsequently (1814), John set up another plant at Waterford, near New London, which he placed in charge of his son Thomas. Meanwhile, John's oldest son, John Scholfield, Jr., after being in Colchester, Connecticut, for a time, in 1804 or 1805 set up a wool-carding shop in Jewett City, then a part of Preston, Connecticut. This business seems to have grown into a regular woolen mill, and by 1816 contained a full complement of machinery.[2] Another son, Joseph, became interested in the Merino Woolen Factory at Dudley, Massachusetts, in 1817.

In yet another direction the influence of the family was felt. A third brother, James Scholfield, who had been called from England as soon as John and Arthur had made a place for themselves, in 1802 bought a mill privilege and fulling mill at North

[1] Of this establishment we know the mechanical equipment: two double carding machines, twenty-four inches wide; two spinning jennies of forty and fifty spindles, respectively, and a billy or slubbing machine of thirty spindles; the spinning machines being operated by hand. The weaving, curiously enough, was done outside, partly on account of Scholfield and partly of individuals who bought the yarn from him (Bagnall, p. 424).

[2] Bagnall, pp. 458–459.

Andover, with the financial assistance of Arthur. Here for ten years he carded wool for customers, adding in time the manufacture of broadcloth. For this purpose he used machinery, spinning jennies and looms, operated by hand, which he placed in his house. In 1812 he sold out this business, becoming thereafter superintendent in Mr. Nathaniel Stevens's mill, which was erected the following year.

Finally, of yet greater influence, it seems,—though of course one cannot estimate the stimulus given by force of example in the cases above mentioned,—was the activity of Arthur Scholfield, who left his brother John in 1801 (apparently because the latter did not like Arthur's newly wedded wife) and went to Pittsfield, Massachusetts. Upon his arrival, Mr. Scholfield, joined soon by his nephew Isaac, also set up a carding machine and for a few years did carding for customers, until in 1804 he began the manufacture of broadcloth on a small scale. But his main contribution was in another line: the manufacture of carding machines. He seems to have built a few almost from the beginning of his residence in Pittsfield. The first advertisement of machines for sale appeared in the *Pittsfield Sun* of September 12, 1803; and in the next year (May 14, 1804) he informed the public that besides having machines to sell, "built under his immediate inspection," he "will give drafts and other instructions to those who wish to build themselves." The terms of these services are not stated; nor is the reason clear, although reading between the lines suggests the competition which was already developing. He gives warning against imposition "by uninformed, speculating companies, who demand more than twice as much for their machines as they are really worth."[1] However, by 1806 the demand for his products was so great that he sold out

[1] Apparently by imitating Scholfield's machines, other men had set up the manufacture of carding engines in nearby towns, notably Giles Tinker who in 1804 began their construction in North Adams (Spear, *History of North Adams*, p. 91). Because of the competition of these men, and perhaps in part by virtue of economies effected as more machines were turned out, Scholfield reduced his prices. At first he is said to have charged $1300 or more. But in 1806 he advertised machines for $253 without the card-clothing (the leather studded with fine wire, which covers the card cylinders), or $400 with it (Smith, *History of Pittsfield*, ii, 169).

his carding business and devoted himself solely to the manufacture of machines for sale.[1] Then, and indeed in after years, no more frequent recommendation of a carding machine was made than that it came from Arthur Scholfield's workshop, and evidently it was believed that none higher could be made.[2]

As a result of Arthur's efforts, or of those of his competitors who were inspired by his example, carding machines sprang up rapidly throughout this section of the country. Town after town secured a carding mill, or the addition of a carding machine to a fulling mill already established; and, before the lapse of a half-dozen years, Berkshire County was dotted with these shops.[3]

Incidentally it may be noted that Arthur Scholfield's activities were not confined to carding machines. In 1806 he was manufacturing picking machines, — machines for loosening the matted locks of wool in preparation for carding, and used then in conjunction with the carding machine at the mill of the custom-carder; and by 1809 he was constructing spinning jennies.[4] Finally he was concerned with the manufacture of cloth during the embargo and war periods, for a time by himself, but in 1814

[1] *Pittsfield Sun*, March 24, 1806.

Taft found no evidence bearing out the statement of Bishop (i, 421), which was taken from the *Census of 1860* (iii, p. xlviii), that Mr. Scholfield was compelled to go to England once or twice to refresh his memory as to the construction of the carding machine; or moreover, that he "smuggled from England portions of the machine or models and plans, concealed in his bedding" (Bishop, ii, 87). In consideration of the events above outlined, the story is on the face of it unacceptable, unless it refers to trips for the purpose of securing English improvements later than 1793.

[2] Similarly, the warmest praise for a journeyman wool-carder was that he had learned the trade under Mr. Scholfield.

In 1807, when the embargo seriously affected his business, at least for a time, he had twenty-two machines on his hands (Smith, *History of Pittsfield*, ii, 170).

[3] A partial list of carding shops in Berkshire County and neighboring towns, drawn from advertisements in the *Pittsfield Sun*, with the dates of their first establishment, is as follows:

1802	Hadley.	1805	Stockbridge.
1803	North Amherst.		Lee.
1804	Lenox.		Bethlehem.
	West Stockbridge.		Great Barrington.
1805	Lower Mills, Hadley.	1806	Tyringham.
	Williamstown.	1807	Cheshire.

[4] Taft, *Notes*, p. 29; Smith, *History of Pittsfield*, ii, 178.

as next to the largest subscriber to the Pittsfield Woolen and Cotton Factory, launched in that year.[1] Like others he suffered from the revulsion and depression that followed the advent of peace, for a while went back to wool-carding, and later acted as superintendent in one of the surviving mills. He died in 1827, apparently little richer than when he came to Pittsfield a quarter of a century before.[2]

The Spread of the Carding Machine. The diffusion of the carding machine through the country was not a symmetrical and orderly affair; and yet, though often the adoption of the machine seems to have occurred in a sporadic and unaccountable manner, there is at least a general movement outward from New England. On account of the rapid spread of the apparatus after the first years, it is possible to give individually only a few of the earlier appearances and leave largely to the imagination the further dissemination. Beside the Scholfield activities and the machines already mentioned as possibly anticipating those of the Scholfields, one was put in operation at Leominster, Massachusetts, in 1800,[3] and simultaneously another in Farmington, Maine;[4] while in the next year a third was set up in New Ipswich, New Hampshire, by one John Saunderson, a Scotchman.[5] At about the same time machines were erected in Manchester, Connecticut,[6] and in East Chelmsford, Massachusetts,—in the latter case by Moses Hale, father-in-law of Nathaniel Stevens who, in the coming decades, became a manufacturer of note and was the founder

[1] Bagnall, p. 265.

[2] John Scholfield had a somewhat greater success. At his death, in 1820, he left three mill properties apparently free from encumbrances (Taft, *Notes*, p. 20).

[3] Hayes, *American Textile Machinery*, p. 21. Two Englishmen, Lees and Taylor, says Hayes, came to this country in 1794. Lees returned to England and bought carding machinery which was shipped to Boston as hardware, and which was put into operation in Byfield about 1796. Consequently, "it is possible that the Scholfields may have been assisted by Lees and Taylor." But there seems to me little to substantiate this idea.

In 1800 Lees went to Leominster and set up wool-carding there.

[4] Butler, *History of Farmington*, p. 263.

[5] Gould, *History of New Ipswich*, p. 229. Bagnall (p. 478) thinks the machine first set up there was of Mr. Saunderson's own construction, founded upon knowledge of such machines which Saunderson obtained in England.

[6] Bagnall, p. 229, who thinks it was probably one of the Scholfield model.

of a family of wool manufacturers.[1] Closely following these earliest establishments came a number in the space of a year or two: Vernon, Connecticut (about 1802); Worcester, Massachusetts (1803); Poughkeepsie, New York (1803), by one George Booth who is said to have brought the machine from England; South Kingston, Rhode Island (1804); and Haverhill and West Cambridge, Massachusetts (1805).[2] Thereafter the movement accelerated rapidly. Five years later, the defective census of 1810 gave the figure of 1776 carding mills in the whole United States;[3] and Gallatin wrote in the same year that "in the Eastern and Middle States, carding machines worked by water are everywhere established, and they are rapidly extending southwardly and westwardly."[4] Indeed, the latter movement began early. Custom-carding was advertised in Lexington, Kentucky, in 1806, and in 1812 Jefferson spoke casually of carding machines in Virginia.[5] With the westward extension of settlement, the carding machine moved along and was always to be found in the newly opened regions.

The Significance of the Carding Machine. The introduction of the improved carding machine was of first-rate importance to the American wool manufacture. It meant in the first place the acquisition by the American wool manufacture of a power-driven apparatus which would replace the old hand cards. The saving in time thus made was great,—indeed, the work of hours being reduced to that of minutes.[6] But other considerations give this

[1] North, *Bulletin*, 1899, p. 236. See also the cases in Berkshire County, Massachusetts; p. 93, above, note 3.

[2] Bagnall, p. 317; Taft, *Notes*, p. 37; Platt, "History of Poughkeepsie," in *History of Dutchess County* (Hasbrouck, ed.), p. 236; Taft, pp. 39, 43; Bagnall, p. 306.

[3] *State Papers, Finance*, ii, 693. In 1820, over twelve hundred carding machines were reported for New York state alone (*Journal of the Assembly of New York, 45th Sess.*, Appendix A, p. 60; quoted in Tryon, *Household Manufacture*, p. 289).

[4] *State Papers, Finance*, ii, 427. See also Bradbury, "Travels," in *Thwaites' Travels*, v, 285.

[5] *Documentary History of American Industrial Society*, ii, 329; Jefferson, *Writings*, ix, 362. See also Clark, p. 518.

[6] The only detailed figures that I have found are English. They show that whereas it took a man ninety-six hours to card seventy-five pounds of wool by hand,

acquisition even larger importance. Whereas in the first attempts at factory production, the carding was perforce done in the families of the surrounding country, now this operation might be brought within the factory walls. This circumstance of itself would assure a more dependable and a better supply of "cardings;" but the machine gave a much superior as well as a much heavier and more regular product. The function of the carding process, it will be recalled, is to open the matted and tangled locks of wool and to mix the fibers of various lengths into a thoroughly homogeneous mass.[1] These purposes at best could be accomplished but indifferently and inconstantly under the hand method. Even in the Hartford factory, which had the services of a crude carding machine, the criticism was made by the English visitor, Wansey, that the wool was "not half worked."[2] Such failure in the primary manufacturing operation rendered inevitable an inferior product all along the line, uneven and faulty yarn, and cloth of uneven if not defective texture. By the manipulation of the wool in the improved carding machine, aided as it usually was by the new picking machine, the basis for effective operation in the subsequent processes was well founded. Much validity, then, attaches to Taft's statement: that "as the introduction of the spinning frame has been recognized as the beginning of the history of cotton manufacture in this country, the introduction of the carding machine may also be regarded as the initial point, the

a machine tended by a child (perhaps a youth) would work the same in fourteen hours (*British Documents*, 1840 (43), p. 439). Under the usual American system where women and children did the hand carding, and at irregular intervals, the time required by the old method would be substantially greater.

[1] In the carding process as first performed, i. e., prior to the introduction of intermediate diagonal feeds or of the condenser (see below), another feature of the operation was the attempt at a considerable parallelization of the individual fibers in the wool. The woolen process smacked somewhat of the kindred worsted manner of manufacture. (For general discussion of this point by one who objected to the change in manner of woolen operation, see Vickerman, *Woollen Spinning*, *passim.*) The introduction of the feeding devices just noted has tended to diminish the extent to which parallelization can be carried, though still in some degree the fibers must be laid parallel in order that a sufficiently strong yarn may be produced. The change, however, is notable and will be considered below (see pp. 353–356).

[2] See above, p. 66.

first proper introduction of the woolen manufacture, or the fabrication by machinery."[1]

The immediate effect flowing from the introduction of this machine was not, however, a strengthening of the factory system. The operation of carding by machine was not a difficult one to learn passably well; and the machine itself neither was expensive nor required an exceptional amount of power. Accordingly, proprietors of fulling mills could easily add this apparatus to their equipment, and others could set up small shops for the sole object of carding by power. The diffusion of the carding machine, which, as we have seen, did take place quickly, was indeed antagonistic to the development of the factory system. It imparted an added virility to the household production. Each locality, except apparently the seaboard towns, now had its carding engine, adequate to fulfill its needs for wool-carding. This arduous process was withdrawn from the household, to be more effectively carried through in the shop of the custom carder; and, being thus assured of a superior finished product, the household manufacture of wool fabrics was enabled to compete to better advantage with the rising factory production.[2] Moreover, the expanding western settlements were given additional strength by means of which to render themselves self-sufficient and to resist the encroachments of the eastern mill products.[3]

[1] *Bulletin*, 1896, p. 17.

[2] Incidentally the "household" manufacture became less strictly deserving of that name than ever before. Now at both ends of the operation — wool-carding as well as cloth-finishing — outside, professional aid was accepted.

[3] An interesting description of custom wool-carding and its connection with the household manufacture, which I ran upon in the *Orange County Gazette* (Goshen, New York), August 11, 1807, deserves to be recorded:

> The season 's pass'd in which the Bear,
> Secluded lies from sun and air;
> He 'll now rejoice at Spring's return,
> That he may feast on buds and fern.
> In some respects, I like the bear
> Have cause to wish the weather fair,
> That agriculture's hardy sons
> May plunge their flocks in gliding runs;
> Well cleanse their fleeces, and prepare
> To fabricate their winter's wear:
> Most cheerfully I take my stand,
> Before the public, heart and hand

Further Improvement of the Carding Machine. The carding machine as first introduced by the Scholfields and others was, judged by modern standards, a diminutive and relatively crude mechanism. While the larger cards of the present time attain a width of sixty or seventy-two inches, the original Scholfield machine was only twenty-four inches wide. The modern carding apparatus is among the heaviest of wool-working machinery; but the first Scholfield card could be moved about by two or three men. Both the frame and cylinders were made of wood, and the single-cylinder machine was not over five feet in total length. The construction out of wood was in itself a check on the width of the machine. We know that John Scholfield, Jr., had by 1816 a double-cylindered "breaker" (the first carding machine in a "set" of two or three), which was three feet wide;[1] but probably most of the early machines were of lesser width. The surfaces of main cylinders, workers, and strippers (the auxiliary, smaller cylinders which, in revolving, alternately take wool from and return it to the main cylinder) must be exactly parallel, lest the teeth of the card-clothing tear the wool or become so worn and broken as to give an imperfect working to the fibers. A single warped board was likely to do considerable damage. Evidently appreciating

To let my gratitude be known,
For all the favours they have shown,
And with petition to appear
For patronage another year,
To whom I'll manifest regard,
While they supply me Wool to Card.
In Deerpark Town's my Fulling Mill,
On that fine stream call'd Shawangunk hill;
I have a well contriv'd machine
To Card your Wool and Pick it clean;
But send a little oil pray do,
A quart to twenty pounds or so,
The girls when they do come to spin it,
I think will find a profit in it.
Should you to Newburgh go,
Or any other Town below,
Bring on your wool, ere you go back
It will be carded, roll'd and pack'd:
While I for trouble, time and wear
Of Mill, and money for repair,
Will only ask for each pound Carding
Eight Cents and thank you in the bargain.

May, 1807. GEORGE F. REEVE.

[1] Bagnall, p. 459.

this weakness in a wooden apparatus, carding-machine builders began rather early to experiment with iron frame and cylinders. Data on the exact course and rapidity of progress are not available, but seemingly about 1820 machines began to be built wholly of iron.[1] Probably within the next decade this practice became better established, though it was several decades thereafter, indeed, not until the post-Civil-War period, before the employment of all-metal apparatus can be said to have been general or perhaps even common.[2]

But the most notable improvement concerned the delivery end of the machine, where the wool, fully worked, was removed from the mechanism.[3] In the early cards, as the wool was stripped from the doffer cylinder by the doffer comb, it was passed between a wooden roller and trough, sometimes called a "shell," and by this means was converted into soft rolls or "cardings" about a half-inch in diameter and as long as the carding machine was wide. In the household manufacture the conversion of these "cardings" into yarn upon the spinning wheel could be easily

[1] An advertisement of a Worcester (Massachusetts) machine maker in 1822 suggests the novelty of the iron apparatus then. He informs the public that he "is now constructing carding machines entirely of iron, the cylinders of which, being, as might be supposed, the most difficult parts to be constructed, are cast in four parallel pieces in such a manner as to combine great strength with light weight, and so contrived as to present no obstacle to fixing on the cards as easily and as securely as can be done upon cylinders of wood." (*Worcester Spy*, July 10, 1822.)

[2] One reason for the delay in wide adoption of the all-iron machines was the great endurance of the framework of this apparatus. Wooden cylinders might be replaced by metal ones, and many sets of card-clothing might be worn out, and yet the wooden frame still be in serviceable condition.

[3] Two minor features of the development may be mentioned. First: the introduction of the finer merino wool necessitated a nicer adjustment of the machine, but apparently this difficulty persisted only a brief time (Livingston, *Essay on Sheep*, p. 154; *Providence Gazette*, August 24, 1811). Again, by 1830 the "set" of carding machines had come to be more or less standardized: three single or two double cards. Dwight's description of the Humphreysville factory (*Travels*, iii, 392) speaks of "a breaker and finisher;" John Scholfield, Jr., in 1816 had a "double breaker" and two "finishing" cards (Bagnall, p. 459). Cf. North, *Bulletin*, 1901, p. 277; and particularly *Bulletin*, 1869, p. 144. According to the latter authority, a "set" of carding apparatus around 1825 consisted "of three carding machines, called the first and second breaker, and the finisher." (This "set" should not be confused with the looser use of the same term, which included the spinning machinery appropriate for carding apparatus of a given type; cf. below, p. 112, note 2.)

carried through,—indeed, more easily than that of the old hand cardings. The only important difficulty arose in attaching the cardings end to end. This was accomplished by rubbing two ends together between the fingers, but in the operation an appreciable thickening of the strand at the point of attachment was likely to result. While the household spinner could make some allowance for these irregularities, in the rising factories such lack of uniformity was a source of much concern.

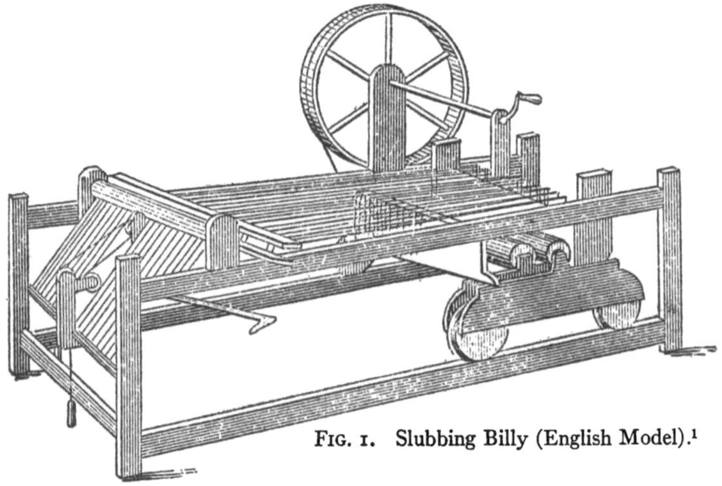

FIG. 1. Slubbing Billy (English Model).[1]

In the manufacturing system as first evolved, a machine intermediate between the carding engine and the spinning machine proper — jenny or jack — had been introduced quite early, a machine called a "billy" or more formally a roping-machine.[2] It was a sort of modified jenny, having a smaller number of spindles

[1] This representation of the billy lacks the feed-table spoken of below in the text (p. 101).

[2] The origin of this machine was probably British. The first mention of it in the United States is that a billy of thirty spindles had been set up by 1806 in John Scholfield's mill at Stonington, Connecticut (Bagnall, p. 424). Whether the Scholfields knew of it upon their first arrival or later received information about it, is problematical. However, whatever the source, by 1810 these machines had become quite well known and quite widespread, the defective census of that year reporting fifty-three; and thereafter they form one item in the normal equipment of a woolen mill, usually in the proportion of one billy to three spinning machines (jennies or other). Cf. Tomlinson, *Encyclopedia of Useful Arts*, ii, 1034.

and a less elaborate form.[1] Its function was two-fold: upon it the cardings were joined together, and by means of it they were somewhat drawn out or elongated, and given a little twist. The bringing of the cardings from the carding engine and the splicing of them upon the feed-table of the billy—by rubbing and rolling them between the fingers—were done by children; and then the drafting and twisting proceeded under the direction of a man, who indeed had general charge over the whole operation.[2] Inasmuch as here the joining of the cardings was done, as it were, in wholesale quantity, the irregularities of the resultant roving were likely to be greater than in the household system. Nor was there opportunity as in hand spinning to reduce these lumps in the subsequent processes. The spinning here was carried through, as has been suggested, on jennies or jacks, machines which spun many threads at one time, and of course the operation had to be performed with mechanical regularity. A yarn lumpy or weak in spots was, however, the inevitable result of this early factory method, with the corollary of a woven fabric uneven of texture. Moreover, since the factory generally aimed at a higher grade of product, the defect was the more annoying. To remedy this situation, attack had of course to be made upon the carding process.

Accordingly, many attempts were soon being made to reform this operation or to introduce more satisfactory mechanisms for use therein.[3] An improvement was reported as early as 1810 which, it seems, looked toward what was ultimately the solution: it was a "perpetual roller" invented by Arthur W. Magill, the

[1] Sometimes a jenny was in the early days used in place of the billy.

[2] This was the most important, practically the only important place in the woolen mill where child labor was employed. Child work on this machine, however, was made particularly severe by the fact that the man in charge of the billy often, perhaps usually, hired the children. There are stories of many hardships that arose through this system: brutality, irregularity of the work, and the like.

[3] Since the apparatus used abroad were similar to those employed in American mills, we find the same criticisms of the process and corresponding attempts at removing the faults. Thus in an account of the processes of wool manufacture as carried on in the West of England about 1810 (*Philadelphia Aurora*, September 7, 1810), the author says: "The present mode of joining the (carding) rolls is very defective, the rolls being larger at the joinings than in other parts, and the thread cannot but be irregular. Many attempts have been made to remedy this defect and to save labor, hitherto without effect."

leading spirit in the Middletown (Connecticut) factory, and aimed, it would appear, at the entire elimination of the billy and the substitution of a mechanism for drawing the wool from the carding machine in a continuous strand.[1] Apparently this attachment was not successful, but experiments along this line continued. John Goulding, who finally found the solution of the problem, himself began experimenting in 1820; and his efforts were aided by inventions pertaining to special portions of the process. One such invention, covering the important ring doffers, he purchased from Ezekiel Hale of Haverhill, Massachusetts;[2] and another for a method of winding the ropings upon the long bobbin from one Edward Winslow, who subsequently coöperated with Goulding in perfecting the new device.[3] Indeed, Goulding stated in the specifications of his patent, which he in fact received in 1826, "I do not claim the construction of the individual parts of the machinery used in the processes before described, but the combination and arrangement by which they are made to produce thread from wool, or other fibrous material, by a continuous operation."[4] The other inventors had contemplated the retention of the billy, but Goulding added to their work by so adjusting the machinery as not only to produce the endless roll but to dispense with the billy and slubbing process altogether. His may not have been an originating mind, but he had the power to grasp the details and to combine them into a practicable mechanism that went beyond the conceptions of his predecessors or collaborators.[5]

[1] *American Watchman* (Wilmington, Delaware), September 19, 1810. Another patent which seems in the same line was that of Alanson Holmes, of Pomfret, New York (January 8, 1810), called "a machine for carding and spinning wool by one continuous operation."

[2] Bramwell, *The Wool-Carders' Vade Mecum*, p. 381. Another ring doffer was also bought up; see North, *Bulletin*, 1901, p. 259.

[3] Bonney, *Bulletin*, 1898, p. 42.

[4] Bramwell, *op. cit.*, p. 385. The patent is No. 5355, May 2, 1826.

[5] A bitter controversy as to the true inventor arose, resulting finally in the lawsuit, Eben D. Jordan *vs.* Agawam Woolen Company, Circuit Court of the United States, Massachusetts District, Boston, 1866. Eben D. Jordan had purchased the renewed patent of Goulding, and sued the Agawam Company for a certain infringement. The latter set up as one of their defenses that Goulding was not the

JOHN GOULDING

The inventor of condensing apparatus for the woolen carding process

THE FINAL (FINISHER) SECTION OF A MODERN CARDING MACHINE

Showing the ring doffer, an essential part of Goulding's mechanism, and the modern rub-roller condensing apparatus

Although Goulding made various alterations in the carding operation proper, the most important feature of his invention was the delivery of the wool from the finisher card. The old roller and "shell" were eliminated, and in their place a rather complicated mechanism was substituted. For the single doffer cylinder on the old machine were set up two cylinders, placed one above the other. The card wire on these was laid on in strips around the cylinders, with uncovered spaces in width equal to the strips themselves, and so arranged that the uncovered spaces on one cylinder corresponded with the strips of wire on the other. By this means the sheet of wool on the last carding cylinder might be seized upon by the strips of wire on the doffing cylinders and separated into two sets of narrow bands.[1] These numerous bands were then drawn off through revolving tubes, which gave them a certain roundness, and wound upon spools the width of the carding engine. These spools, in turn, could be taken to and mounted at the back of the spinning machines, where the roving or more properly roping — the products of the Goulding mechanism — could be directly converted into yarn.

This "American card," as Goulding's device was sometimes called, has been characterized by Hayes as "the most important of all contributions to the card-wool industry of the world" during the nineteenth century; and by North as "almost as great an advance in wool manufacture as the spinning jenny itself." [2] Undoubtedly it supplied the most striking change in the methods

originator but Edward Winslow. Justice Clifford ruled in favor of Jordan, thus supporting Goulding's claim. (There are two volumes of testimony and exhibits; see also Brodix's *American and English Patent Cases*, viii, 56–60.)

See in opposition the contentions of Daniel Bonney, a man who had worked in the mill with Winslow and Goulding when the latter brought his experiments to fruition: *Bulletin*, 1898, pp. 42–43.

An exact apportioning of credit is of course impossible after the century which has elapsed since the patent was granted. Indeed, it must have been difficult at the time of the Jordan-Agawam trial to secure adequate evidence. Wherefore, while many points in the matter remain doubtful in my own mind, I am constrained to follow the opinions of earlier investigators, such as Hayes and North: *American Textile Machinery*, pp. 47–48, and *Bulletin*, 1901, p. 260.

[1] To be exact, under Goulding's plan each roving was kept separate through the operations of the finisher card; but later this practice was dispensed with.

[2] *Bulletin*, 1879, p. 43; and *Bulletin*, 1894, p. 329.

of producing woolen fabrics after the first organization of processes and complement of machinery for factory production had been developed; and the effect of this change upon the quality of the fabrics turned out was also of first importance. Subsequent improvements to Goulding's apparatus, such as the substitution of rub-rollers for the revolving tubes, have of course been made; and the so-called tape-condenser, of Belgian origin, supplies an alternative and apparently better mode of securing roping directly from the carding machine; but these in no way mark an advance upon preëxisting mechanisms comparable with that made by Goulding's contribution itself.

The changes effected by the Goulding apparatus were particularly significant upon two counts: first, the billy and the slubbing process were wholly eliminated and, secondly, a roping of much superior quality was obtainable. Following from these two features is a third rather obvious one, that production was substantially increased. And the savings directly attributable to the new development are in part self-evident. The cost of manufacture was lessened by the reduction of capital outlay, by the elimination of the labor previously occupied in the slubbing process, and by the more effective production.[1] Again, there was a direct social gain through the material reduction in the number of children employed in the woolen industry. But the mechanism also had results upon other apparatus. An impetus was given to the widening of the carding machines themselves by reason of the fact that it was no longer necessary to handle such tenuous articles as the old "cardings."[2] The greater homogeneity of the roping likewise made it possible for the spinner to manage a larger number of spindles on the spinning jack, since there was now less

[1] With respect to the reduction in capital outlay, it may be noted that billies cost about $2.50 per spindle in 1825. A thirty-spindle machine, then, would cost around $75, which was substantially greater than the price of the Goulding attachment. Then, too, the saving in mill space must be considered.

[2] That the long cardings, being handled by children, might drag on the floor, was also a factor which checked the widening of the carding machine (Wheelock, quoted by North, *Bulletin*, 1902, p. 132).

North further states that now forty-inch cards began to appear; and that also the number of revolutions made by the cylinders of the machine could be increased (North, *Bulletin*, 1894, p. 330).

danger of frequent breakages. Previously the jacks had been limited to 120 spindles; now 200-spindle jacks began to appear.[1] Such improvements in carding and spinning meant an appreciably increased effectiveness of the industry.

It is uncertain just how rapidly this new device was adopted in American mills. No complete and immediate scrapping of pre-existing mechanisms could be expected, of course. The manufacturers would be inclined to wear out the old machines. Moreover, there was some hesitation in the trade about adopting the new affair. Thus, the Slater Mills bought a roping billy, a machine which would be useful only under the older methods, as late as 1828.[2] But, seemingly, North's statement was generally correct: that after about 1830 no new sets of cards were started on the previous system.[3] In the Pontoosuc Manufacturing Company, for example, an inventory of 1835 showed two condensers, although one of 1827 had showed none.[4] Moreover, machine-builders began to pay considerable attention to the new apparatus at about this period, a firm in Worcester, Massachusetts, for instance, reporting the manufacture of eighty-five condensers in 1832.[5] A number of years, perhaps a decade, may have elapsed before the Goulding method was universal or indeed predominant; but the beginnings of this change had already been made by the close of the period now under consideration.

The influence of this invention, one may note, was not confined to the United States. Gradually, though after a considerable lapse of time, the Goulding card was adopted in foreign countries. In 1834 a patent was granted in England to one Charles Wilson covering a device which was apparently Goulding's apparatus.[6] However, a book published in 1845, which describes the

1 North, *Bulletin*, 1894, p. 330.

2 Records of S. Slater & Sons Company, of Webster, Massachusetts.

3 North, *Bulletin*, 1894, p. 330.

4 Records of the Pontoosuc Manufacturing Company, of Pittsfield, Massachusetts. The records also indicate in 1835 the presence of four billies at that date.

5 McLane's *Report*, i, 575.

6 Ure, *Philosophy of Manufactures*, 1835, p. 181. It is possible that Goulding received an English patent. North speaks of Goulding making a trip to England in 1825 where he "left his application for a British patent pending" (*Bulletin*, 1901, p. 262).

British method of wool manufacture at that time, explains in full the nature and operation of the slubbing billy, but makes no reference to the condenser method.[1] In the early fifties, for the first time, it was stated that "the operation of slubbing has been lately superseded in many (English) mills by a machine called the Condenser;"[2] but even as late as 1859, Baines gives slubbing as a normal operation in an English woolen mill, although recognizing that "by a new machine, called the Condenser, attached to the carding-machine," this operation may be eliminated.[3] Apparently, then, twenty to twenty-five years elapsed before this particularly valuable apparatus found its way across to England.

The introduction of this invention upon the Continent was apparently not so long delayed as in the case of England, although data upon the point are not abundant. It is stated that the first appearance in France was about 1834,[4] but there is evidence that the apparatus was not extensively employed for ten or fifteen years more.[5] In Germany the course was about the same.

[1] Dodd, *Textile Manufactures of Great Britain*, 1851, pp. 100–101.

[2] Tomlinson, *Encyclopedia of Useful Arts*, 1854, ii, 1035. Ibberson, in his *Woolen Manufacturers' Guide*, 1853, p. 13, says: "The present defective system of piecing the roll-cardings is destined to improvement. If the condenser be only properly managed, it will eradicate a great many defects which are incident to hand-billy piecing, etc.; besides being at its time in a morning, and more economical in its work." Also, in a description of the English woolen processes, given by a special number of the *New York Tribune* upon the occasion of the New York Exhibition of 1853–1854, the slubbing-billy, but not the condenser, is mentioned (*Art and Industry at the Crystal Palace*, p. 223).

[3] *Journal of the Royal Statistical Society*, pp. 5, 26, 27. He states that it "is generally now the case" that "piecing machines are used" (p. 26). In his book, *Yorkshire, Past and Present*, 1870, Baines states that the "old billey has been done away with," as one of the changes in woolen machinery "during the past thirteen years" (p. 665).

[4] From review of Alcan's *Traité du Travail des Laines*, 1866, contained in *Bulletin*, 1870–1871, p. 417.

Picard in his *Bilan d'un Siècle*, after stating that "les cardes à laine fournissaient encore des loquettes, alors que depuis longtemps les cardes à coton produisaient des rubans continus," says: "il fallut en France la loi sur le travail des enfants dans les manufactures pour faire adopter le type de carde enfin dit carde américaine" (iv, 199).

[5] Possibly the Goulding apparatus was earliest used in the manufacture of coarse goods, blanket yarn, etc., and subsequently applied to the production of finer yarns. Thus a British investigator in 1855 remarks of the French industry that "the 'con-

Grothe, apparently thinking of continental Europe as a whole, says that "Goulding's Construction" gained ground very slowly, while for Germany in particular the spread of this device dated from an adaptation made in 1839 by one Götze of Chemnitz.[1]

Obviously, then, if we may suppose the American industry to have adopted Goulding's invention by the middle of the thirties — a supposition not too forced in such a growing manufacture as ours in that period — the domestic producers had secured a substantial advantage over their foreign competitors, an advantage which was to persist for some fifteen or twenty years.[2]

2. *Spinning Machines.*

In tracing the technical development in the spinning process of the wool manufacture, one is venturing upon ground that has been much less well explored than the course of advance in the carding section. Neither in this country nor in England has anyone with a technological bent made an investigation, defining the character of the machines employed at various periods, clarifying the frequently undiscriminating use of names, and recording the spread of the several types of apparatus. Moreover, the employment of machines of similar names in both the cotton and wool-manufacturing industries often leads to confusion or doubt. However, treading his way carefully among these difficulties, one

denser' has been long in use for the manufacture of some classes of goods and is now being employed for the spinning of yarn for woolen cloth" (British Factory Inspector's Report, in *British Documents*, 1856 [2031], p. 64).

[1] Grothe, *Technologie der Gespinnstfasern*, p. 571. He states: "Goulding's Construction gewann Boden, obwohl auch sehr langsam. Seine Vorrichtung ward von Mercier (1835), und von Walton (1837), verbessert. Endlich brachte Götze in Chemnitz (1839) die heute noch gebräuch Continue-vorrichtung am Feinkrempel an und von da ab verbreitete sich dieselbe, und die Vorspinnerei mittels besonderer Jenny trat in den Hintergrund."

[2] The development of automatic operation in the card-clothing manufacture deserves passing notice. At the close of the Revolutionary War card-clothing, then wholly for hand cards in this country, was produced wholly by hand: the holes punched in the leather, the teeth cut, shaped, and inserted into the leather, all by slow, manual operation. Then by a series of American inventions, chiefly those of Pliny Earle of Leicester, Massachusetts, the entire process was made automatic, and within the scope of a single machine (*Bulletin*, 1874–1875, p. 432; *ibid.*, 1899, pp. 235–236; Kittredge, *American Card Clothing Industry*, *passim*).

can yet, I believe, secure a reasonably accurate picture of the advance in this field, and especially the situation in the American industry around 1830.

In many respects there are similarities between the lines of development in the spinning section of the American industry, at least through the first decades of the nineteenth century, and in the carding section already discussed. Superseding the simple colonial implements came an imported apparatus, which for a time dominated the American manufacture, and which had a more important immediate effect upon the household manufacture of cloths. Subsequently, there were improvements in this mechanism, apparently independent of foreign progress along the same lines; and finally came a domestic development—not as commanding as the Goulding card, to be sure, but of substantial merit—which was to form the basis of our operative methods for several future decades.

Already reference has frequently been made to the spinning jenny: its first appearance in Philadelphia in 1775, the use of such a machine at the Hartford factory, and the building of jennies by the Scholfields.[1] Here again the influence of the Scholfields in disseminating technical knowledge of this machine was particularly important; and not enough credit, it seems to me, has heretofore been given them in this connection. Still, jennies had for some years been known and employed in the American cotton manufacture, machines which apparently were more closely akin to the mechanisms of similar name used in the wool manufacture than was the case with the carding apparatus employed in the two industries. Again, there were sources of information concerning the British wool-working jenny, which were independent of the Scholfields. Seemingly Mayall, already referred to in relation to the carding machine's introduction, also had knowledge of the spinning apparatus. In another case, one James Beaumont in 1799 sent to America plans of a spinning machine which he found employed near Huddersfield, England.[2]

In substance this machine was a combination of a number of

[1] See above, pp. 63, 66, 68, 88, 93.

[2] Bagnall, p. 270.

spinning wheels.[1] Numerous strands of roping, already prepared on the billy, were passed between the two jaws of a wooden clasp and fastened to a corresponding number of spindles mounted upon a stationary frame. After a certain length of these strands had been paid out, the portion of the machine containing the

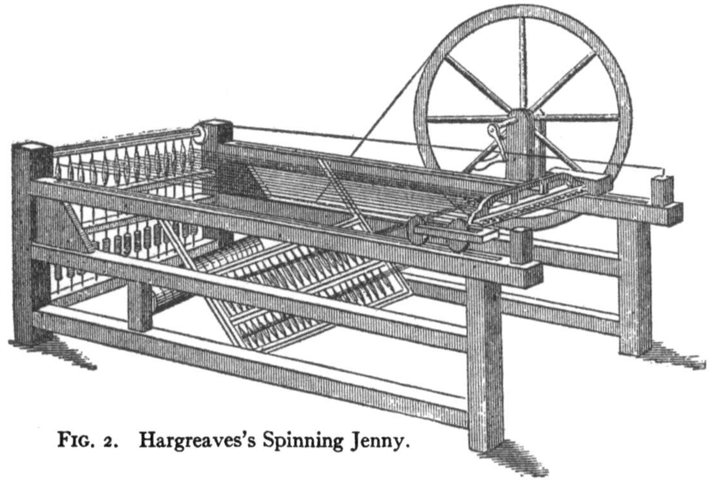

FIG. 2. Hargreaves's Spinning Jenny.

clasp was drawn away from the spindles, the latter at the same time being made to revolve by means of a hand-crank. In this manner, the roping was attenuated and at the same time twisted, reducing the diameter and simultaneously giving strength to the forming yarn.[2] Obviously this apparatus duplicates in a mechanical way the operations performed by the hand of the spinner acting in concert with the spindle of the spinning wheel. But the gain in productivity was astounding. The jennies mounted from eight to fifty spindles, and in some such measure multiplied the yarn-production of the one-spindle spinning wheel.[3]

[1] Indeed, the inventor, James Hargreaves, is said to have conceived the idea of the jenny when his wife's spinning wheel fell over by accident and the wheel continued revolving. The British patent for the jenny is dated 1767.

[2] It is one of the principles of woolen spinning, preserved in the modern woolen "mule," that by drafting (or drawing-out) and twisting at the same time the twist tends to go into the thinner and weaker portions of the yarn, adding to their strength and simultaneously diverting the draft to the thicker portions of the strand. In this way an even yarn is produced.

[3] One relatively small jenny was said to spin more and better yarn, attended by one woman, in one day than in four days at the old spinning wheel (*Massachusetts*

Although the jenny, after its first introduction, became a part of the normal factory equipment, its more immediate effect, as just suggested, was upon the household system of cloth manufacture, particularly in the period after the embargo had been imposed. The jennies which Arthur Scholfield was manufacturing for sale in 1809 (Hayes says in 1806) were intended for family use.[1] Then followed a small flock of similar machines, bearing various names, but apparently all adaptations of the English jenny,—further evidence of the increasing use of this apparatus. Among such new devices, the "Portable Spinner" of Rev. Burgis Allison of Philadelphia is perhaps the one most often mentioned. Mease in his *Archives* describes this as follows: "It is simple and takes up but a little more room than a common spinning wheel. They may be constructed to drive from ten to fifteen spindles, and set to spinning yarn to any degree of fineness admitted by the wool." [2] Ebenezer Herrick's "Domestic Spinner," later recommended by Arthur Scholfield himself, carried only six or eight spindles; [3] and John Brown's "Farmer's Spinner" could spin eight to twelve threads at one time.[4]

But the jenny or other similar apparatus does not seem to have become so widely adopted as was the power-driven carding machine. True, the amount of attention devoted by inventors to

Spy, December 25, 1811); while the larger ones "made by the ingenious Mr. Scholfield," containing twenty to thirty spindles, were alleged to spin from twenty to thirty runs of fine yarn as compared with one and one-half on the old system when the wool was carded by hand, or three when the wool was carded on the machine (Smith, *History of Pittsfield*, ii, 178).

Certain English figures show that while it took two women and three children, employing the spinning wheel, 612 hours to spin a given quantity of yarn, by the use of the jenny a man, a woman, and two children could produce the same amount in seventy-two and one-half hours (*British Documents*, 1840 [43], p. 439).

1 Hayes, *American Textile Machinery*, p. 23.

2 Mease, *Archives*, iii, 191. The machine was patented first April 27, 1812, and was apparently improved in patents of March 3, 1813 and June 28, 1814.

3 *Pittsfield Sun*, March 2, 1811. The dimensions are given as: 6 feet x 2½ x 2½.

4 *Massachusetts Spy*, October 12, 1814; patented May 12, 1813. Other machines might be noted: Daniel Read's "Pleasant Spinner," patented September 10, 1811; and Ebenezer Smith's "family billy and jenny," patented June 28, 1814. Thomas Jefferson had a jenny of six spindles (Bishop, ii, 188, note).

this line of work indicates a considerable market for the product; and, also, as early as 1810 Gallatin speaks of "jennies" and "other family spinning machines" as already "introduced in many places." [1] But there is evidence pointing in the contrary direction. For example, in 1809 a resolution was passed at a gathering of prominent individuals in Pittsfield (met, curiously enough, to organize a "Woolen Manufactory"): "that the introduction of Spinning Jennies, as is practiced in England, into private families, is strongly recommended . . . since . . . it is by this labour saving machine that the American people will successfully rival the Europeans." [2] Again, the *Census of 1810* reported only 299 jennies for the whole country. Moreover, after the conclusion of peace in 1815, references to the household use of this machine are quite infrequent. Apparently it was a phenomenon of the disturbed years of embargo and war, when the household manufacture expanded to fill the abnormal domestic requirements.

In the factories, however, the jenny won a dominant place. From the time of the Byfield factory through 1830, the mill without one or more jennies was indeed the exception. This increased factory use of the machine, one may also note, had led to an enlargement of its capacity. The early ones had usually contained from thirty to fifty spindles; and the largest that was reported during the period before 1815, was one of seventy-two spindles, erected in West Cambridge, now Arlington, Massachusetts.[3] By 1820, however, there seems to have been an appreciable advance: in the census of that year, the number of spindles per machine ranged from forty-four to one hundred and twenty, and the usual

[1] *State Papers, Finance*, ii, 427.

[2] *Pittsfield Sun*, January 7, 1809. Possibly this resolution was dictated by a desire to disarm hostility to the proposed mill on the part of household producers, for the vote ends: "The establishment of an extensive Factory will always go hand in hand with private enterprise." However, ten months later, it could only be said that "a few" jennies had been put into operation "in this vicinity" (*Pittsfield Sun*, November 18, 1809); and as late as September, 1811, it was evidently thought a matter of public interest to see a spinning jenny in actual operation, as such a machine was carried in the procession of the Berkshire Cattle Show of that year (*ibid.*, September 28, 1811).

[3] Taft, *Notes*, p. 44.

number between fifty and seventy.[1] The limit then had apparently been nearly reached; for with every added spindle it became increasingly difficult to control properly this hand-driven machine. The largest jenny to which I have found reference was one of a hundred and fifty spindles, in operation at Uxbridge, Massachusetts, in 1824.[2]

The desire to increase the productivity of these factory spinning machines turned manufacturers' attention to the possibilities of harnessing them to power. For this purpose the jenny was not really suitable, and there are no authenticated cases of this apparatus being adapted to power work. Other machines, however, were tried. William Humphreys, of Connecticut, in 1811 patented a machine for spinning wool by water-power, by means of which, it was said, twelve spindles would perform the work of a forty-spindle jenny.[3] A manufacturer of Northampton, Massachusetts, it was reported in 1812, "employs and moves by water a carding machine and 150 spindles, and by hand 410 spindles." [4] There was another power-driven device, so it is said, built at

[1] *State Papers, Finance*, iv, 28–223; especially pp. 40, 42, 48, 59, and 102, where the sizes are stated or readily deducible.

However, Mr. William H. Vose, later treasurer of the Fitchburg (Massachusetts) Woolen Mill, speaks of working in this factory as late as 1828 and 1829 as spinner upon a jenny of only eight spindles (*Census of 1880*, xx, 392). Possibly, of course, this was a machine kept for learners.

[2] Wheelock, in Chapin, *Address*, p. 142. Some doubt might arise as to whether the larger jennies above mentioned were really driven by hand. I can only say that I have found no clear cases of jennies harnessed to animal or water power.

The jenny had come to be included as part of that rough unit for measuring or stating the capacity of a woolen mill, the so-called "set." Prior to 1830–1840, says North (*Bulletin*, 1901, p. 277), a "set" consisted of three single or two double carding machines with a billy and two jennies.

[3] Warden, *Account of the United States*, 1819, ii, 31: Here, eight years after the date of its patent, this machine is specified as one product of Connecticut genius. Did it survive that long?

There are earlier cases of power-driven machinery, but one is not sure that spinning machines are included. In 1807, the apparatus of the Elkton (Maryland) factory, "made by artists from Europe," was said to be "all moved by water" (Bagnall, p. 235). Clark (p. 565) gives this as a case of wool-jennies worked by power.

[4] *Pittsfield Sun*, January 11, 1812; also Niles, i, 292.

A writer in the *National Intelligencer*, August 6, 1810, states that "the spinning (of wool) is done by water, and horse and steam;" but does not go into particulars as to the type of machine employed.

Providence in 1813 under the direction of an English superintendent, in which the threads were drawn upwards, vertically, instead of horizontally as in the jenny and other wool-spinning machines.[1]

But the course of development which proved ultimately most successful was that employing the spinning jack as its basis. This latter machine was essentially but a modification of the spinning jenny. In it the spindles, instead of being fixed upon a stationary frame as in the jenny, were placed on the moving portion of the machine, the latter part having been enlarged to accommodate them. Contrariwise, the mechanism which held fast the roving during the actual spinning operation was transferred to the rear and stationary portion, and the clasp of the jenny was now replaced by a pair of rollers. Such an arrangement permitted an easier application of power. Indeed, the modern spinning machine, the so-called "mule," is essentially but a power-driven jack, to which some of the structure of the cotton "mule" — really a mule — has been rather recently adapted.[2]

The first "spinning jack" to which I have found reference is the one set up by James Scholfield about 1802 at North Andover.

[1] Edwin M. Stone in the "Semi-Centennial" of the *Providence Journal*, 1870, p. 16.

[2] Inasmuch as modern industrial practice has decided upon the use of the term "mule" for the woolen spinning machine of the moving carriage type, the contention that it is not properly so called would seem a wholly fruitless matter; but I believe an understanding of the difference between the two machines is an aid in untangling some of the technical history. Students of English industrial development will recall that Crompton's mule, first used in the cotton manufacture, derived its name from the fact that it was in a sense a cross between Arkwright's water-frame and Hargreaves's jenny: it embraced the draft between two sets of rollers, which was the chief feature of the one, and the carriage draft and twist, which characterized the other. In no wool-spinning machine of this general sort, however, has there been any roller drawing, but always and solely the type of draft which existed in the original jenny. Yet there is, as suggested above, some justification for the modern use of the term "mule." After the "hand jack" had been made wholly automatic, the heavier framework of the cotton mule was incorporated with the more distinctive features of the wool-spinning apparatus. Probably, then, the most accurate term to describe this particular hybrid would be the old French one, "mule-jenny." However, in the following discussion I have made the text conform to modern terminology, at the same time trying to distinguish between the real and the pseudo mules wherever necessary. Cf. Grothe, *Technologie der Gespinnstfasern*, p. 568, note.

This apparently was an imported product, as James did not come to America until his brothers, John and Arthur, had become interested in the Byfield enterprise.[1] It was a hand-worked machine, and probably the same apparatus which in England came to be called a "wool-spinning mule." Probably other machines of the same sort were the two jacks employed by the Waltham Cotton and Woolen Company in 1810.[2] John Scholfield, Jr., also had a spinning-jack, one of sixty spindles, at Jewett City, Connecticut, in 1816.[3] When next mention is found, however, they were being harnessed to power. A jack is said to have been operated by water-power in the fall or winter of 1814–1815 at Uxbridge, Massachusetts, or perhaps even at a slightly earlier date;[4] and again, in 1819, at Peacedale, Rhode Island.[5]

Just what is meant by the phrase "operated by water-power" in this case is far from clear, nor have I found any means of explication. The mechanical operations of the modern "mule" may be divided into four groups: the delivery of the roping by the rollers and the rotation of the spinning spindles; the outward motion of the carriage, now holding the spindles, the speed of which changes after a distance equivalent to the length of new roping has been traversed; the return of the carriage to its original position with the spindles directly under the rollers; and the winding of the completed yarn upon the spindles, which actually takes place during the return movement of the carriage. Whether one or several of these groups of motions constituted the earliest "operation by water power" seems a question which it is now impossible to solve. Foreign experience, at least in so far as France and Germany are concerned, suggests that the application of power probably came gradually.[6] On the other hand, there is

[1] Bagnall, p. 307.

[2] Starbuck, "Waltham Manufactories," in *History of Middlesex County*, iii, 751.

[3] Bagnall, p. 459.

[4] Taft, *Bulletin*, 1896, p. 21.

[5] Hayes, *Bulletin*, 1879, p. 19. Hayes, however, speaks of it as "the first record which we can find of the application of power to spinning wool in this country."

[6] Alcan, *Traité du Travail des Laines*, 1866, i, 465, distinguishes between the "demi self-acting, ou le renvidage a lieu à la main" and the completely automatic

nothing definite in American data, nor for that matter in the corresponding English data, which intimates this actually to have been the course of development.[1] However, there is negative evidence in the failure of such investigators as Hayes and North to speak of any such change in wool-spinning technique between approximately 1830 and 1860–1870, when the completely automatic mule was introduced.[2] Accordingly, it seems probable that the portions of the process to which power was applied were those which we know were conducted in an automatic or semi-automatic manner just prior to this later development of the modern self-actor or fully automatic mule. These were the first two groups of motions above specified.[3] If this be true, the conduct of the operation was as follows: the roping was delivered automatically, when the carriage of the machine reached the proper position under the rollers; and the spindles were rotated by power at a predetermined speed while the carriage was on its outward traverse. This outward movement itself was accomplished in only a quasi-mechanical manner; some momentum was imparted to the carriage by a loose driving belt, but the rate of motion and especially the intermediate change in rate was controlled by the

machine, the "self-acting." Cf. also Picard, *Le Bilan d 'un Siècle*, iv, 210.

The German data show a further subdivision. For example, Quandt (*Die Niederlausitzer Schafwollindustrie*, p. 177) says: "Das Ein-und Ausfahren des Wagens geschah zuerst durch die Hand des Spinners. Dann machte man das Ausfahren selbstthätig, und nur das Einfahren besorgte noch der Spinner. . . . Nach vielen Mühen brachte es endlich der Techniker so weit, dass er das Ein-und Ausfahren des Wagens selbstthätig von der Maschine ausführen lassen konnte." The second state was called "der Half-Selfactor," as in the French terminology. Cf. Grothe, p. 586, note.

[1] The English used the word "mule" or "wool-spinning mule" for a machine which was apparently similar to our power-driven jack, except perhaps in some of the details of construction. (See below.)

The only reference that I have found with respect to the corresponding English development refers to the English cotton manufacture. Chapman (*The Lancashire Cotton Industry*, p. 68) states that "some time before the self-actor appeared, power was used to drive out the mule-carriage."

[2] North (*Bulletin*, 1901, p. 275) says: "It is a curious fact, in view of the many advances made in other mechanical departments, that the hand-jack (just what he means by this is uncertain) continued to be employed in all our woolen mills until after the Civil War." Then came the "self-operating" jacks and mules.

[3] There may have been some delay in the transfer of all the component motions to power, but probably no considerable delay.

spinner. To check the advance of the carriage, he merely leaned his weight against its front bar. The return of the carriage was entirely the duty of the spinner, though perhaps in the case of the larger machines he had the assistance of another loose belt; while the winding of the completed yarn and the building of the bobbin were also done entirely by the operative.[1]

The adoption of the power-driven jack in this country is particularly difficult to trace, partly because of the loose terminology used in describing spinning machines, and partly because soon the spinning capacity of a mill ceased to be given in terms of machines and was stated only in that of spindleage. The transfer from jenny to jack, however, appears to have come in the latter twenties and early thirties. The manufacturers who testified in the tariff hearings of 1828 spoke, to be sure, only of jennies; but they were chiefly makers of fine cloths; and that section of the industry seems to have retained the hand-machine longer than the rest.[2] On the other hand, certain machine-builders in 1832 reported the construction of jacks alone, but made no mention of jennies.[3] Mr. Vose narrates that after the destruction of the

[1] Obviously, the spinner was still an important factor in the process. More will be said of him later.

My knowledge of the operation as it existed just prior to the introduction of the complete self-actor was derived in part from interviews with men in the industry, especially Mr. Nathaniel Stevens of the M. T. Stevens & Sons Company, and Mr. William Kelly, for thirty years spinner or boss-spinner for the Olney Woolen Company, Cherry Valley, Massachusetts. Mr. Kelly had worked on the semi-automatic jacks; and he did not remember a time and had never heard of a time prior to the introduction of the self-actor when anything but the above-described sort of semi-automatic jack was used.

However, Mr. John P. Wood writes me: "My recollection of mules in use before the full automatic is that their movements were all actuated by the mill power. They were 'hand-operated' only in the sense that the operator shifted the mechanism to change from one function to another by hand. For the full automatic mule the change from one stage of operation or function to another was accomplished without the intervention of the operator." This description does not tally with that given in the text, though it may cover only a mechanism intermediate between that which I have outlined and the fully automatic apparatus. The whole matter is puzzling and I speak with considerable uncertainty.

[2] 20th Cong., 1st Sess., House of Representatives, *Report No. 115*.

[3] McLane's *Report*, 1832, i, 518–519, 572–573. See also *Worcester Spy*, August 20, 1834.

Fitchburg Woolen Mill by fire in the early thirties, the jennies which had been employed were replaced by jacks.[1] The Pontoosuc Manufacturing Company, possessing no jacks in 1827, had acquired four by 1835, although still holding on to some of its old jennies.[2] It seems probable, indeed, that during the decade of the thirties "the roll carding machine, the billy, and the jenny were (all) being thrown aside and no longer retained except by small establishments that depended upon neighborhood trade." [3]

Meanwhile, a somewhat different type of spinning machine had been devised in this country, called the "Brewster," after its inventor, Gilbert Brewster of Norwich, Connecticut. As early as 1813, he was advertising a "Globe-Spinner," a machine which was described as suitable for spinning "Sheep's Wool, Cotton, Flax and Tow, by Water" and which was said to be already in operation in a Rhode Island woolen mill. It was stated, probably with exaggeration, to be manageable by small children, to occupy but about a fourth part of the space required for a jenny of the same spindleage, and to spin equally well at only a third the cost.[4] Seemingly improved later, especially by changes patented in 1824, the Brewster became a real self-operating machine.[5]

[1] *Census of 1880*, xx, 391.

[2] Records of the Pontoosuc Manufacturing Company, Inventories of 1827 and 1835.

[3] H. G. Kittredge in *Dry Goods Economist*, Jubilee Number, 1896, p. 81. He speaks of the decade 1840–1850 as "the end of the transitory period," thinking primarily of the adoption of the fancy loom as completing "the equilibrium . . . in factory operations" and ushering "the era of modern wool manufacturing." Although not clear on the point, apparently the scrapping of the roll carding machine, billy, and jenny had in his opinion been going on for some time before; and the attainment of "equilibrium" etc., was delayed only by the tardy invention of the fancy power loom.

[4] *Providence Gazette*, March 6, 1813. Niles, in 1822 (xxii, 85), speaks warmly of Brewster's machine for spinning wool.

[5] Bishop, ii, 297.

Grothe, *Technologie der Gespinnstfasern*, p. 605, gives credit to Brewster for the development of a self-actor prior to Roberts. He adds: "Freilich ist dieser Selfactor Später durch die Construction Roberts und Smith (1834) überholt, aber er zeigt doch eine bedeutende Combinationsgabe." Richardson, in his *History of Woonsocket* (p. 131), also sets the machine down as a "self-operating mule." He adds that it was a rather clumsy affair and was abandoned after being in use but a short time.

Although hailed at that time as a machine which would soon leave the English manufacturers "much behind us," [1] it apparently came to little. It found scant favor in the cotton trade, and in the wool manufacture was never widely used. Samuel Slater appears to have found it unsatisfactory; [2] and in the investigations of the Committee on Manufactures in 1828 the reports of wool manufacturers were at best half-hearted.[3] After that time the Brewster disappears.[4] It is noteworthy, however, as a predecessor of Roberts's self-acting mule, patented in England in 1825, which in turn became the pattern of most subsequent self-operating spinning machines.

In conclusion, it is of interest and value to compare the development of power spinning here and abroad, especially because of certain misconceptions which have crept into American writings on the subject.[5] In England the hand jenny was the prevailing type of wool-spinning machine throughout the latter years of the eighteenth century, its more general introduction coming after 1785.[6] This apparatus fitted in with the quasi-handicraft

[1] Niles, xxvi, 363.

[2] An entry on the books of his Webster mill reads:

"July 16, 1824.

Gilbert Brewster, Cr.

By Amount of Expenses in Moving Wool Spinning Machine from Middletown (Conn.) to this Place & from this Place to Middletown . . . . $97.83"

[3] 20th Cong., 1st Sess., House of Representatives, *Report No. 115*.

A typical view is that of an Oriskany (New York) manufacturer: "We have a patent machine for spinning called a 'Brewster.' We spin warp on this machine, and consider the mode a very good one. The machine, however, is subject to getting out of repair. We also spin a part of the warp, and all the filling, in the usual mode" (on the jenny) (p. 80). It was generally testified that at best the Brewster was suited only for warp yarn, and that it was likely to get out of order. See pp. 83, 89, 90, 96, 105, 123.

[4] Thus, while a "Brewster frame" appears in an inventory of the Pontoosuc Manufacturing Company of 1827, no such machine is mentioned in one of 1835 (Records of the Company).

[5] For example, North (*Bulletin*, 1901, p. 255) states that "in England power spinning was in general use in the wool manufacture in the latter part of the eighteenth century."

[6] Cunningham, p. 653. Heaton (*Yorkshire Woolen and Worsted Industries*, p. 352) puts the period of its introduction "the third quarter of the eighteenth century;" but it was only invented in 1767!

organization of the Yorkshire manufacture, and there secured a firm root.[1] But in the first quarter of the nineteenth century, wool-spinning factories or fully integrated woolen mills were rising, and in them there was a demand, as in this country, for more efficient and productive machinery. This led to the modification of the mule, which, it is stated, was introduced into Yorkshire about 1824 or 1825, and in the West of England around 1828.[2] This was apparently the "wool-spinning mule" described by Ure, which in fact is exactly the power-driven jack of American experience as far as its automatic action is concerned.[3] The adoption of the fully automatic mule did not occur until a later period.[4]

On the Continent, the progress was slower. In France, hand spinning had scarcely disappeared by 1830, according to Picard; and after that the old hand jenny or "métier à pince" maintained its hold until about the middle of the nineteenth century, when it was replaced by the "mule-jenny" or "mule-jenny ordinaire," the "demi self-acting." [5] Of Germany, less is known. In the his-

[1] The small manufacturers of Yorkshire, who worked in their own homes or small shops, could install one of these machines. In other cases they could "put out" the work of spinning to households which did possess such a machine. On the other hand, there was no place for larger, power-driven machines in such an organization. In Bischoff (ii, 396) it is stated that "the jenny is still (1842) used to some extent in Yorkshire," where the simple handicraft system of production was retained.

[2] *British Documents*, 1840 [43], p. 583; *ibid.* [220], p. 370. Spinning mills were also set up by and operated for a group of small domestic weavers.

[3] Ure, *Philosophy of Manufactures*, 1835, pp. 183–185. A portion of the description of this mechanism is as follows: The "rollers, by means of a peculiar mechanism driven by the main axis of the machine, deliver at each movement of the carriage, the length of roving requisite for one stretch. . . . The spinner is saved from the care and exertion of bringing out the carriage, that operation being performed by the moving power on automatic principles, as in the cotton mule; but he executes the winding of the yarn on the spindles, by pushing the carriage back to the roller beam, and depressing the faller wire," etc. to make a regular cop.

[4] Although William Kelly had in 1792 made the mule self-operating, his mechanism was not practically successful until improved by Richard Roberts in 1825. These devices applied only to cotton spinning. Not until 1832, when Roberts had invented his radial arm, or sector, was the woolen mule made self-acting (Bramwell, *Wool-Carders' Vade Mecum*, p. 381). The adoption of the machine in the wool manufacture took place then but slowly.

[5] Picard, *Bilan d'un Siècle*, iv, 202–203, 209–210.

tory of Niederlausitz, the only German wool-manufacturing region which has been investigated thoroughly, the simple jenny is spoken of as coming in in the forties, while the "Halb-Selfactor" is said to have appeared there only in the beginning of the seventies.[1]

Obviously, then, here as in the carding process the American industry was not tardy in the adoption of labor-saving mechanisms. The advantage or priority was not so great as in the other case,—probably with respect to England it was not appreciable. Still, that we were not behind the British is a sufficient credit to our infant industry. In comparison with the Continental development, the American manufacture was more forward, even as it had been in the case of the carding apparatus.

3. *Weaving Machines.*

The history of improvement in the weaving process is a relatively simple affair. This follows in part from the fact that from the earliest times, even to the present day, there has been no fundamental change in the manner of weaving woolen fabrics. The machines for other portions of the wool-cloth manufacture, such as carding, spinning, and various operations in finishing, have been so modified that only a student of textile history would recognize in them the old hand methods. In the weaving process, however, the modern loom is essentially only the old hand loom with the earlier manual operations performed by power.[2]

The development in weaving prior to 1830 consisted of but three important features: the adoption of the flying shuttle for hand looms, the spread of broad looms, and the application of

[1] Quandt, *Die Niederlausitzer Schafwollindustrie*, pp. 175–177.

Apparently the full self-actor followed closely upon the heels of the half self-actor in this region (p. 177, note).

[2] As a corollary to the above proposition, it follows that in the weaving operation there has not been the saving from improved methods of production that ensued from inventions in the other wool-manufacturing processes. For example, around 1830 the wool-spinning mule could turn out a given quantity of yarn in one-fiftieth of the time required for hand spinning; but the power loom of that period probably did not make a reduction of more than 50 per cent in weaving, even compared with the hand-loom weaving without the fly-shuttle (*British Documents*, 1840 [43], pp. 430–441).

power to both narrow and broad machines. Of the first, little need be said, since the hand loom itself was so soon and so largely superseded. Apparently the flying shuttle, by means of which

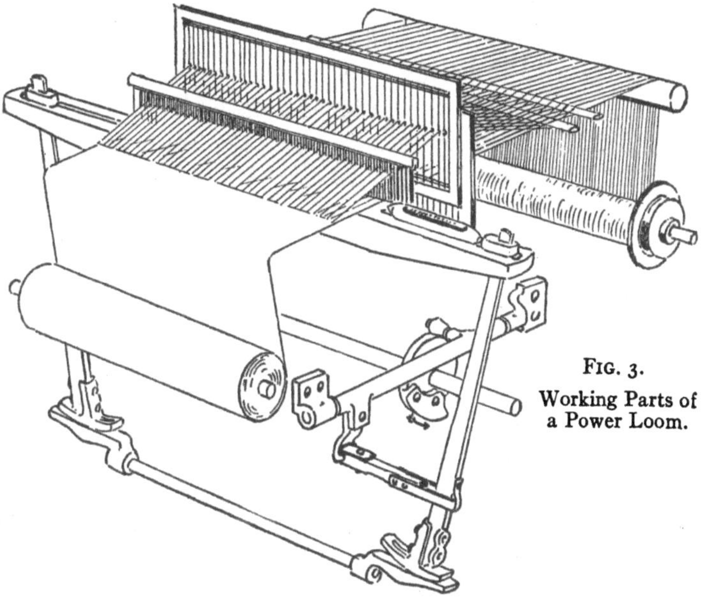

FIG. 3.
Working Parts of a Power Loom.

the labor of a weaver's assistant was eliminated, was first employed in this country about 1788 in Rhode Island.[1] But spread of its use could not have been rapid; for it is narrated that a manufactory of flying shuttles, started in Philadelphia in 1793, shortly moved to Nova Scotia from want of encouragement and support in the United States.[2] As late as 1810, Tench Coxe,

[1] Prior to the adoption of the fly or spring-shuttle, the weaver had to throw or hand the shuttle (which contained the weft or latitudinal threads of the fabric) from one side to the other of the loom; and in the case of a broad loom, it was customary among professional weavers to employ a youth to assist the handicraftsman. The boy stood at the one side of the loom and the weaver at the other, and they passed the shuttle from side to side. The fly-shuttle consisted of a pair of blocks, one on either side of the loom, between which a loose rope was run. The weaver, by grasping the rope near the middle and pulling first in one and then in the other direction, could send the shuttle flying from one side to the other of the loom, the shuttle at the end of its traverse coming to rest against the other block, ready for the next (and opposite) pull.

[2] Bishop, i, 333, note.

commenting upon the figures of looms with fly-shuttles given in the *Census of 1810*, stated that "though it (the fly-shuttle) has been known in this country many years, more than ninety-nine one-hundredths of our shuttles are not of that description." [1] Seemingly it gained little foothold in the household industry, partly because most of the household looms were probably of the narrow variety. In the budding factories it was presumably employed, in so far as weaving departments formed portions of these mills, but there is little definite evidence to indicate this fact.[2]

The wider adoption of the broad loom was a result of the increased manufacture of the famous broadcloth in the period following the Revolutionary War, and especially in that after the imposition of the embargo. As already intimated, the looms of the colonial period and those which were employed in the continuing household production of wool fabrics were probably narrow looms for the most part, looms capable of weaving cloths not exceeding a yard in width. The English broadcloth was always woven, indeed secured its name originally from being woven, in much greater width. This cloth was fulled in an exceptional degree after it was woven, thereby shrinking in width as well as in length. Accordingly it had to be "set" or arranged in the loom to allow for this shrinkage. Broad looms therefore reached the width of ten quarters, or two and a half yards.

Though rarely referred to prior to the Revolution, broad looms are mentioned with increasing frequency as the years roll on. The Hartford factory apparently had broad looms. The Scholfields upon their arrival in Boston constructed a loom suitable for producing broadcloths, and such apparatus was reported at various times as part of the equipment in their several mills. The

[1] *State Papers, Finance*, ii, 677. The Census figures were: looms, 325,392; looms with fly-shuttles, 224 (p. 693).

Another indication of their novelty at this period is the operation of a loom equipped with a fly-shuttle upon "a large stage drawn by Oxen" in the procession of the Berkshire Cattle Show in 1811 (*Pittsfield Sun*, September 28, 1811).

[2] Taft (*Notes*, pp. 46–47) gives one case a mill in Uxbridge, Massachusetts, where the fly-shuttle was used.

Housatonick Manufacturing Company at Pittsfield had four broad and three narrow looms in 1816; and in the same year John Scholfield, Jr., at Jewett City, Connecticut, had an equipment of four broad and seven narrow machines.[1] By that time, the broad apparatus was so widely and generally employed as of itself to suggest a peculiarly large production of broadcloth, a matter to which reference will subsequently be made.[2]

The final step in the development of weaving technique was already in progress. Disregarding the Elkton (Maryland) factory, in which the machinery "made by artists from Europe" was indefinitely stated to be "all moved by water," the first mention of a power loom employed on wool goods is one patented by Messrs. Shepherd and Thorpe of Taunton, Massachusetts, in 1816.[3] A couple of years later, sixteen looms worked by water are said to have been engaged on satinets at Chelmsford, Massachusetts; and in the *Census of 1820* there is notice of eight power looms in a mill of Middlesex County, Connecticut.[4]

In the early years of this next decade, the adoption of power looms became much more rapid. The type of machine at first more generally introduced was that for the narrow fabric, satinet, which was now growing in popularity. This was a rather coarse cloth, made with a cotton warp and a woolen filling. The cotton warp, being stronger than a woolen warp, made the cloth one which could more easily be woven on the early, somewhat crude power machines. Beside the Chelmsford installation above mentioned, power looms for satinets were being made in Philadelphia shortly after 1820; they were in use at Uxbridge, Massachusetts, in 1821; and about 1822 a satinet mill in North Adams, Massachusetts, secured a power loom from Providence, Rhode Island.[5] A "Commercial Directory" published in 1823 indicates that several satinet factories in Massachusetts had adopted this mechanism, mention being made of five separate establish-

[1] Smith, *History of Pittsfield*, ii, 469; Bagnall, p. 459.

[2] See below, pp. 195–196.

[3] Bishop, ii, 233. For similar instance, see Niles, x, 384.

[4] Allen, *History of Chelmsford*, 1820, p. 84.

[5] Scharf and Westcott, *History of Philadelphia*, p. 2304; Wheelock, in Chapin, *Address at Uxbridge*, p. 141; Smith, *History of Berkshire County*, i, 518.

ments in which from four to fifty power or "water" looms were located.[1]

The adaptation of the mechanical loom to broad weaving was not long delayed. Eight such machines were said to have been employed in a Connecticut broadcloth factory as early as 1820.[2] A power loom for weaving broadcloth was set up in Allendale, Rhode Island, in 1822; and in the following year, Messrs. Howard and Hovey commenced the manufacture of broad power looms in Worcester, Massachusetts.[3] The Directory above quoted speaks of broad power looms but once — in Northampton, Massachusetts — where of thirty-five broad looms, twelve were "of a new construction, worked by water." [4] Probably it was after, rather than before 1825, that the new mechanism came into really wide use for the broadcloth weaving.

The use of this machine for the production of other fabrics deserves passing mention. Flannel woven on power looms was exhibited at the Brighton (Massachusetts) fair in November, 1824,[5] and soon afterward the apparatus was generally adopted for that manufacture. The first notice that I have seen of its employment upon cassimere indicates that in the year 1826 ten power cassimere looms were set up in the Uxbridge (Massachusetts) Woolen Mill; and then two years later power looms for the fabrication of kerseys were installed, it is said, at the Peacedale (Rhode Island) Manufacturing Company's plant.[6]

Bagnall states that by 1825 power looms "had already sup-

[1] Kayser, *Commercial Directory*, 1823, pp. 109, 110, 111, and 113. Usually the author speaks of water or power looms in connection with satinet mills, when he mentions the loom equipment at all.

[2] *State Papers, Finance*, iv, 56.

[3] Taft, *Bulletin*, 1896, p. 21; Washburn, in *History of Worcester County, Massachusetts*, ii, 1611.

[4] Kayser, *Commercial Directory*, p. 113.

Other examples of the early adoption of the power loom for broadcloth manufacture: North, *Bulletin*, 1901, p. 278 (Southbridge, Massachusetts); Bishop, ii, 300 (Pontoosuc Manufacturing Company, Pittsfield, Massachusetts). Niles (xlii, 109) speaks of the broad power loom as if it were by that time, 1832, commonly employed.

[5] Bishop, ii, 294.

[6] Wheelock, in Chapin, *Address at Uxbridge*, p. 143; *Providence Board of Trade Journal*, xxiii, 292.

planted hand looms in most of the successful woolen mills, thereby effecting a revolution in the industry." [1] The facts, however, do not wholly bear out the first part of this assertion. The first mention of a power loom in the records of the Slater Mill at Webster, Massachusetts, occurs in 1825,[2] and the Hamilton Woolen Company wove some goods by hand until 1830.[3] Again, in the hearings before the Committee on Manufactures in 1828, when many leading wool manufacturers testified, there are indications that the power machine had as yet failed to acquire full sway. A manufacturer of Dudley, Massachusetts, said: "Our broadcloths are woven partly by hand, and partly by the power loom. The cassimeres are all wove in the hand loom;" and in the Du Pont mill at Wilmington, Delaware, the weaving was said to be "done by hand looms principally." [4] Finally, the long retention of hand-loom weaving in the Philadelphia district must be noted. In 1825 there were said to be forty-five hundred hand looms in the city, at a time when approximately three thousand of the weavers entered into a combination to raise weaving rates; [5] and toward the end of the decade an English observer described that area again as "a great seat of hand-loom manufacturing and weaving." [6] However, it is probably true that by 1825 the introduction of the power loom in the wool manufacture had been well begun, and that within another five-year period the trend was strongly toward a general use of the machine.

This power loom, it should be remarked, was far from being the power loom of today. The machine operated but two heddles

[1] Bagnall, p. 311.

[2] Slater Records: "February 28, 1826.

Hollis Wood, Cr.

By Daughter Almira Labour at Power Loom from May 30th to June 23, 1825, 3 wks. 3¼ days at 7/6. . . . . $4.43"

Other entries indicate that this was the only loom of the sort as yet in the mill.

[3] Pamphlet called *A Brief Record of the Hamilton Woolen Company*, p. 1 (manuscript).

[4] 20th Cong., 1st Sess., *House Documents, No. 115*, pp. 82 and 123.

[5] Niles, xxviii, 159.

[6] Freedley, *Philadelphia and Its Manufactures*, p. 233.

Niles (xlii, 109) speaks even of "the broad power loom" as if in quite common use by 1832.

and one shuttle, and was adapted to the production of only the plainest of cloths, — fabrics which were of the simplest, so-called "plain" weave, and cloths which were of a single color or at least with only the simpler stripes.[1] Such cloths, to be sure, formed the great bulk of the domestic production at this time; but soon textile designs were destined to appear, especially designs imported from abroad, which led to many changes and improvements in the original power apparatus. In addition, the strength of the machine was to be enhanced, and improvements introduced whereby the strain upon the warp threads was reduced and the possibility thus provided for weaving the finest textures.[2]

The newly rising American industry could readily adopt this power mechanism; but the machine did not find place so well in the older European manufactures. In the Yorkshire cloth industry, the small manufacturers working in their homes or tiny shops could make no use of the machine.[3] By 1840 the apparatus is reported to have "made but little progress" in the West Riding. In the West of England, it was not introduced until 1836, and in the so-called heavy woolen district (around Batley and Dewsbury) not until about 1850.[4] In 1856 there were only 14,000 power looms in the English woolen trade, although at the same

[1] The exact type of the earlier woolen power looms cannot now be determined. An old loom preserved in the Slater Mill is of the common cam or tappet variety, and so is similar to the looms early constructed by Lowell for the cotton manufacture. Use was apparently also made of the Scotch or Horrocks loom, which likewise had for some years been employed in the cotton industry (Washburn, in *History of Worcester County, Massachusetts*, ii, 1611).

[2] Among the improvements may be mentioned the increase in the number of heddles which could be operated by the cam loom, the development of the dobby loom, the adaption of the Jacquard loom to power, the increase in the number of shuttle boxes, and the invention of the open and closed-shed apparatus for working the warp movements. Some of these will be noted in later chapters.

[3] The flying shuttle, on the other hand, had been readily accepted in Yorkshire. Patented by Kay in 1733, it was apparently in extensive use about 1760–1770 (Heaton, *op. cit.*, p. 341). In the West of England, however, this device does not appear to have been introduced until 1796 (Cunningham, *op. cit.*, p. 502).

[4] *British Documents*, 1840 [43], p. 587; [220], p. 376 (*Report on the Hand-Loom Weavers*); Bowley, *Journal of the Royal Statistical Society*, lxv, 124. In the worsted trade, the power loom secured a much quicker distribution. It is stated that already in 1846 the hand loom had been banished from most branches of this manufacture (Clapham, *Bulletin*, 1908, p. 308).

time there were 39,000 in the worsted and nearly 300,000 in the cotton industries.[1] The period 1840 to 1860 showed a substantial dropping off of hand weavers in all the English wool-manufacturing centers, and by the latter date the power loom may be said to have secured the upper hand.

The Continent adopted the power loom with the usual tardiness.[2] Just when the first attempts at power weaving were made in France is not certain; but it was not until 1848 that the power loom found place in the manufacture of the light-weight "merinos" or dress-goods;[3] and with respect to the fabrication of broadcloth, it could be said as late as 1867 that the substitution of the power machine was as yet not general.[4] In Germany, the adoption of power weaving had hardly begun in 1850. As late as 1875 there were still nearly 47,000 hand looms in Germany, as compared with approximately 30,000 mechanical looms,—and we know that the large proportion of the latter were to be found in the younger worsted manufacture.[5]

[1] Baines, *Journal of the Royal Statistical Society*, 1859, p. 8. In 1836, only 2150 power looms were reported for the woolen manufacture, of which over half were located in Lancashire where cloths of the mixed, cotton and wool composition were beginning to be produced (Baines, *op. cit.*, p. 8; Lipson, *History of the English Wool Manufacture*, p. 188).

One of the difficulties in way of adoption by the British industry of this new mechanism was the relatively small gain in output obtained from the employment of the power machine, especially in the case of the earlier apparatus and of the finer English fabrics, some of which were woven as much as nine feet wide. For example, in 1840, it was said with regard to the West of England production, that a power loom then could make only forty-two shots per minute, while a hand-loom weaver could make forty if he worked briskly, though, to be sure, he could not keep up that pace with the endurance of the machine (*British Documents*, 1840 [220], p. 435). With the improvement of the power machine, the discrepancy between these two performances became greater.

[2] The adoption of the flying shuttle also came after some delay. Its introduction into France is said to have first taken place in 1788 (Alcan, quoted in *Bulletin*, 1870–1871, p. 412), but for the lighter goods, "merinos," it was not employed until 1817 (Bernoville, *Laines Peignées*, p. 195). In Germany, the flying shuttle is said not to have secured general use until the twenties of the nineteenth century (Schmoller, *Die Entwicklung und die Krisis der deutschen Weberei*, p. 10).

[3] Koechlin-Schwartz, *Rapport sur les fils et tissus de laine peignée*, p. 16.

[4] Chevalier, in *Introduction to the Reports of the International Jury at the Paris Exposition of 1867*, p. 163.

[5] Bachmann, *Organisationsbestrebungen in der deutschen Tuch-und Wollwarenindustrie*, p. 17. See also Clapham, in *Bulletin*, 1908, pp. 311–312. In Niederlausitz,

4. *Finishing Machinery.*

Among the various machines utilized in putting the finishing touches upon the cloth or often in really "making" the fabric, discussion here must be limited to the development of two, the napping and shearing machines. In the colonial period, it will be recalled, napping was accomplished by means of hand cards, similar in form to those used in carding, though with the teeth more closely set. These were drawn over the cloth lengthwise of the fabric, and the nap thus raised. Besides being a slow and arduous process, napping required considerable skill to produce a smooth and equal nap over the whole piece and to avoid the production of tender spots in the goods.[1] The nap was then cut to an even height in the shearing operation, performed in those days with hand shears. These last were large clumsy instruments, often four feet in length and weighing sixty pounds, and calling for much dexterity in their manipulation. In the course of development within the wool manufacture, which tended to make the machinery automatic in action, these processes were destined to undergo marked change.

The line of progress in improvement of the napping operation was the utilization of the cylindrical machine-form already employed in the carding engine. This idea seems to have occurred first, or at least to have been embodied first in a practical machine, by Walter Burt of Wilbraham, Massachusetts, whose patent is dated June 26, 1797.[2] Mease gives the following adequate description of this early "gig mill": it "consists of teazles fixed in numerous small frames, which are again fixed in a cylin-

there were in 1869 a round 800 hand looms in the woolen manufacture, and only 128 power looms (Quandt, *op. cit.*, p. 198).

[1] An alternate form involved the use of teazles. Teazles are the spiny head of the plant called *dipsacus fullonum*, cut off and thoroughly dried. They possess spines which are slightly hooked and which are of just the proper strength to nap woolen cloths, strong enough to pull the wool fibers up from the back of the fabric and yet weak enough to break off if by chance they should go too deeply. They are of sufficient size, around three inches in length, to be handled easily. In the colonial days, they were placed in frames or "hands" about the size of the wire napping cards, and used in the same manner as the latter.

[2] Grothe (*Bulletin*, 1881, p. 60) gives the date of Burt's patent as 1774, before the American Revolution!

drical frame of about two feet diameter and composed of slats or ribs having groves (*sic*) cut through their whole length to receive the frames containing the teazles. The cloth passes over the gig mill sufficiently close to raise the nap, and winds round a cylinder below. The mill is turned by water or steam." [1] Somewhat later a machine of similar structure was devised, in which pointed brass wires upon a cylinder were substituted for the cylinder of teazles, thus initiating the competition between the napping machine proper and the gig, between the pointed wire and the teazle, which has continued ever since. This brass-wire apparatus was in operation in 1812 at the Providence (Rhode Island) Woolen Manufacturing Company.[2] Apparently, moreover, invention continued. Some years later a napping machine is spoken of which worked both ways, backward and forward, over a piece of goods,—a machine of which an English manufacturer is said to have professed ignorance prior to his visit to this country.[3]

Indeed, the English development in this line, perhaps independent of the American experience, at least came somewhat later. The first use of modern gig-mills in England was apparently in Gloucestershire around 1802, though it is uncertain whether these were cylindrical machines or what Grothe speaks of as mere "imitations of gigging by hand." [4] This German in-

[1] Mease, *Archives*, 1813, iii, 343.

Two terms are used more or less loosely in connection with this operation,—gigging and napping. The former, strictly speaking, implies the use of teazles in the nap-raising machine. The latter is a more general term, sometimes used to cover any nap-raising process, and sometimes more specifically implying the use of a machine with a wire-covered cylinder. Again, the whole group of devices are spoken of occasionally as "cloth-raising" machines.

[2] Taft, *Notes*, p. 42.

[3] Luke Baker, a manufacturer of napping machines, wrote in 1827: "I have lately been acquainted with an Englishman who has worked in England for many years in the business of manufacturing woolen cloth; he informs me that he never saw a napping machine that worked both ways, either with cards or teasles, until he came to this country" (quoted by Wheelock, in Chapin's *Address at Uxbridge*, p. 141).

[4] Mantoux, *Révolution Industrielle en Angleterre*, p. 425; Cunningham, *op. cit.*, p. 661. The modern napping machine is quite distinct from the "gig-mills" which were prohibited by Parliament in 1552. As Mantoux says: "It is probable that there was nothing in common between them other than the name" (p. 425). However, see Morris and Wood, *The Golden Fleece*, pp. 146–147: "Gig mills were reintroduced (after the Tudor prohibition) into Gloucestershire and Yorkshire about 1740."

vestigator gives full credit to Burt, the American inventor. It was not until after Burt's time, he says, that "mills with a rotating barrel became common in England with improvements of Lewis, Price, and others. All these English machines were patented after the gig-mills in America" had appeared, the fruit of diverse American inventions.[1] Nor were there any developments on the Continent which throw doubt upon the claim of American ingenuity to priority with respect to the cylindrical nap-raising machine.[2]

Substantial advance in the shearing operation really dates from the machine patented by Samuel G. Dorr, of Albany, New York, under date of October 20, 1792. There were attempts both in this country and in England to adapt the old hand shears to power, but without appreciable success.[3] Dorr's apparatus, which he happily called "the wheel of knives," consisted of a number of sharp blades at first placed parallel to the length of a cylindrical frame, though almost at once (1793) wrapped spirally around the cylinder, and working against a stationary blade. In the latter form, the shearing machine had a structure which has been imitated in the more modern lawn-mower.[4] Other types of machines varying slightly from Dorr's model appeared soon afterward, as for instance the machine with an oscillating shear-cylinder, patented by Beriah Swift, of Washington, New York, in 1806; and

[1] Grothe, *Bulletin*, 1881, p. 60.

Mease states (*Archives*, iii, 344) that by 1813 the cylindrical gig-mills were "partially" in use in New England and New York, although hand cards were still universally used in Pennsylvania (p. 343). However, employment of the earlier process apparently persisted in England much longer. Ure, writing in 1835, makes no mention of the new gig-mills, but narrates: "The hardest work in the cloth-finishing business seems to be that of the hand-raisers," who are still using "teasels fixed in hand-frames" (*Philosophy of Manufactures*, p. 203).

[2] For subsequent improvements, many of which had foreign origin, see Grothe, *op. cit.*, and Wachs, *Die Volkswirtschaftliche Bedeutung*, p. 60.

[3] Mease, *Archives*, iii, 344; Grothe, *Bulletin*, 1881, p. 60.

Grothe states, with regard to the early English inventions: "It will be observed that English inventors from 1792 to 1815 (when the first English copy of Dorr's machine was made) had taken out many patents for shearing machines; but all of them followed the construction of the old hand-shears, or the old shearing machine of Harmer (an Englishman), containing a series of hand-shears."

[4] The number of cutting blades was greater, fourteen blades being embraced in Dorr's original machine, while their degree of curvature was not so great.

a number of these devices gained considerable prominence. Among the names of makers more frequently mentioned were those of William Hovey and his Ontario shearing machine, Molleneaux, and Mussey.[1]

The saving derived from this new mechanism was unquestionably great. David Humphreys, the gentleman who had been instrumental in the introduction of merino sheep and who later set up a cloth manufactory, stated in his testimonial upon a machine of one Eleazer Sprague: "From our experience we judge that this machine will shear as close and as smooth, at one operation, as our best English workmen would do at two with Hand-Shears, and three times as fast at least; that one hand may tend three or four of them at once, when impelled by water — and thus the work of three weeks may be performed in a single day."[2] So great an economy of time and effort inevitably gave a marked stimulus to the use of such machines, and the repeated references to them suggest that by the close of the War of 1812, if not before that time, they had become a part of the normal factory equipment. In addition they were added to the equipment of the country fulling shop, and so with the carding machine and the spinning jenny served as a prop to the household manufacture as well as an aid in factory production.[3]

The imitation of American machines abroad or their introduc-

[1] Another interesting type of machine was that of Edmund Durrin of Wetherfield, New York, patented in 1814. The cutting mechanism was of the zig-zag sort later employed in our common mowing-machine.

Apparently there was an unusual amount of "pirating" in the building of these various machines. Certain Wilmington (Delaware) men, advertising a cylindrical apparatus, state: they "are fully aware that the right of patenting has been so grossly abused, that to proclaim a new patented invention, is considered by many as an annunciation of another method of imposing on the credulity of the public" (*American Watchman*, September 12, 1810).

[2] *Pittsfield Sun*, October 10, 1810. The machine of Eleazer Hovey was said to shear a yard of cloth per minute (Bishop, ii, 176). In 1828, a woolen manufacturer of Northampton, Massachusetts, reported that a superintendent and seven girls attended twenty pair of shears (20th Cong., 1st Sess., *House Documents, No. 115*, p. 90).

[3] A common form of advertisment for these machines was: "price $100 for the narrow machine, and the right to use it at a country stand; for the machine for broad cloth, where it runs steadily, $300." See e. g., *Worcester Spy*, July 31, 1811 and *Pittsfield Sun*, October 10, 1810.

tion into foreign countries has been pretty definitely traced. For example, Dorr's construction is the basis of a machine patented in England by Price nearly twenty-five years later (1815), and, according to Doctor Grothe, the first cylindrical machine brought out in England. Somewhat later, another machine of the same general character was patented by Lewis, of Briscombe, Gloucestershire, by whose name this type of apparatus became known most widely in England. A few years earlier, in 1812, a "machine for shearing cloth with helicoidal shears," apparently an apparatus on the Dorr model, was introduced into France by one George Bass of Boston, though seemingly the mechanism gained little ground until adopted in 1817 by John Collier, the well-known French machine builder.[1] Beriah Swift's apparatus with the oscillating cylinder was dispersed through Europe in a somewhat similar fashion: Swift's English agent, one Thomas Miles, took out a British patent in his own name; some years later it was patented in France by one Nicholson; and subsequently it found its way into Germany.[2] Obviously, then, there can be no question that, with respect to this type of wool-manufacturing machinery, the United States made a distinct and notable contribution.[3]

5. *Conclusion.*

The record of the domestic wool manufacture as regards technical improvements is a highly creditable one for the period before 1830,—and beside the advances already discussed there were

[1] Hayes, *Bulletin*, 1879, p. 43.

[2] Grothe, *Bulletin*, 1882, p. 13.

[3] In addition, there are statements of foreign writers showing the direct relationship. Ure (*Philosophy of Manufactures*, p. 141) says that the English machine similar to that of Dorr's, which came to be known in England as a "lewis," was "suggested by the sight of an American invention for the same purpose." Likewise, according to Hayes (*Bulletin*, 1879, p. 43), Alcan, the French textile authority, clearly admitted the cylindrical shears to have been of American origin.

A single, qualified note of discord is struck by Wachs (*Die volkwirtschaftliche Bedeutung*, p. 62), who discriminates between the original idea of the machine, which he credits to Dorr, and the practical working-out or application of that idea. "Dorrs in praktischer Hinsicht noch mangelhafte Maschine," he says, "wurde dann von Stephan Price (1815), John Levis, und William Davis so sehr verbessert, dass ihre Apparate bereits alles Grundsätzliche der modernen Maschinen, die ihnen freilich an Leistungsfähigkeit weit überlegen sind, enthalten."

others, notably the warp-dressing, and the cylindrical pressing machines.[1] Apparently this industry sensed what Tench Coxe speaks of as "the peculiar value of labor-saving machinery to a nation of moderate numbers, dwelling in a country of redundant soil." [2] Having received eagerly from England the first fruits of British technical advance, namely, the carding machine, the picker, and the jenny, this country pushed forward in a multitude of directions. And our manufacturers registered successes in many lines. As will appear in the sequel, no era in the history of the American industry was so prolific of advances from within the country as this one prior to 1830.

Yet despite the extraordinary technological advance of the American wool manufacture, it should not be imagined that the domestic industry was alone in adding new features to the world's technical equipment. The adaptation in England of the cotton-mule construction to wool spinning, though as yet rendered only partially automatic, was a notable contribution, being adopted in this country as well as abroad some decades later. During these years sundry advances appear to have been made in England in the technique of dyeing, and the useful hydraulic press was also developed there.[3] Likewise, machinery was being

[1] The first is used in a process intermediate between spinning and weaving, a process by which yarn already spun is prepared for insertion in the loom as the warp threads (or the future longitudinal threads of the woven cloth). The process had previously been a purely manual one, and so continued to be in England for some years. The American machine was probably an adaptation from a similar mechanism already devised in the domestic cotton industry.

The roller pressing machine was another case of the utilization of the cylinder in the wool manufacture, the cloth to be pressed being passed under heavy rollers, which were sometimes heated by steam.

Advance in the fulling apparatus should also be recorded. Levi Osborn (1804) and John Dyer (1833) are specially mentioned. The latter is particularly noteworthy since he invented the roller type of fulling mill, which was an important improvement over the old hammer type (Wachs, *op. cit.*, p. 58; Grothe, in *Bulletin*, 1881, p. 60).

[2] *State Papers, Finance*, ii, 676.

[3] The hydraulic press is a device by which great weight is brought to bear upon a relatively small surface. It was invented by Joseph Bramah, an Englishman, in 1796, was subsequently applied to the wool manufacture, and still is extensively employed in the British wool-manufacturing industry. (Wachs, *op. cit.*, p. 63, says that the adaptation to use in the textile trades came in America; but I have

evolved both in England and on the Continent for the fabrication of worsted cloths, a branch of the wool manufacture as yet practically neglected in the United States.

Moreover, in contrast to the progress made during this era by the domestic cotton industry, that of the wool manufacture appears less considerable. The tardiness of most wool-working developments is especially striking. Machine carding and power spinning, the latter on the water-frames of which knowledge was brought to this country by Samuel Slater, were a part of the normal cotton-factory equipment by 1800 at least; and the general adoption of power weaving for ordinary cotton goods anticipated that of similar wool fabrics by something like fifteen or twenty years. Of course this situation was duplicated in other countries. For instance, in England, just as in the United States, the spinning jenny was adopted by the wool manufacture only when it was being ousted from the cotton industry. Power weaving in woolen-goods production in English mills came in much more slowly than in the cotton-goods field. Indeed, all along the line of advance the contrast between the two developments in England is even more disadvantageous to the wool-cloth production. Tardiness of the latter development in both countries is

seen no indication that this is true, although, to be sure, such presses have long been used in this country in greater or less degree.) Whereas in the American cylindrical press the cloth is drawn automatically under heavy rollers, in the hydraulic apparatus the material must be folded evenly and smoothly to fit into the upright chamber of the machine, and the folds must be interlarded with paper. Apparently it is this folding and interlarding that has interfered with the wider use of the hydraulic device in this country.

Besides actual machinery, the British made many advances in the methods of operation. Cold pressing was in 1813 said by Mease to be coming into use in England (*Archives*, iii, 345); and many improvements in dyeing are of British origin. With respect to the latter feature, one may note the comments not infrequently made as to American dyeing. For example, a report to the New York legislature in 1826 states: "The colours of American goods are often fugitive, and their texture frequently impaired by mordants, which would be prevented by a knowledge in the operator or manager of the chemical principles upon which the processes of dyeing and colouring are performed." And a comparison is then made with the superior British methods (*New York Senate Journal*, 1826, p. 441). See also Bagnall, p. 478; Kettell, in *Eighty Years' Progress*, 1864, p. 301; North, *Bulletin*, 1902, p. 316. Incidentally one may note Tench Coxe's suggestion, that "Dying (*sic*) saves the domestic labor and expense of washing" (*State Papers, Finance*, ii, 679).

in large measure to be elucidated on the basis of the greater difficulty in working the wool fiber. But there are certain exceptional circumstances affecting the wool manufacture in the United States which influenced the course of events here, and of these we should make some particular note.

In explaining the slowness of technical development in the American woolen as compared with the American cotton manufacture, Hayes, speaking with special reference to power spinning and weaving, assigned two causes: the fact that there was a "scarcity of fine wool for merchantable or 'boughten' cloth, the only kind which then could be advantageously made in a mill, as the coarse cloths were all home-made;" and the circumstance that "in the early attempts at spinning (by power) woolen yarn adapted for the making of fine fulled cloth, it was found that . . . the (spinning) machinery could not be sufficiently controlled to preserve the looseness necessary for effectual fulling." [1] To some extent he was right. Though the scarcity of fine wool as compared with the "abundant supply of cotton" seems a negligible or at least secondary cause, the emphasis placed by the early manufacturers, and necessarily placed by them, upon the production of "fine fulled cloth" was an important deterrent not only to the introduction of power-driven apparatus in the factories but even to the development of the factories themselves. On the other hand, the cotton manufacture both in England and here was breaking into a practically untouched field. While there had been some importation of Indian cotton fabrics into England and some small household production of cotton goods in this country, especially in the southern states, the factory development met no opposition from or competition with the household (or handicraft) industry such as the organized manufacture of wool cloths encountered in both countries.

This market situation forms the third principal factor bearing significantly upon the development of the small factory of 1830. Already consideration has been given to the two essential features of wool supply and technical advance. Now we may turn to an analysis of the conditions in the American market which mili-

[1] Hayes, *American Textile Machinery*, p. 22.

tated against the rise of factory production, — and against the adoption of improved technique as well; and to this may be subjoined a description of the manner by which these unfavorable conditions were ameliorated.[1]

[1] Considerable weight has sometimes been given in explaining comparative technical development in the United States, to the prohibitions laid by the British government on the exportation of textile machinery, plans, or models from England. These laws date from 1774 and 1781, and were not wholly repealed until 1845 (Clark, p. 260; Hayes, *Bulletin*, 1879, pp. 2–5). It is sometimes said, for example, that the woolen branch of the industry was forced to develop new mechanisms by virtue of such prohibitions, whereas the worsted branch, being introduced into this country after 1845, was under no such compulsion, and accordingly has not made any marked technical discoveries. The story of the American worsted manufacture can wait. It suffices now to point out that as regards the woolen end this statement has little real validity. The importations of machinery or the ideas of machinery, — the introduction of the carding machine, the picker, and the jenny by the Scholfields, or spinning apparatus in the cotton industry by Slater, — are only conspicuous cases of what was frequently going on during the whole period of restriction on export. For example, other carding machines were brought over or erected here without help from the Scholfields (Gould, *History of New Ipswich*, p. 229; North, *Bulletin*, 1899, pp. 215–216); the flying shuttle was introduced from England; and later the Scotch power loom was brought over. The immigration into the United States of foreign workmen and mechanics and their employment in American mills would serve as means whereby European technique would become known here. Furthermore, one cannot examine the contemporaneous literature of this period without feeling that there was a considerable interchange of ideas upon processes and apparatus between the older and the younger manufacturing centers. In short, the effect of the prohibition on exportation of machinery was, to my notion, distinctly minor, if not wholly negligible.

CHAPTER VII

THE EXPANSION OF THE DOMESTIC MARKET

Introduction

The increase in breadth and depth of the domestic market for wool fabrics, though for purposes of presentation made the third of the chief factors relating to the rise of factory production, is undoubtedly the most important of them all. Without the stimulus given by the public demand for mill-made goods, the spread of the fine-wool culture would probably have failed even of such moderate success as it did attain, — the "vital impulse" would have been lacking. Again, the improvement in technical equipment, as has been frequently demonstrated in other lines, is principally the result of "economic necessity," — the demand or incentive afforded by a thriving industrial organism to better the conditions of its existence. Occasionally there are inventions which come apparently by chance alone; but they are wholly negligible.[1] The importation of devices evolved abroad is in an even greater degree the "child of necessity." The extension of the domestic cloth market, then, underlying and influencing the other factors, deserves specially careful consideration.

A proper analysis of market conditions in the United States over the period from 1760 to 1830 carries one far afield. The growth in volume of importations during the earlier decades suggests the broadening of the market area, while the course of this import movement in the later years gives an indication of

[1] Such a fortuitous invention in the textile field was that of the spinning jenny, if one can believe the story usually told of the manner in which Hargreaves chanced upon the basic idea (see above, p. 109, note 1). Another case also in the textile domain was the invention of the coach-lace loom by Erastus B. Bigelow. The lace commonly used in carriages of his day had always been made by hand; and Bigelow's imaginative mind toyed with the idea of manufacturing it by machine. He was at the time (about 1837) a youth, still in his early twenties, and unconnected with a manufacturing enterprise. Subsequent application of the principles underlying this loom to carpet production was, however, the result of business incentive.

the efficiency of domestic production. On the other hand, the experience of the older household manufacture enables one to check conclusions arrived at by other means with respect to the rise of factory output. The types of fabrics issuing from the budding factories, as well as the types of goods imported,—in so far as one can ascertain them both,—throw additional light on the character of the market. Then there are the stimulus to domestic production flowing from patriotic feeling and the more tangible support derived from mounting tariff rates, themselves in part a reflection of popular sentiment; the fluctuations in domestic factory production; and, finally, the changes in the cloth-distributive agencies themselves. A full discussion of all these features cannot be attempted here. The scope of analysis must be limited to indicating the more important elements with respect to each subject, at the same time giving proper weight to each in proportion as it shows the extent or nature of the domestic market.

1. *Importations.*

The case of the Revolutionary War is an excellent one in support of the contention sometimes made that political periods are not necessarily economic periods. The disturbances to normal commercial relations which preceded and accompanied the war passed over the country without producing any far-reaching economic effects, especially any on the industrial side. Many lines of industrial enterprise were in situations approximating that of the wool manufacture, i. e., they were lacking the bases necessary for real progress, — satisfactory raw material, an adequate organization, suitable technical equipment, or a beneficent public regard for their products. Such conditions combined to render this troubled era abortive of enduring industrial change. For the domestic wool manufacture, the course of events is particularly clear if one follows the movement of importations.

English manufacturers of wool fabrics looked forward to the conclusion of peace, confident that it would bring a resumption of the trade relations on lines identical with those of the pre-war days. "Let the dispute with America be settled as it may," wrote a pamphleteer in 1782, "while their wool continues inferior to ours, they (the colonists) must from interest, the strongest tie of friendship, deal with us (for woolen goods). Interest," he adds, "is more binding than any treaty of commerce."[1] Lord Sheffield similarly viewed with complaisance the outcome of the conflict, seeing no danger to British trade from mere political separation, and especially no threat to the British wool manufacture. With the pamphleteer, he fixed upon the most obvious difficulty confronting the American wool-manufacturing industry, that of the wool supply, as the chief deterrent to effective competition from this side of the water.[2] In confirmation of his faith in the future, he instanced the perplexities of the Continental government in securing clothing for the American army, finally having to purchase English cloths in Holland, while at the same period the British woolen industry was in excellent condition and continued so throughout the war.[3] In some respects these writers were justified in their opinions. As to the wool supply, no doubt the sheep in the United States suffered during the war, both in numbers by abnormal slaughter of the animals, and in quality by an even greater measure of neglect than in peaceful years,—a neglect, it may be observed, which continued with little correction till after 1800.[4] Of more importance, however, was the substantial "vacuum" in the American wool-cloth supply, despite the importations which during the war had filtered through from abroad. This lack was particularly felt in the towns, which were accustomed to the use of imported fabrics, and would find little satisfaction, at least after the first wave of patriotic enthusiasm had passed, in the rough home-made goods.

[1] Bischoff, i, 234.

[2] Lord Sheffield considered the American wool supply quantitatively inadequate: the wool in the southern "provinces," he held, tended to become hairy, while in the north the winters were so long and severe that "it cannot answer to raise many sheep" (*Observations*, 1784 ed., p. 10).

[3] *Ibid.*, pp. 11–13.

[4] Wright, pp. 9–10, who accounts for it by the fact that the energies of the new country were directed more to other agricultural products and to the carrying trade and external commerce.

The influx came with the peace. It was not restricted to woolens, of course, nor indeed to goods of strictly utilitarian character. The statement was made in 1785 that "after the peace, vast numbers of adventurers, with goods which they were obliged to dispose of at all events, flocked here from all quarters," [1] until, as another contemporary put it, there was "an amazing Superfluity of all kinds of European goods." [2] But with the "gewgaws and ballooneries," the importations of which seemed to illustrate the unhappy speculative nature of the movement and sorely worried the calmer observers of the period, there was undoubtedly a considerably increased introduction of foreign wool fabrics.[3] There are no statistics of such importations for the years immediately after the war; but the first ones available, figures of British exportations in 1790–1799, suggest what must have been the situation during the previous decade. In these later years, the shipments from England averaged in value £1,826,000 a year, as compared with the shipment already given of £743,000 per annum in 1772–1774.[4] Moreover, there was a marked enhancement during the decade itself, from a figure of £1,488,000 a year in 1790–1792 to one of £2,368,000 in 1797–1799.[5] When com-

[1] *Boston Independent Chronicle*, June 16, 1785; quoted in Hill, *First Stages of the Tariff Policy*, p. 65.

[2] Weeden, p. 819, quoting a letter. For other accounts of the period, see Hill, *op. cit.*, pp. 64–75, and Appendices I to VI; Giesecke, *American Commercial Legislation before 1789*, pp. 126–127.

[3] The allegation is sometimes made in relatively recent writings on the tariff that at this time there was an intentional and organized overstocking of the American market, particularly with wool fabrics. Inasmuch as this alleged plot of English manufacturers to "smother" our infant industries was originally stated to pertain to a supposed fright in English industrial circles after the publication of Hamilton's *Report on Manufactures*, its application to the post-Revolutionary period is at least inaccurate. Moreover, since the charge was first made some twenty years after that event (1816), and since the British wool-manufacturing industry was too loosely organized for effective dumping operations, this allegation probably had no basis in fact. (For the original formulation, see Bishop, ii, 43.)

[4] Brothers, *Wool and Wool Manufactures of Great Britain*, p. 144.

[5] The figure £2,368,000 above given is an unadjusted figure. But during the decade of the nineties there had been an increase in the general level of prices in England amounting to around 33⅓ per cent (Silberling, "British Prices and Business Cycles, 1779–1850;" in *Review of Economic Statistics, Supplement*, October,

pared with the growth of population, as nearly as that can be estimated, these data are even more significant. They mean an enlargement of the per capita consumption of foreign wool fabrics — "English" being in this connection and at this period nearly synonymous with "foreign" — from 65d. in 1772–1774 to one of 85 to 90d. in 1790–1799.[1]

Nor did the up-swing of this movement cease then. For the years 1806–1807 exportations from Great Britain averaged as much as £4,592,000. This figure, however, is subject to important qualifications. Values in England had risen in consequence of monetary inflation, amounting in those years to 15 or 20 per cent.[2] Moreover, a substantial proportion of these shipments was not for our domestic consumption, but for reëxportation to the West Indies, since by reason of the existing naval conflict of France and England direct shipments thence to the West Indian colonies were hazardous. Pitkin estimates this reshipment as a third of our total receipts;[3] but this appears to me a grievous overstatement. Ten or fifteen per cent would seem a better figure.[4] Accordingly, while no exact measure of our imports for consumption in gross or per capita can be made, it is

1923, p. 232); and on the assumption that woolen prices moved with the general movement, adjustment should be made for this change in price levels in order that the figure for 1797–1799 should be more closely comparable with that for 1790–1792. The adjusted figure would be £1,776,000. It is still an increase over that for the first years of the decade, but less considerable.

[1] Estimate of population before Revolutionary War taken from Clarke, p. 103. In the other cases, census figures for 1790 and 1800 are used.

[2] Silberling, in *Review of Economic Statistics, Supplement*, October, 1923, p. 232.

[3] Pitkin, *Statistical View of the United States*, p. 181.

[4] The statistics of reëxports from the United States do not indicate any such volume of reshipments as Pitkin estimates. For example, in 1806, the first year in which all the necessary figures are available, the real value of woolens exported from Great Britain to the United States was £4,894,000; but the value of goods re-exported *to all countries*, which upon their importation had paid a 15 per cent duty, — under which woolen cloths would come, — was only $2,076,000, or approximately £427,000. To be sure, there was perhaps a large smuggling trade to the West Indies; but on the other hand the value of the British goods reëxported must be increased by at least 25 per cent to cover the costs of shipment to the United States, insurance, and the like. It is doubtful, moreover, if the trade in wool cloths to the West Indies with their warmer climate and their large slave populations was considerable as compared with the trade to the continental American markets.

apparent that by this period there had been again an expansion of the American market for foreign fabrics.

The extension of the trade in imported cloths is in part explained by the growth in size and wealth of the towns. According to census estimates, the proportion of population contained in communities of eight thousand inhabitants and greater had increased rather more rapidly than the total increase of population. In 1790 this proportion had been a thirtieth of the country's people (3.35 per cent), and by 1810 it had become a twentieth (4.94 per cent).[1] Moreover, with the encouragement to commerce and shipping which came to American seaboard towns as an indirect result of European warfare, there had unquestionably been an important accession of wealth. This was a heyday of New England commerce, when, for example, Salem came to have, it was said, "a greater per capita wealth than any American town."[2] Indeed, the whole northern seaboard prospered.

The considerable extension of the import trade that did take place was not possible, I believe, without also some enlargement in the geographical basis of the domestic "free" market, — the market in which goods appearing in an ordinary commercial manner were disposable. Trade in such goods began to reach its hands into new regions, particularly into the hinterland of the chief import towns, assisted by the development of radiating turnpikes, improved roads, and the first of our canal constructions. Of Philadelphia, for example, it has been especially pointed out that at this time the importers of dry goods had as customers, not only the retailers of the city, but also "country storekeepers who came in to buy."[3] At the same period there was a marked depression in the allied stocking manufacture which had become established in many communities lying beyond Philadelphia.[4]

[1] The population in such communities increased from 131,000 to 357,000, while the number of people in the whole country rose from 3,900,000 to 7,200,000 (Weber, *Growth of Cities*, p. 22).

[2] Morison, *Maritime History of Massachusetts*, p. 122.

[3] Hazard's *Register of Pennsylvania*, ii, 262; an article by "Lang Syne."

[4] Janson, *Stranger in America*, 1807, p. 195; *Essay on the Manufacturing Interest in the United States*, 1804, p. 28.

In Middletown, Connecticut, a wholesale importing house for English fabrics, especially fine woolen cloth, was set up in 1804, to supply the interior of that state.[1] In addition, there were, it seems, the beginnings of a trade with the newly settled West. Thomas Ashe, a traveler writing in 1806, states: "The chief business of the town and state (Lexington, Kentucky) . . . consists of ordering immense quantities of goods from Philadelphia and Baltimore, and in bartering the same through the State for produce (which is shipped to New Orleans by water). The goods are all British . . . and the merchants of Lexington not only supply their own State, but that of Tennessee . . . and part of the Indian territory which lies to the North."[2] Probably Ashe's account should be taken only with a liberal discount; and I would not exaggerate the movement at this period. But the evidence does suggest that the market for wool fabrics was widening perceptibly during the thirty-odd years, 1774 to 1807.

Apparently there had also been a broadening of the market; that is, the range of quality in the goods it would consume had increased,—although here the data are too scant for satisfactory determination. In the testimony of merchants before a Parliamentary committee in 1811 there is mention of a wider variety of fabrics shipped to the United States than appears in colonial accounts. To the southern states were sent negro blankets, "plains," and the lower grades of wool cloths, while to the northern states, besides the customary broadcloth, came a group of new fabrics, cassimeres, kerseymeres, flannels, and the like, cloths which might be called of medium quality.[3]

For the present consideration, the most important point is that the enlargement of the domestic market for imported fabrics,—in part derived, it seems, through an encroachment upon the old household production,—presented an opportunity to a domestic factory manufacture. The widening of the market in quality was another favorable feature, since a young domestic industry could not at once attain the skill in manufacture necessary to

[1] *Middlesex Gazette*, March 9, 1804.

[2] Ashe, *Travels in America*, 1806, p. 193.

[3] *British Documents*, 1812 [210], *passim*.

compete with the older foreign industries in the production of the finest cloths. Probably, moreover, an American manufacture upon a factory basis could not arise unaided in the face of foreign importations, or at least such a development could not come without a long period of struggle. With a decided change in competitive conditions, due to natural or artificial causes, domestic enterprises would then find a considerable market awaiting their products.

The opportunity for the domestic manufacture came with the commercial disturbances which accompanied the embargo and non-intercourse acts and the War of 1812, and the effect of these events was supplemented by that of the tariff in which the rates on wool goods had been gradually creeping up. To be sure, there was not a complete cessation of importations into the United States. The governmental regulations themselves were not all-inclusive. The non-importation act of 1806 exempted "woolen cloth whose invoice prices shall not exceed five shillings sterling per square yard;" and the embargo of February, 1808, offered similar treatment to cassimeres of the same low values, together with shalloons and woolen stuffs,—such exemptions, it seems to me, being a commentary on the importance of "boughten" cloth to certain sections of the domestic market.[1] Again, the regulations were not always in force, as national policy was somewhat vacillating; and when in force, they were not always observed. Finally, for the war period, a considerable avenue for importation existed through New England, the coast of which was not blockaded during the first part of the conflict.[2]

Yet such modifications do not affect the essentials of the proposition that embargo, non-intercourse, and war meant opportunity for the domestic wool manufacture. Importations from Great Britain fell in 1808 to £1,995,000 from a figure of £4,289,000

[1] The special consideration for the cheaper goods, largely used in the South, makes one suspicious that the Republican or Anti-Federalist party of those days was not above "playing politics"; or perhaps this is merely the beginning of the practice subsequently followed with respect to some wool goods, e. g., flannels and blankets, of giving special consideration, as by lower import duties, to fabrics in large demand among the poorer classes.

[2] See Morison, *Maritime History of Massachusetts*, pp. 205–206.

for the previous year.[1] The testimony of British manufacturers and merchants themselves indicates that there were lean periods in their exportations to America: 1808 was a bad year for shipments, 1809 was somewhat better, and while 1810 was good, 1811 was again poor.[2] Finally, one may note the advertisements of English textiles which appeared not infrequently during these and the war years under the caption of "Scarce Goods." [3] These deficiencies and irregularities of foreign supply, then, were the foundation, slender indeed but adequate, upon which the first real boom in the domestic factory production of wool fabrics was grounded.

After the war came peace; or, in terms applicable to woolen-goods history, after the brief heyday afforded American manufacturers by the abnormal circumstances of 1806–1815 came a flood of goods, even as after the Revolutionary War. Exportations of wool fabrics from England to the United States again reached a figure of £4,200,000 during the calendar year 1815, and in the succeeding three years, too, averaged over £2,690,000.[4] Just how serious this movement was in itself is uncertain: the indirect trade, through the United States to the West Indies, was probably now a negligible quantity, but there was at this time still a considerable inflation of values in England due to the monetary conditions.[5] Perhaps, however, the prices of wool goods, by reason of some improvements in technique of manufacture, had not risen so high as the general level of prices. One cannot surely judge the resultant of these forces. At least it is evident that taking into account the new factor in the situation, the expanded factory production in the United States, the influx of an unusually large quantity of foreign woolens was a momentous affair. There

[1] Pitkin, *op. cit.*, p. 294.

[2] *British Documents*, 1812, [210], especially pp. 127, 205, 210, 214, and 244. As to 1812, Niles speaking of English goods in general said that there was "a very great supply" with "additional ship loads daily arriving" (iii, 110).

[3] For example, see *Middlesex Gazette*, April 11, 1811.

[4] These figures exclude a small value of carpets.

[5] Prices in England moved from 100 in 1790 to 156 in 1799, 152–166 in 1806–1808, and in 1815 were at 166. During the next three years, 1816–1818, they averaged 143 (Silberling, *Review of Economic Statistics*, October, 1923, p. 232).

had been some basis of actuality for Niles's proud exclamation in 1814, after stating that for two years the country had been largely self-dependent for wool goods: "Has any real want been experienced?"[1] The enlarged domestic production, mainly upon the factory system, had in a marked degree filled in the area previously controlled by the importations. But the domestic market was neither broad nor deep enough to absorb easily a suddenly much-enhanced supply of wool fabrics. Some of the consequences flowing from this situation will engage our attention later.[2]

The crisis of 1818–1819 brought to an end the post-war speculative movement, with which the large cloth importations of the period apparently were connected.[3] The tariff was retained at the moderately protective level instituted by the act of 1816; and the projected decrease in rates that had been specified by that act to occur three years later was canceled. But, perhaps more important than these other factors, the domestic industry

[1] Niles, vii, 275.

[2] It is interesting to note incidentally that after the War of 1812 there was in English manufacturing circles none of the complacency which had characterized the British opinion subsequent to the Revolutionary War, e. g., Lord Sheffield's utterances. Instead there was evident worry in the minds of British manufacturers, to be seen in their testimony before Parliamentary committees. An extreme expression of this attitude, and one that long stuck in the minds of American protectionists, was made by Mr., later Lord, Brougham on the floor of Parliament: "It is worth while to incur a loss upon the first exportation, in order, by the glut, to stifle in the cradle those rising manufactures in the United States, which the war has forced into existence, contrary to the natural course of things" (Niles, xi, 284).

For further discussion of the effects of these importations, see below, pp. 161–164, 182–183, 249, and Chap. IX, *passim*.

[3] The relationship between the heavy importations of the years 1816–1818 and the boom which was then affecting the business of the country, is evident in the literature of the period. For example, a "rage for shopkeeping" is noted by one writer (Niles, ix, 350), in which men set up stores with unreasoning profusion, abetted by the "litter of banks" that had sprung up in many parts of the nation. The purpose of these stores was largely the sale of imported goods, among which woolen cloths were a prominent feature. A traveler in the western country found even there an extraordinary array of English products: at Pittsburgh the dry goods and grocery stores were "literally stuffed" with goods of English manufacture; at Natchez three-fourths of the stock of every store was so constituted; and at Cincinnati the main street had such a supply as to resemble Cheapside. The writer remarks: "Shopkeeping has been very profitable, but it certainly is now very much overdone" (Fearon, *Travels*, pp. 208, 234, 271).

underwent severe readjustment. The methods and aims of the young manufacture, — a manufacture which had some features of a mushroom growth, — were overhauled and made to fit more effectively with the existing peace conditions of international competition.[1] As a result of all these various factors, importations decreased in both value and quantity. From the average value of £2,690,000 in the years 1816–1818, British exportations of wool fabrics to the United States fell during the next decade to an average of only £1,074,000 in 1828–1830.[2] As to quantity: whereas in the earlier years there had been an exportation of 509,000 pieces and 3,948,000 yards of goods, — some fabrics being measured in the one and some in the other manner, — by the turn of the decade (calendar years 1828–1831) these figures had declined to 465,000 and 1,682,000, respectively. Inasmuch as these statistics include worsted stuff goods, — as yet not directly competitive with our factory manufactures, — the relief to the domestic woolen manufacture was indeed greater than these group figures show.[3] The early years in the thirties showed some reaction from this downward trend, but not until the boom years just prior to the crisis of 1837 did importations return to a level comparable with the former one (1815–1819). And even when they did return to such a level, the country was so prosperous and so much more populous that the enhanced supplies were accepted without complaint from the domestic manufacturers.[4] During the same period, it may be added, there was an even greater decline in the per capita con-

[1] For tariff history, see below, pp. 163 ff.; and for reform of the domestic industry, see below, pp. 195 ff.

[2] Exclusive of worsted stuff goods, which did not compete directly with the domestic woolen manufactures, the figures are: for the period 1816–1818, £2,400,000; and for the years 1828–1830, £664,000. All figures here and in the text are, approximately, for calendar years. The British data pertain to years ending January 5. So the official year of, say, 1818, I have called equivalent to the calendar year 1817.

[3] Exclusive of worsted stuff fabrics, the quantity of pieces in the two periods (worsted stuffs being measured in terms of pieces) would be, respectively, 240,000 and 129,000.

[4] During the next decade the course of gross imports, — exclusive of carpets, worsteds, hosiery, and clothing, — was as follows by fiscal years:

sumption of imported wool-manufactures. By the years 1822–1824 this average had reached 85 cents, and at the end of the decade it had sunk still lower, to 57 cents per capita.[1]

In this movement it is probable that certain general causes were operative. For instance, during the years 1819–1824 the British wool manufacture was seriously burdened by a duty on its raw material. From a rate of 5s. 3d. per hundred weight in 1802 and 6s. 8d. in 1813, the duty was in 1819 pushed up by the Conservative reaction which followed the Napoleonic wars, to 56s. per hundred weight, or 6d. per pound. Inasmuch as Spanish and German wools played an important rôle in the production of the finer English cloths, this increase of rate was significant. The years until 1824, one may note, were just those in which the American industry was getting upon its feet again and beginning its more healthful advance.

Again, the fact is well known that in the early twenties the interest of the British traders generally was in the newly expanded South American market, and to some extent British woolen merchants participated in this new adventure. At the turn of the decade, the calendar years 1819–1821, the average annual shipments of wool goods to the principal South American states had been only £360,000 in value; but in the calendar years 1823–1825 the trade had reached a value of £685,000 per year, and in the single year 1825, one of £836,000.[2] The effects had become evident in America toward the end of this movement. Niles spoke in 1825 of the great and sudden rise in the price of British goods in the United States, "caused by the immense supplies that have been sent off or ordered for Mexico and South America."

In terms of thousands of dollars

1826	$6554	1833	$8062
1827	6471	1834	5837
1828	6286	1835	9636
1829	4727	1836	12,345
1830	4068	1837	4148
1831	8950	1838	6556
1832	6886		

[1] Clark, p. 609. These figures include all wool goods imported, even carpets.

[2] *Parliamentary Papers*, 1826–1827 [532]. The countries included in the above figures are Brazil, Mexico and Guatemala, Columbia, Peru, Chile, and Argentina.

Curiously enough for Niles, the ardent protectionist, he comments: that this situation "will do many times more for our manufactories than the tariff accomplished. . . . If this state of things continues for two or three years, the industry of the people will protect itself." [1] A year or two later, though the crisis of 1825 in England had somewhat disabused British traders, comment is still made of "the madness in England to make shipments to South America," and its effect on prices in this country.[2] Moreover, that region could still be spoken of at a Parliamentary inquiry as "a wonderful market" which was "becoming more steady."[3] Though shipments to these chief South American countries never reached a value half that of shipments to the United States, still the psychological influence and a substantial, purely business incentive effected a diversion of interest from our trade and thus gave an additional impetus to domestic production.

More important than these factors, it seems, in influencing the general trade movement was the series of changes within the domestic industry itself, — the improvement in technical equipment, the change in the character of the domestic output, the accumulation of capital, and the like, features which have been or will shortly be considered. It was these more fundamental and enduring changes which made possible the subsequent development of the manufacture. Even the tariff cannot compare with these internal adjustments in laying the foundation for the young industry. To be sure, protection tempered the wind to the struggling manufacture and compensated it for the tax upon the raw material; but the course of importations under these early tariffs, irregular and uncertain, suggests that at best such protection was of only secondary value.[4] The influence of these internal factors is well evidenced by a closer survey of the course of importations, an examination into importation by types of fabrics.

A glance at the accompanying diagrams is sufficient to suggest

[1] Niles, xxviii, 84. He is speaking of commodities in general, but specifically mentions "cottons, woolens, and hardware."

[2] *Ibid.*, xxxi, 227.

[3] *Parliamentary Papers*, 1828 [515], p. 297.

[4] See table, above, pp. 147–148, note 4.

the variation in the experience of the several fabrics.[1] It is evident that in the case of "cloths," chiefly broadcloths, importations struck a rather constant figure after the decline in

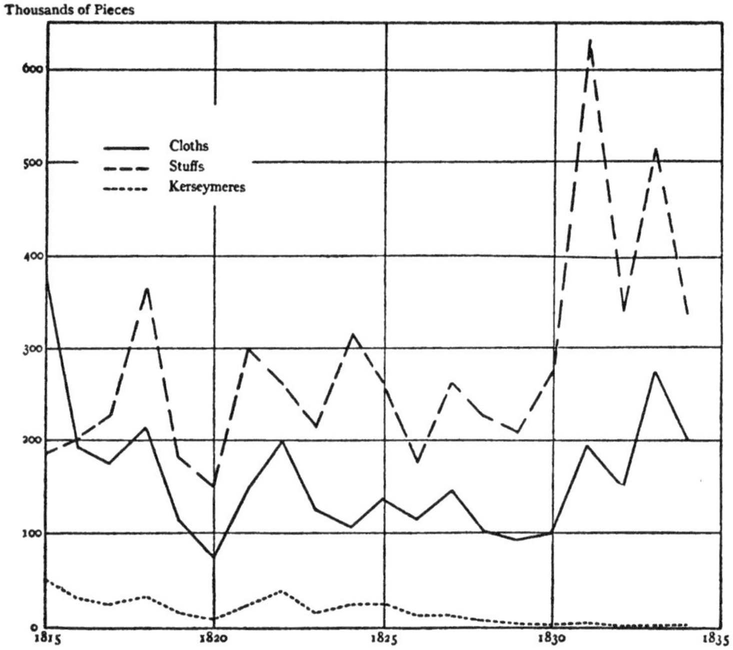

FIG. 4. Exportation of Cloths, Stuff-goods, and Kerseymeres from the United Kingdom to the United States, 1815–1834.

1816–1820, though to be sure with a slightly downward tendency until the lift in the thirties. This situation indicates that with regard to this particular commodity the American manufacture was only partially successful in meeting the foreign competition and satisfying the domestic requirements: there was still a fairly

[1] These diagrams are based on statistics of English exportations to the United States. There are no American (import) figures upon quantity in this early period, and the categories of the statistics of value are not as numerous as those of the British data on quantity. To be sure, the proportion of British goods to the total volume of wool fabrics imported into the United States tended to decline during the decade of the twenties, although, on account of difficulties in comparing British (export) figures with American (import) data, one cannot be sure by what degree such decrease occurred. Yet British exports probably formed 80 to 85 per cent of our imports. And so one is not much in error to speak of "importations" as equivalent to "British exportations to the United States," as I have in the text.

steady demand for foreign goods; while the dip downwards suggests a gradually strengthening position of domestic mills as their processes improved and their costs declined.

With respect to this finer fabric, there is additional evidence of the lack on the part of American producers of real competitive power. During the period under consideration there was a marked change in the position of the fine-cloth manufacture. From a place of dominance among factory products, it fell until several fabrics, notably satinets, flannels, and negro cloths, were of larger and more general production.[1] Again, there is suggestion in the fact that the broadcloth manufacturers were the men prominent in the affairs of the Harrisburg Convention and in the hearings of the Committee on Manufactures in 1828, both these proceedings being concerned with higher tariff protection. They set the tone of these hearings, as when one of them remarked that "the best investments in broadcloth manufactures in the country are not worth over 50 cents on the dollar." [2] Moreover, testimony from England is available. For instance, a manufacturer asserted before a Parliamentary committee in the same year, 1828: "We send (superfine cloths) very largely to the United States; they (the Americans) will have great difficulty in interfering with any of our cloths that are worth more than 10s. a yard; I do not think they can manufacture them." [3] It seems, accordingly, that broadcloth was an article in the production of which Americans were under a comparative disadvantage, an article the manufacture of which did not fit into American economic conditions,—at least American economic conditions of that date. Because of the better workmanship and other advantages of the British manufacturer, importations could continue despite natural and artificial protection to American production.

A somewhat similar situation as regards importations is ap-

[1] See below, Chap. IX, *passim*.

[2] *State Papers, Finance*, v, 827. Out of fourteen men who testified before the Committee on Manufactures, all but three indicated an interest in the production of broadcloth. For the Harrisburg Convention and the Act of 1828, see below, pp. 168–171.

[3] *Parliamentary Papers*, 1828 [515], p. 295 (or *Journal of the House of Lords*, lx, 1828, Appendix 3, p. 886).

parent in the case of blankets, though here the downward inclination of imports remarked in connection with broadcloths is less decided. Blankets were a type of fabric in the production of which American mills were not sufficiently successful to be able to drive out foreign goods. At most the American industry could

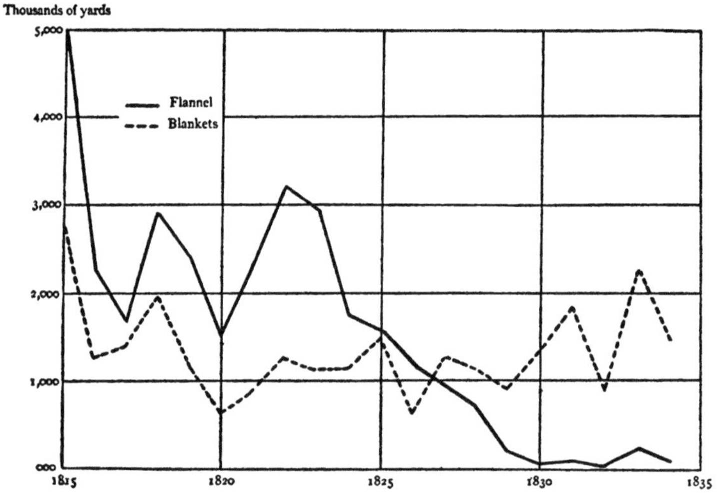

FIG. 5. Exportation of Blankets and Flannels from the United Kingdom to the United States, 1815–1834.

only prevent an increase in volume of importations commensurate with the growth in population. While explanation of the tardiness in the development of blanket production is difficult, and probably lies chiefly in lack of proper technical equipment, sufficiently broad power looms, or in the less considerable protection accorded this article by the tariff laws, it is at least plain that, as an Englishman explained in 1828, "blankets are an article they (the Americans) have not got on so fast in the manufacture of."[1]

Worsted stuff-goods are a third commodity of which the importation seems indifferently affected by affairs in America, whether industrial expansion or the tariff. Here, however, the solution is simple. There had as yet been no real development of

[1] *Parliamentary Papers*, 1828 [515], p. 214 (or *Journal of the House of Lords*, lx, 1828, Appendix 3, p. 847). See discussion of American blanket manufacture below, pp. 202–204.

the worsted manufacture in this country. Some handicraft production of worsted fabrics seems to have persisted, at least for a time, on lines of the earlier colonial methods, though the evidence is scant. At any rate, the factory production was negligible. Two attempts at factory manufacture had been made around 1820 in Rhode Island, one of them, the Pawtucket Worsted Company, formed for the production of fine vestings. Again, a mill at Dedham, Massachusetts, is said to have turned out worsted yarns for some years after 1822. And a few mills are reported as turning out small quantities of worsted fabrics in 1832.[1] However, thirty years were yet to elapse before the worsted manufacture could be said to be established in this country. Moreover, it may be noted again that, as suggested already, the types of worsted fabrics imported were for the most part not directly competitive with American wool manufactures. The chief group was that of worsted dress-goods for women's wear, a sort of article entirely different from the flannel, linsey-woolsey, or homespun which had been used for that purpose theretofore and which still supplied an important part of the demand for women's garments. Accordingly, the continued importation of worsted fabrics, with the rather wide fluctuations in that movement, are really of but secondary value in estimating the position of the American wool-manufacturing industry.

The course of importation in the case of the other fabrics, as shown in the diagrams above, is of special significance. Moreover, what is presented as occurring in the import movement of flannels and kerseymeres, holds true for other categories itemized in available statistics: coatings, baizes, and to a less extent "woolens mixed with cotton, linen, etc." These fabrics had in a degree a common character: they were of lower grade than the lordly broadcloth, did not require so great skill in their production, and appealed to a clientèle less exacting and less affected by style. The most important and most spectacular case is that of flannels. Exportation from England had amounted to over 5,000,000 yards in the calendar year 1815, and had averaged

[1] Clark, p. 573; Field, *State of Rhode Island and Providence Plantations*, iii, 363; McLane's *Report*, i, 379; Bishop, ii, 361.

2,285,000 yards for the next three years. But thereafter the outward movement to the United States fell until in the five years 1828–1832 it was only a tenth of the latter figure,—only 228,000 yards. Nor was there an appreciable reaction in the thirties when the general course of woolen imports was upward.[1] The rather precipitant decline of flannel importations, especially in the twenties, at a time when American production, as will be shown, was mounting steadily, together with the failure of the movement to recover substantially in the thirties, indicates that unquestionably with respect to this article American manufacturers had command of the domestic market. That flannel and in only less degree the other fabrics mentioned above were types of cloth easily manufactured,—requiring little technical skill,—and enjoying a wide, popular demand, suggests the lines upon which the American wool manufacture had found it more advantageous to proceed.

In brief, the volume of importations, which had risen prior to the embargo and war period and which had indeed been harmfully great after the war, tended to decline substantially in the decade of the twenties. Reaction to a higher level of importations was, it is true, destined to occur in the next decade, when the speculative boom of that period offered a peculiarly easy market for foreign goods. But the level thus subsequently reached was by no means so significant to the young domestic wool manufacture as the import movement of the early post-war years had been. Apparently, on the whole the American industry was gathering competitive strength and was finding it possible to supply an ever greater proportion of the domestic demands for wool fabrics. In this movement, however, certain lines or classes of cloths experienced much more decisive changes in status than did others,—a feature of the situation fully as im-

[1] It is noteworthy that the only manufacturer who before the Committee on Manufactures in 1828 admitted passable conditions in the wool-working industry was also the only flannel manufacturer, Abraham Marland (*State Papers, Finance*, v, 818).

The tariff of 1828 was an important factor in accounting for the particularly low figures of flannel importations in 1828–1832; but as will be shown below (pp. 204–206), the tariff at best merely expedited a change which was already started.

portant to note as the general course. For example, the domestic manufacture of flannels tended rapidly to increase, while the importations of that fabric declined in a steady fashion. Again, the production of satinets, never much disturbed by competition from abroad, grew in volume until it supplied an important section of the American demand for wool goods. On the other hand, the domestic broadcloth manufacture decreased as unfavorable conditions supervened, while imports of this fabric persisted at a substantial and a fairly even figure. In this divergent experience, finally, one should note that the character of the goods whose importations tended definitely to decline corresponded closely with that type which knowledge of American conditions would lead us to believe most advantageous for domestic mills to produce. These were goods of medium quality, free of any considerable style influence, and subject to a large domestic demand. Already the dominant economic forces of the country were beginning to mold the wool manufacture in the form which was to characterize so many American industries.

The Organization of the Import Trade.

Disturbance to the American wool-manufacturing industry arose not only by reason of the amount or variation in the amount of goods imported but also of the method of their distribution within the country. It is noteworthy, too, that the method of distribution for imported fabrics had by 1830 become on the whole less satisfactory from the viewpoint of the domestic manufacturer than the method employed in the early days of domestic factory production,—in this respect contrasting with what we shall find was the case with the distribution of American-made goods. A fairly orderly method of sale for domestic cloths had been arising despite the influence of the auction system, but dealings in imported goods continued to be characterized chiefly by instability and uncertainty.

Subsequent to the colonial period, when goods were "generally sent (to America) at the risk of the shop-keepers and traders of England," [1] there had been a considerable growth in the number

[1] Gee, *Trade and Commerce of Great Britain Considered*, p. 171.

and importance of American importing houses. While the representatives of foreign exporters did not by any means disappear, the trade seems, before the outbreak of the War of 1812, to have drifted largely into the hands of resident American merchants. This period was, we may recall, one of great commercial expansion in the United States, when our merchants were willing, as it were, to fish in troubled waters. After the close of that war, conditions within the United States changed to the detriment of these importing concerns of domestic origin.

Chief among the unfavorable factors were the dumping, in the immediate post-war years, of stocks previously accumulated by British merchants, and the development of the auction system of sale. The importation of woolens in 1815 and 1816 had been accompanied by the invasion of "adventurers," seemingly men dispatched by English merchants to expedite the sale of the surplus stocks. This was the beginning apparently of the "foreign agent" system which aroused so much complaint in later years. Evidently, too, the auction sale came then for the first time into prominence, employed at that time for the quick distribution of these surplus goods. The joint action of these two factors, heavy importations and the sales system, is evident in the contemporaneous comment of a traveler: "Both here (Philadelphia) and at New York, I have seen British goods sold this way (by auction) for less than they cost in England; I hardly recollect seeing them sell for more." [1]

As time went on, the practice of sale on "foreign account" and that of auction sales became more firmly fixed in the distribution of foreign goods, these two methods tending also to give strength to one another. In Baltimore, said Niles in 1828, there was hardly one large importing house; but a dozen would be established were this desolating system (agents and auctions) restrained as it should be.[2] Mr. Mallary spoke even more emphatically, and with particular reference to the woolen import trade. Before the war, he said, this business was almost exclusively in the hands of our own merchants. The number in Boston, New

[1] Palmer, *Travels*, p. 257. See also Carey, *Crisis*, pp. 34–35.

[2] Niles, xxxv, 241.

York, Philadelphia, and Baltimore was about one hundred and sixty. Now (1830) there were but about twenty. "As I am informed by a most intelligent merchant, there were in New York at the period to which I have alluded, forty-three, whom he recollects; now only five. One of the appraisers recently informed me that there were at least six!"[1] Meanwhile, the auction sale had grown in prominence with respect to imported goods. Indeed, the utilization of this method for imported textiles seems to have reached its height around 1830. Statistics of foreign dry goods sold at auction in New York City indicate a hundred per cent increase in the value of such stuffs sold between 1818–1820 and 1827–1829: from $6,567,000 to $12,426,000.[2] Then, too, the wave of agitation against the "auction system," as reflected in the contemporary literature, with the insistent demand for control and suppression by taxation or otherwise, reached its greatest intensity around 1830, suggesting that at that time the effects of the system were most deleterious. The intensity of the domestic feeling in these years is evident in a memorial from "Sundry Merchants, &c. of New York City:" "Of all the evils with which the American Merchants, manufacturers, and tradesmen have to contend, in their competition with foreign capital, skill, and enterprise, there is none, perhaps, of equal magnitude, or fraught with consequences so ruinous and demoralizing, as those which flow from the present pernicious system of selling goods at auction. The numerous evils of this system have grown with its growth; and strengthened with its strength; its paralyzing in-

[1] *Congressional Debates*, 21st Cong., 1st Sess., p. 800.

Mr. Mallary continues: in most of our cities, especially in New York, woolen cloths are generally sold on foreign account,—"as far as I can ascertain, four-fifths; many suppose nine-tenths." Even Gallatin in his *Free Trade Memorial* indicates the same situation, though he does not go back so far: "The importations from England were, before the tariff of 1828, about equally divided between the American importer and the British manufacturer, who, though the whole amount of the woolen branch is curtailed, engrosses now more than two-thirds of what is still imported" (Taussig, *State Papers*, p. 194). See also *Report of the Convention of the Friends of Domestic Industry:* "Your committee (on evasions) are informed, and believe, that four-fifths of all the importations of dry goods into this port (New York) are on foreign account; and in the particular branch of woolen cloths, seven-eighths of the whole amount are thus imported" (p. 33).

[2] *New York Documents, Report of the Comptroller*, 1843, pp. 130–131.

fluence is felt in almost every branch of business, and by every class of the community." [1]

The two phenomena, sales on foreign account and sales by auction, as already suggested, were directly connected. The sale by foreign exporters through agents located in this country permitted the importation of goods at somewhat lower prices than if they had been sold to domestic merchants. Intermediate profits, those required by the foreign exporting merchant, were wholly or partly eliminated; goods invoiced at cost of production bore lower import duties; and the stocks of these foreign dealers could be carried at lower rates of interest.[2] Some such advantages, to be sure, have always favored the foreign-agent system, but in that period, particularly with slower turnover and presumably higher rates of profit, the advantage was probably greater than in more recent times. Again, the agent, as well as the domestic merchant, could take advantage of the credit on import duties extended by the government. Moreover, the sale through agents permitted fraudulent entry of values, a practice which was to some extent incited by the system of minimum valuations begun in the tariff of 1824 and expanded in that of 1828. The constant allegation of fraud at the period, too, intimates that the opportunity was not neglected nor the incitement (of the minima) wholly resisted. But the possibility of ready sale by auction was the foreign manufacturer's or merchant's greatest asset. No elaborate office was necessary, and storage facilities were reduced to a minimum. There was no need of advertising, nor attempt to maintain cordial relations with particular domestic purchasers. Furthermore, the auctions provided means of an immediate sale. At first, to be sure, it was the practice of importers generally to extend credit of three, six, and even nine months to purchasers, but the note of the purchaser was discountable at the banks.[3] Later, when the auction system was more

[1] 18th Cong., 1st Sess., *Executive Reports, No. 22.*

[2] The foreign agent was frequently said to have an advantage over the regular domestic importer of 7½ to 10 per cent,—whatever that may mean exactly.

[3] For practice of credit extension: *State Papers, Finance,* iii, 585; Holmes, *Account of the United States,* p. 210. The custom of purchasers' endorsing one

firmly established, the auctioneer came to occupy a more important position, and one more favorable to the foreign agent. In 1829, it was said to be the general practice, not only for the foreign agents to hand over their invoices and to endorse their bills of lading to the auctioneer, leaving him to enter their goods at the customs house and to give bond for the duties, but also for the auctioneer to make advances upon the goods thus placed under his control. An amount equal to two-thirds the value of the goods was at once advanced, and the balance was paid over upon actual sale. On the side of internal distribution, too, the auctioneer had acquired obligations, especially that of endorsing the notes of purchasers.[1] Under such conditions, obviously, neither the position of the foreign agent nor that of his principal was a particularly arduous one.

To contemporaries, the operation of this general system seemed to savor of what we now designate as dumping. For example, the Woolen Circular in 1826 stated that Europeans "export the surplus of their fabrics to this country, leaving their home-market free from an excess of goods, and producing a glut in our markets, which paralyzes the exertions of our manufacturers." [2] But the practice was too common and continuous to be properly designated "dumping."[3] The fact that, as we shall see, the auction was also employed to a considerable extent by domestic manufacturers themselves, suggests that that portion of the system did in some measure fit into the market conditions of the period, featured as they were by the lack of a well-organized distributive system in a steadily expanding trade. Perhaps, in fact, the evils

another's notes, is said by Holmes to have induced over-speculation: "a sort of chain, or house of cards was formed . . . so that when one man failed, several others went down too."

[1] *New York Assembly Journal*, 1829, p. 392; Niles, xlv, 395, quoting from the *London Spectator*. The general result is stated thus in the latter account: "So that it has repeatedly happened that bills for two-thirds of the value of the goods exported have been on their way back to England, before the goods themselves have been landed, or the necessary papers passed through the customs house."

[2] Niles, xxxi, 201.

[3] More accurately, the foreign export trade was not organized in a manner — monopolistic or quasi-monopolistic — to induce profitable long-run dumping,

of the system were not quite so great as its critics alleged. With the wide utilization of auctions as a means of distribution, agents or auctioneers would perhaps be inclined to hold goods from the block, at least in times of ordinary good business, until a fairly satisfactory sale was in prospect. Especially if the auctioneer had made advances on the goods, he would not heedlessly overstock or oversell the market.

Still the agent-auction system at best was not a factor favorable to the domestic production of woolen goods. It made foreign competition more severe and more quickly felt than would otherwise have been the case. The chief effects were perhaps three in number. This system would tend to make more pronounced the normal fluctuations in business, especially if industry in England happened to be simultaneously depressed. More goods might be sent to the American market than would appear if domestic merchants were importing "on their own;" and auction sales might put these goods more rapidly into distribution. Again, the way to fraudulent dealings in importations was made particularly easy; and the evidence adduced in the courts and in the literature of the period indicates that frauds were not infrequent or trivial. And, finally, the development of a better distributive system in the sale of woolen cloth was impeded. Jobbers and even retailers could make purchases at the auction sales; and under such circumstances orderliness in selling arrangements was rendered difficult. In short, then, the peculiar situation with respect to the marketing of foreign wool fabrics that arose in the period before 1830 was of much import to American wool manufacturers, affecting both the industrial and commercial aspects of their business.

2. *Public Encouragement to the Domestic Manufacture.*

The difficulties in which the American nation found itself in the years preceding the second war with England — a rude awakening from the dream of independence and isolation — induced a recrudescence of that desire for economic self-dependence

while the phenomena above referred to were too persistent to be called sporadic dumping.

which was so manifest in the pre-Revolutionary days. Such was the ardor that inspired the couplet:[1]

Of foreign gewgaws let's be free,
And wear the webs of Liberty.

Such was the spirit that prompted the formation of numerous houses in the larger cities for the distribution of domestic manufactures.[2] It communicated itself to Congress, too, where a reprint of Hamilton's famous "Report on Manufactures" was ordered, and the Secretary of the Treasury was directed to collect information in regard to the various industries of the country,—and, as Mr. Stanwood has noted, these from a Republican Congress![3]

In the several states, the popular enthusiasm found even more complete expression. The New York legislature of 1811 recommended that all its members present themselves at the next session clad in fabrics of American manufacture.[4] The legislature of Massachusetts offered to contract with the general government for the supply of blankets and clothing to fill the need in any contingency, which goods were to come principally from the manufactures of that commonwealth.[5] In addition, there were state premiums, as well as those offered by private societies, for the encouragement of household production.[6]

A somewhat similar wave of popular commendation for domestic manufactures arose in the years after the war, when it was supposed to be the British hope to "stifle in the cradle" the infant American industries. In New York, Governor Tompkins recommended the extension of "patronage and protection" to the clothing industry; and the legislature passed an act exempting wool and other textile factories from taxation and excusing all persons engaged in such business from militia duty, except in extreme necessities, and from jury duty in minor cases.[7] In New

[1] *Philadelphia General Advertiser*, January 2, 1809.
[2] See below, p. 209. [3] Stanwood, *American Tariff Controversies*, i, 135.
[4] Niles, i, 312. [5] *Ibid.*, ii, 17. [6] See below, p. 178.
[7] *New York Messages of the Governors*, ii, 855; Laws, 1817, Chapter 64, passed February 28, 1817. In addition the earlier law giving premiums for household manufactures of woolens was revived: Laws, 1817, Chapter 240, passed April 15, 1817.

Jersey, a tax heretofore laid upon cotton and wool manufactories was discontinued, and these objects specifically exempted from other taxation.[1] Patriotic societies raised their heads again, or now for the first time saw the light, — some state and some city organizations. The city societies owed their origin frequently to the efforts of a national institution, the American Society for the Encouragement of American Manufactures.[2] Moreover, the spirit spread westward, associations being formed in Kentucky in 1817, and in Cincinnati in 1819.[3] With the patriotic enthusiasm, expressed in resolutions to abstain from the use of imported goods and to give preference to domestic manufactures, the latter society, curiously enough, mixed the spirit of economy: members should not purchase liquors, fruits, nuts, or preserves except in case of sickness; they should go without black clothes for mourning, and the like.

This ebullition of patriotic sentiment for domestic manufactures, it may be noted, is the last one in which there appears to have been any substantial amount of popular feeling. From the associations above mentioned, it was but a step to a primarily propagandist organization, such as the Philadelphia Society for the Promotion of National Industry, which was then under the influence of Matthew Carey, one of our earliest protectionists.[4] Other societies of somewhat similar character followed,—and since that time the country has not lacked organizations of this type. Thus the phenomenon which is commonly spoken of

[1] Niles, ix, 194. Also, the governor of New Hampshire recommended the exemption of such establishments from taxation (*ibid.*, x, 280).

[2] Bishop, ii, 238. Societies in Delaware and Pennsylvania are mentioned. John Adams, Jefferson, Madison, and Monroe were elected to membership in the New York Society for the Promotion of Useful Arts; and they accepted, Monroe in person (Niles, xii, 311, 412).

[3] Lippincott, *History of Manufactures in the Ohio Valley*, p. 94; Flint, "Letters from America," in Thwaites, *American Travels*, ix, 270.

[4] Of this Society, a representative from Massachusetts complained in Congress that it "has its branches in every part of the Union, with which it corresponds, and which it directs and instigates and sets in motion by the means of pamphlets and newspaper essays. Its inflammatory and unfounded statements have pervaded every part of the Union. Each member of the present Congress has been favored with enough to make two large volumes" (quoted in Stanwood, *op. cit.*, i, 189).

vaguely as "protection" may be considered to have roots in other soils than merely the self-interest of the "protected" industries. Both in form and spirit, the beginnings of the modern propagandist organizations may be traced back through this group of societies just mentioned to even the simpler, purer, and more fiery associations which arose in the heat of the Revolutionary War, — indeed, to those ephemeral but popular societies that refused to drink tea or use imported woolens in the years prior to the Revolution.

In addition to this more demonstrative type of aid to the budding industry, though probably not unaffected by it, was the increase in tariff rates upon wool fabrics. From the first duty of 5 per cent ad valorem, imposed by the tariff of 1789, the rates had gradually risen until in 1804 they reached 15 per cent.[1] In 1812 the rate was raised to the distinctly protectionist figure of 25 per cent, though by reason of the unsettled conditions that obtained during the life of that act the existence of such a duty probably had little influence. But with the act of 1816 begins the modern period of protection, the commencement of that struggle and argument surrounding the import taxes upon wool and wool manufactures which was to continue to the present day. Without attempting to follow the early movement through all its convolutions, something must be said as to its general course in the period to 1830.

Niles had written in 1813, "Let Congress keep 'steady' for five years, and we shall not want fine cloths from abroad;"[2] and in fact Congress maintained relatively "steady" conditions for much more than five years. The tariff of 1816 contained the same rate upon the great majority of wool cloths, 25 per cent, that had been adopted in 1812. For the less important classifications, blankets and worsteds, a duty of 15 per cent was imposed. To be sure, a charge amounting to 15 per cent was laid upon raw wool imported, but not until the closing years of this tariff period did the purchases of wool from abroad become of quantity suffi-

[1] The rates had been as follows: 1789, 5 per cent; 1792, 7½ per cent; 1794, 10 per cent; 1800, 12½ per cent; and 1804, 15 per cent.

[2] Niles, iv, 294.

cient to affect the situation.[1] The rates upon wool manufactures carried in this tariff act had strong support among those interested in domestic manufactures. They followed substantially the recommendations made by Dallas, then Secretary of the Treasury, in his well-known report on manufactures presented in 1816. He had suggested a duty on all woolens of 28 per cent, and, in his classification of industries, had separated blankets and worsted goods from most of the manufactures of wool as subject to other considerations than pure protection.[2] Again, one as fervent for national self-dependence as Niles expostulated with a critic, that "the present tariff, in our opinion, is sufficient to protect our domestic manufactures under the regular state of things, to which we shall arrive bye and bye."[3] And, on the whole, events tended to justify this statement. After the exigencies of 1819 had been met, the industry progressed tranquilly, not with a feverish prosperity, but at least undepressed by inordinate importations from abroad. To this situation, the imposition of the 6d. duty on wool by the British Parliament and the other factors already discussed made important contributions. In the American industry itself, the technical advance and the increase in the number of factories are witnesses to the relative strength of the domestic position.

In 1824, however, after a narrow escape four years earlier, the tariff underwent revision. Apparently considerations affecting the adolescent wool manufacture had little influence in determining the course of the general tariff measure; at least they played a much less prominent part than in many later tariff revisions. The western and middle states passed the bill, with the South opposed and the New England states divided. At the final vote Massachusetts and Vermont, a large wool-manufacturing and an important wool-growing state, respectively, were decidedly opposed, while Connecticut, which was considerably interested in both industries, voted in favor of the act. Nor is an examination of the Congressional debates upon the bill fruitful

[1] Wright, pp. 62–63. In the years prior to 1820, some small amounts of wool were even exported (*ibid.*, p. 63).

[2] *State Papers, Finance*, iii, 89–90, 93.

[3] Niles, xi, 79.

of much evidence concerning the forces which shaped the wool duties. Seemingly there was both lukewarmness on the part of Congress and divided counsel in the camp of the beneficiaries. The latter fact is indicated by the *American Annual Register* in its subsequent account of the 1824 rates on wool cloths: "It is true, however, that opinions on these points (rates, etc.) were not unanimous, even among the parties interested. The manufacturers feared that an increased duty on foreign cloths would be accompanied (and its beneficial effects to them counterbalanced) by an increased duty on wool. The capitalists who had (recently?) embarked in the industry, with extensive resources and improved machinery, were inclined to ascribe the (hitherto?) languishing condition of the manufacture to the imperfect manner in which it had been hitherto attempted; and feared that the effect of an increased protection would be destructive to domestic competition. From this and other causes the efforts of those engaged in this manufacture to obtain a substantial increase of protecting duties were less united and earnest than might otherwise have been expected." [1] This situation, it may be remarked, was adequately remedied prior to the succeeding tariff campaign. At all events, the schedule of rates on wool manufactures carried in the act of 1824 was perhaps bound to be unsatisfactory to a large section of the manufacturing industry because of the manner of its enactment. In the eyes of this section it undoubtedly deserved the epithet afterwards applied to it: "a meager and reluctant tariff." [2]

Upon manufactures of wool in general, the rate of duty, to be sure, was at once raised to 30 per cent ad valorem, and after June 30, 1825 to 33⅓ per cent. Likewise, the rate on blankets and worsted stuff-goods, still considered separately, was increased to 25 per cent. But there were corresponding drawbacks. A proviso — that legislative device which later was to make tariff schedules so complicated — was inserted to the effect that goods, except flannels and baizes, valued at less than 33⅓ cents per

[1] *American Annual Register*, 1826–1827, i, 103; quoted in Stanwood, *op. cit.*, i, 229–230.

[2] Niles, xxxiii, 105, "Address of the Harrisburg Convention of 1827."

square yard should bear the special rate of 25 per cent, like the blankets and stuffs. This would let in some cheap fabrics of special interest to the South. Of more importance: Congress, as yet in happy ignorance of the "proper" relation between duties on the raw material and on the finished product, of compensatory duties, and the like, imposed duties on the unmanufactured wool nearly as great as those on the manufactures themselves: 20 per cent at once, and after June 1, 1826, 30 per cent. Of small comfort was the proviso here attached, that wool valued at less than 10 cents per pound should pay only 15 per cent duty, since such cheap (and coarse) wool would go chiefly into the carpet industry.

When the rates on wool and its manufactures reached their final positions, the wool-manufacturing industry had theoretically a poorer defense against the foreign producer than under the preceding tariff. A domestic manufacturer employing the more expensive foreign wools would, upon the assumption that the raw material amounted to one-half the total cost of production, have a protection of only 18⅓ per cent against the European manufacturer using similar wool. An American producer of cheap fabrics, such as abroad were valued at less than 33⅓ cents per square yard, who utilized the cheap foreign wools valued at less than ten cents a pound, would with the same assumption have a net protection of but 17½ per cent. If the prices of domestic wools were raised by the full amount of the duties, the American manufacturer would, whatever type of raw material he bought, have the benefit of only these net rates. At the same time, the 6d. duty imposed in 1819 upon wool imported into England was repealed, — a feature of the so-called Huskisson reforms of the early twenties.

Yet there is room for doubt whether the domestic industry, even with both these factors changed to its disadvantage, suffered peculiarly during the continuance of this tariff law. The brevity of the tariff's duration, particularly after the various wool duties became finally adjusted, prevents an accurate judgment; but, more than that, the commercial crisis in 1826 obscures the action of the tariff alone. Surely there is nothing in the statistics of importations to indicate that the domestic manufacture was especially hard pressed from the foreign source. The complaints which led to the assembly of the Harrisburg Convention in 1827 and in the succeeding year to an increase in the tariff on woolens were, it seems, primarily the result of general rather than particular business conditions. The circumstance is significant that the manufacturers who testified in the inquiry of the Committee on Manufactures in 1828 for the most part dated their hard times from 1826, not 1824.[1] Finally, the increase of the wool duty was probably a minor hardship. It is doubtful if the market for wool in this country was sufficiently well organized to take advantage of the variations in the import duties. With the modification in the character of domestic wool manufactures which was then gradually taking place, — the increasing production of medium-grade fabrics, in which wools of corresponding quality could be employed, — the effect of import duties on wool was further minimized. In the manufacture of such goods, the conditions after 1824 were by no means so bad as in the portions of the industry having to do with the finer grades of cloth.[2]

However, the failure of Congress to deal fully and fairly with the tariff upon wool products in 1824, the special reaction upon the wool manufacture of the subsequent business depression, or perhaps other factors, caused special attention to be devoted to that industry in Washington during the succeeding years. In 1827 a tariff bill dealing with wool and wool manufacture alone was introduced. The chief points of interest concerning this bill are the minima. Provision was made that the general rate of duty (it happened to be 33⅓ per cent) upon wool cloths should be assessed upon all fabrics valued at or below 40 cents per square yard as if they were all worth the 40 cents; all between 40 cents and $2.50 per square yard as if they were valued at the latter figure; and similarly for those valued between $2.50 and $4.00. Obviously, the nominal rate would in practice be the actual one

[1] *State Papers, Finance*, v, 792–832. To be sure, some allowance must be made for the slower communication of those days, — a factor which would delay the effective operation of our tariff laws. But I doubt if this is sufficient explanation of the above-mentioned fact.

[2] *Ibid.*, p. 820.

only in the case of cloths valued at exactly the minima. As soon as the value of a cloth exceeded a given minimum point, the actual rate immediately became exceptionally heavy. This special bill, however, never became law, being defeated in the Senate by the deciding vote of Vice-President Calhoun.[1]

The fate of this measure, however, instead of discouraging the protectionists, simply urged them on to greater efforts. Within three months after the defeat of the bill the call had gone out from the Pennsylvania Society for the Promotion of Manufactures, for a meeting at Harrisburg, Pennsylvania, of representatives of those interested in wool and wool manufactures in each state: "to deliberate on what measures are proper to be taken, in the present posture of their affairs." [2] In response, informal conventions for the election of delegates were held all over the northern states, and at the Harrisburg meeting thirteen states, including even Virginia and Kentucky, were represented.[3] Before a half year had elapsed after Calhoun's decisive vote, the general convention had been held, a proposed tariff bill drawn up, and an address to the country promulgated.[4]

The proposals of the convention contained the following chief points. As regards raw wool, they urged freedom of ingress for the cheapest grades, those valued below eight cents per pound; and for the higher qualities, virtual prohibition.[5] With respect to wool cloths, the provisions were practically those contained

[1] In the light of future events, it is interesting to note that before the bill had passed the House, a minimum of $1.50 sponsored by Mr. Blaney of Maryland had been inserted.

In the bill drawn up by the Committee on Manufactures in 1824, minima of 40 and 80 cents were proposed; but these were removed on the floor of the House (Stanwood, *op. cit.*, i, 227).

[2] Niles, xxxii, 237. The call sent to the counties of Pennsylvania was somewhat more general. The object was there stated to be: "to take into consideration the present state of the wool-growing and wool-manufacturing interests, and such other manufactures as may require encouragement" (*ibid.*, p. 238).

[3] North, *Bulletin*, 1900, p. 236.

[4] The convention at Harrisburg met on July 30, and continued to August 3. See account of it in Niles, xxxii, 388–396. The address to the people was dated October 10, 1827; reprinted in Niles, xxxiii, 100–108.

[5] For wool valued above 8 cents a pound, the duty was at once to be 20 cents, and to be increased steadily until it reached 50 cents.

in the bill which had just missed passing a few months previously. The system of minima was retained, with steps at 50 cents, $2.50, $4.00 and $6.00. The ad valorem rates at these points, however, were increased to an ultimate 50 per cent.[1] The most important step in this ladder was that between 50 cents and $2.50. Within these two values would come the great majority of the cloths which would compete with American-made fabrics. What was essentially a specific duty of $1.25 was to be levied upon all cloths valued from 51 cents to $2.50. Upon the goods of which the value did not reach fairly close to $2.50, this tax would be prohibitive. Thus the Convention aimed at a virtual exclusion of both wool and manufactures of wool which would come into competition with American products.[2]

The passage through Congress of the tariff bill embodying these proposals is a matter which needs no special comment here.[3] The political jockeying, the significance of the investigation made by the Committee on Manufactures, and the attempted chicanery are not pertinent to a special study. It will suffice here to indicate the changes made in the bill before it became law.

With regard to raw wool, the Harrisburg proposals were moderated in one respect and aggravated in another. A composite duty of four cents per pound plus 40 per cent, and later 50 per cent ad valorem replaced the high specific duties contemplated by the convention. On the other hand, this duty was made applicable to all wools, even the low grades which the wool-growers had been willing to admit free.[4] With respect to the

[1] The rate was at first to be 40 per cent, but was to increase until 50 per cent was reached. The customary exceptions among wool cloths, blankets and stuff-goods, were made; but it was petitioned that protection be given to blankets adequate "to secure their manufacture in the United States" (Niles, xxxii, 396).

[2] It should be added that recommendations were submitted with regard to other manufactures also, — iron, hemp, flax, spirits, and printed cotton goods, while (mirabile dictu!) the committee on glass reported that further protection was not needed by that industry.

[3] See Taussig, *Tariff History*, pp. 87–103.

[4] The Committee on Manufactures declared, in what we know now to have been false tones, that it "will not disguise the fact, that it has been their intention

manufactures of wool, the changes were apparently less extensive. The ad valorem rate was lowered to 45 per cent for most goods, though the rate of 50 per cent was retained for the highest grade. The system of minima was also retained. But one feature of that system was varied: a minimum was inserted at $1.00, breaking the long straddle between 50 cents and $2.50. Over this apparently minor change, feeling ran high. The "dollar minimum" was said to be "planted in the very midst of the woolen trade," ruining the whole scheme of the bill. Largely on its account, Niles proposed that the title of the bill be changed to: "An act to prohibit the manufacture of certain woolen goods in the United States, and prevent the increase of sheep, and for other purposes." [1]

Much could be written about the effects of this tariff: the net protection afforded by the duty on wool manufactures after allowance for the possible action of the wool duty; the variation in this theoretical net protection at the minima as compared with that at other points; the qualities of cloth most affected by the location of the dividing lines finally determined upon, and especially by the insertion of the heartily condemned "dollar minimum;" and the extent of the "frauds upon the revenue" committed in the valuation of imported fabrics, frauds which were incited by this precious system of tariff duties. But adequate treatment of such themes would take us far afield. We can note only a few points. First, we should observe that the character of the tariff schedule made for wide differences of view concerning the real onerousness of the duties imposed. If one

. . . to extend every protection which the nature of the case would admit to the grower of American wool" (*State Papers, Finance*, v, 780). For the true situation, see Taussig, *op. cit.*

[1] Niles, xxxiii, 385.

Certain Treasury rulings coming at about this time made the situation more difficult from the point of view of the manufacturer. The lists and headings of cloth — portions of the fabric necessary to the weaving operation but discarded in the making of garments — were now excluded from the measurement made at the customs to determine the amount of dutiable cloth. Also, there was an abandonment of the principle, hitherto observed, of adding 10 per cent to the invoice value, for charges incidental to exportation, and reckoning the duty thereon (Niles, xxxv, 211; *Convention of the Friends of Domestic Industry, Report*, p. 37. Cf. Taussig, *Tariff History*, p. 99, note).

looked at the tax placed upon goods valued at 50 cents, $1.00, $2.50, etc., — goods whose value agreed exactly with the minima, — the net protection was no greater, perhaps less, than that under the preceding tariff act.[1] If one considered the goods whose value just exceeded the several dividing lines, — for example, a cloth worth $1.01 per yard, — the tax seemed inordinately high.[2] As a matter of practice, however, inordinate duties were for the most part avoided by importers through prudence or deceit. Those cloths which could not be brought in readily at or just below the minima, or which by hook or by crook could not be made so to do, were, it seems, not imported at all.[3] Nor does there appear to be any question but that the cupidities of foreign exporters and domestic importers were stimulated to an extraordinary degree, and that such men frequently gave way to their evil promptings. Yet viewed after the lapse of a century, the whole affair can best be considered as no more than an episode, — interesting, to be sure, but of no appreciable consequence on the general course of the industry.

Even in the years immediately following the law's enactment,

[1] The net protection at the $1.00 minimum may be computed as follows: Assuming an average price of 30 cents a pound for the wool entering the cloth (Niles uses that figure in xxxiv, 109–110, and 37½ cents in another place, xl, 404), the value of that wool abroad before the imposition of the duty would have been, roughly, 24 cents. Upon that the rates of the 1828 tariff would have amounted in ad valorem terms to 66⅔ per cent when the act was in full effect. Utilizing the assumption that the cost of the wool equals half the total cost of the cloth, the net protection on the latter would be:

Duty on cloth	50 per cent
Deduct duty on the wool, ½ of 66⅔ per cent . . .	33⅓ per cent
Net protection on the fabric	16⅔ per cent

A manufacturer declared in the Free Trade Convention of 1831 that, when the duty on the raw material was taken into account, wool cloth received a protection of not more than 25 per cent, generally speaking (Lee, *Exposition of the Evidence*, No. IV, p. 8).

[2] This followed, of course, because a cloth like that mentioned above came under the next higher classification: the $1.01 fabric paid duty as if it were worth $2.50, and 45 per cent of $2.50 meant over 100 per cent of $1.01.

[3] As the protectionists said: the importer "would descend in the rates below the respective minimums until the increased rate of duties should entirely absorb his profits. . . . The intervals would be supplied by the domestic manufacturer" (Niles, xxxii, 120); in other words, the importer would hug the minima.

the influence of the act was almost negligible, or at least largely lost in the action of more powerful forces. In 1829, despite the fact that the duty on raw wool had been materially increased and that the importations of wool declined both in 1828 and 1829 as compared with the preceding year, foreign wool was said to be 7 per cent and domestic wool 25 per cent lower than in 1827.[1] Nor was there a change for the better until the latter half of 1830.[2] This situation perhaps might be ascribed to the circumstance that "the domestic growth of wool is amply protected, but the domestic consumption of it is not."[3] Such, however, does not seem to have been the fact. To be sure, Samuel Slater wrote in January, 1829, in a melancholy vein,[4] and a wool manufacturer in the same year stated his belief that "there is scarcely a woolen manufacturer in New England making a cent at present."[5] But this situation was apparently quite independent of the tariff. The quantity of importations did not increase in 1829 and 1830; they declined. And, when after 1830 the volume of imports mounted exceptionally, the domestic industry was said to be doing "an excellent business."[6] Before the tariff rates were modified, the manufacture had recovered from what was apparently a substantial business depression, — one which was due chiefly to the condition of general business, — and was on the road to prosperity.

In sum, the period from 1760 to 1830 was one of transition in

[1] Niles, xxxvi, 82–84.

[2] See prices in Wright, p. 347.

[3] Niles, xxxiv, 266.

[4] Ammidown, *Historical Collections*, i, 473: "It is rather a pinching time here for money; though many borrowers of money say times are becoming more easy. Since the failure of Hurd (a wool manufacturer of Lowell), money-jobbers and anti-tariff folks have propounded almost every one who has seen or at least touched of late a cotton or woolen factory, that he must go down stream."

[5] Niles, xxxvi, 298. He adds, however: "Indeed, the factory at which I am engaged has been continually losing since 1825; and, although in that year we paid 60 cents for wool and 25 cents per yard for weaving, but now, at the low price of wool (he had quoted 33 cents for full-blooded Merino and Saxony) and paying only 6 cents per yard for weaving by power, we are losing."

[6] Niles, xxxviii, 369. In 1830 the Middlesex Manufacturing Company of Lowell, the largest establishment for the manufacture of wool that had yet been started in the country, was incorporated (North, *Bulletin*, 1894, p. 330).

the public attitude toward the industry. It began with popular incitement to manufacturing expansion flowing from the patriotic aspirations of the young country; and something of that same nationalistic spirit was preserved in the slogan of an "American system" which protectionists of the twenties and thirties extolled so warmly. However, in the interim, another bulwark to protection was being constructed, that of vested interest. Indeed, one of the extraordinary and most interesting features of the period as far as the tariff is concerned was the celerity with which the wool manufacture set about claiming for itself special protection against foreign importations, although of course this notoriety was shared with the wool-growing industry. No other industries but these had the temerity to call a general conference of the parties interested, and to draw up a tariff schedule for the adoption by Congress. This feature may or may not be considered a portent of the special position which Schedule K was to play in more recent tariff discussions. Interpretation would depend upon one's bias. Surely, however, the assumption of this attitude by the wool manufacturers of the latter twenties is indicative of the new position and status of that industry. The manufacture had ceased to be a "precious embryo," as Hamilton denominated the Hartford experiment, and had become a thing asserting rights and privileges. A new stage of development had been attained.

But when one turns to a consideration of the net influence of the tariff in bringing about this new condition of affairs, he is not so sure that protection played as important a part as some of the manufacturers and writers of that period seemed to believe. No doubt the duties aided in the maintenance of the manufacture during the time of reorganization after the second war with England, supplying a screen behind which the forces of the domestic industry might be reformed; perhaps without this artificial assistance the more secure erection of an American wool-cloth production would have been somewhat longer delayed; but on the whole the tariff cannot, it seems to me, be considered of primary significance. Factors of more positive influence and of more permanent effect upon the industry are to be found in other lines, especially in the fields of technical development, changes in the form of industrial organization, and changes in the character of production. To the latter, accordingly, greater emphasis is given in this study of the wool-manufacturing industry.

CHAPTER VIII

DIMINUTION OF HOUSEHOLD PRODUCTION

The history of the household manufacture of wool fabrics is for the period 1760 to 1830 quite a different story from that of the factory manufacture. At the first date the former system was the predominant form of production, occupying the whole field except for the minor handicraft production of worsted fabrics. By 1830 the ultimate extinction of household manufacture was clearly forecast. The factory was then growing in competitive strength, and its influence was extending with the improvement in transportation and the better organization of the distributive agencies. The end might be considerably delayed, but the course was set.

The United States, to be sure, was of too great a size and at the time too little settled to permit the break-up, at one time throughout its length and breadth, of a system of production so well suited to frontier or quasi-frontier conditions. One must, then, discriminate among the various sections of the country. For example, the volume of household manufacture was unquestionably at its height for the eastern states at the close of the Revolutionary War. Subsequently, while there evidently were intervals of increase, the tide was in the main flowing outward. But in the meanwhile other sections of the country were experiencing an enhancement in production under this system, which indeed had not begun to fail by the end of this period.

Of the changing situation in the eastern part of the country information is most adequate. The interruptions in commercial transactions with England prior to the War of Independence and during that seven-year conflict apparently caused an increase in the area of household manufacture as the slack occasioned by decreased importations was taken up. Typical of this period was the case of Massachusetts: during the war, it was said, this state "got into the manufacturing of almost all the clothing which each family had occasion for; . . . Scarce a country man but had his own clothing, which was the produce of his farm, and the industry of his family. . . . In these extensive manufactures of woolens, linen, cloths, and hosiery, the call for imported articles was every day decreasing, the demand lay principally among those whose pride would not permit them to wear the manufactures of their country, or the sudden demand for the army rendered it out of our power to furnish a full supply."[1] But with the advent of peace, the household manufacture of wool fabrics returned to approximately the same status as it had held before the war, retreating before the extraordinary importation of English goods. The General Court of Massachusetts, for instance, declared in 1785: "The quantity of woolens imported, their superior fabric, and the cheapness of them, have not only in a great measure put a stop to our looms, and to the several modes of manufacturing our wool, but have thereby been a principal cause of the decrease of sheep in the Commonwealth."[2] Seemingly the situation in 1790 and even after 1800 was not much different from that in 1760, except that as time went on importations were penetrating somewhat farther into the country, and that here and there small factories were turning out a moderate quantity of machine-made or partially machine-made fabrics.[3]

The most adequate and probably the most accurate description of the household industry with respect to various sorts of commodities during the early nineties is that of Hamilton in his *Report on Manufactures*. Unfortunately, however, he usually does not discriminate between wool and other fabrics. At the

[1] *Boston Independent Chronicle*, August 12, 1784; quoted in Hill, *First Stages of the Tariff Policy*, p. 134. Note the emphasis even here upon the country districts, which, as already outlined, were particularly the field of household operations.

[2] *Acts and Laws of the Commonwealth of Massachusetts*, 1784–1785, p. 840; quoted in Tryon, p. 125.

[3] Quite unacceptable, as far as wool fabrics are concerned, are the statements derived ultimately from Tench Coxe, which appear in Bishop (i, 413–414) and are used by Wright (pp. 9–10): that "the importation of foreign manufactures was (about 1790) less by half than it was twenty years before;" and that throughout the state of Virginia, "three-quarters of all the Clothing was manufactured by the people, who before the war, had imported seven-eighths of it." W. C. Ford, writing in 1791, also was exaggerating when he stated that "in that part of the United States situated to the south of Pennsylvania, there are no manufactures whatsoever" (quoted in Beer, *Commercial Policy*, p. 72, note).

only point where he is dealing with wool goods alone, he says the household manufactures thereof "are carried on in different parts of the United States to a very interesting extent." [1] Elsewhere he gives a fuller discussion of the home industries in general: "There is," he says, "a vast scene of household manufacturing which contributes more largely to the supply of the community than could be imagined without having made it an object of particular inquiry. This observation is the pleasing result of the investigation to which the subject of this report has led, and is applicable as well to the southern as to the middle and northern states. Great quantities of coarse cloths, coatings, serges and flannels, linsey-woolseys," hosiery, and various cotton, tow, and linen fabrics, "are made in the household way. . . . It is computed in a number of districts that two-thirds, three-fourths, and even four-fifths of all the clothing of the inhabitants are made by themselves." [2] Contemporary testimony, however, emphasizes the point that these "districts" were chiefly rural.[3]

Nothing occurred markedly to change the conditions under which the household industry existed until the introduction and dissemination of the carding machines and spinning jennies in the

[1] Taussig, *State Papers on the Tariff*, p. 98. The manufacture of wool hats is the only production using that fiber which had "acquired maturity," i. e., control of the domestic market (*ibid.*, p. 98).

[2] Taussig, *State Papers on the Tariff*, pp. 49–50. Hamilton states in passing that the household textiles are produced "in many instances to an extent not only sufficient for the supply of the families in which they are made, but for sale, and even in some cases for exportation" (p. 50). He must here refer, however, to linen or cotton fabrics, perhaps hosiery, other knit-goods, or wool hats. As will appear shortly, there seems never to have been any considerable sale of home-made wool cloths, and the possibility of their exportation is even more remote.

Another account, nearly contemporaneous with, but less optimistic than Hamilton's, is to be found in a letter of Phineas Bond to the Duke of Leeds, written in 1789: "Many useful domestic manufactures have been resumed in the Eastern and middle States — from motives of economy, formerly most families raised a certain portion of the articles of their own domestic consumption; but the same reasons which caused a decrease of tillage operated in some measure to lessen the quantity of home manufactures" (American Historical Association, *Reports*, 1896, i, 631. See also, pp. 651–652).

[3] Phineas Bond's "Letters," in American Historical Association, *Reports*, 1896, i, 631–632, 651–652; Drayton, *View of South Carolina*, p. 150; Melish, *Travels*, i, 99, 115; "Hamilton Papers," quoted by Tryon, pp. 140-141; Martin, *History of Louisiana*, ii, 234.

last years of the eighteenth and the beginning of the nineteenth century,—a development which was followed shortly by the addition of napping, shearing, and pressing machines to the equipment of the "fulling" mills or clothiers' works.[1] Moreover, just as these new mechanisms were giving increased strength to the household system, another occasion arose for more widespread household production, in the disturbances which ushered in the War of 1812. While the output of the new-sprung factory, which had been stimulated by the same events, probably absorbed the greater part of the demand surrendered by the decreased importations, a portion of the deficiency was supplied by an enlarged home manufacture.

When the difficulties with foreign nations began to disorganize the preëxisting course of supply, popular attention at first turned to the possibility of increased household production rather more than to that of enhanced factory output. Voluntary societies in various communities offered premiums upon woolen cloth from household looms;[2] and the country fairs almost invariably awarded prizes and premiums for such products. The state legislatures fell in with the same policy. In Ohio the general assembly voted that "each person who had a family should be allowed to hold twelve sheep, the wool thereof, and all yarn and cloth manufactured by such family, exempt from all attachments, distresses," etc.[3] Again, in Delaware sheep were exempted from taxation by a law of 1809, and ten or less could not be seized for debt.[4] Tennessee and New York went further, granting premiums upon the best cloths produced in the households of their respective states. The latter had the more elaborate law, distributing $2500 to $3500 each year from 1809 through 1814.[5]

[1] See above, pp. 87 ff.

[2] E. g., pamphlet of the Philadelphia Society for the Promotion of Domestic Manufactures, dated July 25, 1808.

[3] Niles, i, 393; Warden, *Account of the United States*, ii, 275.

[4] *Laws of Delaware*, iv, 267; quoted by Tryon, p. 148, note.

[5] Melish, *Travels*, ii, 193; *Transactions* of the New York Society for the Promotion of Useful Arts and Manufactures, iii, 225–226, 237–250; iv, Appendix 6. Cf. Tryon, pp. 148–152. The New York Society above mentioned made the first recommendation to the legislature with regard to such a law, and itself distributed nearly $2000 in premiums upon household fabrics during the five years. Factory

The first attempt at a statistical measurement of household textile production was in connection with the *Census of 1810*. The actual figures are of little value. As a test of normal output they would be unacceptable because at this period a peculiar strain was being put upon the family production. Moreover, a high degree of error unavoidably attached to the collection of such figures at so early a date.[1] Yet certain general and approximate deductions from them are possible. The total quantity of cloths listed as woolen was roughly 9¼ million yards, out of a total textile production of some 72 million yards. The output of cotton fabrics was half again as large as that of woolen, and the manufacture of linen cloths over twice as great.[2] With respect to the woolen fabrics alone, however, such other data, statistical and otherwise, as are available suggest the paramount position of this household production in the total domestic consumption of wool cloths. In contrast with the 9½ million yards of household output, the factory product in 1810 as estimated at the time by Tench Coxe was only 200,000 yards. Allowance in total consumption must of course be made for importations,—of which we have no satisfactory figure in terms of quantity.[3] But, seemingly, Gallatin was conservative when he

products were excluded from competition. Specimens of cloths awarded prizes are preserved in the library of the Albany Institute.

[1] The difficulties in securing an enumeration of this sort would at any time be well-nigh insurmountable, and at this period the novelty of census undertakings and the obstacles to communication probably heightened the error.

[2] The quantity of woolen fabrics was not separated from the aggregates in the cases of Massachusetts, Maryland, North Carolina, Kentucky, and in two of the territories. Another heading, "mixed and unnamed" fabrics, may contain some cloths of which wool was a component part, linsey-woolseys, cotton-warp negro cloths, and the like; and the total quantity so entered is over a third of the grand total — 26.8 million yards as compared with 72.4 million yards. However, in three instances, — the entries for Vermont, New York, and Delaware, — this "catch-all" category contains but a negligible yardage. Apparently in these cases, mixed goods were thrown into some other subdivision, probably placed under woolen goods, since such fabrics were commonly spoken of as wool cloths. Presumably, then, the 26.8 millions of yards comprise cloths of which the character was not ascertained.

[3] *State Papers, Finance*, ii, 691 (Report of Tench Coxe). On importations, Clark (p. 253), quoting Pitkin, gives the quantity at this period as 5 million yards; but Pitkin's figures are all in terms of value, and Clark does not indicate the

made the contemporary estimate: that "about two-thirds of the clothing . . . worn and used by the inhabitants of the United States . . . is the product of family manufactures." [1]

The statistics also present a picture of the proportionate importance of the household production in the various sections of the country. Over 92 per cent, it appears, came from the states north of the Mason and Dixon line; some 1½ per cent is given as the quota of the northwestern states and territories; and only the remaining percentage, approximately 6 per cent, was produced in the South. That these proportions are approximately correct is indicated from a similar analysis of the number of carding machines and of fulling mills. Enumeration of these adjuncts to household manufacture was also made in this census and presumably was made more accurately.[2] The geographical distribution of these facilities was as follows: carding machines, northeastern states, 89.6 per cent; West, 2.2 per cent; South, 8.2 per cent; and fulling mills, northeastern states, 90.1 per cent; West, 3.3 per cent; and South, 6.6 per cent. Obviously, the states from Pennsylvania northward were still predominantly the home of the household industry; the West was just beginning to make a showing in this regard; and the South, with at best but a 10 per cent ratio, was in proportion to her size and population much less dependent upon the household system of wool-cloth manufacture.[3]

A third feature of the family production brought out in the

way in which he made the translation. Nor have I found any means of doing so with even moderate accuracy.

[1] *State Papers, Finance*, ii, 427. Gallatin confines his estimate to the people who "do not reside in cities;" but, in view of the relatively scant city population at the time, his statement would not have been far different presumably if he had included the whole country.

[2] It might be contended that inasmuch as the carding machine was first employed in New England, and spread thence southward and westward, a deduction from the number of them erected in 1810 would tend to underweight the southern and western states. However, the proportions with respect to this apparatus agree so closely with those regarding fulling mills as to give them greater apparent validity.

[3] When the states for which woolen-fabric production was not reported have been excluded, the per capita production of such cloths was in 1810: for the northeastern states, 2.8 yards, and in the South, only .3 of a yard. Again the ratio of approximately nine to one is evident.

Census of 1810 was the relatively small per capita output in regions which were easily reached by internal commerce, or which included the larger towns.[1] This situation is illustrated by the conditions in the state of New York, of which a map is presented

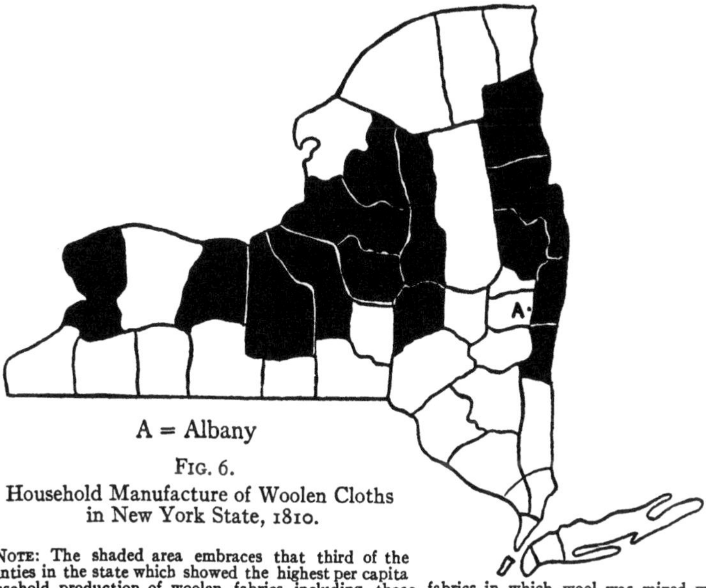

A = Albany

FIG. 6.
Household Manufacture of Woolen Cloths in New York State, 1810.

NOTE: The shaded area embraces that third of the counties in the state which showed the highest per capita household production of woolen fabrics, including those fabrics in which wool was mixed with cotton or linen.

herewith (Figure 6). It will be observed that the production of wool fabrics per head of population was relatively small in the counties which embrace New York and Albany, and those bordering upon the lower reaches of the Hudson River. To some extent, too, there was a correlation between the wool-growing counties and the counties producing a large per capita value of wool cloth. For example, Washington, Cayuga, and Onandaga would appear in both lists.[2] Such a picture of the household production is in accord with the analyses already made, and gives considerable confirmation to the interpretation of the colonial period earlier presented.

[1] Cf. Tryon, p. 184.

[2] Dutchess County, curiously enough, was not a county of large cloth production. Possibly this is indicative of a growing trade in the finer wool for which Dutchess County was beginning to be famed.

With the further growth of factory production, the household manufacture entered upon still another phase, at least in certain sections of the country. As will appear later, the early "manufactories" not infrequently carried on commission work for people in the surrounding region even after they had acquired a full complement of machinery for cloth manufacture and were indeed producing for a more distant market. Such concerns often maintained an additional carding machine for custom work; and sometimes they advertised to spin, weave, finish, or indeed to carry through the whole series of processes in cloth production for their patrons.[1] This, however, was probably the last stage in the household manufacture. The mills at the same time or shortly afterwards adopted a policy of exchanging cloth for wool, or of keeping a supply of cloths ready for local sales; and from that it was but a small step to a complete extinguishment of production in the household.[2] With the increase in the number of factories after 1807 this phase of joint household-mill production became a significant one in the central and New England states; and after the peace in 1815, it was temporarily of still greater importance, when the factories, suddenly exposed to impetuous competition, sought any means of keeping their machinery running.[3]

The household manufacture suffered a reaction after the con-

[1] See below, pp. 222–224.

[2] The stages might be arranged somewhat as follows:

1. The simple household production, with the operations carried on solely in the home — usually of a brief duration in any community.
2. The household-fulling mill stage, in which the finishing was customarily given out.
3. The household-carding machine-fulling mill stage, in which both the carding and finishing were done on commission by outside agencies, or perhaps, as often as not, both at a single combined shop.
4. The household-mill stage, the final one, in which any, several, or all the operations were conducted in the small wool factory upon command of its patrons. If all the processes were carried through at the mill, the only remaining tie connecting it with the home was the ownership of the raw material; and properly speaking, this is not a sufficient justification for including this type of production among the varieties of "household" organization. It would rather be one form of factory production.

[3] *State Papers, Finance*, v, 808, 811, 814; Benedict and Tracy, *History of Sutton, Massachusetts*, p. 535; Lippincott, *Manufactures in the Ohio Valley*, p. 75; Niles, xx, 86.

clusion of peace as did the factories, only a part of which may be laid to the transfer of a portion or the whole of its operations to mill-commission work. The committee on domestic manufactures at the Pittsfield Fair in 1817 called attention to a decrease in domestic productions that year, "probably occasioned by the peculiar condition of the times." [1] In Middletown, Connecticut, an "alarming diminution of our household manufactures" was observed in 1819, laid more specifically to the influx of foreign cloths.[2] In one town in Hampshire County, Massachusetts, the home production of wool fabrics, according to one historian, ceased in many families before 1822, though it continued longer in some.[3]

Nor was there in the eastern states a subsequent return to household manufacture that had any vigor or persistency. Rather there was a steady diminution in output, assisted in part by the greater attention being paid by the factories to cloths of the medium and common grades, — cassimeres, satinets, flannels, and the like,—and also in part by the steady improvement in the means of transportation. To be sure, there are exceptions to this statement as to nearly every generalization respecting the household manufacture in any section of the United States. For example, in the district of Maine, a sparsely settled area in 1810, only 75 carding machines and 59 fulling mills were reported in that year. By 1832, however, as many as 350 carding machines and 345 fulling mills were enumerated, distributed quite generally through the state.[4] In addition, there were increases subsequent to 1810 in portions of several states, such as Pennsylvania and New York, as noted below. Nevertheless, the trend was predominantly in the opposite direction. Such, for instance, was the testimony of well-informed persons who in 1832 were interrogated by the Secretary of the Treasury, McLane, in his inquiry as to the status of manufactures in the country. Among the questions which he put them were the following: "To what extent and

[1] Niles, xii, 47. [2] *State Papers, Finance*, iii, 454.

[3] Judd, *History of Hadley, Massachusetts*, p. 380, note.

[4] McLane's *Report*, i, 65. There is a disagreement within this Report; an addition of the individual entries gives a total of 345, though McLane's summary has the figure of 299.

upon what kinds of articles is household manufacture carried on in the county (where the addressee resided)? Has it increased or decreased, and to what extent, since 1824?"[1] Replies to these queries from New England were nearly unanimous in indicating a reduction in family productions, though estimates vary widely from place to place. New Hampshire reported a decline of 20 or 25 per cent, although in certain towns a much higher percentage is suggested by the individual statements. In Massachusetts, the coastal counties contained little or no household production of any sort, although considerable was still retained in the hinterland. With regard to the whole region it was said: "A few coarse woollens, and probably a trifling quantity of cottons, are produced by household manufacture, but probably not one-tenth part so many of either as in 1824."[2] In wool-growing states such as Vermont, the higher price of wool (probably after 1829) encouraged farmers to sell their wool clips and buy cloth in the open market.

In the middle states somewhat the same change appeared to have occurred, although the data are not here so full. In New Jersey and seemingly in eastern Pennsylvania household production was declining, at least in the years shortly before 1830; but in western Pennsylvania, as yet difficult of access, such manufacture had even recently increased.[3] Of New York, no reports were received in the inquiry of McLane above mentioned, but the course of events is discernible in the state census figures. In 1810, New York had been credited with a production of approximately 3¼ million yards of woolen cloth, with the heaviest output in those counties which either held considerable numbers of sheep or lay to the northern or western parts of the state (see Figure 6 above). In 1820, the production of wool fabrics in the households of the state, including both fulled and unfulled cloth, is given as nearly 4½ million yards; and five years later, as approximately 6⅜ million yards.[4] The enhanced production for the state during

[1] McLane's *Report*, i, 82. [2] *Ibid.*, i, 87. See also pp. 78 and 136 of the same.
[3] *Ibid.*, ii, 404, 407.
[4] Statistics of the 1820 Census are contained in *Journal of the New York Assembly*, 45th Sess., 1822, Appendix A, p. 60. Those of the 1825 census in *Journal of the New York Senate*, 49th Sess., 1826, Appendix.

this period, as in Massachusetts and Pennsylvania, was due primarily to the large increases in the northern and western counties. But in 1825 the production had reached its zenith. With the completion of the Erie Canal, feeder canals in the central part of the state, and the Champlain Canal, came an added facility of commerce, an easier marketing of the products from these communities, and consequently a higher purchasing power and greater desire for cloths either from domestic factories or from foreign workshops.[1] This altered situation is reflected in the yardage of household wool-cloth production ascertained by the next state census, that of 1835. At that time, the output in both fulled and unfulled woolens amounted to less than 5 million yards.[2] A similar story is told by the number of carding machines and fulling mills enumerated in the several censuses.[3]

Such figures illustrate the fact already noted, that it is difficult to speak in generalizations of any section of the country, even of a single state. However, despite exceptions, it may, I believe, be truly said that after 1815 the tendency was definitely toward a lessening household production of wool fabrics in the old East, that which one visualizes as the settled portion of the middle and New England states at the close of the Revolution; and likewise that after 1825 no state as a whole nor any considerable part of a state experienced an increase of such production. By the close of the period under discussion, 1830, the decline was well under way.[4]

[1] See below, pp. 279–282.

[2] Statistics contained in the *New York Census for 1835*, a separate volume.

[3] The full figures for cloths, carding machines, and fulling mills are given below. The statistics for cotton, linen, and other fabrics are also presented. They suggest that the condition spoken of in the text was not peculiar to the wool manufacture.

	Fulled cloth	Flannel and woolen cloth not fulled	Cotton, linen, and other cloths	Carding Machines	Fulling Mills
1810	....	....	....	431	427
1820	1,958,712	2,451,107	5,635,985	1,233	991
1825	2,918,233	3,468,001	8,079,000	1,584	1,222
1835	2,183,951	2,790,069	3,799,953	1,061	965

[4] The weakening economic pressure behind the household manufacture begins in the twenties to be evident in the pleas for its maintenance or increase which the "reformers" of the period were putting forward. In place of the call of patriotism or the needs of national aggrandizement was now placed such twaddle as the fol-

Of the southern states, where the household production of wool cloths was never important, with perhaps the exception of the Revolutionary War period, little need be said. Apparently the manufacture was maintained in some parts of the region, such as North Carolina and the upper sections of South Carolina and Georgia. Of the first named, it was asserted as late as 1828 that there were "thousands of families in the state hardly consuming one yard of imported cloths annually, being supplied from their own looms." [1] But with the rise of cotton to kingship in the South and Southwest, the growth in rice and the spread in tobacco culture, these areas became more and more completely agricultural, and, with the exception of the "back country," were supplied with "money crops" readily exchangeable for their requirements in manufactures.

In the West, however, including Kentucky and Tennessee, there was an increase in the household manufacture of wool fabrics during these years, a reproduction of the conditions which had existed in the more easterly regions ten or twenty years earlier. In the frontier days, as about 1785 in the Ohio settlements, the women had to spin and generally to weave all the cloth for their families.[2] Similarly, Michaux in his travels wrote of Kentucky and Tennessee at the beginning of the new century, that in both states "the wealthiest people, as much from patriotism as economy, wear garments of the stuffs manufactured in the country." The invocation of patriotic endeavor is common in the period; but what was probably the real cause is suggested in the succeeding sentence: "They also find this the only method of keeping the little money which they have in cir-

lowing: "To encourage family industry is to destroy idleness, and to substitute in its place an honest rivalry for excellence, tending to make the fireside happy and independent" (*New York Assembly Journal*, 1825, p. 799). Similarly Niles, noting that "tens of thousands of amiable, respectable and lovely young women" are engaged in household manufactures, sees as the primary gain thereby that it drives away "the diseases and distresses of inanity" (xxi, 35).

[1] Niles, xxxv, 260. Other references to southern wool manufacture: *Documentary History of American Industrial Society*, i, 191–192, 334; ii, 329; Warden, *Account of the United States*, 1819, ii, 161; Clark, "Manufactures during the Ante-Bellum and War Periods," in *South in the Building of the Nation*, v, 314–334.

[2] *American Pioneer*, ii, 160.

culation and preventing it from passing to England."[1] By reason of poor transportation facilities, the crops of the area had little effective purchasing power over non-local goods.

Soon after the wave of permanent settlers had reached the West, the fulling mill made its appearance, and by 1810 Ohio was credited with twenty-one, Kentucky with thirty-three, and Tennessee with two such establishments.[2] Then in about 1805 carding machines had reached the other side of the mountains. The *Census of 1810* reported a total of thirty-nine such machines in Ohio and Kentucky, and at about the same time the manufacture of cards and of spinning machines for family use began in Kentucky and Tennessee.[3] Simultaneously small factories were rising, but apparently as yet neither they nor importations played for any considerable period a significant rôle in the supply of wool fabrics to these interior regions.

The period around 1815 has been called "the supreme age of the handicraft system and home manufacturing" in the inland areas of the country, principally Kentucky, Tennessee, and the Northwest Territory;[4] and indeed, as in the eastern states around 1800, the family production was as yet free from significant competition on the part of domestic factories or foreign imports. But in volume of output the household manufacture continued to increase for a decade or two, and in relation to total consumption it was apparently able to retain its place until possibly as late as 1825. The *Census of 1820*, defective as that was, showed a considerable multiplication of carding and fulling shops over the number in 1810.[5] In the same year, Hall in his *Letters* wrote: "A very large portion of the western people manufacture their

[1] Michaux, *Travels*, 1805, p. 296. See also *Autobiography of Rev. J. B. Finley*, p. 154; Hildreth, *History of a Voyage from Marietta to New Orleans in 1805*, p. 31; Hildreth, *Pioneer History*, p. 394.

[2] Probably these figures are defective, less accurate than those for the eastern states.

[3] Howells, *Life in Ohio*, p. 8; Clark, p. 518.

[4] Tryon, p. 269.

[5] *State Papers, Finance*, iv, 447–455. In some cases there were several carding machines in one establishment. For instance, some shops in Ohio were said to hold six carding machines, and one was reported as containing forty-nine cards, all "employed by customers" (p. 191).

own clothing; among the farmers the practice is universal: and it extends so far to other classes that it is not at all unusual to see professional gentlemen in affluent circumstances and men of high official rank clad in plain domestic fabrics." [1]

Another observer of about the same date, in what appears to have been a conservative estimate, said: "It is supposed that nearly two-thirds of all the clothing, linen, blankets, &c., of those inhabitants who reside in the interior of the country, are of home or household manufacture." [2] Of Kentucky the ratio was placed higher: "Not only all the servants and poorer class, but nine-tenths of the most wealthy and respectable owners of the soil are clad in homespun." [3] In spite of improved navigation upon the Mississippi and Ohio rivers and of the betterment of overland transportation from the eastern ports, the western farmer who in 1820 brought his produce only as far as Pittsburgh had to give 12½ barrels of flour for a single yard of superfine broadcloth.[4] Obviously under such conditions the economic necessity for household manufacture was strong upon large sections of the population.

Yet in the western states the rate of industrial development was much more rapid than in the older communities. The introduction of fulling mills and carding machines always followed closely upon the heels of settlement, and likewise there was an early erection of "woolen manufactories." The first "manufactory" of the western country, that at Steubenville, Ohio, had commenced operations already in 1814–1815; and three years later Flint enumerated two mills in Pittsburgh and one each in Steubenville, Chillicothe, and Cincinnati, Ohio.[5] Something of the peculiarly complicated conditions which prevailed in the West may be secured from Flint's comment about the town of Millersburg, Ohio: "Today I have seen a number of young women on horseback, with packages of wool, going to, or return-

[1] Hall, *Letters*, p. 68. See also Howells, *Life in Ohio*, pp. 123–124; and Melish, *Travels*, ii, esp. 193, 215.

[2] Holmes, *Account of the United States*, 1823, p. 208.

[3] Kayser, *Commercial Directory*, 1823, p. 55.

[4] Niles, xx, 180.

[5] Flint, *Letters from America*, 1822, pp. 85, 102, 118, 150.

ing from, the carding-machine. At some of the houses the loom stands under a small porch by the door;" and yet "Miss does not wear the produce of her own hands."[1] Evidently, while economic pressure impelled an extensive family manufacture, commercial and industrial progress had placed factory-made goods, — perhaps from the Steubenville factory, — at the disposal of the fastidious element in the household. By 1825 the proportion of total consumption derived from sources other than the home activities had probably become a significant factor in such states as Ohio and Kentucky, but if one is to judge by the experience of western New York and Pennsylvania, the volume of household production continued to increase for many years longer. In the regions still farther west, such as Illinois and Michigan, the home manufacture was perhaps as yet hardly past the "supreme age;" there it was still to acquire the preeminence and the well-organized form which it possessed in the East about 1800 or in Ohio, Kentucky, and Tennessee around 1815.

Now what can be said for the country as a whole? How in 1830 did the quantity of household products compare with that of the young factories? Was the proportion of household production in the total domestic output increasing or decreasing? To the last question a confident answer can be given. Undoubtedly each year the mills were winning the industry away from the homes. Even with due allowance for the westward expansion of the household manufacture, the share of household production in the nation's wool-cloth output must be put down as decreasing. The *Census of 1810* had indicated that twenty-four yards out of every twenty-five in domestic output had come from the home. Never again, at least after 1815, was the proportion to be so great.

As to just what was the share retained by the household in 1830, it is difficult to say. Even contemporary estimates differed widely. Mr. Mallary, chairman of the House Committee on Manufactures, stated in the debates of 1828–1829 that home-made woolens reached forty million dollars, but factory-

[1] Flint, *Letters from America*, 1822, p. 129.

made goods scarcely twenty-two millions in value.[1] Randall, who was interested in and was writing about wool-growing and wool-manufacturing throughout this period, implied in after years that "the proportion of home-made to factory woolens was, no doubt, annually decreasing" during the thirties, but that as late as 1839 a fair estimate would set the two down as even; and one might infer from this analysis that a substantial excess of household over factory production existed in 1830.[2] On the other hand, we have the straightforward assertion of the Friends of Domestic Industry in 1831 that the proportion between the amount of wool worked up in factories to that wrought in families was as three to two.[3] How shall one reconcile these divergent opinions? Taking into account the biases or prepossessions of these gentlemen, and also the imponderables of less definitely expressed opinions, less frequent references to household production, and the like, I am inclined to steer a middle course, not wide of that set by Randall. The volume of household production for the whole country was probably still in excess of that proceeding from domestic factories. Perhaps a ratio of four to three would not be far off. But this situation, it should be remarked, was chiefly due to the renewal of household production in the West and in the frontier areas of the eastern states, e. g., in Maine. For the older communities a ratio such as that offered by the Friends of Domestic Industry would apparently be more proper. Moreover, the household manufacture was already doomed. The factory had displayed its superior productive power. Families in the neighborhood of

[1] *Congressional Debates*, March 4, 1828, col. 1733.

[2] Randall, *Sheep Husbandry*, 1848, p. 127. Randall confessed that he had no data upon the subject; but, then, neither had anyone else. He quoted Mallary's estimate (see above) and that of the Friends of Domestic Industry (see below), and remarked: "It strikes me, however, that Mr. Mallary's estimate is too high, and that of the *Report* of the 'Friends of Domestic Industry' too low."

[3] *Report* of the Convention held by the Friends of Domestic Industry, p. 79. The New York Census of 1835, from which alone one can secure data upon household and factory woolen manufactures at a given time, sets down a household production of 4,974,000 yards and a factory output (including cotton-mixed goods) of 7,312,000 yards. If such were the situation in New York as late as 1835, surely the estimate of the Friends of Domestic Industry must be erroneous for the country as a whole five years earlier.

mills, if not as yet depending entirely upon "boughten" cloth, were utilizing more extensively the facilities of the factory through such arrangements as the manufacture of their wool on shares, or the spinning of their wool, or the weaving of their yarns in the mills. Where the means of communication permitted an easy marketing of factory-made goods, the household production tended rapidly to disappear, — and the coming of railroads meant an ever-widening area which would be affected by this force. The period of predominantly household manufacture in the newly settled parts of the country would not be so prolonged as it had been in the East. Even for the whole of the United States, the complete extinction of this primary form of manufacture could be foreseen.

Household Production for Sale.

It is a characteristic feature of the household manufacture in all cases that its products do not enter into commerce; and the American wool manufacture supplies no significant exception to this general rule. As has been pointed out, in 1760 the production in the families was carried on almost wholly "without the least design of sending any of it to market." Certain later periods of stress led to occasional modifications of this situation. The general position and character of household manufacture remained the same, but the exceptions are sufficiently numerous to warrant passing attention.

In the period of agitation that preceded the Revolution, for example, homespun is said to have been sold in New York. Indeed, the artificial demand of the times sent the market price of homespun so high that, according to the report, the producers were able to purchase good English cloths for themselves with the proceeds of its sale.[1] Again, there are instances of communities producing such large quantities that probably some part of the output must have been surplus. Thus a "small country town" in Massachusetts, it is recorded, manufactured thirty thousand yards of cloth in 1767.[2] So, too, during the Revolutionary War

[1] *Documentary History of New York*, i, 734.
[2] Weeden, pp. 732–733.

itself, occasional references are to be found to trade in household fabrics. The contemporary newspapers carry advertisements of domestic cloths for sale, and there are a few cases where the prices of such fabrics were fixed by public authorities.[1] Indeed, one can find mention of what were apparently small "putting-out" operations.[2] But on the whole, even in this period specially favorable to the household manufacture, the appearance of household products in the local markets or in wider commercial activities was unquestionably the abnormal phenomenon, and could have cut no considerable figure in the industrial or commercial operations of the time.[3]

In the period subsequent to the Revolution, evidence pointing toward a commercialization of the family production is no more abundant. Country storekeepers would sometimes accept wool cloth in exchange for other goods; but the amounts never were large. A typical case is that of Manna Wadsworth & Company, of Pittsfield, Massachusetts. Their ledgers covering the years 1791 to 1796 show a total of forty-one entries of this sort, or only seven a year; and the average quantity per entry is only fifteen yards.[4] Advertisements of such storekeepers, however, rarely mention a willingness to barter goods specifically for wool fabrics, although not infrequently inserting so extensive a list of

[1] E. g., the town of Dudley, Massachusetts: see Ammidown's *Historical Collections*, i, 418.

[2] See *Boston News Letter*, December 31, 1825; Weeden, pp. 789–790. In the former case, it was stated that "one gentleman only, at Barnstable, about fifty miles from Boston, who has, not long since, set up the woolen manufacture, receives from the Spinners 500 Skeins of Yarn one Day with another." The data presented by Weeden refer to payment for spinning as well as for weaving in a single case at Andover, Massachusetts, and to the fixing of spinning rates for woolen and worsted yarns at East Greenwich, Connecticut.

[3] Obviously no account is here taken of local inter-family exchanges of cloth for other articles, of cloth for services, and the like, which might well be quite numerous, as in the colonial period (see above, p. 33).

[4] Ledgers of Manna Wadsworth & Company, preserved in the Berkshire Athenaeum, Pittsfield, Massachusetts. The entries covered mostly checked or plain flannel, some few yards of "fulled cloth" and rarely "Broad cloth." Cf. Tryon, pp. 134, 141. Phineas Bond (1789) implies that there was sale of home-made cloths in the stores (American Historical Association *Reports*, 1896, i, 632). He also gives a case of putting-out of wool-spinning (*ibid.*, p. 651), but apparently the purpose was relief to the poor.

acceptable "country produce" as: "Flax, Flax-seed, Wheat, Rye, Indian Corn, Barley, Butter, Tallow, Beeswax, Old Pewter, Brass, Cotton and Linen Bags, and Ashes." [1]

In the period of 1807 to 1815, when household operations were again specially stimulated, references to trade in homespun become more numerous. Gallatin intimated in his Report that as early as 1810 some cloths of this manufacture were finding sale; [2] and there are isolated glimpses of the trade, such as the shipment from Berkshire County, Massachusetts, to Albany, New York, of thirty bales of woolens, the most of which, it is said, were manufactured in private families.[3] The storekeepers and others perhaps spoke more frequently now of wool cloths wanted or acceptable.[4] In addition the Federal government showed a desire for household manufactures. Thomas Melvill, Jr., with the title of United States Superintendent, came to Pittsfield, Massachusetts, soon after the outbreak of the War of 1812 and purchased cloth, not only from the local "factories," but from the households, one purpose of his work being said to be "the encouragement of manufactures in private families." [5] He offered to purchase chiefly kerseys, checked and striped flannel, blankets, and stockings.[6] The persistence of his efforts speaks of success in the procurement of household cloths. Moreover, it was reported in 1815 that whereas "at the commencement of the war Berkshire could only furnish, beyond her own consumption, two thousand

[1] *Pittsfield Sun*, February 25, 1809. In addition, occasionally proprietors of wool-carding shops and fulling mills accepted cloth or yarn in payment for their services (see e. g., *Documentary History of American Industrial Society*, ii, 328).

[2] *State Papers, Finance*, ii, 427.

[3] Bolles, *Industrial History*, p. 376.

[4] Positive mention of wool cloths was still far from numerous: in the *Pittsfield Sun*, three or four advertisements in the course of a half dozen years; in the *Middlesex Gazette* (Middletown, Connecticut), perhaps half a dozen; and in other current newspapers, such as the *Massachusetts Spy*, the *Philadelphia Democratic Press*, the *Vermont Republican*, and the *Baltimore Federal Gazette*, only one or two in the country and none in the city papers.

[5] *Pittsfield Sun*, August 15, 1812.

[6] *Ibid.*, October 15, 1812, March 4, 1813, December 2, 1813, December 22, 1814, and July 20, 1815. In the last advertisement, he states that he has, as agent for Thomas Melvill, Sr., 500 pounds of wool on which he wished to receive proposals for manufacture into cloth, probably by the factories, — another unusual situation.

yards of woolen cloth, last fall (1814) one gentleman (presumably Melvill) alone purchased thirty thousand yards of soldiers' cloths, manufactured in the county," besides the finer goods that came from her factories.[1] The advent of peace closed this period.[2]

After the flood of importations which greeted the peace and the consequent decline of household manufacture in the eastern states, one hears even less of purchase or sale of family productions. Of Connecticut it was said in 1816 that a part of the home output "is regularly sold to the country stores;" but probably this refers to the previous war conditions.[3] The practice probably passed away in such areas; but, as one might expect, it was transplanted to the back country. A report from Spartanburg, South Carolina, as late as 1826 stated that of the woolens and cottons of coarse quality produced in the households of the community, some were made for sale;[4] and apparently the same usage prevailed in the West, though never in any greater measure than earlier in the eastern states.

The failure of household productions to enter commerce further than, for the most part, in local barter is not hard to understand. The cloths were coarse in quality and the supply uncertain. They could not hope to compete either with the imported fabrics or with the goods flowing from the domestic "manufactories." Special exigency might for a time give them a little wider currency, but the return of normal conditions would pen them again in their narrow field. Always commercial transactions in such goods were the exception, and household production for household use was the rule.

[1] Niles, viii, 56; quoting from the Albany *Argus*.

Arthur Scholfield and his nephew, Isaac, are said to have sold "considerable quantities of gray mixed broadcloth . . . to the officers stationed at Pittsfield" (Holland, *History of Western Massachusetts*, ii, 558).

[2] Apparently this episode at Pittsfield was the only one of its kind. Search of government documents and of newspapers in other wool-manufacturing centers fails to reveal any other such affair. However, perhaps they occurred without leaving the record that appears in the Pittsfield case.

[3] *State Papers, Finance*, iii, 104; and a somewhat similar account, Niles, x, 82.

[4] Mills, *South Carolina Statistics*, p. 730.

CHAPTER IX

CHANGES IN QUALITY OF DOMESTIC MANUFACTURE

IN 1760 the available market for goods produced outside the households was narrowly restricted. It consisted almost wholly of the more fastidious town population, supplied at the time, in fact, chiefly by the superior English fabrics imported from the mother country. And such continued to be the general character of the market down to the War of 1812. Goods to be salable had to be pleasing to the "city beaux" who, as it was said, could "look beyond convenience to elegance."[1] Only gradually, with the expansion of the market, which has been spoken of in connection with increased importations, came the possibility of manufacturing the inferior qualities of wool cloths for general sale.

In accordance with the market situation during the early years, when domestic factory production of cloth was first beginning, the efforts of such production were directed to a peculiarly large extent toward the fabrication of the finer goods, especially broadcloths. The Hartford mill, it will be recalled, was particularly interested in broadcloth manufacture. The whole project for the acquisition and wider culture of merino sheep was inspired largely by this consideration. The broadcloths in which succeeding Presidents were inaugurated attracted wide comment; the premiums offered by the various societies for promoting domestic manufactures were highest in the case of broadcloths; and, generally speaking, the discussions of wool-cloth production centered upon this fabric to the practical exclusion of all others.[2] Similarly, any list of the more prominent concerns that existed in the period prior to 1815 would include mainly broadcloth manufacturers: e. g., the Scholfields, Colonel Humphreys of Connecticut, the

[1] Livingston in *Transactions* of the New York Society for Promoting Arts and Manufactures, 1806, ii, 91. Similarly, i, p. 32, "our beaux."

[2] Cf. pamphlet of Pennsylvania Society, dated July 25, 1808; and *Transactions* of the New York Society, iii, 226, for premiums offered.

Northampton Woolen Manufacturing Company in which James Shepherd was the dominant factor, the Du Ponts of Delaware, the Middletown (Connecticut) mill, Derby of Salem who imported eleven hundred merino sheep, and the Steubenville (Ohio) factory. Of the fourteen mills spoken of by Gallatin in 1810, the greater number were, it appears, chiefly interested in fine-cloth production.[1] Indeed, as one writer said at about this time: "the finer the goods or the material proposed, the more ready (was) the disposition (of manufacturers to make them), the more abundant the quantity in proportion to the demand, and the more moderate the price." [2]

Only gradually did the production of coarser fabrics gain ground. The increased demand for such goods on the part of the army occasioned somewhat greater manufacture. In 1812 considerable quantities of domestic kerseys were reported to have been contracted for by the government, a single woolen manufacturer in New Hampshire agreeing to supply five thousand yards per month;[3] and in the succeeding year the government was able to secure practically all its coarser fabrics from within the country.[4] Again, the demand of the southern states, in some degree shut off from English supplies, encouraged the production of such inferior cloths. Gallatin spoke of a few mills in the vicinity of Philadelphia and Baltimore, more closely in touch with the southern market, as engaged upon "coarse cloth and cassinet," and the like.[5] In addition, some northern mills began to seek this trade. For example, the Hazard mill in South Kingston, Rhode Island, took up the production of kersey, which soon met with great demand in the southern market.[6]

[1] *State Papers, Finance*, ii, 434, Table E. Other broadcloth mills of this period are spoken of in *Census of 1860*, iii, p. xxx.

[2] *Pittsfield Sun*, October 5, 1811, quoting the *Philadelphia Democratic Press* with reference to "the late experiments to procure homemade articles of military clothing for the United States." Some years later (1819), the Commissary-General of Purchases, charged (probably with much exaggeration) that the manufacturers "during the war, with two or three exceptions, when the finer cloths commanded very high prices, and great profits, would not make a yard of (coarse) cloth for our suffering troops" (*Senate Documents*, 16th Cong., 1st Sess., No. 21, p. 8).

[3] Niles, iii, 60.

[4] *State Papers, Finance*, ii, 816–817.

[5] *Ibid.*, ii, 434.

[6] Gammell, *Life of Rowland G. Hazard*, p. 7.

Then, after the close of the war, came a still greater movement. This had its roots in the increased division of labor within the country. Cities were growing up in which industrial and commercial life played an ever larger part. The enhancement of this city population alone is significant. Communities of 8000 souls and more had contained only 131,000 people in 1790, whereas by 1830 they held 864,000. In proportion to the country's total population, too, they were advancing: from 3.35 per cent to 6.72 per cent.[1] Moreover, the outlying districts had been brought closer to the budding factories with the development of turnpikes, and later of canals. Exchange of rural with urban production was facilitated, and in this trade wool-cloth output from the expanding mills had its proper share.

Equally important with the growth in total volume of such trade in wool fabrics was the broadening in type of goods that this extension of the market required. The restricted and specialized market of the earlier period was becoming that broad and diversified market which the country has afforded ever since. The chief varieties of fabrics inferior to broadcloth which came to be more widely manufactured in domestic mills were: cassimeres, satinets, kerseys, cassinets, flannels, and blankets. The derivation of these manufactures and their increased production through the period to 1830 deserve brief consideration.

The leading variety among these new goods, at least from the viewpoint of quality, was the cassimere, a cloth of English origin. Another cloth of somewhat similar character, frequently met with in this period, was the kerseymere. In these fabrics the fulling, napping, and shearing were not carried so far as in the case of broadcloths. The texture, accordingly, was not so firm as that of broadcloths, and the face did not have the smoothness and sheen which were characteristic of the latter. Since these fabrics were then made up in what today would be called heavy weights, — probably twenty ounces per yard or more, — they probably resembled more the kersey or heavy overcoating of the present time than the cassimere now turned out. In color or design there seemingly was no difference at first between broadcloths and these

[1] Weber, *Growth of Cities*, p. 22.

cassimeres and kerseymeres. All were manufactured in solid colors, — plain black, blue, and the like, — although perhaps gray mixtures were also produced.[1] However, in the cassimere and similar cloths lay the possibility of far greater use of design than in the more highly finished broadcloth, for design and heavy fulling are not compatible. And ultimately, in the "fancy cassimeres" of the forties and fifties, style was introduced into woolen-cloth production through the manufacture of these newer fabrics.[2]

Cassimeres and kerseymeres, then, were goods inferior in quality to the noble broadcloth. The chief market for them, consequently, was at first among the less prosperous classes of the population, as the wealthy insisted upon the finer and older fabric; but, with some improvement in methods of production and with change in fashion of dress, they came more and more into use with the well-to-do. Moreover, the manufacture of cassimere and kerseymere, — especially the former, — seemed to thrive in the United States. Reference to their production in American mills became more frequent as the years went by; and the shipment of such goods from England to this country declined materially in the decade of the twenties.[3] This branch of the woolen manufacture had become acclimatized in the United States.

Ranging in quality below broadcloth, cassimeres, or kersey-

[1] There are various ways in which color may be imparted to wool cloth. The two most important ways, and the two concerned here, are the dyeing of the woven fabric, and the dyeing of the loose wool. In the latter case, — that employed in the construction of mixtures, and sometimes for medium or light shades of colors, — only a portion of the unwrought wool is usually dyed; and that portion is mixed with the undyed fiber in the proportions necessary to secure the desired effect or shade.

[2] By style is here meant style in the way of pattern. Already style in the way of cloth-finish had been used.

[3] The classification among British export statistics which presumably covered cassimeres was that of "coatings." Exportation of coatings to the United States, which had averaged nearly 17,000 pieces in the years 1815–1818, dwindled until, in the early thirties, e. g., 1830 and 1832, none at all were reported or, as in other years, only a negligible quantity. Similarly, the exportation of kerseymeres, for which there was a separate classification in the British figures, declined steadily from approximately 38,000 pieces in 1815–1818 to little over 2000 in 1830–1832.

meres, were yet two other cloths, satinet and cassinet, — the latter being a coarse variety of the former, and indeed one of the coarsest types of cloth produced in this period. These cloths, however, have a particular significance. They were made with cotton warps, and this was a new departure, not only for the American industry, but really for the wool manufacture everywhere. There is no reference to any considerable employment of cotton warps in the British or other foreign wool manufactures prior to its use in the English worsted trade about 1834;[1] and, by reason of the differentiation in England of the old-established wool manufacture from the up-start production of cotton cloth, together with a marked geographical localization, it is not improbable that such should have been the case. In the youthful American industry, where all textiles were new and where manufacturers frequently shifted from one branch to another, the discovery of the value of cotton-warp woolen fabrics was not a strange or surprising phenomenon. In addition, there was the impetus, especially great in this country, toward the production of cheap fabrics, if at the same time these were still serviceable goods. Satinets and the similar, though coarser cassinets fulfilled these conditions. Of these particular cloths, one may add, there surely was no mention in accounts of British manufacture during this period.

The first mention of satinet in this country occurs as early as 1788;[2] but the really large production of these fabrics did not begin until about 1808. James Beaumont of Canton, Massachusetts, and one John Hill of Philadelphia were early manufacturers in this line; and they were followed closely by others, of whom the best known men were Abraham Marland of Andover, Massa-

[1] Baines, *Yorkshire Past and Present*, p. 684; James, *Continuations and Additions*, p. 228; Butterfield, *Notes on the Worsted Industry*, p. 42.

I may have been overconservative with respect to the use of cotton warps in mixed cotton and wool goods in the British industry. I have seen no direct statement concerning the woolen branch of the industry, and no clear indication that a cotton warp was ever employed in any type of woolen fabric prior to its use in the American manufacture. However, information is most meager respecting the exact types of cloth turned out in the British woolen industry. In so far as types are indeed mentioned, they seem all to have been all-wool fabrics.

[2] Scharf and Westcott, *op. cit.*, iii, 2314.

chusetts, and Delano Abbott of Vernon, Connecticut.[1] The establishments engaged in this production were usually small affairs, mostly one-set mills, and neither so large nor so prominent as the broadcloth concerns.[2] The case of Mr. Abbott is typical. He started life as a farmer, and was attracted to the wool manufacture through accidentally running upon a piece of this novel fabric called satinet — the story alleges that the cloth was an imported affair, but probably it was merely sold as "imported."[3] A billy of thirty spindles and a jenny of sixty were built for him by a local machinist and set up in an outbuilding near Mr. Abbott's house, while in another were placed two hand looms. Only the spinning and weaving were undertaken, the carding and finishing being entrusted to the custom shops of the neighborhood.[4] Such, with variations, was probably the history of many satinet establishments.

However, the manufacture in general prospered. The fabric fitted into the growing need for a serviceable and moderately priced cloth, especially at this time when more and more of the town population were discarding the knee-breeches of colonial times for the full-length trousers, theretofore worn only by workingmen. Reliance upon the more efficient cotton-manufacturing industry for the warps not only reduced the expense of plant to the wool manufacturer but gave him some advantage over the

[1] Bagnall, pp. 275, 339, 603–604; *Philadelphia General Advertiser*, January 2, 1809. Beaumont wrote in his autobiography: About 1808 "I then (leaving cotton) began to manufacture all wool cloth, carcys (kerseys?) and sattinets. For the last article I got great credit, making my own cotton warps of Sea Island cotton, and employed English workmen, who beat them up well in the hand loom, so that when afterwards finished you could scarcely tell the back side from the face. I sold the finest of them for $3.50 a yard, both before and during the war of 1812" (Bagnall, p. 275). This was probably a case of relatively fine production in this grade of fabric.

[2] A "one-set mill" was one containing one set of woolen carding machines, with the complement of spinning machinery and looms that would be kept busy on the wool which such carding machines would normally turn out. A "set" of carding machines, in turn, meant the two or usually three individual carding machines — first breaker and finisher, or first breaker, intermediate, and finisher — that were combined for a proper treatment of the wool in the carding process.

[3] The practice of misrepresentation was early a feature of the wool-cloth sale, at least among tailors.

[4] Bagnall, pp. 603–604.

producer of all-wool goods. Furthermore, since the fabric did not aim at fineness of texture, the producer did not have to pay a premium for the less abundant high-quality wool of the country. But perhaps chief among the favorable influences was the relatively smaller amount of skill required in this line of manufacture. The lower grade of wool made the wool filling yarns less tenuous, the strong cotton warp gave added facility in weaving, and the plainer finish eliminated many of the difficulties in the final manufacturing operations. So great, indeed, was the success of this manufacture that by the third decade in the century probably not far from half the factory production in this country was of this character. And meanwhile there had been a distinct drop in price. As one manufacturer reported, goods which ten years earlier had sold for $1.40 a yard, changed hands in 1832 for only 60 cents,—and this despite the fact that there had been no importation of satinets from England.[1]

The experience of the cheaper grade of cotton-warp fabrics, the cassinets above mentioned, or, as more frequently called, the "negro cloths," is not quite so happy. These fabrics, to which might be joined the older "linseys," were the lowest qualities of wool or part-wool cloth produced in this country. While satinets employed domestic wools, these goods were manufactured mainly out of cheap foreign wools; and accordingly were subjected to certain vicissitudes which the former escaped. The earlier protective tariffs imposed simple ad valorem duties upon incoming wool, but in the "Tariff of Abominations" a mixed duty, four cents a pound plus forty and later fifty per cent ad valorem, was enacted, a duty which fell with special weight on the cheaper foreign staples. In the period of the 1824 tariff, according to the address of the Harrisburg Convention, "the consumption of British manufactured negro cloths . . . had materially decreased

[1] Hazard's *Register of Pennsylvania*, xiv, 389; McLane, ii, 221.

Already in 1828 domestic manufacturers were complaining of internal competition in this article. Mr. William W. Young of Brandywine, Delaware, stated before the Committee on Manufactures: "The low price of sattinets is wholly owing to domestic competition and I do not know any other branch of the woolen manufacture in which domestic competition is felt to any considerable extent except in relation to foreign as well." *State Papers, Finance*, v, 821. See also pp. 813 and 825.

and importers had not been able to sell any quantity of them at prices to cover cost." [1] But in the subsequent period the domestic production was sensibly checked, though apparently the American mills were still able to keep some of their machinery going. Except for this short period, however, the production of these inferior cloths, which had increased materially in the earlier twenties, formed a significant element in the American wool-manufacturing industry.

Two other fabrics demand attention, blankets and flannels. Although these two have in later times been frequently classed together, as in tariff legislation, and although by reason of the relative simplicity of manufacture in both cases they might well be grouped together, their respective histories in the period under consideration were quite different. The production of blankets, except occasionally in the household way, is rarely, if ever, mentioned in the years before the embargo and war. Then some manufacture appears to have developed. A committee of the Massachusetts legislature in 1812 secured engagements from individuals to supply at least fifty thousand blankets for war purposes; and two establishments, it is known, those of Abraham Marland in Andover, Massachusetts, and of Aaron Buckland in Manchester, Connecticut, furnished goods of this sort "for the government" during the war.[2] Yet the references to blanket production continue to be infrequent; and as late as the thirties blankets remained an important article of importation. Failure to develop this line of manufacture was at times laid to the character of our wool supply. For example, Niles once stated that "our coarsest wool is too fine, soft, and short for blankets." [3] His idea seems to have been that there was a definite technical difficulty. However, this explanation is inadequate. Practically any type of wool can with greater or less facility be made into blankets, and surely fineness or shortness of staple was no real obstacle. Be-

[1] Niles, xxxiii, 190. Niles stated elsewhere (p. 208) that "homemade negro cloths are cheaper and better than the British."

[2] *Ibid.*, ii, 17; Abbot, *History of Andover*, p. 196; Bagnall, p. 229.

[3] Niles, ii, 9. The English were said to have an additional advantage in that the by-product of their worsted manufacture, the noils from the combing process, was available for use in the production of blankets (*ibid.*, p. 52).

sides, there is testimony, such as that of Mr. Marland, that there was "no wool more suitable for the making of blankets than the native wool of this country."[1] There is more validity to the latter's explanation of this failure to develop an American blanket manufacture. He found the difficulty in the fact that this native wool "has always borne too high a price to warrant the manufacture from it." In other words, domestic wools could be used in other ways more advantageously. Blankets at that time apparently were made of much coarser wool than is now customarily employed. Wool akin to carpet types was utilized, and such fiber never was grown in any considerable quantities in the United States. Supplies were in some degree available from abroad, and, except for the period of the "Tariff of Abominations," they might be brought in under simple, low ad valorem duties.[2] Some of this coarse, low-priced wool did in fact come into the country; but apparently there were inadequacies and uncertainties in such importations, arising presumably from the lack of organization in the world's wool trade, which made reliance upon foreign staple a definite check to increased blanket manufacture. Surely there is a consensus of opinion, of contemporaries and subsequent writers, that difficulty in the raw material end was an important obstacle to expansion in this section of the industry. However, the more significant cause seems to lie in the condition of technological equipment. Some of the cheap wool, especially that from South America, contained burrs which it was then impossible to eliminate easily. Not until the invention, by Mr. M. H. Simpson in 1833, of a burring mechanism to remove this vegetable substance was it advantageous to use this staple even in the manufacture of blankets.[3] Again, on account of the unusual width in which blankets must be woven, the power loom was not readily adaptable to this production; and accordingly the American industry possessed no marked advantage over its foreign competitors. Whatever the cause, suffice it to note that though, as Mr. Marland

[1] *State Papers, Finance*, v, 798. Mr. Marland adds: "I do not think the manufacture of blankets is carried on to any extent in this country at present (1828)."

[2] A specific or compound duty would tend to increase the actual duty expressed in ad valorem terms upon the wools of lower unit value.

[3] *Bulletin*, 1879, p. 44.

said, "the process of making blankets is very simple, easy, and cheap," no considerable production of them actually took place prior to 1830.

On the other hand, the flannel manufacture was, it seems, more successful than any of the phases of manufacture already noted. At that time flannel had a wide use, especially for underclothing and shirts. As such there was less need of a fine finish than in the case of broadcloth, cassimere, or even satinet. Indeed, the finishing operations for flannels are peculiarly simple, — little more than washing and pressing. The fabric is practically complete as it comes from the loom. Moreover, the common wool of the country was said to be particularly adapted to employment in flannels, while the type of yarn employed in its fabrication and the simple character of the weave contributed to the ease with which this cloth could be produced.

Prior to the disturbances which ushered in the War of 1812, flannel for the domestic market came almost wholly from abroad, except for that produced in the household manner. The factory production of flannel was, as Tench Coxe said, one of the "extensions of the woolen manufacture, produced by interruptions of the importations from Europe." [1] Among the first domestic wool manufacturers to enter this new line, indeed, the man who has been called the pioneer in the flannel production in this country, was Nathaniel Stevens of Andover, Massachusetts, who in 1814 turned his whole mill to that venture. Another early producer was Abraham Marland, already mentioned.[2] Subsequent to that time the flannel manufacture made steady progress. By 1824 it was reported that as much as 690,000 yards of this fabric had been produced the previous year within forty miles of Boston.[3] Soon production went forward in an even quicker pace. In 1827 it was remarked that "American flannels are rapidly driving the foreign article out of the market," [4] and then within a couple of years that

[1] Coxe, *Arts and Manufactures*, p. xxx.

[2] *250th Anniversary Souvenir of Andover, Massachusetts*, p. 10; Bailey, *History of Andover*, p. 590; Bagnall, p. 340. The Stevens mill continued to run wholly or chiefly on flannels until 1876.

[3] Niles, xxv, 338, quoting the *Boston Daily Advertiser*.

[4] *Ibid.*, xxxii, 290.

"flannels now used are almost wholly American." [1] A rapid change in the status of the American flannel manufacture, though perhaps not quite so marked as these contemporaneous opinions suggest, is also evident in the course of flannel importations. Whereas in the calendar years of 1820–1824 the importation of flannels from England had averaged 2,346,000 yards, thereafter our imports thence steadily declined, until in 1834 the amount reported was but 211,000 yards. Rarely in the study of our industrial and commercial history would one find such a change in the brief space of a decade. The explanation of this change seems to lie especially in the technical development of the whole industry. Because of the fabric's simple construction, the flannel production received benefit from all the improvements secured anywhere in the wool manufacture, — Goulding card, spinning jack, or power loom. For example, we know that the power loom was early employed in the domestic flannel mills, at a time when other branches of the American cloth manufacture were still using the hand loom.[2] But another factor in determining the course of the flannel manufacture was the tariff. In common with duties on other sorts of woolens, the tariff rates on flannels had been rising, but a specially high imposition was placed upon flannel importations by the act of 1828. The duty on cheap flannels was described by Nathan Appleton as "a higher protection than on any other species of woolen goods." [3] Again, the whole group of rates covering flannels was declared "fully adequate," as Clay put it; while Niles went so far in 1832 as to "admit the fact that flannels are as if prohibited by the act of 1828." [4] Protection of this sort unquestionably had a considerable influence. It gave valuable support to the young flannel manufacture. On the other hand, protection alone cannot be credited with the result attained. It was effective largely because of the ready adaptability of this production to existing American conditions. The fact that the volume of importations had been declining even within tariff

[1] Niles, xxxvi, 284.
[2] See above, p. 124.
[3] *Congressional Debates*, 22nd Cong., 1st Sess., col. 3808 (June 27, 1832).
[4] *Ibid.*, i, 280 (February 2, 1832); Niles, xlii, 75.

periods, and that domestic production continued to hold the field even after the extent of protection had been subsequently modified, indicates that the fundamental conditions were quite ready for the new development.

This survey of the types and character of domestic manufacture shows, then, a decided change in the character of factory output: whereas the early emphasis had been upon the manufacture of the finer qualities, especially broadcloth, by 1830 the domestic market for wool goods had expanded, or perhaps we might say deepened, until the greater bulk of the output was of medium and lower-grade cloths. Typical of the movement is the case of Dickinson, the Steubenville (Ohio) manufacturer. In 1819 he had begun operations with the manufacture of broadcloths. In 1828, after a few years of unprofitable operation, he states: "Our late determination has been to make mostly coarser cloths."[1] The newer development, to be sure, had not been uniformly successful in all lines, — the production of blankets especially proving to be of peculiarly slow growth. But other cloths, particularly cassimeres, had begun to cut away the ground from under the broadcloth manufacture, inasmuch as such goods offered a possible substitute; flannel production was in full swing until, as one observer stated, "the quantity manufactured is ample for the consumption of the whole country;"[2] and in the satinet manufacture, the industry had developed a new fabric specially adapted to American needs and specially suited to American manufacturing conditions.

The situation in American manufacture resulting from these several changes is pictured in a census of the industry taken by Benton and Barry. This enumeration really pertains to 1836, but the conditions of that date probably did not differ markedly from those obtaining at the beginning of the decade.[3] The 1488 sets of woolen machinery reported were divided on lines of output into the following groups and proportions:

[1] *State Papers, Finance*, v, 822.

[2] Appleton, *Speech on the Tariff*, January 23, 1833, p. 31.

[3] Benton and Barry, *A Statistical View of the Number of Sheep and an Account of the Principal Woolen Manufactories.*

The word "set" as used in this enumeration has the meaning presented in previous discussion; see above, p. 112, note 2.

Type of Fabric	Sets of Machinery	Per cent of Total
Broadcloth	344	23.1
Cassimeres	178	11.9
Satinets	574	38.5
Flannels	158	10.6
Linseys	210	14.1
Blankets, hats, and yarns	24	1.8

Obviously, almost four-fifths of the output was on fabrics which were distinctly of medium and coarse character. Broadcloth, once the chief aim of the American manufacture, was now a poor second among the several groups; and all signs pointed toward a yet further decline in its importance within the succeeding decades. Adjustment in manufacture to the production of fabrics better adapted to American conditions of production had begun, and many years were to pass before the American industry could again aspire to any large manufacture of fine cloths.

CHAPTER X

THE DEVELOPMENT OF DISTRIBUTIVE AGENCIES

THE expansion of the market for domestic wool manufactures, with the decline of importations and of household production and with the change in factory production to the lower-quality fabrics, had its more tangible side in the rise of agencies for the distribution of wool goods. While this development is to some degree confused by the intermingling of the cotton with the wool textiles, sufficient evidence is available to trace the general course of evolution in the latter industry and to picture the situation as it obtained around 1830.

The early mills apparently enjoyed but a rather narrowly restricted local market for their products. The Hartford factory sold largely through the store of the Hartford merchant, Elisha Colt; and, indeed, this continued for some time to be a common means of selling at least a portion of the factory production. Leonard & Geddes of Wilmington, Delaware, who styled their establishment a "commission store for domestic manufactures," advertised in 1812 that they had, and would continue to have, a general assortment of Du Pont's cloths and cassimeres.[1] So, too, Jeremiah Van Rensselaer of Utica, New York, kept broadcloths and satinets as agent for the Oriskany Manufacturing Company.[2] These operations, supplemented frequently by direct sales at the mills themselves,[3] sufficed for local distribution; but the

[1] *American Watchman*, January 6, 1813.

[2] *Utica Patriot*, March 21, 1815. Other cases, though seemingly of less regular correspondence with manufacturers: *The Bee* (Hudson, New York), December 20, 1808; Niles, i, 390; *Massachusetts Spy*, several instances in 1814 and 1815.

[3] *American Watchman*, September 15, 1810; *Philadelphia Democratic Press*, December 2, 1813; *Providence Gazette*, December 3, 1814; *Massachusetts Spy*, August 3, 1814.

Occasionally a well-known manufacturer might have even wider personal influence. For example, a tailor in Utica, New York, advertised in 1812 the receipt of cloths from Arthur Scholfield, then located in Pittsfield, Massachusetts (*Columbian Gazette*, November 3, 1812).

thriving concerns soon found it necessary to establish wider contacts.

The initial step in this development, as already intimated, came through the patriotic spirit of the times. Persons interested in aiding the new American industries established warehouses for the disposition of manufactures in several of the larger cities, — institutions which also made advances upon these products. The Philadelphia Society for the Encouragement of Domestic Manufactures seems to have been the pioneer in this movement. It was incorporated in 1807 with a capital of $10,000 and empowered to make advances either in cash or raw materials upon American manufactures, especially textiles, to the amount of half their value. The goods were to be deposited at the Society's warehouse and, after their sale, the balance above the advances was to be paid over with deductions only of the legal interest on the loan and a 5 per cent commission.[1] Similar institutions were soon erected at Baltimore and Alexandria.[2] That they proved to be among the most useful investments of patriotic zeal is indicated by their financial success or by the growth in their sales. The Philadelphia Society during its first six years of existence paid dividends of 6 and 8 per cent; and the volume of transactions at the warehouse of the Athenian Society at Baltimore rose from a value of $17,000 in 1809 to one of $80,000 in 1812.[3]

But the success of these enterprises is perhaps still better illustrated through the imitation of their efforts by purely business concerns. Commercial undertakings of this character were also stimulated by the dislocation of normal international commerce in the period after 1807. Such new concerns — organized to sell on commission any sort of manufactures, but especially cotton and wool fabrics, and, by reason of the example or competition of the earlier Societies, to make advances upon goods deposited with them — were quickly established in such centers as Philadelphia, New York, Baltimore, and Boston, and had become quite numer-

[1] Bishop, ii, 118.

[2] There seem to have been two such warehouses in Baltimore; see *Massachusetts Spy*, July 18, 1810, and Niles, i, 461–463. As regards Alexandria, see *National Intelligencer*, July 4, 1810.

[3] Bishop, ii, 118; Niles, iii, 395.

ous before the close of the war. Perhaps as ambitious an undertaking as any was the so-called Commission Company of New York, incorporated in 1812 with a capital of $600,000. According to its announcements, it dealt in all the textiles — wool, cotton, flax, and hemp — upon which it agreed to make "liberal" advances. Agencies were erected in various cities "in such a manner as to form a Chain of Connexions, and open Channels for the Disposal of Goods to every Point of the Union;" goods received in New York were forwarded to the "appropriate and best market;" and traveling agents were employed "to exhibit Patterns and Samples of Goods in the Ware-Houses of the Company." [1] The increasing scope of business done by such companies is also suggested by the fact that the possession of a partner "generally well acquainted" with Ohio and the western country was considered a point worth calling to the attention of possible clients.[2]

After the close of the War of 1812, and more particularly after the period of distress which followed hard upon the peace, came a development of even greater significance, the transference of various enterprises from the distribution of foreign cloths to that of domestic fabrics. A case in point is that of A. & A. Lawrence, for years thereafter a famous house in the cotton and wool-textile trade. Previously it had been engaged over a considerable period solely in the sale of foreign goods, but after 1816 it came gradually to deal in American fabrics, cotton and woolen, selling on commission.[3] Merchants began to turn their faces away from the sea, and to find in the increasing industrial development of the country an ever-broadening field for their activities. Probably not unconnected with this change was the rise of the agent-auction system in the sale of imported fabrics.[4]

Now the establishment of new commission houses proceeded rapidly. Typical of their experiences is that of Joshua Clapp, a graduate of the house of Lawrence, who in 1821 set up a store in Boston.[5] His opening stock "consisted of twelve pieces of red

[1] *Providence Gazette*, May 22, 1813 and November 20, 1813.

[2] *Ibid.*, February 5, 1814; this advertisement pertained largely to cotton goods, but the concern also dealt in wool fabrics.

[3] Appleton, *Memoir of Abbott Lawrence*, p. 7.

[4] See above, pp. 156–160.

[5] *Massachusetts Spy*, January 17, 1821.

flannel, manufactured by Abraham Marland, of Andover; about the same quantity from the mill of Nathaniel Stevens, also of Andover; a few pieces of heavy, unsaleable specimens of American broadcloth, from the Crowinshield mill in Danvers, I think, and a bale of American cotton cloth (though it may have been of India manufacture) . . . to fill up the shelves. Once in ten days or two weeks, the stock was replenished or increased, by the receipt of goods manufactured in the meantime in the factories. These were brought from Andover to Boston in a one-horse wagon, each load consisting of from twelve to twenty pieces of flannel." At the start the accounts were only three in number, but in a year or two they had expanded to twelve or more; and thereafter the concern enjoyed a considerable measure of prosperity.[1] Besides this establishment of Clapp's, other leading companies organized in this period were Lewis Tappan & Company; Tucker, Sayles & Hitchcock; and Joel Carter & Company, the last of whom advertised at one time that he had consignments from ninety to a hundred different factories.[2] Most of these firms had their head office in Boston, near by the important wool-manufacturing centers; but some commission merchants located in other cities. When Bela Tiffany, who had been connected with Samuel Slater in the cotton manufacture at Dudley, entered the commission business together with his brother, Lyman, and one Samuel Wyman, they established their central office in Baltimore, and had branch houses in New York and Boston.[3] Tucker, Sayles & Hitchcock also had a New York office. However, up through 1830 Boston maintained a distinct leadership in the systematic distribution of domestic cloths; and not for some years thereafter did New York begin to draw ahead.[4]

[1] Emmons, "Early Commission Houses," *Bulletin*, 1891, p. 314.

[2] Shaw, *Wool Trade of the United States*, p. 29; *Massachusetts Spy*, February 12, 1823 (Carter's advertisement).

[3] *Massachusetts Spy*, January 22, 1817; Ammidown's *Historical Collections*, i, 477.

[4] It may also be observed that in a commercial directory of the period, that edited by Kayser in 1823, the differentiation among various merchandising concerns is carried much farther in the case of Boston than in that of other cities. This seems to indicate a greater development of the trade in that region.

The early mills seem at first to have sent their products to several commission houses, the number of such houses employed and the quantity of goods sent to each varying from year to year. But from this practice it was an easy and wholly reasonable step to the employment of a single merchant for the sale of a mill's total output. Thus we find the concern of Lewis Tappan & Company in the twenties acting as the selling agent for the Wolcott Manufacturing Company, which had mills at Southbridge and Woodstock, Massachusetts;[1] and the mill records of the Stevens mill at Andover and of the Slater plant at Webster show that at least from time to time a single selling house took the whole production of these establishments.[2] In fact, I am inclined to think that by 1830 this practice was by no means uncommon in the American industry.

Among the various points of contact between the factory and the commission merchant or selling agent, none is of so great significance in the present connection as the credit relation. Apparently the earlier practice of making advances on goods consigned for sale continued without change throughout this period. Advertisements of commission houses frequently carried the formula: "Cash liberally advanced on consignments."[3] But this was only one of the great liaisons. A less satisfactory type is described by Mr. George W. Bond. When the demand for wool was particularly keen — as in the period 1824–1828, according to Mr. Bond — "manufacturers had to go into the country to secure their supply for the year. This could be bought only for cash. To enable themselves to do this, many were obliged to mortgage their mills and machinery to their selling agents. . . . Sooner or later nearly all of these mills failed and their agents were obliged to take possession under their mortgages."[4] Illustrations of this result are not wanting, though probably causes other than that

[1] Shaw, *Wool Trade*, pp. 29, 33; Ammidown's *Historical Collections*, ii, 371.

[2] Records of M. T. Stevens & Sons Company, and of S. Slater & Sons Company.

[3] For examples, see *Massachusetts Spy*, February 18, 1818; January 10 and 17, 1821.

[4] *Report on Wool and Manufactures of Wool*, 1887, p. lviii.

The conditions in the purchase of wool as suggested by this case are of interest in view of the trend toward improvement of methods in wool-dealing, which was evident at about this period (see above, pp. 82–84).

given by Mr. Bond contributed to the same end. Joshua Clapp in time controlled and managed the Litchfield mill, for the products of which he had acted as a distributor.[1] Amos Lawrence was treasurer and general agent for the Amesbury Flannel Manufacturing Company in 1823.[2] The Wolcott Manufacturing Company in 1831 passed into the hands of Sayles & Hitchcock, who incorporated as the Hamilton Woolen Company, with Hitchcock as president, Sayles as clerk, and these two and another as directors.[3] Finally, in the floating of new companies, the commission merchants played an important part. According to Mr. Bond, the stock of such concerns was largely taken by these houses.[4] In at least one case, the formation of the Middlesex Woolen Company, the evidence is quite clear. Here the trading house of W. & S. Lawrence was the prime mover in the enterprise, and remained for years closely allied to that concern.[5]

But commission houses apparently did not confine themselves always to selling on commission alone. Merchants of somewhat similar position in the importing field had been accustomed to purchase goods outright, and presumably this example had influence in the distribution of domestic fabrics. A case in point concerns one of the earliest commission houses, that of Mr. Joshua Clapp. "During the summer of 1821," Mr. Clapp said in later years, "commission No. 3, the proprietor's own, furnished the largest part of our business. Having ascertained the probable amount of importations in plaid worsted goods for the coming autumn, and finding the quantity limited, the merchant (Mr. Clapp) exercised his full credit and bought up in advance the stock due in Boston and largely in New York. As the season advanced, these goods were sold at a profit."[6] Probably this was

[1] Emmons, *Bulletin*, 1891, p. 314.

[2] Kayser, *Commercial Directory*, 1823, p. 108.

[3] Ammidown's *Historical Collections*, ii, 374.

To those above instanced, there might be added the case of the Fitchburg Woolen Mill in which at one time Farnum & Kimball, commission merchants of Boston, became part owners (Vose, in *History of Worcester County*, i, 271).

[4] *Report on Wool and Manufactures of Wool*, 1887, p. lvii.

[5] Hunt, *American Merchants*, ii, 372; Lothrop, *Life of William Lawrence*, p. 16.

[6] *Bulletin*, 1891, p. 315.

not a conspicuous feature in the business of commission houses, and indeed such a practice might easily lead to a situation of conflicting interests. However, perhaps we have here an indication of the manner in which commission houses changed into more independent concerns.

Meanwhile, agencies other than the commission houses and selling agents were springing up. With the extension of the market for wool fabrics, it became necessary or advantageous for selling houses, located chiefly in the larger cities, to turn over a portion of their work to others, to concerns who would make it their business to be familiar with the varying conditions of the divers smaller communities, and who would act as relayers in the transmission of goods to the increasing number of retailers.[1] This elaboration of the distributive system apparently did not occur before the twenties; at least there is no trace of it prior to that time. In that decade, however, one finds such a merchant as Joshua Clapp dealing with regular customers, Isaac Osgood, Charles B. Shaw, and others, who are described as "prosperous and solid jobbers, influencing and holding largely the country trade."[2] A Committee of the New York legislature likewise includes them in a brief description of the dry-goods sales organization which it incorporates in one of its reports. The jobbers, it says, "are an intermediate grade of merchants, between the wholesale and importing merchants and the retail shopkeepers." But seemingly the distributing system had not as yet settled into what was later to be its normal form; for, as the description continues, these jobbers "purchase largely at auctions, at the package sales, from wholesale importers, and in such other ways as they can obtain merchandise on reasonable terms. Some of them are also importers to a limited extent, and others occasionally receive goods on consignment."[3] Still it is obvious that, generally speaking, a commercial organization of somewhat modern character had developed to take care of the growing internal trade in wool manufactures.

[1] These intermediate merchants were chiefly located in the larger cities, especially Boston, New York, and Baltimore.

[2] Emmons, *Bulletin*, 1891, p. 316.

[3] *New York House Journal*, 1829, p. 393.

That the degree of development in this system would differ between the several sections of the country need hardly be suggested. Just as the industrial organization in the West went through many of the stages which had earlier formed the course of evolution in the East, so in a measure did the western commercial organization tread in the footsteps of eastern experience. As late as 1832 many of the factories in the middle states were still selling largely to local consumers,—and sometimes not even for cash. For example, the Xenia Woolen Factory of Greene County, Ohio, reported that "one-third of the goods made are sold at the factory, principally in barter for wool, provisions, and in lieu of wages to the workmen." [1] And the story was the same for the Licking County and Springsborough mills.[2] Indeed, considerable local distribution of their products was for many years thereafter a feature in the operation of many western mills.

Before we leave this phase of our subject, however, something must be said of that type of distributive agency — "auctions" and "package sales" — mentioned just above, and discussed in connection with the import trade.[3] The auction system was, in fact, *l'enfant terrible* of the whole distributive organization. It was a serious disturbing factor, not only on account of the instability which it gave to values, but because it broke in upon the arrangements made and being made by the other agencies. As one observer put it: "A greater evil to the regular resident merchants and manufacturers of New York (and indeed of other cities) than the auction system does not exist under the sun." [4] The import trade, as previous analysis has indicated, was most seriously affected, since there the auction method of sale played directly into the hands of the foreign merchant, relieving him from the necessity of maintaining any considerable organization within the country; but the commerce in domestic goods was also embarrassed to a very considerable degree. Dealers in American fabrics found themselves faced with a severe competition, and a

[1] McLane's *Report*, ii, 862.

[2] *Ibid.* The Old Town Factory, Old Town, Ohio, made the report that it "carded last year 6000 pounds of wool for household manufactures, and dressed, and dyed, and finished 1500 yards in addition."

[3] See above, pp. 156–160.

[4] Niles, xxxiii, 388.

competition which tended to make all their business extremely speculative. Moreover, they could not control the jobbers, who instead sought bargains in the auction sales. Unless these jobbers were purchasers, remarked the New York legislative committee above mentioned, these sales "would be but small, compared to what they now are." And, again, these jobbing houses complained because their business too was seriously disrupted: country dealers and shopkeepers went over the jobbers' heads and bought directly of the auctioneers.[1] So prevalent did this become, that the retail trade was itself rendered subject to violent fluctuations. Speaking of a certain type of cotton fabric — but there is no reason to suspect different conditions in the woolen trade — a retailer wrote: "I have known prints to sell at 28 cents and go down to 21 cents in less than five minutes. I have known an article that was not very plenty, to advance in a few days from 35 to 65 cents, by the competition in the auction room. And that article in a few weeks after sold in large quantities at 22 to 25 cents; and had it not been for the auctions, they would never have been higher than 35 cents, as they could be well afforded at that price." These fluctuations, he said, kept the retailer always with one eye on the auction sales instead of both on his legitimate business, and always readjusting his prices lest his competitor across the street, who had just replenished his stock at the auctions, should undersell him.[2] While these accounts are probably exaggerated, for suppression of these sales was a subject of much debate in this period, there can be little doubt that the system

[1] *New York Assembly Journal*, 1829, pp. 392–393. See also *Emigrant's Guide*, by an Old Scene Painter, 1816, p. 48; and Flint's Letters, in *Thwaites's Travels*, ix, 59. However, there is some indication that regular merchants dealing in domestic textiles were not averse to using the auction system themselves if it served their purpose. For an example involving cotton goods, see Appleton, *Introduction of the Power Loom*, p. 12.

[2] Niles, xxxiv, 350.

In a private letter, dated September 27, 1833, Mr. David Campbell, Jr., New York agent for the Pontoosuc Manufacturing Company of Pittsfield, expressed his concern over the effects of the auction system: "I am a good deal staggered at the vast quantity (of cloth) thrown into auction, but the holders must realize upon them to pay duty. That is the squeezer upon them and what is our safety in future?" (Letter reproduced in the *Pittsfield Sun*, December 26, 1895.)

was a cause of substantial disturbance and unsettlement in American commercial transactions.[1]

Yet despite condemnation of the system by various advocates of American manufacturing development, it is interesting to note that domestic manufacturers and merchants of textiles came to utilize this method of distribution in increasing volume. Certainly references to the sale of domestic wool fabrics at auction become more frequent as the years approach 1830. Typical perhaps of the manner in which American producers became interested in this form of sale is the case of Mr. Sykes, wool manufacturer of Baltimore. In 1824, "his stock being heavy," he sold some portion of his goods at public auction. Apparently the results were most satisfactory. "They so well sustained the competition with the British goods," it is stated, that he proposed in the succeeding year to dispose of a greater quantity of cloth in that manner.[2] Others followed Mr. Sykes's example. On September 12, 1826, a single auction sale was held to dispose of one hundred and sixty packages and over fifteen hundred pieces of American wool fabrics.[3] Again, several of the manufacturers who testified before the Committee on Manufactures in 1828, stated that their sales were sometimes or always effected in this manner.[4] For American textiles as a whole, moreover, data relating to sales in New York City give confirmatory evidence. These indicate that whereas in the years 1818–1820 "American Dry Goods" formed only an eighth of the total volume of "Dry Goods," by the closing years of the decade they comprised nearly one-third.[5]

[1] A memorial from the Friends of Domestic Industry in 1819 attacked auction sales of domestic goods, not merely because of their disturbing effect on prices, but also of their reaction upon quality of production. Such sales, they said, "tend to encourage the manufacture of inferior fabrics, and thereby injure the reputation of American fabrics generally" (*State Papers, Finance*, iii, 442).

The city of New York apparently was the chief center of these auction sales, although Philadelphia and Baltimore also participated in the trade. The importance of the New York dealings of this type is suggested by the figures, to be presently adduced, of "Dry Goods" sold in this manner.

[2] Niles, xxix, 49.

[3] *Ibid.*, xxxi, 116. See also *ibid.*, xxxv, 103.

[4] *State Papers, Finance*, v, 808, 817, and 819.

[5] *New York Documents, Report of the Comptroller*, 1843, pp. 130–131: "Statement showing the amount of the various kinds of goods sold at auction in the city

It is, of course, impossible even to estimate the proportion of American wool fabrics which was marketed through the auction sales, but the evidence points to a substantial, and during this period an increasing, importance of this sales method in the American trade.

Yet the alternate and better organized system of distribution was making headway even during these years, whatever the disturbing influences of the auction system. And the steady evolution of a better articulated system is of special significance in the history of wool manufacturing. The auction method, unorganized as it was in this period, was distinctly the sign of an immature market for wool fabrics. It suggested a lack of regularity in the demand for such goods and the failure of woolen factories to provide an even and orderly flow of products to the consuming areas. The elaboration of the newer system was a natural result of the growing maturity of wool-cloth manufacturing and marketing, while the development of that "intermediate grade of merchants," the jobbers, indicates the increasing geographical expansion of the trade. That the complete modern system of distribution had not been worked out before 1830 is not surprising. The manufacturing end had not as yet reached full maturity, nor had the commercial agencies had time to work out entirely their relationships with the mills and among themselves. The feature most noteworthy in the development before 1830 was: that the marketing organization manifested the effect of a widening trade in wool fabrics, the same widening trade which made possible the establishment of manufacturing upon the factory basis.

of New York, from 1818 to 1841." Averages by three-year periods are as follows in thousands of dollars:

Years	American Dry Goods	Foreign Dry Goods	Total of all Goods
1818–20	$922	$6567	$11,707
1821–23	1564	8745	14,420
1824–26	3166	11,851	20,394
1827–29	4320	12,426	22,535
1830–32	4647	9546	20,921

CHAPTER XI

THE RISE OF FACTORY PRODUCTION

1. *The Development of the Factory.*

THE examination which has been made into the technical progress within the wool manufacture and especially into the changes that were taking place in the market for domestic cloths, has unavoidably given advance notice of the central feature in the industry's development up to 1830: the rise of the factory. In 1760 no wool-working factory existed, merely a widespread household production of woolen fabrics,—to which the numerous fulling mills lent their aid, — and a minor manufacture of worsted cloths upon the handicraft system. By 1830, however, production of wool cloth in factories was undoubtedly the most significant, if not the predominant method of wool-working at that time. In volume of manufacture, factory output might not hold first place by reason of the continued large production of household goods in the less advanced sections of the country; but the market dominated by the factory was steadily expanding, and all signs pointed to the factory's ultimate full ascendancy. The steps by which this transformation came about, the source of the capital and the character of labor attracted to the new enterprises, the magnitude of factory production at that period, and the characteristics of the typical factory of that era, — these are the matters which now invite consideration.[1]

[1] The exact definition of a "factory" is not here a matter of prime importance; nor does it seem necessary to follow Clark in differentiating between a "mill" and a "factory" (Clark, p. 447). However, Clark is right in that it is difficult to determine just when a concern becomes a "factory." "It is not a question," he says, "of specialization, nor ownership, nor completeness of process, nor size, but rather depends upon a combination of equipment and organization" (*ibid.*, p. 447). I am inclined to stress these latter features: a complete or nearly complete mechanical equipment for turning raw wool into finished cloth, and an organization in which the proprietor is occupied with management alone and the workers with supervision of actual manufacturing operations. The latter consideration, of course, is tied up intimately with the matter of size, but organization is the more significant factor.

In tracing the steps by which the manufacture of woolen fabrics passed from the household into the factory, it is easy to become too dogmatic, to give the appearance of a precise series of changes when, as a matter of fact, such regularity of development did not obtain. Neither here, nor, as I suspect, in most similar developments, was there the same usual sequence of forms in all sections of the country and at all times. Exceptions to any generalization are frequent. Nevertheless, in the rise of the American wool-working factory before 1830, certain organizations are often met with at one stage and during a limited period, which with quite frequent occurrence give way somewhat later to a different form. One may therefore arrange a sequence of considerable validity, admittedly not a series through which each and every establishment was bound to go, yet one which represents the normal and typical history for the whole industry.[1]

After the introduction of the new technical equipment, the first manufacture of cloth for sale took place in establishments operating on a very small scale. Indeed, the method of production was more nearly akin to the handicraft than to the factory system. A typical case is that of James Scholfield. In 1802 he came to North Andover, Massachusetts, and set up a manufacture of woolen cloth. His house, which in fact still stands, was scarcely larger than the ordinary country woodshed. He devoted a part of this house, or a part of the house and an out-building, to spinning-jacks and a loom, or perhaps two looms. With the aid of these mechanisms, and assisted by his family, he produced a little broadcloth.[2] Similarly, Samuel Mayall, who contests with the Scholfields priority in the introduction of the carding machine into the United States, later conducted a shop for wool-carding and cloth-dressing in Gray, Maine, and manufactured cloth in a small way.[3] Even as late as 1812, or shortly after that, two Englishmen "reg-

[1] Tryon (p. 272) gives a fairly workable series of stages: (1) Home absolutely independent of factory; (2) Factory supplementary to home; (3) Factory preparatory for home; and (4) Factory independent of home. Yet, as will appear, these stages are subject to some emendation and interpretation.

[2] Bagnall, p. 308. The attempt does not appear to have been successful financially, perhaps by reason of its location so near the port of Boston.

[3] North, *Bulletin*, 1899, pp. 215–216.

ularly brought up at the manufacturing of woolen cloth in all its branches" were setting up in Kennebunk, Maine, a comparatively small-scale production of such goods, while conducting the ordinary business of custom wool-carding.[1] Establishments of this sort, where the proprietor worked by himself, or at least only with the assistance of his family or of one or two helpers, and where the product could have been intended only for the local market, were but little in advance of the purely handicraft shops of the colonial worsted industry. They now possessed or had access to a machine for the carding operation and, in some cases, the new spinning machine; but surely they were not factories.

However, it was around the recently acquired carding machine, or around the combination of this apparatus with the older fulling mill, that the larger establishments were destined to grow. One can find various cases in illustration. For example, the Hazards of South Kingston, Rhode Island, first purchased a half-interest in a fulling mill, then they added a carding machine, and after the break with England acquired further equipment for the complete manufacture of cloth.[2] John Scholfield, Jr., erected a custom carding mill at Jewett City, Connecticut, in 1804 or 1805. Gradually he added other machinery, until at the close of the War of 1812 he had a full complement of apparatus for the manufacture of wool cloths.[3] The Sawyer Woolen Mills of Dover, New Hampshire, arose in a similar manner, but at a considerably later period. In 1823 Alfred I. Sawyer commenced the business of carding and cloth-dressing, and nine years later added a single set of machinery for the manufacture of flannels.[4] Of course, other concerns, such as those of the Du Ponts at Brandywine, Maryland, and of Abraham Marland at North Andover, Massachusetts, apparently began at once with a complete mill equipment. Indeed, once the

[1] Remich, *History of Kennebunk*, pp. 237–241. Other instances are numerous: James Saunderson at New Ipswich, New Hampshire (Gould, *History of New Ipswich*, p. 230); Arthur Scholfield at Pittsfield, Massachusetts; Albert Stone at Grafton, Massachusetts (*Massachusetts Spy*, August 3, 1814); Daniel Stearns at Pittsfield (Field, *History of Pittsfield*, p. 20), among others.

[2] Gammell, *Life of Rowland G. Hazard*, p. 7.

[3] Bagnall, p. 458.

[4] *Awards and Claims, Exhibition of 1876*, p. 209.

industry was on its feet in a given area, such was the normal procedure,—as might be expected. But during the period of incubation, so to speak, the process of growth was intermittent and slow, and cases of the gradual change from carding and fulling shops to full-fledged factories are sufficiently numerous to authenticate this course of development as the usual and natural one.[1]

The halting development of these mills is further illustrated by the amount of custom work which they performed and the extent to which they employed workers outside their own walls. Besides the custom carding and fulling which one would of course expect of them, other operations were undertaken by the new enterprises for local patrons.[2] The Abbotts, who bought the old Scholfield plant at Andover, seem only to have spun for customers, and Amena Braman of Dudley, Massachusetts, advertised only to card and spin for his patrons, perhaps because in neither case did these establishments have looms, or at least surplus weaving capacity.[3] More generally, however, the mills were ready to carry the manufacturing process as far as their patrons desired. Arthur Scholfield announced in 1810 that "customers can have their wool made into Rolls, Roping, or Cloth, as best suits them."[4] The proprietors of the Pittsfield and Housatonic factories at Pittsfield

[1] Other cases: Bagnall, pp. 229, 285–286, 424; Taft, pp. 44, 45; *Pittsfield Sun*, May 27, 1813; Abbott, *Women in Industry*, p. 46; *Worcester Book*, p. 91; Field, *History of Middlesex County*, 1819, p. 59; Temple, *History of Whately, Massachusetts*, pp. 170–171; *History of Androscoggin County, Maine*, p. 385; *Census of 1880*, xx, 389; North, *Bulletin*, 1899, pp. 215–216; American Woolen Company, *Sketch of Mills*, p. 108; Temple, *History of Palmer, Massachusetts*, p. 270; Larned, *History of Windham County, Connecticut*, ii, 539.

Kayser in his *Directory* of 1823 seems to have caught the beginnings of factory development in Maine, long known as a state of many woolen mills. He writes (p. 58): the carding-fulling mills "which abound in every part of the country," besides carding machines and finishing apparatus, "occasionally likewise contain a spinning frame, and sometimes one or two looms."

[2] This sort of activity on the part of the early mills has also been referred to in the discussion of the declining household manufacture (see above, p. 182) since it really lies intermediate between purely household and purely factory work. The importance of such action in the development of the factory warrants some further comment here.

[3] Bailey, *Andover*, p. 594; *Massachusetts Spy*, June 8, 1814. See also *American Watchman*, July 17, 1813; and *Massachusetts Spy*, June 21, 1815.

[4] *Pittsfield Sun*, May 9, 1810, and July 6, 1811.

advertised in 1814 that "arrangements are making to take in wool to card, spin, or weave on shares." [1] Perhaps as typical a case as any is that revealed by an advertisement of 1808 with respect to a concern of New Hartford, New York: [2]

> Jacob and Lewis Sherril have erected machines for picking, breaking, carding, and spinning wool.
> Picking, breaking, oiling, and carding — 8¢ lb. cash, or 10¢ credited.
> Spinning warp — 10¢ a run; filling, 8¢.
> Will pay cash for wool, and keep on hand Yarn and Rolls.
> Will also Weave any width, from 5 to 10 quarters.

In such devious ways, by carrying through various processes, by manufacturing on shares, and, in general, by supplementing and coöperating with the earlier household production, factories secured their start. Gradually they gathered the strength necessary to stand alone, especially through the growth of a market. This temporizing, it may be added, was not always a phenomenon of the first years in development alone. Not infrequently manufacturers continued to lean somewhat upon the local demands for commission work or for production of cloth on shares, even after they had been able to establish a relatively wide market for their products. This was especially true of concerns located in country districts, where the practice of household manufacture persisted most tenaciously, and in periods of depression, when the general market requirements were curtailed. Moreover, as the industry moved westward, these phenomena were repeated. For example, the "new steam wool carding factory" of Lexington, Kentucky, announced in 1829 that it would card or spin on commission, as well as keep on hand a supply of fabrics, from the coarsest negro-cloth to the "finest (fabric) that can be made of the best Merino

[1] *Pittsfield Sun*, June 9, 1814. Other instances: Oriskany Woolen Factory (*Columbian Gazette*, Utica, New York, May 28, 1811); Abner Cunningham (*Orange County Gazette*, Goshen, New York, September 6, 1814); factory at North-Killingworth, Connecticut (*Middlesex Gazette*, June 16, 1814); Stockbridge Woolen Factory (*Pittsfield Sun*, May 20, 1814).

[2] *Utica Gazette* (Utica, New York), July 26, 1808.

Other cases of similar character: *Documentary History of American Industrial Society*, ii, 329–330; Spear, *History of North Adams*, pp. 73, 92; Sibley, *History of Union, Maine*, p. 109; Remich, *History of Kennebunk, Maine*, p. 249; Lippincott, *History of Manufactures in the Ohio Valley*, p. 75.

wool."[1] But even in the eastern region, instances where the new-sprung factory as late as this was still catering to the needs of the local household manufacture are not wanting.

To satisfy the other deficiency wherein the early factory failed of entire self-dependence and of the complete organization of the modern plant — the "putting-out" of certain operations — contact was again had with the household industry. The factory always contained the carding and finishing processes, and the spinning jenny or jack early formed part of its equipment. The jenny, to be sure, was not unknown to the household industry; but, for some reason, perhaps the impossibility of close control over the operation and a consequent greater unevenness in the yarn, spinning never (or almost never) seems to have been "put out" to household workers.[2] Not so, however, with weaving. Even John Scholfield, who had woven cloth himself and so was competent to supervise factory weaving, possessed no looms in his Stonington (Connecticut) mill. The woolen yarns of his production were woven on hand looms outside, either on his account or on that of individuals who had purchased yarn from him.[3] Dwight's account of the mill started by Colonel Humphreys gives an equipment of only four broad and eight narrow looms for factory work, and states that "most of the weaving has been done in private families."[4] As late as 1827 it is reported of the Glenham (New York) woolen factory that approximately thirty persons out of a total of one hundred and fifty were employed "without" the mill.[5]

[1] *Documentary History of American Industrial Society*, ii, 335.

[2] The Hartford factory appears to have sent out the wool to be spun (cf. above). Also Rowland Hazard once said in reminiscence of his early life, "In 1816 and later I used to employ scores of women to spin at their homes" (North, in Davis's *New England States*, p. 204). These are the only indications of such operations that I have found. Indeed, there is no hint of such work elsewhere.

The reason I give for this situation might be criticized in the light of English experience, where spinning was put out to household workers for many years. However, the weaving in that case, at least in Yorkshire, was in the hands of particularly skillful workers, the small "manufacturers." They could make allowance for irregularities in the yarn when perhaps American weavers, less well-trained, could not.

[3] Bagnall, p. 424.

[4] Dwight, *Travels*, iii, 392, 393.

[5] Niles, xxxiv, 76.

SAMUEL SLATER

"Father" of the cotton manufacture in the United States, but also a pioneer in the allied wool manufacture

DAVID HUMPHREYS

An early enthusiast for the merino sheep and the founder of an early wool-manufacturing establishment

Finally, the extensive use of hand-loom weaving in the Philadelphia district should be noted. The practice followed in that area of employing hand-loom weavers was begun in this period, and was occasioned probably by forces similar to those that caused its appearance elsewhere; but the long persistence of this practice in Philadelphia—that is, for a considerable time after 1830—gave that region subsequently something of a peculiar status.[1] While the evidence available does not indicate that weaving outside the walls of the factory was the prevailing method of production, it does show that this practice was by no means an uncommon affair until the middle twenties at least.[2] The occasion of the decline in hand-loom weaving thereafter was the appearance and wider adoption of the power loom. Hand-loom weaving, if performed by skilled handicraftsmen, as was the case in Yorkshire, could compete with power-weaving, — at least until the mechanical loom had been substantially improved over its original form; but hand-weaving in the household, as occurred here, had to give way more quickly.[3]

To summarize the general development, we may say: that the American woolen factory found its origin in carding-fulling mills frequently enough to suggest this course of evolution as the normal one. With the custom business of these shops as a secure basis, manufacturing expanded, apparently at first only as a quasi-handicraft occupation, but soon on a broader scale. Yet the persistence of the household system of manufacture made advantageous the retention, for a number of years, of a rather close connection with the needs of that production, — through the acceptance of commission work in various forms for the inhabitants of the surrounding country. Again, the factory did not at

[1] Wilson, *Picture of Philadelphia*, 1824, p. 11; Niles, xxviii, 159; Freedley, *Philadelphia and its Manufactures*, p. 233.

[2] Other cases of outside weaving: Taft, pp. 44, 45; Bagnall, p. 229; *American Watchman* (Baltimore, Maryland), August 21, 1813; Wheelock, in Chapin's *Address*, pp. 134–135; Bishop, ii, 207; Greene, *Providence Plantations*, p. 71; Niles, i, 292; Massachusetts Historical Society *Collections*, 2nd Ser., iii, 263; "Petition of the Citizens engaged in manufactories on the Brandywine, December 9, 1815," in *Congressional Papers*, 1806–1816.

[3] As to the English case, see Heaton, pp. 357–358; *British Documents*, 1840 [43], p. 587; and Clapham, *Bulletin*, 1908, pp. 308–309.

once acquire self-dependence, maintaining for some time, especially in weaving, a reliance upon outside help. But the youthful establishments step by step gathered strength and breadth of action until by 1830, except in the more western parts of the country, they had attained a position not unlike that of more modern enterprises.[1]

2. *The Source of Capital and the Course of Profits.*

The deficiency of capital was asserted by Gallatin to be "the only powerful obstacle" to the "introduction and advancement of manufactures in America;"[2] and in the wool-manufacturing industry too this scarcity was a deterrent upon a rapid extension of production. The gradual evolution of many factories suggests the difficulties in the situation. These mills apparently were expanded out of profits which were squeezed from the unfavorable

[1] General comparison of the course of development in the United States with that abroad cannot be made. For the most part information on the foreign development is scanty; and, besides, conditions differed much from area to area. Within England alone, the course of advance in the West of England seems to have varied much from that in Yorkshire. In the former region, a hesitant and gradual development such as that which came in the United States appears to have taken place, although it is not at all evident that the carding-fulling mills served the same purpose as in this country. For the Yorkshire district, the firm establishment of the handicraft operations — shops of the Yorkshire "clothiers" — made for a dissimilar evolution. As late as 1840, the organization in this region is described as follows: "All the processes to which the wool is submitted previous to that of spinning, are carried on in factories, called 'scribbling and slubbing mills.' The spinning of the yarn, and the weaving of the cloth, though sometimes carried on in factories (especially in the case of superfine cloths made in the town of Leeds), are generally performed in the cloth-maker's family; whilst all the finishing processes subsequent to weaving . . . are completed in factories" (*British Documents*, 1840 [43], p. 528). The "scribbling and slubbing mills" would of course correspond roughly to our carding mills, though perhaps with the operation of roping or slubbing with the billy added. Incidentally, it is odd to find that some of these "scribbling and slubbing mills" were put up and owned by groups of clothiers, who apparently had all their wool prepared at them. At the other end of the fabrication, stood the finishing "factories," which probably were comparable with our fulling mills. But in between stood the independent clothier, who indeed clung long to his position. When real factories came, they apparently had to supersede the whole earlier organization. However, as already intimated, evidence is scarce respecting even this English development.

[2] *State Papers, Finance*, ii, 430.

market conditions of the times. But one wishes also to learn the source of those initial supplies of capital by means of which manufacture was started. It is of course impossible to ascertain all the sources of these first increments, and especially to estimate their respective contributions; yet there is opportunity to catch glimpses of the transfer of capital to the woolen industry.

A considerable amount of capital was attracted to the youthful manufacture from foreign trade. The Hazards of South Kingston, Rhode Island, had long been interested in commerce, but gradually Rowland Hazard, the head of the family at the time, drew away from it, and began to pay attention, first, to carding and fulling, and later to wool manufacture also.[1] So also the Derby of Salem, Massachusetts, who brought over a large flock of merino sheep and soon after erected a factory, came from a prominent family of shipowners and traders.[2] Here and elsewhere it is evident that the capital amassed and the profits earned through the commercial ventures of the troubled period before 1815 were finding new employment. And the latter was to be found not only in the rising cotton manufacture, but in the still younger factory production of wool cloths.[3]

In yet another way commercial capital found its way into the new industry, when firms that had been engaged in the import trade turned their eyes inland as their business hesitated and then halted in the period of troubled commerce. The Hartford factory had numbered among its important stockholders, George Phillips and Company and Peter Colt and Company, merchant

[1] Gammell, *Life of Rowland G. Hazard*, pp. 41–46. Hazard is said to have known nothing about the manufacture, and to have had to take a partner, Knowles, who superintended the operations (Bagnall, pp. 285–289).

[2] Bishop, ii, 195.

[3] Other instances: Providence Woolen Manufacturing Company, funds secured from "men possessed of capital," presumably Providence traders (Field, *State of Rhode Island and Providence Plantations*, iii, 361); Newport capital in a Plainfield, Connecticut, mill (Larned, *History of Windham County, Connecticut*, ii, 427); Quaddic Manufacturing Company of Thompson, Connecticut, capital from Rhode Island men of means (*ibid.*, ii, 439).

For cotton manufacture, see Clark, pp. 367–369; Copeland, *Cotton Manufacturing Industry*, pp. 3–5, 196.

traders of the town.[1] The Merino Wool Factory Company, of Dudley, Massachusetts, similarly had included among its shareholders the Boston mercantile firm of French & Everett.[2] Arthur W. Magill, the prime mover in the Middletown (Connecticut) mill, had been interested in a wholesale importing store of that town.[3] Indeed, the testimony of a British cloth exporter in 1828 was undoubtedly accurate; he said, "I know many respectable merchants in New York, Baltimore, and Boston, who used to be importers . . . who have turned their capital to manufacture the cloth in their own country."[4]

From other lines of business, there were some contributions. Conspicuous among them are the examples of Du Pont in Delaware, who, after success in the manufacture of gunpowder, turned in 1811 to take advantage of the opportunities in the production of fine woolens and ultimately possessed three woolen factories;[5] and of Samuel Slater, the early prosperous cotton manufacturer, who in 1814 became interested in wool-cloth production at Dudley, Massachusetts.[6] Less conspicuous, but probably as numerous as any of the foregoing (perhaps barring commercial capital) were the cases where farmers, like Delano Abbott, of Rockville, Connecticut, began the manufacture on a small scale out of their slender savings.[7]

Yet, as has been suggested, the profits accruing to the industry,

[1] Maine Historical Society, *Collections*, iv, 55–56.

[2] Ammidown's *Historical Collections*, i, 436.

[3] *Middlesex Gazette*, March 9, 1804.

[4] *British Documents*, 1828 [515], p. 43. The "managers" of the Middlesex Company of Lowell had been importers for many years (*Awards and Claims, Exhibition of 1876*, p. 187).

[5] Bishop, ii, 171.

[6] Ammidown's *Historical Collections*, i, 468. Slater entered into partnership with one Edward Howard, an Englishman skilled in the woolen manufacture. In 1824, the Village Factory, established in 1824 at Dudley, passed into Slater's hands (*ibid.*, i, 437).

[7] With regard to Abbott, see Burr, *Connecticut Magazine*, vi, 64. The Stevens mill at North Andover had as its original promotors local farmers and a country doctor. Again, a mill in West Cambridge (now Arlington), Massachusetts, was bought by the local tavern-keeper (*History of Middlesex County*, iii, 183).

especially in the period of interrupted commerce and of rising prices, were as much responsible for the successful development of factories as the increments of capital flowing from outside sources. One could begin in a small way and build more widely out of earnings. And in fact the resources necessary to commence operations in the wool manufacture were by no means great. In one instance, an enterprise located at North Adams, Massachusetts, the initial expenditure on plant was only $1100, — $300 for the water-power site and $800 for the construction of the mill.[1] This was probably about the minimum. However, if the start were made, as so frequently was the case, through the erection of a carding-fulling mill, the initial outlay of course could not have been considerable. Once started in such modest ways, the concern must rely on the profits in subsequent years to consolidate its position and expand its operations; and not infrequently in the early stages of the factory production of wool cloths, returns were high. A mill near Newport, Delaware, was reported in 1810 by one close to the concern to have cleared 25 per cent annually on the capital employed.[2] Another at Danville, Pennsylvania, is said to have yielded 40 per cent.[3] Nathaniel Stevens of North Andover apparently cleared five dollars on every piece (sixty yards) of flannel made at his mills.[4] In addition, there is negative evidence in the fact that no mill seems to have failed during the period before 1815. There is little likelihood, to be sure, that the mills throughout the country made earnings that averaged the figures above adduced. Yet unquestionably returns were good; and this circumstance assisted materially in the growth of the new enterprises.

In subsequent years, in the period of readjustment that followed the peace and even in the twenties, profits were probably on a lower level, at times undoubtedly displaced by actual losses. Statements of extraordinary earnings cease to appear, and instead there are constant complaints to Congress—partly perhaps for

[1] Spear, *History of North Adams*, p. 73.

[2] *National Intelligencer*, August 6, 1810, quoting the *Philadelphia Aurora*.

[3] Warden, *Account of the United States*, iii, 268.

[4] Clark, p. 376; quoting *Bagnall Papers*. This refers to the year 1816, and presumably profits were even higher in the earlier years.

effect—of the peculiarly great difficulties in the wool manufacture. A concern in Walpole, Massachusetts, started in 1810 with a capital of $16,000 to $20,000, is said to have wholly exhausted its capital by 1817.[1] A mill in South Kingston, Rhode Island, apparently that of the Hazards, is reported to have been run at a loss of 15 per cent in the decade 1814 to 1824.[2] But seemingly conditions improved as the years went by. With the expansion of the domestic market, giving greater stability to the industry, and with the improvement in methods of manufacture, giving greater freedom from embarrassing importations, there is every probability that such should have been the case. To be sure, there is evidence to the contrary. One factory in Delaware stated its profits to have been 12 per cent in the period 1815–1824, 8 per cent in 1824–1828, and 6 per cent in 1828–1831; and another manufacturer estimated in 1832 that all money up to that time invested in American woolen mills had been lost to the original owners.[3] But in the same document, McLane's *Report on Manufactures*, there are many cases of substantial profits in the years just preceding. The loss of the South Kingston mill above noted had been turned into a net gain of 12¾ per cent in the years 1824 to 1832. Satinet mills in Maine were said to yield 15 to 20 per cent, if properly conducted; and in several other cases earnings of 10 or 12 per cent were reported.[4] The balance of the testimony clearly indicates a marked improvement in the industry in the latter part of the twenties and the beginning of the next decade. In other words, the data available as to profits suggest, as does information regarding technical development and marketing conditions, that by 1830 the industry was well established

[1] McLane's *Report on Manufactures*, i, 396.

[2] *Ibid.*, i, 964.

[3] *Ibid.*, ii, 672; and i, 68. See also *State Papers, Finance*, v, 808 *seq.*, where several manufacturers at a tariff hearing in 1828 testified that they had been losing money.

[4] McLane's *Report*, i, 23; and i, 290, 919, 1004, 1017; ii, 69, 467. See also Clark, p. 377; and *Congressional Documents*, 27th Cong., 2nd Sess., *House Report, No. 461*, pp. 56–57. There is, of course, the probability that in some of these cases, insufficient deductions were made to cover depreciation and obsolescence. But one cannot gauge the general significance, at least in rates and percentages, of these faulty accounting practices.

in this country and had in good measure outlived those uncertainties of return which frequently accompany industrial immaturity.

3. *Business Organization.*

Discussion in the foregoing section has in part prepared us to appreciate the character of the typical business unit within the wool-manufacturing industry when the working of wool reached the factory basis. Concerns began usually as the enterprises of individuals, families, or at best of partnerships. David Humphreys, Rowland G. Hazard, and Delano Abbott commenced operations alone, as the Scholfields did also, apparently. Again, several members of the Du Pont family coöperated in the establishment of the Brandywine mills that bore their name, while the Stevens enterprise at North Andover, Massachusetts, got its start when a small group of friends and neighbors joined forces in setting up a partnership. And the individual enterprise or partnership remained during the period to 1815 the typical business unit.[1]

The joint-stock form, to be sure, put in an early appearance among wool-manufacturing concerns. For example, the Hartford mill of 1788 and the Newbury-Port Woollen Manufactory of 1794 were chartered enterprises with divided ownership, as was also the Cecil Manufacturing Company of Maryland (1794). But on the whole the employment of this form was rare until after 1800.[2] In the period of more rapid manufacturing development commencing after 1807 a larger use of incorporation began. Charters of concerns in the New England and middle states that gave "cotton and woolen goods" or merely "woolen goods" as the proposed production of their plants rose from three in 1807 to

[1] Davis in his *Essays in the Earlier History of American Corporations* (ii, 256) says: "In America, as in England, the great bulk of manufacturing enterprises, as they emerged from the household stage, were individual or partnership undertakings." And I have seen no evidence to indicate that the manufacture of wool formed an exception.

[2] Davis (ii, 269) records only eight companies incorporated for manufacturing purposes of all sorts in Massachusetts, Connecticut, New York, and New Jersey before 1800.

seventy-one in 1814.[1] Then, too,—if we may judge from later experience,—there were some concerns organized on the joint-stock basis, although they were unincorporated.[2] On the other hand, the above enumeration is subject to various deductions. It is likely that many of these chartered companies never actually went into operation, and that many others in fact turned their efforts to cotton goods alone. Hence, the number of joint-stock enterprises in the period 1807–1814 with which we are directly concerned was small indeed.

The trend, however, was already clear. Succeeding years showed a gradually expanding use of the joint-stock form, although, because of the relatively small size of some woolen mills, the individually owned enterprise and the partnership establishment continued to play a large part in the American wool manufacture. This situation is evident in McLane's *Report* of 1832. One of the prearranged questions which were submitted to manufacturers was the character of ownership, and some fifty replies are recorded. Of these mills twenty-three indicated the joint-stock form, and thirty-four the private or partnership form,— or ratios not far from one-third and two-thirds.[3] The course of a particular Massachusetts enterprise is suggestive of the general

[1] The tabulation by states during these years is as follows:

	1807	1808	1809	1810	1811	1812	1813	1814	1815
N. H.	..	1	1	5	3	5	3	9	1
Mass.	..	..	3	1	3	8	15	24	15
Conn.	..	..	..	..	..	2	1	7	6
Vt.	2	1	3	4	2	3	2	4	2
N. Y.	..	..	3	6	13	13	19	24	9
N. J.	..	..	1	..	..	..	1	2	1
Pa.	1	..	..	..	..	1	..	..	2
Md.	..	1	..	..	1	..	2	1	..
Total	3	3	11	16	22	32	43	71	38

(*State Papers*, *Finance*, iv, 397–429.)

It should also be noted that the proportion of these enterprises that gave the manufacture of woolen goods alone as the purpose of their formation was not high, perhaps a quarter.

[2] McLane gives several cases of enterprises which in 1832 were reported as "joint, but not incorporated" (*Report*, ii, 62, 64).

[3] McLane's *Report*, *passim*. Rhode Island is reported (i, 974) to hold nineteen mills of which six were joint-stock and the rest private. No information is available for the important group of Massachusetts mills. Apparently the local agents failed to insist upon an answer to this stock inquiry.

movement. One James Shepherd began the manufacture of wool in Northampton in 1809. A year later a charter was secured as the Northampton Cotton and Woollen Manufacturing Company; but the enterprise was never organized as a "company." Messrs. Thomas, James, and Charles Shepherd carried on the business as a family affair through the war, although using the name of company always. Subsequently James Shepherd bought the concern, and continued its operations either as "sole owner partner" or in copartnership with one James M. Robbins. These men were induced by the satisfactory trade of the times "to employ a larger capital and extend their business;" and subsequently, after a period of difficulty under the tariff of 1824, the establishment came under the control of a joint-stock company and was so conducted thereafter. Larger capital and expanding operations brought the advantage of joint ownership.[1]

This trend toward joint-stock ownership is significant for our purpose. It suggests the growing scale of manufacturing operations in the industry, and the increasing general confidence in the industry. The basis was available upon which could be reared the strikingly large enterprises of later years. Yet at the period of the twenties and early thirties, too much emphasis might easily be given this phenomenon. Form of business unit was as yet no decisive indication of size and importance. Probably there was often little difference in scope of operations between the individual or partnership and the joint-stock enterprise. Subsequent decades were to see the more striking developments. It suffices for the present to note that a commencement had already been made by 1830.

4. *Labor Supply.*

To appreciate the early conditions in the American wool manufacture, a knowledge of the sources and composition of the labor supply is as important as that of the sources and earnings of capital. Information here is, if anything, scarcer than with regard to capital, and, partly on account of the wider distribution of the wool-working industry, it is less abundant in connection with

[1] McLane's *Report*, i, 310–311.

that manufacture than with respect to the kindred manufacture of cotton.

There is evidence that mill-owners in the early wool manufacture had difficulties in gathering a working force and enticing it within the factories, as was the case also in the early cotton industry. A small contingent of woolen workers, to be sure, and an important contingent, was available in the foreign artisans who had come or had been induced to come to this country. A group of them — men who like the Scholfields had early set up a quasi-handicraft manufacture of woolens — has already been mentioned. Not infrequently others are spoken of. At Colonel Humphreys's mill, an Englishman, who, it is said, had come from Lancashire for the purpose, had charge of all the processes of manufacture.[1] The factory at Steubenville, Ohio, "had the advantage of a few skilled foreign workmen;" and so too the mills at Oriskany, New York, and elsewhere.[2] It was said in 1810 that "the convulsions of Europe have driven hither every description of artist employed in the woolen manufactory;" while Tench Coxe, writing in 1814, summarized that "no branch of manufactures receives so great an accession of foreign workmen as the woolen branch, because the raw material and manufacture are universal in Europe."[3] Unquestionably such men, placed in positions of responsibility in the new mills, would have influence in the improvement of operation far in excess of their numbers, both directly and through the training of other workmen.

Yet despite the presence of these artisans, the greater part of

[1] North, in Davis's *New England States*, i, 205.

In the Hartford venture, it will be recalled, the proprietors were reported by Henry Wansey to be wholly dependent for the technical side of the business upon an Englishman, a skillful sorter (Bagnall, p. 207).

[2] Niles, xxi, 367; Capron, *Bulletin*, 1881, p. 127; Bagnall, p. 234.

[3] *National Intelligencer*, August 6, 1810; *State Papers, Finance*, ii, 679. See also Niles, x, 82; and Carey, *Appeal to Common Sense*, p. 54. The Wolcott Woolen Manufacturing Company at its start in 1816 is said to have employed "mostly foreigners" (Ammidown's *Historical Collections*, ii, 370). See also *State Papers, Finance*, iii, 104. The character of these workers is reported by one writer as follows: ". . . generally English operatives, who, as a class, were ignorant about all things but their trade of weaving, and much inclined to intemperance, which introduced a class of population about each establishment noways creditable to morals or respectable society" (Ammidown, i, 493).

the operatives had to be secured from the native population, and here manufacturers met difficulties. Appreciation of the obstacles in this field was apparently responsible for that method whereby legislatures (e. g., Connecticut) sometimes extended aid to the young industry: the exemption from the poll tax for a certain number of years of all workmen in wool manufactories. To speak more specifically: the Hartford factory, although the scale of its operations was not extensive, was reported to have been to "heavy expense in procuring and retaining workmen who had competent skill in the different branches of Woolen Manufacture," and had been compelled to "raise up an entirely new set of workmen from amongst our own Youth, at a heavy expense." [1] And the emphasis placed on skilled foreign workers suggests that similar trials confronted later manufacturers in greater or less degree. Again, it was difficult to secure an adequate number of children. According to Dwight, "discreet parents" at the start of Colonel Humphreys's mill were reluctant to place their children within the factory; [2] and apparently as one result of this situation, Colonel Humphreys sought pauper apprentices, just as the early English cotton manufacturers had done before him. At one time he got seventy-three boys from the New York Almshouse, and others from nearby villages, all being duly bound under the form of indenture.[3] In other localities the same difficulty seemingly was no less considerable; for frequently in contemporary newspapers appeared advertisements of mills in search of apprentices, usually boys twelve to fifteen years old.[4]

Another method of securing labor, and one widely employed, was that of hiring whole families, with the provision that the families should contain a number of children. Usually these families occupied the company houses, and each member found a place in the mill. Illustrative of this means of procuring employees is an advertisement that appeared in a Baltimore newspaper:

[1] Bagnall, pp. 103–104.

[2] Dwight, *Travels*, iii, 393.

[3] Bagnall, p. 357.

[4] *Middlesex Gazette*, June 27, 1811 and November 14, 1811, June 16, 1814 and June 23, 1814; *Pittsfield Sun*, June 9, 1814, July 14, 1814, and August 31, 1815; *The Bee* (Hudson, New York), August 9, 1814; *American Watchman* (Baltimore, Maryland), August 21, 1813.

"Wanted: several families who have a number of children who can be employed in a factory. Such families will be furnished with convenient accommodation on application at the Madison factory."[1] This method, moreover, freed the proprietor from the supervision which was necessary for large bodies of "apprentices."

Yet the evidence available does not point to a mere exploitation of this child labor. The sentiment of the times was distinctly in favor of the employment of children. As Niles said, they are thereby "inured to habits of industry, order, and regularity, which generally adheres to them through life."[2] Moreover, the welfare of the apprentices was given special consideration, at least by Colonel Humphreys, and probably elsewhere. Somewhat the same attitude that led Samuel Slater to the establishment of the first Sunday Schools in Rhode Island, led Colonel Humphreys to seek legislative protection for the children in woolen mills. At his instance the legislature of Connecticut passed a law requiring the proprietors of such establishments not only to supervise the morals of their workmen, but also to educate the children "as other children in plain families throughout the state are educated." And Dwight remarks that, as far as Humphreys's mill was concerned, the "discreet parents" who had earlier

[1] *American Watchman*, March 23, 1814. See also same for April 26, 1815. Other cases are not infrequent.

An interesting document indicating the conditions in both branches of the textile industry at the time is a contract made at the Oxford Cotton Mill in which Samuel Slater was interested:

Oxford, March 10, 1815.

This certifies I Cyrus Logee have this day contracted to move my family to Slater and Tiffany's factory in Oxford consisting of My Son Duty Logee and Stephen and to furnish two other efficient Girls to heel or tend Twister for the term of one year from the first of April next ensuing and to occupy the Tenement in common with William Clark, upon the following terms (Viz.) myself to work in the Carding Room at any part they Judge the most proper @ 5/ per day. Oldest son Spin on mule @ 4/ per day. Second son Spin or work in Carding Room @ 7/6 per Week and the Girls are to have 13/ each per week for the term of one year.

His
William Clark. Cyrus X. Logee
Mark.

(Records of S. Slater and Sons Company.)

[2] Niles, xvii, 89.

kept their children out of the factories, later offered them "in more than sufficient numbers." [1]

Indeed, the situation at Derby under Colonel Humphreys's administration has an idyllic cast, at least on the surface. Model tenements were erected for the employees, gardens were maintained to supply them with vegetables, and workmen were discharged for immorality.[2] Here, and elsewhere, the hiring of whole families was regarded as particularly desirable, since other workers could be induced to live with them, — to the improvement of moral health.[3]

The utilization of children, however, though a feature of the early wool manufacture, was by no means a predominant factor in that industry. Indeed, there was in reality less need for children there than in many other industries of the time. The working of wool was rather noteworthy for the large proportion of adult male labor. The chief reliance in the early mills for the sorting, carding, spinning, weaving, and some of the finishing operations was upon such labor, both for the actual work and for superintendence. Women could be employed as helpers in some of these processes, and in repair of defects in the completed fabric. Children were used for the most part also as assistants, especially in the spinning process, and even more particularly in the operation of the billy. Work generally was too arduous or required too much skill for the employment of women and children as responsible machine tenders.[4] The Census figures of 1820, fragmentary

[1] *Travels*, iii, 393.

Another observer stated: "The apprentices appear extremely well satisfied with their condition, being well fed, clothed, and lodged, like the members of a well regulated and happy family" (Bagnall, p. 356).

[2] Dwight's *Travels*, iii, 393.

[3] Massachusetts Historical Society *Collections*, 2nd Ser., iii, 264; Records of S. Slater & Sons Company.

[4] Niles pointed out: "The manufacture of wool is less adapted to the labor of women and children than that of cotton . . . male spinners, weavers, dyers, fullers, shearers, etc., etc." (xii, 277).

Slater wrote in 1827: "There is less young help in the woollen than in the cotton manufactures;" and again: "The wool business requires more man labour" (White, *Memoir of Samuel Slater*, pp. 128, 131). On the other hand, Carey gives an instance of a satinet mill of 1822 which employed "about 27 adults and 25 children" (*Crisis*, p. 24).

as they are, demonstrate this great reliance on adult male labor. In the Massachusetts factories for which data are given, the averages among employees were: twelve men, seven women, and six children; in New York mills, twelve men, two women, eight children; and for the country as a whole, nine men, three women, and six children.[1] But such relationships were typical only of the earlier factories. Technical changes in the next decade were to produce substantial changes, both as regards the employment of children and with respect to the proportions between men and women.

The adoption of the Goulding card was a potent force in the reduction of the number of children employed in the woolen mill. By the elimination of the roping billy, the province of children was narrowed to that of helpers in the several processes, especially spinning. Whereas the maintenance and elaboration of the drawing and spinning operations caused the continued employment of child labor in the cotton and worsted manufactures, the obviation of drawing through the use of the Goulding device spelled the decline of such labor in the woolen industry.

The adaptation of woolen spinning to power, on the other hand, did not occasion any significant change in the type of labor employed, since the work was still too arduous and skillful for women. This was especially true of the early spinning-jacks in which some of the movements — the recession of the carriage, for example — continued to be manual operations. The only exception to this situation was in the case of the Brewster machine. Here, as was brought out by Colonel Shepherd in the inquiry of 1828, girls could replace the more highly paid men.[2] But the Brewster apparatus was never widely used.

In the weaving process, the introduction of power looms had effected greater change than had come from improvements in the spinning operation. One manufacturer said in 1828, "We do not

[1] In the case of the larger concerns, a somewhat similar ration obtained:

Men . .	48	46	31	41	46	= 42 Average
Women . .	27	23	20	13	10	= 19 "
Children . .	40	23	19	16	25	= 24 "

[2] *State Papers, Finance*, v, 814.

pay as much now for weaving as formerly, since the power loom has been introduced, and we now employ women, instead of men, to do the work."[1] And, indeed, the substitution of women seems to have been quite frequent.[2] The strenuous work of operating the harnesses and "beating-up" the cloth as it was woven was now obviated; and it is probable that the change to the production of lower-grade fabrics was not without effect. In the manufacture of the finer goods, such as broadcloths, men were still necessary, — even as today the male weavers still have an important place in the weaving of similar fabrics, — but in the production of satinets, negro-cloths, and the like, the work could be satisfactorily attended to by female weavers.

Finally, by the improvement of the finishing operations, some small increase in the employment of women was possible. After the introduction of mechanical shearing machines, for instance, it was stated: "One superintendent and seven girls attend to twenty pair of shears;"[3] and perhaps, too, in the case of the cylindrical napping and pressing machines, a few additional women might be employed. But in all these processes, the handling of heavy rolls of cloth was an obstacle to the wide use of female labor. While economizing in the employment of men, these improvements in finishing did not, generally speaking, lead to any considerable substitution of women for men.

The result of these various innovations is apparent in the statistics of labor presented in the inquiries of 1828 and 1832. In the hearings before the Committee on Manufactures in 1828, seven manufacturers representing the leading concerns of the country gave definite accounts of their labor forces. The 735 employees contained in these establishments were divided into 41.4 per cent each of men and women, and 17.2 per cent of children.[4] In 1832,

[1] *State Papers, Finance*, p. 822.

[2] *Ibid.*, p. 808; *Massachusetts Spy*, July 5, 1826; Niles, xxxiii, 141. The employment of hand-loom weavers in and about Philadelphia, which persisted for many years, presumably gave a different complexion to the industry in that center, since most of these weavers were men.

[3] *State Papers, Finance*, v, 814.

[4] *Ibid.*, pp. 809–831. In two other cases, the proportion of women was apparently even greater: in one, the manufacturer stated that he employed "mostly"

the mills of Massachusetts, for which the reports seem quite full and accurate, the ratios were: 42 per cent of men, 49 per cent of women, and 8 per cent of children.[1] In short, as compared with conditions of 1820, a substantial change in the composition of the normal labor force had occurred. Adults had become, as Niles remarked at the time, "always numerous in and about woolen factories."[2] Women had reached a place at least of equality with men, while the utilization of children had shrunken decisively. The proportion of women is of particular interest. It marks in fact the high-water level in the use of such labor in the American woolen industry, and reflects probably the condition of labor at that time in the United States, especially the scarcity of adult male labor. Subsequently, the proportion of women in woolen mills tended to become lower.

The substitution of women for men was of special advantage to the woolen manufacturers by reason of the marked spread between the wage scales of men and women. From the evidence of manufacturers at the inquiry in 1828, it appears that the wages of men in the mills averaged around $20 to $25 per month, or $4.50 to $5.50 a week. Women and girls, on the other hand, received only about half that amount, — from $2.50 to $3.00 a week. In the investigation of 1832, approximately the same situation appears: men in the Massachusetts factories averaged around 90 cents a day, while women secured only 40 cents.[3] Occasionally piece rates took into account the sex of the worker. Thus, Abraham Marland said in 1828, "If I hire females to weave, I pay 83 cents for what I pay men $1.00;" and the Amesbury (Massachu-

women. The average for the seven mills was 44 men, 44 women, and 16 children. In the seven concerns for which definite figures were presented, there was considerable variation. Three mills, for example, reported as follows:

Men . .	19	30	60
Women . .	3	15	104
Children . .	4	25	36

[1] McLane's *Report*, i, 66–577.

[2] Niles, xxxii, 226.

[3] Rates of wages for men and women in Massachusetts woolen mills ran from 60 cents to $1.33, and from 31 cents to 83 cents, respectively. Some of these wide variations are explicable probably by the fact that table board or other factors often entered into the matter.

setts) flannel mills had a weave rate for women only half that for men.[1] The adoption of improved machinery, then, had an important indirect influence toward the cheapening of American wool fabrics and adding to the competitive strength of the domestic industry, — that is, an influence beyond the direct contribution to productive power. Women with lower wage scales could be substituted in appreciable degree for the higher paid men. At the same time, through the diminution in the proportion of child workers, a distinct social advantage was gained.[2]

The picture of labor conditions in the early wool manufacture would not be complete, however, without a brief notice of at least two further matters: some peculiar relations between wage-earners and the mills, and the hours of labor.[3] Of the former, some mention has already been made, particularly with regard to Colonel Humphreys's establishment, one of the first mills. The conditions there suggested seem to have continued to prevail throughout the period under consideration. Woolen mills, being attracted to water-power sites, were usually located some distance from the larger towns, and in the little communities that subsequently grew up, the factory was always the center of the village. Then, an important adjunct to the mill was the company store, at which claims acquired by work in the factory — money wages often being dispensed with — were convertible into consumable goods. The situation at Oriskany, New York, is typical.

[1] *State Papers, Finance*, v, 820; Niles, xxxiii, 141.

[2] The higher wage rates for adult male weavers were compensated in some measure by higher productivity. Not only could they turn out a larger volume of goods, but they would produce more perfect cloth. Moreover, they could probably assist in mounting the warp in the loom and could handle the heavy rolls of completed fabric. Yet the spread of wages was so great that some net gain must have accrued to the industry through the employment of women weavers.

[3] Discussion of the prevailing rates of wages might be included except for the fact that *per se* they are of little significance. The rates themselves are not always uniform, sometimes including board and sometimes not; they were probably often affected by the policy of the company store; and of course they were subject to the general movements in the value of money. Moreover, dissimilarity of conditions would make an international comparison of questionable value, even if foreign figures were obtainable. It has been thought unwise to go into this subject further than to show relative wages of men and women, the influence of improved machinery upon wage scales, and the like, — features scattered through the text.

According to the account given in 1828, "a large proportion of the labor at the factory has heretofore been paid at the company's store. The company keeps a general dry goods and grocery store, and has sold to the laborers at the usual profit of country trading stores. . . . The practice is, to give the laborer a due bill, which is current at some of the neighboring stores for goods, as well as at the company's store, which bills are redeemed at the factory in their cloths. The company does not pay any more cash for labor than formerly. The agreement with the hands, generally, is to pay one-half cash." [1] Other concerns were not so liberal as this in all respects. For example, the Slater mill at Webster usually included in its wage agreements a clause to the following effect: "and I further promise and agree that I will not trade, or make purchases, at any store whatsoever, during the above period" except at the stores "belonging to Mr. Slater." [2] In this manner, in common with most manufacturing establishments of the period, the woolen mills acted as purveyors for their employees,—frequently at a substantial profit to themselves.[3]

Another point in the close relations of factory and worker was the arrangement whereby "board" was provided the latter. Four of the manufacturers who appeared before the Committee on Manufactures in 1828 supplied board for their employees, and another for his apprentices.[4] In others, like the Slater plant at Webster, only a portion of the workers were taken care of in this way, although it appears that in this case the factory secured certain fixed rates from local boarding houses.[5] By this means, as

[1] *State Papers, Finance*, v, 810.

[2] Records of S. Slater and Sons Company, e. g., "Agreement of March 24, 1831 with one William F. Knapp."

[3] Note that the Oriskany company sought "the usual profit of country trading stores." It may also be noted that the proprietor of the Steubenville (Ohio) mill counted among his advantages "an extensive well-assorted retail store, where we sell and barter goods to the amount of $30,000 or $40,000 per annum" (*State Papers, Finance*, v, 823).

[4] *State Papers, Finance*, v, 815, 817, 819, 831.

[5] See, for instance, a contract of slightly later date: "I hereby agree to work for Saml. Slater & Sons from this date to 1st April 1837 at wool sorting and am to have $16.66 per month boarding myself, it is understood I am to be furnished with board at 10/6 per week. Dec. 3d, 1836, Webster. Oliver M. Russ."

The company received payment from a man who ran a boarding house and he well as by the medium of the mill store and by the usual practice among early mills of housing part or all of their employees in "company" tenements, the life of the early factory operatives was controlled by the "company" to a much greater extent than it has been in later decades.

The working days in the early woolen mills strike the modern observer as extraordinarily long, but in fact they were the common duration of factory hours at that period, not only in other American industries, but also in English woolen mills. This matter formed one of the stock questions in the inquiry of the Committee on Manufactures in 1828, and so plenty of evidence on this point relative to the American wool-manufacturing industry of that date is available. Representative replies are as follows: "We expect to get sixty-eight hours per week, the year round, and this is all we insist on;" "In the summer time we work twelve hours, over and above the time allowed for meals, and we fall but little short of that in the Winter;" and "In the Summer we begin to work at about sun-rise, and continue until about sun-set, allowing half an hour for breakfast, and from one hour to one and a half hours for dinner. In the Winter we begin as soon as possible after light, and work until about nine o'clock at night, allowing about half an hour for meals."[1] But surely not all was pure exploitation. As a curious contrast, and illustrating again the closeness of the factory to the life of its employees, is the statement of another manufacturer: "The strictest attention is paid to the order, morals, and general conduct of every person about the establishment," and "it is made the duty of the boys to attend Sunday School, otherwise to be discharged."[2]

In short, the early woolen factory was the center of a paternalistic system. The worker spent all or nearly all the daylight hours within the mill; he lived in the company houses; he frequently boarded at company establishments or houses controlled by the company; he traded at the company store; and to some

was in turn authorized to charge certain rates. In 1834, the rate per week for men was 9s. 9d. and for women 7s. 3d. (Records of S. Slater & Sons Company.)

1 *State Papers, Finance*, v, 821, 819, 817.

2 *Ibid.*, p. 823.

extent he found even his morals supervised by the company. The situation was not beneficent in all respects, but on the other hand it was not without some good points. For our purposes, to recognize it as the normal situation in this, the early stage of the American wool manufacture, is sufficient.[1]

[1] The acquisition and training of a factory force was itself not always a simple and unruffled affair. Occasionally there were outbreaks. Such for example is the suggestion of a rather picturesque advertisement in a Baltimore newspaper: the Madison Woolen factory states that "a few of our weavers through ignorance mistaking impudence for independence and licentiousness for liberty, have been the cause of our loosing not only what we were willing to part with (themselves) but also a number of the opposite character;" and accordingly places were open to the proper applicants (*American Watchman*, January 29, 1814). Again, there were occasional disturbances in opposition to the installation of power looms (Ammidown's *Historical Collections*, i, 493; ii, 371; North, *Bulletin*, 1901, p. 278; *Brief Record of the Hamilton Woolen Co.*, p. 1); and there was a "combination" of the hand-loom weavers of Philadelphia (Niles, xxviii, 159). Apparently, however, much of the trouble may be traced to the presence of foreign workmen, whose character, as already noted, was apparently not high. As yet there was of course neither labor organization nor labor troubles in the modern sense.

CHAPTER XII

THE FACTORY IN 1830

1. *Volume and Geographical Distribution of Factory Production.*

THE problem of estimating quantity of production in the days when reliable statistics were few and far between is a difficult one. No Federal census of manufactures goes as far back as 1830; state censuses supply figures for only two or three limited areas; and the general estimates of contemporary observers are often conflicting in whole or in part. And yet various questions relating to the volume of domestic factory manufacture, hitherto avoided, press for consideration: the absolute growth in factory production during the early decades of the nineteenth century; the extent of this production in 1830 as compared with household production; and proportions in domestic consumption of wool fabrics supplied respectively by factory production, household manufacture, and importation. Such problems must be tackled; and despite the shortcomings of the existing data, there is sufficient evidence, I believe, to give us an approximately correct view concerning these matters.

The number of factories established in the period prior to 1807–1808 is small, indeed, even if one should include enterprises which, properly speaking, were only handicraft shops. They would not exceed six or eight concerns at best.[1] From that time on, however, mills were organized with considerable rapidity. The *Census of 1810*, though admittedly incomplete, gave in all twenty-four wool manufactories, turning out some 200,000 yards of cloth annually. The size of these concerns is suggested by the number of persons employed: in the various mills reported by the Census, it ran from eight to twenty-nine. A better view of the growth in the first boom period of the industry is gained from a consideration of the situation at the close of the War of 1812, — since the

[1] I have listed in Appendix B the early mills of which I have record.

year 1810 falls in the middle of the movement.[1] By 1816, Connecticut alone was credited with twenty-five woolen factories, which could manufacture 375,000 yards of narrow or 125,000 yards of broadcloth per year.[2] Six establishments in Delaware were said to be driven by the waters of the Brandywine; and the Census of New Jersey in 1814 reported fifty-six woolen factories, scattered pretty generally throughout the state.[3] Similar progress was made in Massachusetts and New York, if one may judge from the number of separate enterprises of which information is available. Taking the country as a whole, the Committee on Commerce and Manufactures estimated that in 1816, $12,000,000 of capital was invested in the domestic wool manufacture, from which issued a volume of goods valued at $19,000,000. By this manufacture, moreover, 50,000 persons were said to be employed "constantly," and as many more "occasionally," — the latter presumably referring to household weavers who took out work from time to time.[4] These latter figures, however, are probably much exaggerated, though one is at a loss to tell by exactly what measure. The best possible conclusion is that the industry had unquestionably shown marked expansion during the Embargo and war periods.

The progress between this earlier period and 1830 is no less difficult to estimate. Data upon the value of wool manufactures, the number of persons employed, or the amount of capital invested are all unsatisfactory. Some are mere guesses by individuals, such as Bishop's statement that the volume of capital invested in the industry rose from 10 to 50 millions between

[1] Reference has already been made to the number of incorporations in the chief New England and middle Atlantic States of concerns which mentioned wool among the articles that they proposed to manufacture.

The totals for the several years 1807–1815 ran as follows: 1807, 3; 1808, 3; 1809, 11; 1810, 16; 1811, 22; 1812, 32; 1813, 43; 1814, 71; 1815, 38.

These figures also do not include partnerships which at that time were apparently an important form of business organization in this industry. (Cf. above, pp. 231–233.)

[2] *State Papers, Finance*, iii, 104; but the *New York Columbian* reported 14 woolen factories in New London county alone (Niles, viii, 291).

[3] Niles, ix, 95; *ibid.*, viii, 151.

[4] *State Papers, Finance*, iii, 104.

1815 and 1827.[1] Other data lack homogeneity between dates in the two general periods. One is driven to attempting comparison on the basis of the amount of wool consumed. The nature of the information available compels a comparison of 1810 with 1830, although, as indicated above, the former is not the most useful date for our purpose, — it falls in the midst of the early development. And there are other objectionable features to the basis chosen.[2] Still, as far as statistics are concerned, one is here treading on surer ground than when he is considering capital and the like; and a comparison of 1830 with 1810 will offer some picture of the general progress.

The *Census of 1810* reported a production of wool cloths in American factories amounting to 200,000 yards; and on account of the few mills then existing, one may perhaps accept that figure as approximately correct. The total wool consumption, then, would be around 400,000 pounds, on the assumption that two pounds of raw wool were required for each yard of cloth.[3] But the estimate for the period around 1830 is not so readily secured. We have no information concerning factory production of cloth, and so must resort to a more roundabout method of estimate. The wool clip of the country according to Wright was 30 to 32 million pounds in 1830, to which 1½ to 2 million pounds of wool available for the cloth manufacture were added by importation.[4] The proportion of foreign wool employed in the cloth manufacture, all of which was probably wrought up in the factories, to the total

[1] Bishop, ii, 314.

[2] Other objections are concerned with the adequacy of wool consumption as a test of real productivity. A change in the nature of the wool consumed, with a change in the degree of shrinkage, would affect the situation; a given increase in wool consumed might mean a greater increase in cloth turned out. Again, the adoption of cotton warps or of new and lighter-weight fabrics would mean greater yardage per pound of raw wool.

[3] Fabrics at the time averaged much heavier than they do now, perhaps around ten ounces per running yard three-fourths (or twenty-seven inches) wide. But this is ten ounces of wool in the cloth. To make allowance for shrinkage in scouring and for losses in manufacturing, one must assume a raw wool basis of around two pounds for each ten ounces of finished cloth.

[4] Wright, p. 75. Importations averaged at this time around 2,500,000 pounds of which I have estimated three-fifths to four-fifths to have been of the type usable in the production of woolen fabrics, the rest going into carpets, hats, knit-goods, etc.

amount of raw material so wrought was variously estimated by contemporaries. Some of the manufacturers who testified at the inquiry of 1828 stated that they used a quarter of imported wool, some as much as a half.[1] But these ratios are undoubtedly far above the average. The sponsors were in the main eastern men, proprietors of establishments of relatively large size, and producers of fine goods, — men such as Colonel James Shepherd of Northampton, Massachusetts, and Aaron Tufts of Dudley. Manufacturers located elsewhere — in New York State, as also Mr. Dickinson of Steubenville, Ohio, and even Messrs. Du Pont of Delaware, except in their cheapest goods — used little or no foreign staple.[2] Estimates indicating small use of foreign wool are available from other sources. The able memorial of the citizens of Boston, presented to Congress in 1827, said that "the manufacturers are supplied almost to the full extent of their demands by domestic wool," and placed the ratio of imported material at 4 or 5 per cent. Similarly a memorial of the New York Chamber of Commerce put the proportion "not to exceed, perhaps, a twentieth part." [3] No doubt these latter estimates were somewhat extreme in their way, for the memorialists in each case were not without bias. However, we may perhaps steer a middle course. If we take the actual wool importations at 1½ to 2 million pounds and a proportion of foreign to total wool consump-

[1] *State Papers, Finance*, v, 793, 795, 798, 799, 803, 804, 805, 807.

[2] *Ibid.*, pp. 793, 797, 801, 802, 805. The same alignment of manufacturers is evident in the *Report on Manufactures* of 1832. The great majority of mills for which evidence on this point is available reported the use of native wool alone; but certain concerns indicated a considerable employment of foreign fiber. These concerns were of two types. One was the fine-goods production. The Fitchburg Woolen Manufacturing Company reported the use of one-third Spanish wool and two-thirds American (McLane's *Report*, i, 486); the Middlesex Woolen Company, one-third from Vermont and the rest from abroad (*ibid.*, p. 342); while for the Northampton mill above mentioned, three-quarters of the wool consumed was said to be foreign (p. 308). The other group was composed of the producers of very cheap fabrics. Thus the Canton Woolen Manufactory, turning out a large proportion of negro cloth, indicated the use of 300,000 pounds of Smyrna wool and only 50,000 pounds of domestic staple (p. 376). However, the general impression, which one secures from an inspection of McLane's *Report*, does not differ from that stated in the text.

[3] "Memorial of the Citizens of Boston" (reprinted), p. 12; 20th Cong., 1st Sess., *Senate Document, No. 53.*

tion in the mills at some intermediate figure,—say, an eighth,—obviously the factories were employing a weight of raw material much greater than twenty years earlier. Assuming a rough figure of 15 million pounds for the total factory consumption, this was a tremendous increase over the 400,000 pounds of 1810.

Just what relation may be assigned to the growth in the two periods, 1810–1816 and 1816–1830 respectively, is somewhat uncertain. Assuredly, the statement of North that "the actual progress of the (wool-manufacturing) industry in this decade (1820–1830) was relatively less than in any other in our history" cannot be accepted.[1] The development in this later period, of course, was not in some respects so spectacular as in the hot-house period of interrupted commerce, but after the reaction in 1815–1816 there apparently came a steady and solid growth which put the industry of 1830 far ahead of the industry even at the previous high point, say, in 1815. Indeed, I am inclined to allocate fully a half of the increase in manufacturing capacity to the period after the conclusion of peace. This advance was not so much the result of an increase in the number of establishments as a growth in the average size of such concerns. A substantial increase in the number of mills, to be sure, did take place in this period, especially with the western movement of settlement; but these mills were of greater average capacity than those established fifteen or twenty years before. Meanwhile in the eastern states the trend was distinctly toward establishments of larger size, — a trend caused by the widening of the domestic cloth market, the change in the character of goods produced, and the adoption of improved machinery. Mills of somewhat larger size, devoting their efforts to the production of goods which did not demand special care and skill, and utilizing a considerable complement of power-driven machinery, necessarily called for a much larger quantity of raw material than the upstart mills of 1815 or even 1820.

Geographical Distribution. The growth of wool factories in the period prior to 1830 was not limited to any one section of the country. To be sure, the development in the southern states was

[1] North, *Bulletin*, 1901, p. 206. From any point of view other than that of productive capacity, the statement above quoted is even less true.

not great; yet, in an enumeration of 1823, fifteen factories using wool alone or with other fibers were reported for Maryland, four for Virginia, and even two for Georgia.[1] New England had already jumped into the lead with ninety-seven establishments out of a total for the whole country of two hundred and twenty; but New York boasted the greatest number of any state (thirty-six mills), and Pennsylvania was not far behind this with thirty-three. While the absolute figures for the several states are perhaps much in error, the general picture is, I believe, correct.[2] A somewhat similar view pertaining to the next decade, indeed to 1836, is presented in the following tabulation, — based, however, upon sets of machinery instead of separate mills:[3]

DISTRIBUTION OF SETS OF WOOLEN MACHINERY, BY FABRICS AND BY STATES — 1836

	U. S.	Me.	N. H.	Vt.	Mass.	R. I.	Conn.	N. Y.	N. J.	Pa.	Del.	Md.	Oh.	Ky. and Tenn.
Broadcloths	344	3	..	37	150	4	17	100	..	18	3	3	6	3
Cassimeres	178	15	10	23	59	..	4	60	..	1	..	3	3	..
Satinets	574	5	19	37	195	16	93	100	20	58	7	4	5	15
Flannels	158	..	10	3	77	..	9	40	..	19	..	..	..	..
Linseys	210	..	..	..	18	60	15	51	..	21	2	5	16	22
Blankets, hats, and yarn	24	1	4	..	10	..	9	..	..	..	..	..	..	..
Total	1488	24	43	100	509	80	147	351	20	117	12	15	30	40

This enumeration, like that of 1823, indicates the growing dominance of New England; and now this section is credited with approximately 60 per cent of the total capacity. Probably in the number of establishments, New England did not possess that ratio, but her mills were on the average larger affairs. The tabulation also indicates a substantial localization in the production of the finer fabrics. Over three-quarters of the machinery devoted to the manufacture of broadcloths and cassimeres was to be found in the three states, Massachusetts, New York, and Vermont, the

[1] 18th Cong., 1st Sess., *Senate Document, No. 45.*

[2] The *New York Census of 1825* gives a total of 189 woolen factories, and 28 more cotton and woolen factories, for that state, an enumeration which undoubtedly gave too liberal an interpretation to the term "factory."

[3] Benton and Barry, *Statistical View*, 1837, p. 124.

ratio in the case of broadcloth running to nearly 85 per cent. In the case of satinets, less than 60 per cent, and in that of linseys, only a third of the total capacity was concentrated in those states. On the whole, the production of satinets was the most widely disseminated, linseys finding little place at all in the manufacture of New England except Rhode Island. Satinet was a product meeting the general public needs with particularly wide success. Flannel was also a fabric with a wide popular demand, but its factory production was in 1836 more largely concentrated in a few states, perhaps because of the relatively short period since importations had played a considerable part in supplying the domestic market.

Another noteworthy feature in the geographical distribution in 1830 was the production in western states. The development of woolen mills west of the Alleghanies had, as a matter of fact, followed pretty closely the establishment of factories in the East. As early as 1811, Lexington, Kentucky, contained three woolen factories, though it is uncertain what size of mill they were;[1] one man helped to build a woolen factory in western Virginia or in Ohio in each year of the war;[2] and the steam mill at Steubenville, Ohio, and that of Mr. Arthurs at Pittsburgh, Pennsylvania, stood out as conspicuous establishments even for the whole American industry. The success of the Steubenville concern seems to have been considerable. It was frequently spoken of as a "celebrated establishment;" and its standing was the occasion of the following comment by Niles in 1822: "The reflecting man will ponder not a little on the fact that wool is transported from New Jersey to be manufactured into cloth at Steubenville . . . and that such cloth is sent to the New York, Philadelphia, and Baltimore markets."[3] The enumeration of 1823, above mentioned, credited

[1] Niles, vi, 249. [2] Howells, *Life in Ohio, 1813–1840*, pp. 8–19.

[3] Niles, xxi, 367; xxviii, 82, note. The Steubenville mill was also noteworthy as being one of the earliest steam-driven plants.

Another interesting case of competition flowing back from the frontier concerns the Piscataquis Manufacturing Company of Dover, Maine,—at that time a frontier settlement. By 1837 this Company was making cassimeres which were trucked thirty-five miles through the woods to tidewater at Bangor, the teaming being done by oxen. Thence the goods were sent to Philadelphia by sailing vessel, where they were consigned to a commission house and sold on account (*Sketch of the Mills of the American Woolen Co.*, 1901, p. 108).

Ohio with thirteen, Kentucky with eleven, and even Indiana with two wool-working establishments. By 1836, the number of mills in this region was probably much increased, Ohio being shown with thirty sets in the tabulation just presented, and Kentucky and Tennessee together with forty. Incidentally, a feature worthy of note in connection with the sets operating in these states is that almost all were being employed in the manufacture of linseys and satinets, products particularly well adapted to western use.

Probably, however, these western mills were less mature affairs than most of the eastern establishments, at least on the marketing side. Except for one or two concerns like that at Steubenville, they sold almost wholly to the countryside close by their plants, and frequently not for cash. A typical case is that of a "factory" in Clarkville, western Pennsylvania. Around 1830 "a great part of the wool" was being "worked on shares; some little purchased;" only a small amount of cash was actually paid out in wages, the "work being done by persons composing the company;" and while some sales were for cash or credit, part of the product was sold for wool and part for "produce." [1] The "New Steam Wool Carding Factory" of Lexington, Kentucky, presents a somewhat similar picture. The proprietors advertise in 1829 that they will card, spin, or weave on commission for household workers; that they "keep constantly on hand and for sale at the Factory" linseys, negro cloths, and like fabrics; and that they will "receive in payment for Carding, Spinning, Colouring, Weaving, or for any of the above articles, Wool, Wood, Pork, Lard, Feathers, Bacon — in short, they will receive all most any article the farmers may have to dispose of." [2] Obviously, then, such mills were substantially behind eastern mills in development, perhaps ten years behind. But it is of significance that westward expansion had already made considerable advance. Already one can see the beginning of that relatively wide distribution of woolen factories which was to characterize the industry for many decades to come.

[1] McLane's *Report*, ii, 423.

[2] *Documentary History of American Industrial Society*, ii, 335.

2. *The Character of the Representative Establishment.*

Much has already been brought out from time to time concerning the character of the factory in 1830,— its technical equipment, its practical self-sufficiency, the nature of its products, and the like. However, an assembling of these various points in a summary fashion seems desirable in an effort to picture more adequately the typical mill of that period.

The growth of the wool manufacture in the early decades of the century, as has already been noted, was not merely an expansion of total capacity: there was also an appreciable growth in the size of the representative manufacturing unit. The first general type of establishment to develop, the quasi-handicraft shop, was a diminutive affair, — perhaps a shed and two or three workers. But the early mills were often not much larger. The first mill in Uxbridge, Massachusetts, beginning as a fulling-carding shop, had at the outset a building of two stories (of which one was perhaps the basement) measuring twenty feet by forty. To convert this into a complete manufactory of cloth, an addition, twenty-five feet by thirty and possibly three stories high, was built. The equipment was, of course, small,—just the carding machines, billy, and jenny that went to make up a single "set," — the weaving apparently being done outside.[1] Nor had the Cecil Manufacturing Company at Elkton, Maryland, a much larger establishment. While we have no information as to its equipment, the building, it appears, was only sixty feet long by thirty-six feet wide, and possibly three stories high.[2] With the Middlesex Woolen Manufacturing Company, however, one reaches a concern of somewhat greater size, although here the volume of production was distinctly low. The principal building was forty feet by thirty-six, and five stories high; to which was added a rear building forty by twenty (one story high?), a dyehouse, and other outbuildings. The machinery for washing, carding, reeling, fulling, and finishing, as well as for warming the building in winter, was driven by a steam engine,— a rather unique feature, — but a steam en-

[1] Taft, pp. 46–47.
[2] Bagnall, p. 235. This mill was built in 1794 or 1795.

gine of only twenty-five horse power. Sixty to eighty hands were employed at the mill, the weaving here, it seems, being done on the place. But with all this equipment only forty yards of broadcloth were manufactured in a day.[1] Colonel Humphreys's factory in Connecticut was somewhat larger yet, and, indeed, was one of the most extensive of the times. In 1811 it contained a picker, four carding machines, two jennies, a billy of forty spindles, four broad and eight narrow looms, two newly invented shearing machines, and four fulling mills, besides eighteen stocking frames. A building one hundred feet long and thirty-six feet wide, of four stories, housed this equipment, and for the operation of this apparatus contained a working force numbering as many as one-hundred and fifty persons.[2] But the usual mill at that time was of the one-set character, — for example, John Scholfield's establishment at Stonington, Connecticut, and Daniel Stearns's at Pittsfield, Massachusetts.[3] The period around 1810 was the era of the small factory, a factory often dependent upon household workers for the weaving of its own fabrics and not infrequently dependent upon patronage from the household system for much of its activity. Several of the operations in such a mill, especially spinning and weaving, were still hand processes, and the volume of daily production very low. Correspondingly, the market which it supplied was quite restricted. Much of the output

[1] Field, *Account of Middlesex County, Connecticut*, 1819, p. 41; Bishop, ii, 180. This concern began operations in 1810.

[2] Dwight, *Travels*, iii, 392; North, in Davis's *New England States*, i, 205. Other typical mills might be instanced. The equipment of the Housatonick Manufacturing Company at Pittsfield, Massachusetts, was: three double-carding machines, a picker, three spinning jennies of 140 spindles in all, a roping jack, four broad and three narrow looms, besides finishing machinery (Smith, *History of Pittsfield*, ii, 469). That of John Scholfield, Jr.'s mill at Jewett City, Connecticut: one carding machine called a "double-breaker," two finishing carding machines, one roping machine of 40 spindles, two spinning jennies of 40 spindles each, one spinning jack of 60 spindles, four broad and seven narrow looms, and one twisting frame of 70 spindles (Bagnall, p. 459). The Providence Woolen Manufacturing Company, it is said, was "intended to manufacture daily 200 yards of Broadcloth" (Dwight, *Travels*, iv, 494). Even the mixed cotton and wool manufactory of Lexington, Kentucky, was "a stone building, of 120 feet by 40 and five stories high with power both of steam and water" (Kayser, *Commercial Directory*, 1823, p. 55).

[3] Bagnall, p. 424; Smith, *History of Berkshire County*, ii, 342.

was disposed of at the mill itself, though occasionally some portion was sent to nearby towns.

From 1810 to 1830 the change in the character of the factory was not altogether a steady process. The advance prior to 1820 was, I fancy, not great; and the movement became considerable only after that date. Nor did the change produce a complete transformation in the domestic industry. Small mills were still the common run in many sections of the country, especially in the less well-developed regions. In looking over McLane's *Report on Manufactures*, for example, one is impressed by the large number of small mills scattered through Maine and Vermont, western New York State, and such newer areas as Ohio and Kentucky. Representative of these establishments is the Bristol (Maine) Satinet Factory. Housed in a wooden structure twenty-six feet by fifty, and two stories high, were four sets of cards, one hundred and fifty-five spindles, and four looms; while the labor force of the "factory" consisted of only nine persons.[1] Again, the *Report*, after presenting data from some fifty concerns in New York State which it describes as "almost all the large woolen establishments in the State," notes that, according to a contemporaneous Register, the total number of wool-working enterprises within the state reached two hundred and two. The greater part of the other one hundred and fifty are described as "small establishments, engaged in manufacturing to a limited extent only, and depending very much on what is called 'custom work,' i. e., carding, dressing cloth manufactured in families, and taking wool to manufacture at 'halves,' the manufacturers and the persons furnishing the raw material sharing equally the manufactured article." [2] Indeed, the country was still dotted with small "man-

[1] McLane's *Report*, i, 6.

[2] *Ibid.*, ii, 90.

The term "factory" was loosely used in this period before 1830. For example, in 1826 it was reported that Vermont had 287 "small factories," although they possessed only 242 carding machines altogether, and although only "about one-third are now in order to work in the several branches of picking, carding, roping, spinning, weaving, fulling, dyeing, and dressing," i. e., in the complete wool manufacture. To put these other two-thirds into "a complete state for manufacturing in all its branches," however, all that needed to be added to the equipment of each was "a billy or roping machine of 20 spindles, a jenny of 50 spindles, and 3 looms"!

ufactories" which perhaps should better be designated shops than factories. Not until a much later date was manufacturing concentrated into particularly efficient, large mills which by force of their comparative strength and with the aid of improved transportation conditions could drive the small, local enterprises from the field.

Because of the persistence in 1830 of many small concerns, averages of capacity or labor force by states or sections are of little value. Thus, one can point out that according to McLane's *Report on Manufactures* the twenty-two Rhode Island mills possessed a total of only thirty-nine sets of woolen machinery.[1] Again, he can show that the average number of employees in the factories of Connecticut in 1832 was twenty-eight, in those of Massachusetts thirty-seven, and in those of Rhode Island only seventeen.[2] These averages of employees, to be sure, do indicate substantial growth when compared with the similar figures recorded by the *Census of 1810* for the factories of that time. But such statistics are not, to my mind, the most significant.

The trend of the industry rather than the average of the period is the feature that seems the most suggestive, and this trend is indicated by the evolution during the twenties of factories with a considerable manufacturing capacity. The number of such establishments, too, was sufficiently great to eliminate the possibility that the development was a chance affair. A few examples will make evident the new situation. Samuel Slater & Sons' mill at Webster, Massachusetts, was producing broadcloth, cassimere, and satinet to the quantity of 80,000 yards annually, and employing 128 persons; the Hamilton Woolen Company manufactured 50,000 yards of broadcloth and had a working force of 104 persons; while a woolen factory at Dedham, Massachusetts, turned out 150,000 yards of cloth and employed 100 men, 12 boys,

(*Memorial of Vermont Manufacturers and Growers of Wool*, pp. 9–10, to be found in the Boston Public Library). In McLane's *Report*, too, many carding or fulling mills are entered as "factories," especially as to the western states.

[1] McLane's *Report*, i, 976.

[2] *Ibid.*, i, 112–577, 982, 976. The fifty-four largest New York mills averaged twenty-seven employees (*ibid.*, ii, 91).

and 150 women.[1] The Pontoosuc Manufacturing Company at Pittsfield was started in 1825 with a brick building, 145 feet by 50, and 4 stories high; and its initial equipment included 6 carding machines, 5 jennies, a Brewster frame, and 20 power looms.[2] At Somersworth, New Hampshire, were 2 large plants: the Great Falls Manufacturing Company, partly cotton, but also turning out 130,000 yards of broadcloth yearly; and the Salmon Falls Manufacturing Company, with its 220 employees, producing over 40,000 yards more of the same article.[3] The flannel factories near Amesbury and the negro-cloth mill at Canton, Massachusetts, are likewise noteworthy.[4] New York State, too, boasted a significant development. The thirty largest mills averaged nearly three sets apiece, and such well-known establishments as the Oriskany Manufactory and the Glenham Company reported working forces of 147 and 130 respectively.[5] But most conspicuous and promising of all was the essay of the Middlesex Company at Lowell, commenced in 1830. It started with the ample capital of $100,000; and in 1832 was reported to be producing 135,000 yards of cassimere and 30,000 yards of cassinets, and to be employing a working force of 185 persons. Equipped with the most improved machinery, and organized somewhat after the pattern of the cotton mills in its neighborhood, it stands out as a conspicuous example of the development which had for some time been going on.[6]

[1] McLane's *Report*, i, 576–577, 536–537, 378–379.

The Hamilton Company is said to have possessed five sets of machinery in 1831, and twenty-eight broad looms (Ammidown's *Historical Collections*, ii, 374).

[2] Smith, *History of Pittsfield*, ii, 485; Records of the Company.

[3] Niles, xxxi, 205; xxxiii, 157; McLane's *Report*, i, 581–582; Clark, p. 566.

[4] Niles, xxxii, 178; McLane's *Report*, i, 210–211, 252–253; Canton: Niles, xxxi, 206; Harrisburg Convention, *Proceedings*, p. 66; McLane's *Report*, i, 376–377.

[5] McLane's *Report*, ii, 60–62, 75–79, 91.

[6] *Ibid.*, i, 342–343; Clark, p. 566; North, *Bulletin*, 1902, p. 311. In addition to concerns mentioned in the text, additional references may be given: Wheelock, in Chapin, p. 143 (Uxbridge Woolen Mill); Martin, *Seventy-three Years' History of the Boston Stock Market*, p. 20; Niles, xxxvii, 150; xxviii, 309; xxxii, 226, 306; North, in Davis's *New England States*, i, 208; *State Papers, Finance*, v, 599; Bishop, ii, 378; McLane's *Reports*, i, 134–135, 166–167, 212–213, 278–279, 308–309, 328–329, 356–357, 484–485, 502–503, 506–509, 526–527.

Such mills, in fact, marked the dawn of a new era. The preceding years had brought the adoption of power machinery by the larger and more progressive concerns, the introduction of new fabrics better adapted to general American consumption, and the broadening of the market for these goods. To be sure, most of the mills still relied wholly or chiefly upon water for motive force, and in consequence were scattered pretty widely through the country; but the occasional introduction of steam power indicated the beginning of the modern period. Despite the persistence of many small and immature establishments, undoubtedly the factory had now made a place for itself, — indeed, had become the characteristic feature of the American wool manufacture.

3. *Place of Factory Production in Supply of the Domestic Market.*

The narration of the increase in factory production of woolen fabrics, of the geographical spread of the industry, and of the expansion in size of the representative manufacturing concern may give an exaggerated idea of the part played by factory operations in the years around 1830. Lest this should be the case, it may be well to compare the volume of factory production with the total domestic consumption of wool fabrics. Domestic factory output, domestic household manufacture, and foreign importations must be considered together, and an attempt made to assess the share in consumption contributed by each. Already the relation between the first two factors has been pointed out: that household production in the United States probably exceeded in volume the output from factories in something like the ratio of four to three.[1] But to correlate domestic household and factory production with foreign imports is a difficult problem, since homogeneous and trustworthy statistics of quantity or value covering these three fields do not exist.

A glance at the contemporary estimates in the matter of value will give some idea of the obstacles encountered in arriving at a sound conclusion. The annual production of Massachusetts factories alone was placed in the early thirties at 6½ million

[1] See above, p. 190.

dollars.[1] For the whole country the yearly output of factories was in 1830 placed at 14½ millions by a Congressional committee, — a figure, incidentally, which North accepts in his sketch of the industry's history.[2] But data presented by the Friends of Domestic Industry in 1831 lead to a much higher estimate. The Friends put household and factory production together at 40 million dollars annually; and from this figure we can deduce the factory production alone as from 24 to 30 millions, — this by inference from the Friends' guess as to volume of output in the two sections of the industry.[3] Finally, one may quote the figures of Mr. Mallary, chairman of the House Committee on Manufactures. In 1828 he gave 22 millions as the value of factory-made goods, and 40 millions as that of household production, or a total of 62 millions.[4] With which of these estimates shall one compare the data upon importations, — an average of slightly over 7 million dollars (duty-paid) for the years 1829–1831?[5] And how shall one place a sure valuation upon household production? There exists in fact no adequate basis for discriminating among the several estimates of value put upon factory production, nor any means of arriving at a sound valuation of household output. Therefore, a comparison upon the basis of value of factory, household, and foreign contributions to the domestic market obviously is impracticable.

A somewhat better basis is that of wool consumption, i. e., a comparison of the wool consumed in domestic household and factory production with the amount embodied in the fabrics im-

[1] *Census of 1860*, iii, p. xxxii.

[2] North, *Bulletin*, 1901, pp. 206–207.

[3] *Report of Convention of the Friends of Domestic Industry*, p. 79.

The *Report* gives the ratio in terms of volume between factory and homemade fabrics as three to two; but in terms of value the ratio would presumably give greater weight to the factory output.

[4] *Congressional Debates*, March 4, 1828, p. 1733.

[5] This figure excludes importations of carpets, knit-goods, and stuff-goods. The first two are excluded with obvious propriety. Stuff-goods were also noncompetitive, except in a minor, indirect way, with American woolen fabrics. No domestic manufacture of such goods existed, — at least, no significant manufacture. Even protectionists of the period paid little or no attention to this particular form of importation.

ported. Even here one must adopt indirect and rather approximate methods. We may begin with the total amount of wool available. This would include the domestic clip, 30 to 32 million pounds around 1830, according to Wright's careful study, and the quantity of imported wool, between 1½ and 2 million pounds.[1] At a maximum, then, 34 million pounds of wool were available for domestic cloth production; and this would, according to our previous surmise, be divided between household and factory use in the ratio of something like 4 to 3: say, 19 or 20 millions for the household and 14½ or 15 millions for the mills.[2] Now, what of importations? Here we have another estimate, that of Mr. Mallary, made in the course of Congressional debate during 1828. According to his calculation, an importation of cloths, flannels, and blankets valued at $6,100,000 represented raw wool to the amount of 9,000,000 pounds.[3] Applying this estimate as well as one can to the actual importations in the period 1829–1831, valued at $7,022,000 duty-paid, one arrives at a figure for raw-wool content of 10,900,000 pounds.[4] This result, however, ought, I believe, to be subjected to a liberal discount. Mallary was interested in showing the relation between the volume of wool imported in the form of goods and the domestic wool clip; and accordingly would be tempted to exaggerate the raw-wool content of given fabrics.

[1] This matter was brought out above, p. 247.

[2] This checks fairly closely with the estimate of 15 millions of factory wool consumption arrived at above (p. 249) by a somewhat different method.

[3] *Congressional Debates*, March 4, 1828, p. 1739. Mr. Mallary was computing the amount of wool which would be required if all imports of raw wool and of wool manufactures were prohibited. For wool manufactures, his method of estimation was as follows:

	Value	Raw Wool Equivalent
Cloths and cassimeres imported	$5,000,000	6,500,000 lbs.
Flannels and baizes	500,000	1,000,000 "
Blankets	600,000	1,500,000 "
Total	$6,100,000	9,000,000 "

[4] For the period 1829–1831 the total values (duty-paid) of the three groups of imports mentioned by Mallary were as follows:

Cloths and cassimeres	$5,895,000
Flannels	123,000
Blankets	1,003,000

Moreover, I have attempted, with the assistance of the trade, to check Mallary's estimates by calculating the wool content of the British exports of wool goods, for which statistics of yardage are available.[1] I should be inclined to place the figure for importations on a good round basis of 7,500,000 pounds.

Finally, taking this estimate into comparison with domestic consumption, we reach the following summary: wool used in American household manufacture, 19 to 20 million pounds; that employed in American factories, 14½ to 15 million pounds; and that represented in importations, 7½ million pounds, — or, roughly, ratios of four, three, and one and a half respectively. And these ratios, it may be added, tally closely, at least as far as the part played by importations is concerned, with certain contemporary opinions on the subject: the statement of Mr. Tufts, a prominent mill-owner of the times who, before the Committee on Manufactures in 1828, remarked that something like four-fifths of the total domestic consumption of woolen goods was of domestic manufacture; and the comparison, made by Mr. Mallary in 1828 upon the basis of value, between domestic factory-made goods and importations, — namely, that the former amounted to a value of 22 million dollars, and the latter to one of only 10 million dollars.[2]

Factory production, in short, supplied little more than a third of the domestic demand for wool cloths at the close of our present period. Undoubtedly it had made great progress since even so recent a date as 1810, when it added merely 200,000 yards to the total domestic supply. Nevertheless, much ground was yet to be gained from the household industry; and if importations bulked anywhere near as large as I have assumed, serious effort still remained to be made in ousting foreign goods. While hold-

[1] Particularly I had the help of Mr. Nathaniel Stevens of M. T. Stevens & Sons Company; and arrived at the figure of 6,500,000 pounds. Even with a 25 per cent added to cover possible underestimates and importations from other countries, the total would be only 8,100,000 pounds.

[2] *State Papers, Finance*, v, 813; *Congressional Debates*, March 4, 1828, p. 1733. I have given considerable weight to Mallary's proportion between domestic mill-made goods and those imported, since it seems unlikely that he would underestimate the part played by the latter.

ing forth promises of a splendid future, the domestic factory of 1830 could not be said to have dominated the local markets of that period.[1]

[1] Incidentally one may note that the relationship between importations and domestic factory production may well account for the intensity with which American manufacturers demanded protective duties. They were competing with a foe who could still push large weights of goods over the existing tariff wall, at least weights which bulked large in comparison with the quantities of goods that they themselves could turn out.

PART III

THE MATURE FACTORY

INTRODUCTION

SUBSEQUENT to the appearance of the factory as a distinct industrial form in the wool manufacture, another satisfactory stopping place is difficult to find, i. e., another period or point of time at which one may pause to discover the status of the industry. Superficially at least, the course of development seems to have been without any important changes in direction, and, to be sure, one must admit that continuity of movement has always played the more dominant rôle. Yet forty years, or about forty years, after the era which we have just been considering, came a turning point of considerable significance. Conditions which had surrounded the industry during the intervening decades were then beginning to change rapidly, and within the manufacture itself important new features were just appearing. Accordingly, by breaking into the evolution of the industry at this point it is possible not merely to summarize the preceding experience but also to understand the nature and sources of subsequent development.

The criteria which have determined the interruption at or around 1870 differ from those which made 1830 a natural stopping point. For the latter the elements of industrial form and technical equipment were paramount. But there is no essential change in industrial form after 1830 until the combination movement of relatively recent years; and while there are factors on the technological side which make 1870 a not unreasonable point for pause and review, they would not be conclusive of themselves. Rather, the elements of most significance are: quality in production, predominance of the factory over competitive methods, geographical distribution, and the commercial policy of the country. In quality of output the years around 1870 cover an important transition. The developments of the preceding years are reflected in the output of the mills, and yet the changes of the succeeding decades are quite distinctly foreshadowed. The years around 1870 also mark the close of that long movement through which, at least for the greater part of the country, the household production of wool fabrics was blotted out; while they also disclose a pronounced dispersion of factories throughout the country, — a feature of the industry not unrelated to the extirpation of the household manufacture. Finally, the Civil War, working many changes in the industry, had bequeathed not only a situation of temporarily extended manufacturing capacity but also a policy of tariff protection which gave a new basis in this regard for subsequent industrial development. To these features, then, special attention will be given.

CHAPTER XIII

GROWTH OF THE INDUSTRY

1. A MARKED expansion in production is one of the most important phenomena in the history of the wool-manufacturing industry during the period between 1830 and 1870. The strength of the young manufacture, as indicated in previous chapters, forecast a considerable growth; but in some ways the subsequent development was more appreciable than could have been anticipated. There had been a marked increase in population, — from 13 millions in 1830 to 39 millions in 1870, — a steady westward extension of settlement, a rapid growth in transportation facilities, and an appreciable tendency toward urban concentration. These together with factors more closely connected with the manufacture itself, e. g., the decline of household fabrication and the initiation of the worsted-cloth production, gave a peculiarly great stimulus to factory output in the whole wool-manufacturing industry. The general net effect of these various forces is portrayed in the following statistics, covering as fully as possible the forty years now under consideration, of the number of mills, the machine equipment in terms of sets, the number of employees, and the consumption of raw material, — although, it may be noted, some of the individual figures presented on the following page are doubtless quite inaccurate.

Obviously the expansion of the industry in the forty years between 1830 and 1870 was extraordinary. The woolen branch alone, measured in terms of sets, increased six-fold. Other significant criteria which permit the woolen and worsted sections to be grouped together indicate even larger growth. The number of employees in 1870 was nearly five times that thirty years before, 1840; and presumably there had been a marked advance in the decade preceding the latter date. But perhaps the best index is that of the consumption of raw materials, picturing as it does the volume of goods turned out. The quantity of wool used in the factories around 1830 has been estimated as something like 14½ or 15 million pounds.[1] As compared with this, the consumption of raw wool alone had advanced to 71 million pounds in 1849 and to 189 million pounds in 1869, — an increase of above twelve-fold by the latter date. But in the meanwhile the utilization of cotton and cotton yarn had undoubtedly increased somewhat more rapidly, particularly with the expansion of the worsted manufacture; while the intermixture of shoddy in wool fabrics, not begun until after 1830, was in 1869 contributing another 19 million pounds of material. Accordingly, measured in terms of all the material employed in the industry, expansion had been substantially more than twelve-fold, though perhaps not quite so much as fifteen-fold. Such a growth of the industry cannot be regarded otherwise than as remarkable.

WOOLEN MILLS[2]

	1837	1840	1845	1849	1859	1869
Number of Establishments	....	1420	1021[3]	1559	1260	2891
Number of Sets	1488	....	1730	....	3209	8366
Number of Employees	....	21,342	....	39,252	41,360	80,053
Raw Material Consumed: millions of pounds[4]	31[5]	....	....	71	99	212

WORSTED MILLS

	1837	1840	1845	1849	1859	1869
Number of Establishments	....	....	....	....	3	102
Number of Employees	....	....	....	....	2378	12,920
Raw Material Consumed: millions of pounds	....	....	....	....	5	22

[1] See above, p. 260.

[2] The sources of data for this tabulation are the Censuses of 1840 to 1870; Benton and Barry, *Statistical View* (p. 124), for the 1837 figures; while those for 1845 are derived from a booklet entitled "Statistics of the Woolen Manufactories in the United States," which is usually attributed to William H. Graham (hereafter referred to as Graham).

[3] A somewhat similar figure, one of 1067, is given by Fleischmann, *Erwerbszweige, Fabrikwesen, und Handel der Vereinigten Staaten von Nord-Amerika*, 1845, pp. 40–43.

[4] The data through 1849 are for wool alone. Thereafter, as the figures become available, cotton and other raw materials are added.

[5] This is, I believe, an overestimate. The estimate previously made in this study (p. 260, above) for the consumption in 1830 was 14 to 15 million pounds. One reason for thinking this figure of Benton and Barry too high is that they assign only 12 million pounds of wool for consumption in the households of the country while estimating the factory consumption at 31 million pounds. Probably 20 to 22 million pounds for the factory consumption, even at the peak of production before the crisis of 1837, would be a liberal estimate.

2. However, this expansion did not take place in a wholly regular and methodical manner. Despite some contradictory data, it is quite clear that the industry experienced two chief periods of growth. One was between 1830 and 1850, which may be considered a continuation of the expansion prior to that time. The second was the decade of the sixties, tied up of course with the conditions imposed by the Civil War. During the decade of the fifties, there was small total expansion: wool consumption, even including the new worsted industry, increased only from 70 to 86 millions of pounds; the number of employees rose but about four thousand; and the number of establishments actually declined. To be sure, there was by no means complete stagnation within the industry. The character of production, the geographical distribution of the manufacture, and the technique of the industry all underwent important modification. The diminution in the number of establishments might even turn out to be connected with certain advantages. Yet on the whole one must conclude that this was a period of relative backwardness. And this fact becomes especially clear if we consider the general situation in the country. The population of the country was increasing from 23 to 31 millions, the kindred cotton manufacture was expanding materially, and indeed the nation as a whole was enjoying a prosperous era. The forces which produced such a pause in the spread of the domestic wool manufacture, as well as those which induced the growth of the other periods, will appear in the later discussion. Chiefly they concern the technical advance, the tariff, and the wool supply, besides the more obvious influence in the last decade of conditions imposed by the war.

The development of the industry, again, concerns more than the increase in total manufacturing capacity. Of scarcely less interest is the geographical location of the industry. At first confining attention to the woolen branch, it is evident that in this regard the decade of the seventies forms a real dividing line. While transportation facilities remained inadequate, mills at a distance from the coast or from the larger centers of wool manufacture could profitably take advantage of the cheap water power, local supplies of wool, and the local markets; provided of course that they confined their production to those fabrics which the local wool permitted them to turn out and which the local markets were willing to purchase. The status of transportation facilities was the most important factor in the earlier decades. For example, British cloths were reported in 1842 to cost in our port cities double their original figures, but, says this account, "as they proceed west they become three times the price they cost to the English consumer."[1] In similar manner the price of domestic goods, if shipped westward, would be much enhanced. It was not strange, then, that factories were established in the western states as population moved forward. Factories in Ohio and western Pennsylvania were noted in the earlier period. The first one in Illinois is dated 1842; by 1847 a mill was in operation at Milwaukee; and by 1856 mills had been set up as far west as Cedar Rapids and Washington, Iowa.[2] In the year 1856, operations in the far western states commenced also. The Willamette Woolen Manufacturing Company was founded at Salem, Oregon, and only three years later, the Pioneer Woolen Mills of San Francisco, California, were established.[3]

The gross effect of this westward movement is reflected in such figures as we have of the proportion of establishments and sets in the several sections of the country:

	Percentage of Establishments			Percentage of Sets		
	New England	Middle States	All Others	New England	Middle States	All Others
1837[4]	....	....	....	60.6	34.6	4.8
1845[5]	45.6	42.7	11.7	56.7	34.9	8.4
1849	30.9	45.9	23.2	....	....	....
1859	31.6	37.8	30.6	51.8	28.7	19.5
1869	21.0	26.9	52.1	40.1	27.9	32.0
1879	24.6	26.6	48.8	49.0	26.8	24.2

[1] 27th Cong., 2nd Sess., *Senate Documents, No. 357*, p. 6.

[2] *Western Monthly*, i, 247; Riley, *Development of Chicago and Vicinity as a Manufacturing Center*, p. 55; Parker, *Iowa Handbook*, 1856, pp. 76, 92.

[3] *Bulletin*, 1869, p. 62; *Hunt's Merchants' Magazine*, xxxix, 127.

[4] Benton and Barry. This enumeration is avowedly an estimate with respect to several states, including Kentucky and Tennessee, and probably if anything understates the proportions in the western communities.

[5] Graham. The same qualifications apply here as with regard to Benton and Barry.

While at all times the New England states held a more important place than any other section with respect to the more significant feature, that of machinery, the decline in their position, apparently steady from the thirties on to 1869, is very suggestive of the changing conditions.[1] The western industry was growing more rapidly than that of New England or that of the middle Atlantic states, both in number of establishments and in amount of equipment,— no considerable change in fact occurring with regard to the industry of the South. And the geographical dissemination of the manufacture was proceeding at a really extraordinary rate.

This westward expansion of the industry even up to the close of our present period was the more remarkable when it is realized that in the latter decades railroad and commercial facilities were increasing with considerable rapidity. The trunk-line railroads were in process of building or consolidation; the transcontinental roads were launched; and the network of the mid-western states was being filled in.[2] Then, purely commercial factors had increased the competitive strength of eastern mills, especially the rise of a more stable distributive system for wool fabrics, while the possession of larger amounts of capital by the eastern manufacturers and merchants would aid them materially in the extension of their trade. Indeed, it was sometimes charged that the

[1] The utilization of "sets" as the basis of comparison, the only basis possible with the earlier years, probably puts the eastern sections in a worse light than if some other measure of manufacturing capacity could be employed. While the proportion of sets in the New England states for 1869 was only 40.1 per cent, that of spindles and of looms was 56.1 and 48.4, respectively. The "set" had by 1869 ceased to be a homogeneous unit. With the broadening of the woolen card by the more progressive eastern establishments, the "set" was a somewhat different thing there than it was in the smaller, less progressive western mills. However, it is doubtful if the picture is much in error on this account. The earlier enumerations, those of 1837 and 1845, probably overvalued the eastern industry, and the decline in ratio of sets in the East between 1859 and 1869 was too great to be compensated by the increase in unit capacity of machines in eastern mills. With the utmost concession, it seems true that the eastern manufacture was making no relative headway in the fifties and sixties, and probably was falling somewhat behind the growth in the rest of the country.

[2] See MacGill, *History of Transportation in the United States before 1860*, ch. 16, and maps.

larger concerns in the East were deliberately "crowding their stuffs into the West in exchange for wool, aided by cash capital not possessed by small operators in the West." [1] But some of the factors which were of force in the earlier decades, — cheap water-supply, local wool supplies, and local markets, — were still of considerable significance. In addition, the extraordinary demand and high profits of the Civil War period brought new concerns in the West as well as increased production in the older eastern centers. Then, too, in some degree the westward movement and wider geographical distribution of the woolen industry is attributable to the peculiar nature of this manufacture. The woolen branch of the wool manufacture in foreign countries as well as the United States has at no time displayed the tendency toward the geographical concentration of industry and large-scale production which has marked the development in other industrial lines, such as the cotton manufacture, the steel industry, and even the sister branch of worsted production. Because of the close attention which the directing head of the establishment must pay to the manufacturing processes, because of importance attaching to the style factor, and for other less significant reasons, the woolen branch is today distributed more widely and is prosecuted on a smaller average scale than the worsted manufacture and many other branches of the textile industry.[2]

Yet there were certain developments in the decades between 1830 and 1870 which foreshadowed some degree of concentration in the eastern states in subsequent years. First, the growth of cities in the East and the early rise of the wholesale clothing trade there were of influence. With the launching and expansion of the clothing manufacture in Chicago and Cleveland some years after, to-

[1] 62nd Cong., 1st Sess., *Senate Documents, No. 72*, p. 1989; quoted in Clark, p. 574.

[2] It is interesting to note that whereas the New England states in 1869 held only 40 to 50 per cent of the woolen manufacture, they contained between 75 and 80 per cent of the cotton-manufacturing industry, as measured by spindleage. As early as 1853 Wallis noted: "Whilst the cotton manufacture is located more exclusively in the Eastern States, the woolen manufacture is extended in almost equal proportions over the whole of the Middle States, and extends itself into the western regions and toward the South" (*British Documents*, 1854 [1717], p. 16).

gether with the growth of cities in the West, the force of these factors was moderated; but always they have been of some influence. Even today the larger part of the clothing industry, including women's with men's clothing, is still in the East. Again, the textile-machine industries arose in the eastern states. From the time that Pliny Earle and his competitors set up the production of card-clothing around Leicester, Massachusetts, in the last years of the eighteenth century, and from the time that a group of machine-builders arose in Worcester, Massachusetts, and in Philadelphia, respectively, the tendency for producers of textile machinery to locate in the eastern states has been steady.

A third factor relates to the facilities for the purchase of raw materials. The early manufacturers, one will recall, sought after their wool by journeys through the countryside, by offers to exchange cloths for wool, and by similar devices. But rather soon the evolution of a specialized trade of wool dealers began; and in this development Boston played an important rôle. For example, as early as 1828, one James Vila was conducting a wool warehouse at 1 Bath Street, near Hancock, Boston; and by the fifties there were about fifteen wool merchants located in Boston.[1] Moreover, as the years passed, Boston came to hold an ever-expanding position in relation to the total wool dealings of the country. In the swelling importations of foreign staple, the city was coming to have a particularly large share. By the years around 1870, Boston merchants were securing 40 per cent of the import movement in wool of all sorts;[2] while of the domestic clip, they were supposed in these years to be receiving at least a third.[3]

Finally, the element of labor supply should be noted. Popu-

[1] Shaw, "The Wool Trade of the United States:" 61st Cong., 1st Sess., *Senate Documents, No. 70*, pp. 29, 42, 52. This account is most fragmentary and extends only to 1870.

[2] The total importation of wool (including carpet wools) increased ten-fold between 1830 and the decade of the fifties. By the seventies this movement had again expanded, until it was now over three-fold the figure of the fifties.

[3] Boston Board of Trade, *Report for 1872*, p. 23. This was probably an underestimate. Comparison of receipts of wool at Boston during the early seventies, with the total domestic clip (as estimated), indicates a ratio of over 40 per cent.

lation was greater in the East than in the West or South, and it was more concentrated. Not only were the growing cities a broadening market for the products of the wool manufacture, but they also served a good recruiting ground for mill help. Moreover, immigrants were strongly inclined to settle in the older communities, especially in the New England and middle-Atlantic states, and these foreigners contributed in this period a large contingent to the working force of American wool-manufacturing establishments.

With opportunities of special value as regards purchase of raw material, supply of machinery, supply of labor, and sale of finished product, obviously there was reason to expect an effect sooner or later upon the localization of the wool manufacture in New England or at least in the eastern states. And, indeed, for these or for other reasons, such localization did at last take place. The westward movement ceased between 1869 and 1879 (see above tabulation), and subsequently the East, especially New England, has secured a constantly stronger position in the industry, — of which more later.

On the other hand, the worsted manufacture had by 1869 already become localized, — indeed, localized in a higher degree than it is today. The newly acquired industry was to a peculiar extent concentrated in Massachusetts. While only 35 mills out of a reported total of 102 were situated in the state, these mills contained 118 out of the whole 161 combs given for the country.[1] Such might perhaps be considered a natural condition for a young industry, especially when the products of that industry were confined to a rather limited range.[2] With a greater maturity and with an increased diversity of output, some greater

[1] Some of the establishments reported by the *Census of 1870* as worsted mills were apparently engaged solely or largely upon woolen goods. Thus for New York State, seven establishments were indicated, containing one comb but eight sets of carding machinery. Similarly, Pennsylvania's thirty-one mills held only twenty combs but seventy-four sets of cards. The confusion of the two branches will later be seen to have occurred quite frequently in the earlier days.

[2] In part the concentration of the worsted manufacture in 1870 may be explained on the basis of the supply of capital. The new worsted mills called for considerable capital investment and would tend to seek those areas where capital was most plentiful, that is, the eastern states.

geographical distribution took place. In part this movement was caused by the adaptation of the newer branches to conditions in the several sections of the country, and in part by the changes in our general economic status; but it never led to a geographical dispersion for the worsted branch that was as great as in the case of the woolen manufacture.

3. A third important feature of the industry's development between 1830 and 1870 was the growth in size of the representative establishment. While this phase of the development will be touched upon frequently in the succeeding pages, we may here note the evidence which statistical data have to present. On account of the relatively recent development of the worsted manufacture prior to 1870, consideration of that branch may for the present be omitted. In the woolen end, the number of workers per establishment according to the earliest figures available, those of 1840, was only fifteen. By 1869, the average had increased to twenty-eight per establishment, or nearly 100 per cent. In number of sets per mill there had also been advance, although such information runs back only to 1845. In the latter year, according to Graham, the establishments of the country averaged only 1.7 sets, but twenty-five years later this figure had increased to 2.9 sets. Yet such data do not tell the whole story. One must examine the several sections of the country, at least as far as possible.

The situation in the western communities is particularly significant, not only because it mirrors in a measure the preceding development in the East, but because it explains why the average for the country in number of employees or sets per establishment did not increase as rapidly as one would expect in the forty-year period now under discussion. As already intimated, the western woolen mills were chiefly small affairs. In 1845, apparently there were few western mills indeed with more than one set of machinery. Even Ohio's seventy-nine mills were reported by Graham to contain but ninety-seven sets. As late as 1869, too, the average size of western woolen establishments was still low. For the whole area of the Ohio and upper Mississippi valleys, the mills averaged less than two sets apiece, although New England factories could boast an average of five to six sets, — and more productive sets, too. Furthermore, the connection of these establishments with the local markets remained intimate. A western writer states in 1870 that manufacturers in that region "buy their wool and sell their cloth near home. In some cases, they exchange as much as 70,000 pounds of wool in a year directly with the farmers for cloth." [1] And an inquiry in 1876 elicited frequent remarks from western mills such as "we sell our own goods at the mill," or "goods made for home consumption." [2] Mr. John L. Hayes, moving spirit and first secretary of the National Association of Wool Manufacturers, summarized the situation when he reported of western producers: that they were "confident that if they did not attempt to make their mills too large, and continued to seek their principal markets in the counties and local districts where they are established, . . . they should be prosperous." [3]

On the other hand, the period 1830 to 1870 had witnessed the development of production on a substantially larger scale in the eastern states. By 1830 the evolution of fair-sized mills was already an important feature in the eastern, and especially in the New England manufacture; and this movement proceeded with no appreciable pause in the subsequent period. The equipment of New England woolen mills was reported by Benton and Barry in 1837 to average a little more than two and a quarter sets per establishment. By 1859 this average had risen to over four sets, and by 1869, as already stated, to five and one half sets. That the increase was not more rapid nor more decided may be attributed to the slower development of Vermont, New Hampshire, and Maine, where mills retained somewhat the same character that western mills possessed. In Massachusetts alone, where the industry was most highly developed, the mills had averaged two and three-quarters sets apiece in 1836; by 1845, according to Graham, they had increased that average to nearly three and one-half; while by 1869 they had attained an average of over seven

[1] *Bulletin*, 1870–1871, p. 450.
[2] *Awards and Claims, Exhibition of 1876*, p. 443.
[3] *Bulletin*, 1870–1871, p. 217.

and one-third sets.[1] Similarly, in number of employees per mill, the Massachusetts establishments were drawing away from the rest of the country. The average for the country in 1840 had been fifteen, and in 1869 only twenty-eight; but Massachusetts, already possessing approximately thirty-seven per mill in 1837, had increased that figure to nearly eighty-five by 1865. This section of the country, moreover, was destined to become of even greater significance as the site of large establishments, and its experience serves as advance notice of subsequent experience for the country as a whole. Indeed, it is significant to add that for the whole country the year 1870 was in this matter of average size of mill as in other considerations a real dividing line. Forces were gathering, and in fact had been slowly and inconspicuously increasing in vigor since the commencement of the industry in this country, which were to lead in the following decades to a substantial change in the preëxisting situation. The number of individual establishments was destined to decline from the high-water mark of 2891 mills in 1869, until it reached a low point of 501 in 1914; and meanwhile the number of employees per mill — and other similar indices of size — was to rise rapidly. The smallest mills tended to drop out, both in the East and West, and despite the advantages of small-scale production, improvements in technique and administration allowed an appreciable growth in the size of the representative concern.

Finally, we may return to a brief notice of the worsted manufacture. Accurate evidence concerning the increase in number and size of establishments does not run back far; and yet such as exists does indicate that the years around 1870 were for this manufacture as much a turning point as they were for the woolen branch. From the three or four mills which were turning out worsted goods in 1830,[2] increase in number apparently was slow

[1] Between 1837 and 1845 the increase in size of Massachusetts mills is better shown in the following comparison:

	1-set	2-set	3–4 set	Over 4-set
1836	70	45	49	19
1845	49	33	34	25

(Benton and Barry, and Graham.)

[2] See above, p. 153.

until the fifties; but even by 1859 probably not over ten or a dozen mills were wholly or principally engaged on this type of work.[1] Thereafter came a prodigious outburst of activity, the number of establishments jumping to 102 in 1869, — according to the Census for that year. The succeeding decade witnessed a decrease to 76; and then came a steady increase until 1909. The years before 1870 were years of growth partaking somewhat of a hothouse character; and then came a period of maturing and acclimatization, so to speak, which rendered possible a subsequent era of renewed expansion. Even in the decade of the seventies the number of combs in worsted mills increased from 161 in 102 mills, to 288 in 76 establishments; and the number of employees from an average of 127 per establishment to one of 247. In short, at the time when the woolen industry was drawing free of the conditions which the westward expansion and the slow and uncertain growth of a half century or more had imposed, the younger worsted branch was just recovering from the overextension induced by a rather impetuous development. In this respect, as in many others, the course of development in the two branches of the wool-manufacturing industry supplies interesting and significant contrasts.

[1] The *Census of 1860* reports only three establishments in the worsted manufacture, but, as will appear later, this figure is inaccurate.

CHAPTER XIV

THE DECLINE IN HOUSEHOLD PRODUCTION

To the sketch above given of the growth of factory production in the American wool manufacture may be contrasted another, which in a large measure is the complement of the first, — the decline in the household output of wool fabrics. With respect to the period up to 1830 it was observed that while the household industry was declining in some parts of the country, there were evidences of much vigor in other sections. By 1870, however, the forces of decay had changed the whole aspect of that production.

The earlier decades, the thirties and forties, manifested substantially less change than the subsequent period. References to the household production, to be sure, become less and less frequent throughout this time, but this is in part explicable on the basis of the peculiar interest evoked by the new factories, and in part by the disappearance of the household system from the regions nearer the towns. The statistics of New York State, for example, indicate a decline of only a third in the family manufacture of wool fabrics between 1825 and 1845.[1] At the latter date, too, Fleischmann remarks that "in every state there exists still . . . many carding-mills, which prepare for spinning" the

[1] The data for New York State are as follows:

	1825 (yards)	1835 (yards)	1845 (yards)	1855 (yards)	1865 (yards)
Amount of fulled cloth mfd. in the domestic way	2,918,000	2,184,000	1,664,000	198,000	259,000
Amount of flannel and other non-fulled cloth similarly mfd. . .	3,468,000	2,790,000	2,650,000	380,000	632,000

The figures for 1865 probably represent a recrudescence of household production stimulated by the patriotic sentiment — the desire to be useful — or by the exigencies of the Civil War. Thus the experiences of the War of 1812 were in some degree repeated, and, again, those of the World War — the knitting of socks and sweaters — were in a measure foreshadowed. The declining influence of successive wars upon this family manufacture of wool goods is of peculiar interest.

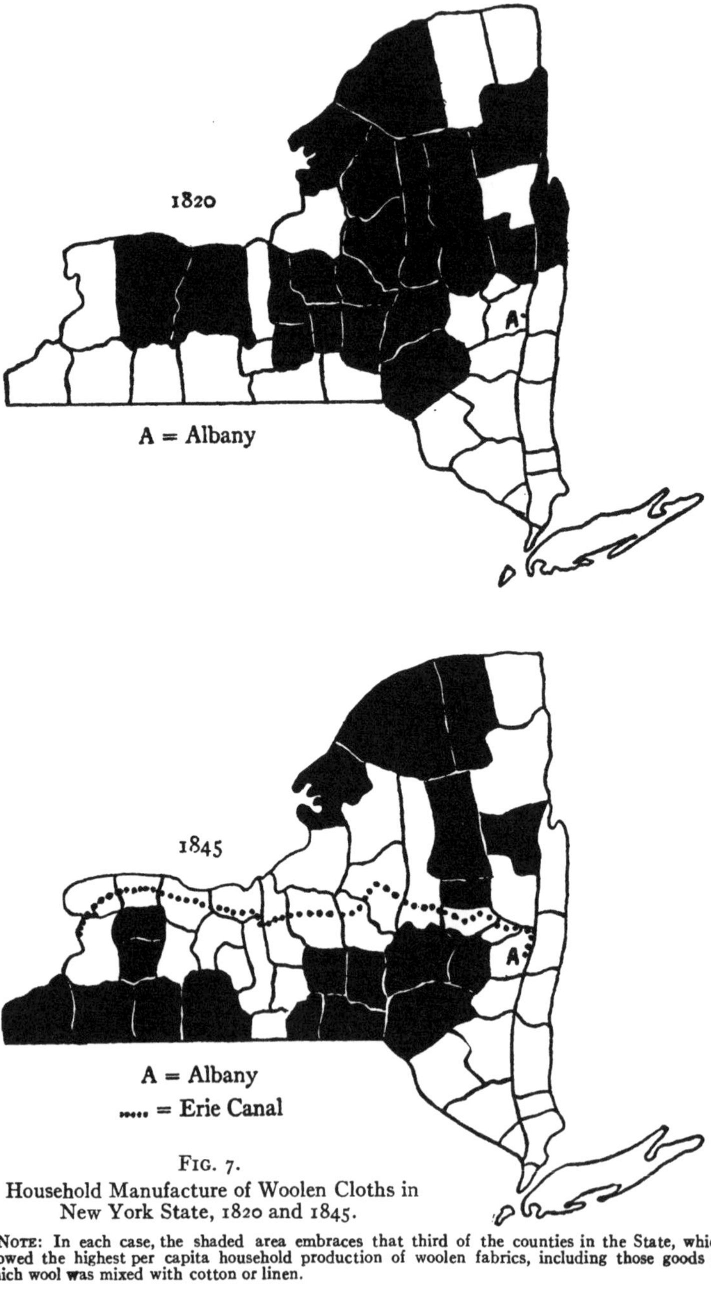

FIG. 7.
Household Manufacture of Woolen Cloths in New York State, 1820 and 1845.

NOTE: In each case, the shaded area embraces that third of the counties in the State, which showed the highest per capita household production of woolen fabrics, including those goods in which wool was mixed with cotton or linen.

farmers' wool.[1] And even as late as 1860, 712 carding and fulling mills were recorded by the Census, — and this was probably a serious underestimate.[2]

But as Wallis suggested in 1854, the home manufacture was "becoming daily more and more exceptional."[3] And this could hardly be otherwise with the growth in the factory production, the cheapening and improvement of its output, and with the advent of better distributive and more adequate transportation facilities.[4] The operation of these forces was so slow and inconspicuous that a picture of the movement cannot often be caught. However, the figures of household production in New York State, though probably far from accurate of themselves, do give us an intimation of what must have been the experience of the country as a whole. In the accompanying maps, the shaded areas represent that third of New York counties which in the Censuses of 1820 and 1845, respectively, showed the heaviest per capita household production of woolen fabrics. It is evident that in 1820 the counties nearer the City of New York and those on the line of the Hudson River had already been affected by the domestic factory production or had been influenced by the importation of woolen goods; or, contrariwise, the counties with the highest household manufacture were those located at some distance from the distributive centers. It is also noteworthy that two counties which were among the heaviest wool-growing areas, Washington and Otsego, were also in this latter group. By 1845, however, a curious split had occurred. The counties of heaviest per capita production were now either in the northern, less well-developed section of the state, or along the southern border. To one at all familiar with the history of transportation the reason is plain. In the interval between 1820 and 1845 the Erie Canal had been completed, and some portions of railroads reaching out westward from Albany, both traversing counties which had now

[1] Fleischmann, p. 45.

[2] As late as 1880, 570 carding and fulling mills were reported in *Census* (ii, 963).

[3] Wallis, *Report*, *British Documents*, 1854 [1717], p. 16.

[4] As to the improvement of the distributive organization for wool cloth, see the following chapter.

ceased to have heavy per capita production. The introduction of transportation facilities had occasioned a decay in the household industry.

But in explaining the general decline in family production in New York State, another factor should be added: the establishment within the region of many wool-manufacturing concerns, especially small enterprises dependent upon a strictly local market for their goods. The number of woolen mills had increased from 217 in 1825 to 345 in 1845, a high-water mark from which there was recession in subsequent decades. The expansion of wool-factory production before 1845 impressed Randall, together with the effect of this production upon household manufacture. The number of carding-fulling establishments, those adjuncts to household work, "is decreasing in New York," he says, "as manufactories of the common fabrics, worn by farmers and other laboring men, are increasing in every direction — many of them doing custom work either at the halves, or at a fixed sum per yard — and all of them exchanging cloth for wool. By either of these methods, the cloth can be obtained as cheaply, perhaps cheaper, than to manufacture it in families."[1] Small wonder, then, that there was a flagging interest in the premiums offered by the New York State Agricultural Society for domestic wool manufactures. Even as early as 1845 the officers reported with a regret which was apparently blind, that except in such articles as blankets and flannels "there was but a meagre competition" at the Utica fair. The failure of competition was particularly noticeable in woolen cloth, "which ought to be a staple of home manufacture. Instead of fifty pieces being presented for premiums, which might be considered a moderate estimate, there were but two, and those manufactured by machinery!"[2] The country was surely headed straight for destruction. But the course of development was already set, and by 1855 the volume of household production as reported by the state census amounted to less than 10 per cent of the corresponding output in 1825.

[1] Randall, *Sheep Husbandry*, 1848, p. 89. See also Fleischmann, p. 36.

[2] *Transactions* of the New York State Agricultural Society, v, 154.

Such, in general, was the experience of other eastern communities, although detailed information with regard to these others is much less adequate. The most concrete evidence relates to the number of fulling mills. While the *Census of 1840* showed nearly 2300 such establishments in the eastern and middle states, that of 1860 reported only 160. In the seaboard southern states there was a somewhat similar movement, although apparently less rapid. With a more stable basis of the economic system, the change in methods of production or rather in sources of cloth supply was slower. Even as late as 1858 the Milledgeville (Georgia) Manufacturing Company was calling "the attention of the public to their new and improved machinery for carding wool and weaving kerseys."[1] However, unquestionably the household manufacture in all the eastern area was in process of steady decline.

Nor was the decline of household production in the eastern states accompanied by so considerable an expansion of such manufacture in the western communities as one might expect from the earlier history of the household industry in this country or from the westward expansion of the factory production. No doubt a substantial amount of household manufacture went on in the western states unnoted by contemporary writers because of its very normality: it was not worth mentioning. However, there are evidences that the manufacture in this manner did not have the prevalence nor the persistence there that it had had in the eastern regions. It is true that such manufacture of this type as did exist in 1860 was localized chiefly in the West and in the South (especially in the Southwest): of the 712 fulling and carding establishments reported by the *Census of 1860*, 328 were accredited to the western states and 217 to the southern. But references to home production in these communities are peculiarly infrequent; and the references that do occur are often inconclusive. Thus it was reported in 1854 that from the considerable production of yarn by Pennsylvania woolen mills, a large proportion went "for the supply of the West in the materials of home weaving;" but the note was appended that this industry

[1] *Documentary History of American Industrial Society*, ii, 330.

was declining steadily.[1] Statistics of household manufacture in the western states in the years 1840–1860, while undoubtedly far from accurate, may yet be quoted to show the general trend. The only figures available cover all homemade manufactures. For this miscellaneous group of commodities, but including wool cloth, the per capita production in representative western states was in terms of value as follows:[2]

	1840	1850	1860
Ohio	$1.22	$0.87	$0.26
Kentucky	3.36	2.50	1.81
Indiana	1.88	1.65	0.63
Illinois	2.09	1.35	0.54
Missouri	2.99	2.45	1.59

Apparently the establishment of woolen mills followed rather closely upon the heels of settlement, or at least mills which, providing an opportunity for wool carding or fulling, also carried on some production of cloths. Typical perhaps was the concern at Milledgeville, Georgia, just mentioned. While "to the public" it called attention to its new machinery for carding wool and weaving, the advertisement continued: "to Merchants, We recommend the kerseys of our own manufacture."[3] The erection of mills which manufactured on commission, bartered cloth for wool, and in other ways cultivated the local markets, in a con-

[1] Wallis's *Report, British Documents*, 1854 [1717], p. 16. A diligent search of local material with regard to the West has yielded less than a half-dozen references to household production of woolen fabrics. Typical are the following: Riley, *Development of Chicago and Vicinity as a Manufacturing Center* (p. 55), states that "a coarse cloth called linsey-woolsey was manufactured to a considerable extent in the homes throughout the territory" in the period prior to 1850. Again, in Wilson's *Description of Iowa*, published in 1865 (p. 85), the need of "woolen and fulling and carding mills" is mentioned, "to make the yarn required for our woolen socks, making no allowance for that needed for domestic cloths for farmers' use." Such statements taken in connection with the known spread of woolen mills through the West do not suggest a very widespread practice of household manufacture.

[2] Lippincott, *Economic Development of the United States*, p. 201. It is noteworthy that in the more easterly states and the states with better transportation facilities, the per capita decline was greater than in the others.

The total value of such manufactures manifests a decrease in the decade 1850–1860. For all the states above mentioned, the total values were as follows: 1840, $7,909,000; 1850, $8,633,000; and 1860, $6,585,000.

[3] *Documentary History of American Industrial Society*, ii, 330. For western mills, see discussion above.

siderable measure cut the ground from under the household production, especially in the West where a more adequate supply of wool was available and where the development of these small factories was more frequent.

Again, the improvement of transportation facilities came rapidly in the western regions, treading more closely upon the heels of settlement than was true of the East. To the freight route of the Mississippi River and its tributaries were added the more effective and more direct east-and-west lines of the Erie Canal and railroads. Such improvement meant much to the western farmer, particularly the possibility of substituting money crops for subsistence farming. The farmer was no longer so restricted in his operations, but could now turn to the production of commodities which would command a wide market, and in exchange for which he could purchase his requirements of cloths and of anything else from the industrial communities.

In short, then, it seems probable that while household production of woolen cloths may possibly have played a substantial part in the thirties and forties, the subsequent decades saw a marked decline until by the seventies it was a negligible feature even of western economic life.

CHAPTER XV

CHANGES IN MARKET ORGANIZATION

AMONG the factors responsible for the expansion of the factory production of wool fabrics in the period now under consideration was, as already intimated, the development of a more stable and better integrated system of distribution. In some respects, this development was of course but a continuation of that which was shown occurring in the decades before 1830; but the future of the new system was not wholly clear at that time. In particular, the position of the rising system was then undermined by the auction sales method, which indeed was increasing in importance even as the "orthodox" system was feeling its way to a better coördination; and peace in the distributive end of the wool manufacture would not be safe so long as the auction sale held such a substantial place. The course of the development in the decades before 1870, however, was something more than a removal of handicaps. In an important measure it marked the evolution of the modern avenues of distribution, the institution of new forms and methods by means of which wool fabrics were transferred more satisfactorily from mill to ultimate consumer.

As just suggested, the suppression or elimination of the auction sales system was of necessity a primary step. All evidence, in fact, points to the view that this factor in the distributive system reached its zenith in the years around 1830, at least in so far as textiles are concerned. Statistics of the value of dry goods sold at auction in New York City, the chief auction center of the country, show a substantial decline between 1829–1831 and 1839–1841, the last years for which such figures are available. In the earlier three-year period, the sales of domestic dry goods had averaged $4,419,000 and of foreign dry goods, $10,125,000; while a decade later the quantities had diminished to $3,149,000 and $8,538,000, respectively.[1] The decrease was obviously greater

[1] *New York State, Report of Comptroller*, 1842, pp. 130–131.

in the case of domestic goods; and this situation would be anticipated, since the more orderly methods of distribution were more advantageous to domestic producers and the auction sales more attractive to the importer.

In subsequent years, too, the position of the auction sale seemingly became not only relatively but absolutely less important. This is surely true in the case of imported fabrics. The Comptroller of New York State in his report for 1849 called special attention to the falling off which had occurred in the auction duties during the preceding decades. Whereupon, with the lack of insight which is sometimes conspicuous in official quarters, he stated: "With an increasing population, and an increasing commerce, it is incredible that there should be a decrease of sales by auction. How is this falling off to be accounted for?" And with reasoning in line with the rest of his argument, he fell back on the proposition that no doubt "it has arisen from fraud."[1] This accusation elicited remonstrance from auctioneers and merchants, and in their responses there is much of interest in the present connection. The greater bulk of their testimony refers to imported goods, as already suggested, since articles of domestic produce and manufacture had been freed from auction duty in 1846. With regard to foreign goods, however, besides stressing the substitution of domestic for foreign fabrics and the decline in value of textiles,[2] arguments against the Comptroller's accusation asserted: that "the intercourse induced by steam navigation has brought together the agents of foreign commission houses and the jobbers of this country, thus lessening the inducements for a speculative or uncertain importation," and that "many articles which were formerly sold at auction largely, are now . . . sold through brokers." Among these goods now sold through brokers, woolen fabrics were mentioned; and an elaborate summary was presented of the advantages to both seller and buyer flowing from "private sales." Furthermore, it was stated that "in Boston, the auction business is reduced in a greater ratio than in this city (New York). In Philadelphia there has

[1] *New York Assembly Documents, No. 5*, 1849, p. 88.

[2] The duties were assessed on an ad valorem basis.

also been a falling off. In Baltimore it amounts to nothing as compared with private sales."[1] With such a situation in the distribution of imported fabrics, for which sale by auction would be more attractive than for domestic goods, it appears unlikely that the auction system in the latter connection could have maintained any considerable sway. To be sure, there was no complete elimination of auction sales for domestic fabrics. Notices of auction sales appear from time to time. Indeed, what is said to have been till then the largest auction sale of woolen fabrics ever held in this country occurred in 1878. The increased manufacturing capacity of the American industry derived from extensions of the Civil War period led finally to "so great a glut of production in blankets that the largest manufacturers of blankets found it indispensable to relieve the market by an auction sale in New York."[2] But episodes of this sort do not make a system. The position of the auction sale as an independent factor in the distribution of wool fabrics may be said to have declined steadily in the thirties and forties until by the succeeding decade that method had become a negligible feature of the marketing organization.

The "regular" method of distribution, developed in the preceding period, experienced some important changes during the years that followed. With the expansion and diversification of textile manufacture in this country came a specialization in the

[1] *New York Assembly Documents, No. 218*, 1849, pp. 8, 12.

Among other reasons noted was the "facility of bonding merchandise, enabling importers to hold from the hammer the surplus, at least until the market is prepared to take it for distribution in the regular mode of private sale as demanded for the immediate consumption of the country" (p. 8).

Private sales are alleged to be to the interest of owner and of commission merchant, because the former gets more for his goods and the latter receives his full commissions, which apparently he had otherwise to split with the auctioneer. Then "the buyer prefers to buy at private sale, because he gets a credit of from eight to ten months, instead of six, a great convenience to the jobbers of dry goods, who are obliged to give very long credits to their country customers without any positive or fixed period of payment" (p. 12).

On the decline in importance of auction sales generally, see Westerfield, *Early History of American Auctions*, p. 208.

[2] *Bulletin*, 1881, p. 386. See also Hayes, *Report on Exhibition of 1876*, p. 49, giving a case of an auction sale of flannels; it was "by a single house" representing 157 sets of machinery in different mills, and netted $2,500,000.

distributive system, placed by one writer in the decade of the forties. The classification of goods was carried to a finer point than theretofore, and commission merchants arose who handled distinct lines such as cloths and cassimeres, or silks and dress goods.[1] Moreover, the relation between mills and particular dealers became closer. During the first part of the period under consideration, it was frequent, and perhaps usual, for manufacturers to sell through several commission houses. Thus, the Pontoosuc Manufacturing Company of Pittsfield, Massachusetts, in 1835 was doing business with four concerns, though one of them, Hutchinson & Tiffany of New York, handled three-quarters of the sales. Again, S. Slater & Sons Company, of Webster, Massachusetts, in the forties and fifties, dealt chiefly with four or five houses, but sent smaller weights to three or four other concerns. The Stevens mill in Andover, Massachusetts, at about this period operated in a similar fashion, though in a typical year such as 1844 consignments were made to as many as nineteen concerns with amounts running from 14 to 1428 pieces.[2] But already change was coming in the trade. When the Middlesex Manufacturing Company was established in 1830, Lawrence, Stone & Company became the selling agents.[3] The sales of the Hamilton Woolen Company, founded in 1831 under that name, were subsequently handled by the wholesale house, Tiffany, Sayles & Hitchcock, which had taken over the enterprise in the preceding

[1] Beach, "Dry Goods Trade," in Depew, *Hundred Years of American Commerce*, p. 556. The writer makes the exception of "the regular dry-goods jobbing houses" in his statement that "the general trade, both wholesale and retail . . . began to make more or less separate distinctions in the goods which it sold."

[2] Records of Pontoosuc Manufacturing Company, S. Slater & Sons Company, and M. T. Stevens and Sons Company. The Slater and Stevens mills had earlier shown a tendency to trade with only one selling house. Why they shifted back to the use of several agents, does not appear. Where so many houses are mentioned, it may be that the data in the records refer to shipments rather than consignments, i. e., shipments on advice of the regular selling houses; or they may refer to sales direct to jobbing houses or even perhaps retailers. Variation from the "regular" method of distribution does not seem wholly unusual. Of the Hamilton Woolen Company it is said that "in very early days it is apparent that goods were frequently shipped to nearby markets, such as Hartford and Albany (instead of to Boston), and some of the correspondence was direct with local merchants in these centers" (private letter from an official of the Company).

[3] Middlesex Manufacturing Company, *Report of 1897*, p. 3.

year.[1] Apparently other manufacturing concerns followed in this lead, although data in this matter are scarce. At least by the sixties, the practice seems to have become quite general for a selling house to be the exclusive selling agency for a given mill. Pomeroy, Adams & Company of New York were described as "agents" for the Rock Manufacturing Company and the Hockanum Company, both of Rockville, Connecticut, and for the North Adams Woolen Company of North Adams, Massachusetts; and similarly A. T. Stewart & Company, long a prominent house in the dry-goods trade, was agent for a group of mills, including the Pontoosuc Manufacturing Company, above mentioned, and the Utica Steam Woolen Mills, of Utica, New York.[2] In general, as the trade in wool fabrics became more specialized and as the "regular" system of distribution became better established, the employment of special selling agents grew to be the dominant feature of selling practice on the part of domestic mills; and, one may add, this custom has continued to form an important feature of selling practice since that time.

There were a few instances of a phenomenon, sale through a mill agency or direct selling, which became of particular significance only in more modern times. In the crisis of 1857, the Middlesex Company found itself in a bad way by virtue of the "mistakes and irregularities" of its selling house, Lawrence, Stone & Company. To free the company from possible future embarrassment flowing from the same source, provision was made in the following year that the mill's production should be sold through the office of the treasurer. As Cowley remarked, "Until now, all our manufacturing companies had sold their products through commission houses in Boston and New York, whose compensation was determined by the gross amount of the sales,—not by the amount of the profits;" and the Middlesex Company now substituted a method whereby not only was the business of selling kept directly under the control of the Company, but the interest of the selling agent was made for the most part identical

[1] Brief record of the Hamilton Woolen Company (manuscript).

[2] *Bulletin*, 1869, pp. 352–370. There is evidence of the ownership of woolen mills by selling houses: e. g., that of the Fitchburg Woolen Mill by Rufus S. Frost & Company of Boston, wholesale merchants and selling agent for this mill.

with that of the enterprise.[1] This example was followed by a few other concerns. For instance, S. Slater & Sons Company is said to have begun selling its own goods in 1866, and the treasurer of the Assabet Manufacturing Company, of Assabet, Massachusetts, is reported in 1869 as its selling agent.[2] But apparently this type of organization was rather exceptional before 1870. With the growth of larger manufacturing units in subsequent decades, the increase in direct selling came as an appropriate corollary.

But too much attention might readily be paid to the wholesale end of the distributive system. Essential to the orderly marketing of fabrics were the jobbers, although, unfortunately, of these merchants little definite information is available. During the greater part of this period they undoubtedly were the most important, perhaps in the early days almost the sole customers of the commission houses; and as such they are said to have "ruled the trade." [3] At first they apparently were located exclusively in the chief eastern commercial centers, Boston, New York, Philadelphia, and Baltimore, where they stood in convenient geographical interposition between the commission houses or selling agencies and the scattered retail stores of the East. However, when the area of sale for eastern products increased with the expansion of internal commerce, jobbing houses were established in the larger interior cities, e. g., Chicago and St. Louis, and trade in wool fabrics for the western region went largely through their hands. To be sure, the erection of wool-working mills in the West during the period before 1870, — mills which turned out goods especially suited to their local clientèles, — handicapped the development of a nation-wide distributive system. But ultimately these enterprises were destined to give way before the growing competitive strength of eastern mills; and by 1860 even, the products of the latter were already serving a much broader market than they commanded, say, at the close of our previous period.

[1] Cowley, *History of Lowell*, 1868, p. 54. See also Reports of the Company for 1857 and 1858; and North, *Bulletin*, 1902, p. 318.

[2] *Slater Mills at Webster, 1812–1912*, p. 33; *Bulletin*, 1869, p. 370.

[3] *Bulletin*, 1873, p. 128.

With the increase in size of market area for eastern cloths came the evolution of a somewhat more complex system of distribution than that which had previously sufficed. In the earlier decades, it seems to have been the custom for the country storekeepers to come to the shops of the New York and other eastern cloth sellers; and to some extent this practice continued. As late as 1853, Greeley speaks of "the country merchants" as present in New York during October of that year "busily selecting their winter stock."[1] But subsequently the commercial traveler developed in this trade as he did in others, and the selling houses sought out the retailer.[2] Possibly the rise of the commercial traveler was due in part to the efforts of eastern jobbers to keep control of the whole domestic market. If so, that device was not sufficient for the end in view; and, as I have just indicated, later decades saw the appearance of western jobbing houses. Finally, one may note the rise of a new distributive agency in the eastern centers. To serve as intermediaries between western jobbers and the eastern mills, certain houses which had heretofore been doing a simple jobbing business in a more restricted field, seem to have set themselves up as wholesalers or general dry-goods jobbers. Such general jobbing houses were at first located wholly in eastern cities, notably in New York — where indeed they were always most numerous — but later they put in appearance in the larger western centers. And such wholesalers apparently had by 1870 become significant factors in the distributive organization. Accordingly, commission houses, selling agencies, general jobbers, local jobbers, and retailers all took part by the sixties and seventies in the transmission of wool fabrics from the mills to the ultimate consumer.

The "regular" distributive system as elaborated and developed by the middle of the century, however, was hardly established before the rise of new forces began to disturb its symmetry. One such force was the rise of the wholesale clothing industry. In the middle thirties came the first stirrings of this manufacture

[1] *Art and Industry at the Crystal Palace*, p. 229.

[2] Beach, in Depew's *Hundred Years of American Commerce* (p. 556), mentions the development of the "commercial traveller system."

and trade. Beginning with the production of overcoats, the industry grew rapidly despite a setback in the crisis of 1837, receiving encouragement subsequently from the California demand after the gold discoveries, and particularly from the army requirements during the Civil War and those of demobilized soldiers immediately afterwards. It was also aided by the invention and introduction of labor-saving machinery, notably the Singer sewing machine, devised in 1850, but also a button-holing machine, and, scarcely less important than the sewing machine, that for cutting the cloth, invented by Isaac Fenno about 1870. As yet the industry had not developed the localization and intimate connection with city slums which later blackened its history;[1] but by 1870 it had become a distinctly important industry, promising yet bigger things in the future. Statistics of the wholesale clothing industry bear out this impression. Between 1849 and 1869, the number of establishments increased from 4278 to 9705, and the value added by manufacture from $22,581,451 to $67,595,752.[2]

The influence of this development upon the American wool manufacture can hardly be overemphasized, its effect upon the

[1] A considerable amount of "putting-out" existed in the industry down into the seventies, the employment by Boston houses extending "into New Hampshire, Vermont, and Maine, and particularly the latter state. . . . A single large concern in the city will employ as many as forty or fifty firms, in all parts of New England, who undertake (being supplied with the cut cloth and trimmings) to return the garments made up and ready for the warehouse. One of these firms will sometimes employ as many as eight hundred persons" (*Bulletin*, 1873, p. 132).

However, one writer instances "the cheap labor of women and indigent foreigners" as one means enabling "the dealers in ready-made clothing to undersell their rivals" (Winslow, *Biographies of Philadelphia Merchants*, p. 92), and Kettell speaks of immigrants, "Germans and others," as taking in sewing, and of some of the abuses which we would now cover by the general term "sweating" (*Eighty Years' Progress*, p. 310).

For other accounts of the early industry, see Greeley, *Great Industries of the United States*, 1872, p. 590; Winslow, *Biographies of Philadelphia Merchants*, 1864, p. 92; Browning, "Clothing and Furnishing," in Depew, *One Hundred Years of American Commerce*, pp. 562–565; Kettell, *Eighty Years' Progress*, p. 310; Hayes, *Bulletin*, 1873, pp. 135–137; and *Census of 1860*, iii, p. lxiv.

[2] These figures refer only to the manufacture of men's clothing. Even as late as 1880 the manufacture of women's clothing was confined almost entirely to cloaks (*Census of Manufactures*, 1914, ii, 187).

scale of operation in the industry, upon the quality of product, and upon commercial practices in the trade. At present, the development is important from yet another aspect. The rise of the cutting-up industry brought about a significant change in the distributive organization. It was recognized in 1860 that the "wholesale clothing merchants" united "the jobbing business with that of manufacturers and dealers in clothing on a large scale," i. e., they overreached the jobber and squeezed him out.[1] That this evolution of direct selling did not take place without opposition on the part of the established system is apparent in an account of that period written by Mr. John L. Hayes. Speaking in 1873, he said: "Clothing manufacturers in Boston, and not old men either, remember the time when they could not, on any terms, purchase their cloths directly of the commission houses selling the goods of American mills. At that time, the jobbing houses were the most important customers of the commission houses; and the jobbers refused to purchase of the commission houses which dealt directly with the clothier." And, for a time, the jobbers seemingly had their way. But they could not stave off the inevitable. As the clothing industry increased in scale and the possibilities of that industry as purchaser of goods became more obvious, the desire of the wholesale clothiers was bound to secure more attention. Indeed, by the era at which Hayes was writing, he found that "no customers are more eagerly sought for by the agents of the mills, than the now rich and powerful clothing houses."[2] From the overcoats, and then the linen dusters and summer suits, the production of the clothing industry had broadened until it covered practically the same field as it does at present in so far as men's garments are concerned. The trade in women's suits and dresses had hardly commenced, and therefore the sale of dress-goods remained almost wholly in the hands of the jobbers.

The development of intimate relations between wholesale clothiers and the selling agents for the mills was fruitful of im-

[1] *Census of 1860*, iii, p. lxiv.

[2] *Bulletin*, 1873, p. 128. The use of the words "agents of the mills" in this connection suggests that this type of sales organization was not unknown at that time, although no attempt is here made to differentiate the "agents" from the "commission houses."

portant results. Not all were beneficial to mill operations. The jobber had stood as a sort of buffer between the manufacturer and the retailer, between the distinctly industrial process and that section of the distributive operations most closely related to the consumer. He collected the individually small orders of the retailers and transmitted them in terms of individually sizable commands to the cloth manufacturer, — and, incidentally, commands that were firm and dependable. If business conditions changed for the worse subsequent to the placement of the orders, the jobbers were accustomed to keeping their word and themselves shouldering the losses. On the other hand, the development of the wholesale clothing trade meant, especially at first, a multiplication of orders for the cloth producers and a diminution in the average size of orders. Later, to be sure, consolidations among establishments in this trade tended toward an increase in the scale of operations on the part of clothing manufacturers, particularly as far as standard types and qualities of clothing were concerned, and a consequent increase in the size of order to the cloth-producing mills. But it is doubtful whether this latter tendency had much influence before 1870. Diversity of product and small unit orders seem to have prevailed, — perhaps, indeed, with the clothing manufacturers themselves stimulating the tendency in this direction by their competition in opening a new and still uncertain market. Secondly, the clothing trade came ultimately, and perhaps had by 1870 already come, to indulge itself in more frequent cancellation of orders to cloth producers than had been the practice of the old-time jobbers. Such a worsening of trade ethics signified increased difficulties for the cloth mills.

But consequences of this new development advantageous to cloth production were not lacking. Inspection of fabrics was carried out more systematically and thoroughly than had been the case when the jobbing houses were the immediate purchasers; and this change could not fail to have marked effect in spurring the mills to more efficient and careful operation. Secondly, there unquestionably was a cheapening in the costs of distributing wool cloths, as conversion of fabrics into consumable form was more directly accomplished. At least one middleman with his profits and his costs of handling was eliminated.

The results of these changes were in part evident at once, that is, in the events and experiences of the American wool manufacture during the period before 1870. Of the trend toward diversity in mill production, sufficient is said in the ensuing chapter. Undoubtedly the alteration in methods of cloth distribution had an influence in this regard. But we may also note that the reduction in distributive costs together with the special activities of the wholesale clothiers which would tend to stimulate sales was a large factor in enhancing the use of factory-made cloths. These fabrics in the form of ready-to-wear garments could more effectively compete with the home-made cloths. And thus the growth of the wholesale garment industry was responsible in no small measure for the extraordinary decline in the production of the latter which marked the years of the mid-century.

CHAPTER XVI

INCREASED DIVERSITY OF PRODUCT

While the outstanding and distinctive feature of the period before 1830 was the change in industrial organization based upon the expansion of the domestic market and upon the developments in technical equipment, that of the period between 1830 and 1870 is unquestionably the increasing diversity in the production of domestic mills, equally dependent upon the broadening of the home market and the improvement in technique. The growth of the country, the improvement in transportation facilities, and the decline in household manufacture had given an impetus to the factory production of goods in greater variety. And of hardly less importance to the same end were the increasing prosperity of the country, the increasing differences in wealth, and the rise of the wholesale clothing industry ready to capitalize changes in fundamental conditions. A hundred years before, even fifty years before, the market for "merchantable" cloth had been restricted to the moderately prosperous classes of the colonial towns. By 1870, however, practically the whole nation served as the market for factory goods, except for the steadily dwindling minority which insisted upon fabrics of foreign origin. Farmer and city housewife, mechanic and well-to-do merchant, were now within the reach of the expanding factory output. On the other hand, increased diversity of production was possible only after the invention of new, or the improvement of old machinery. Fancy goods could be turned out on the spinning machines, and particularly on the looms of, say, 1820. Increasing diversity of production, then, cannot be considered apart from the improvement in technical equipment.

The contrast between the character of fabrics turned out by American mills in the twenties and thirties and that of goods produced in the early seventies is especially striking. The chief types of cloth in the earlier years were black and colored broadcloths and cassimeres, satinets, flannels, and blankets, together with such low-quality articles as jeans, kerseys, and negro-cloths. Almost all these goods were made in solid colors only. Fineness of material and character of finish determined the relative quality of the fabric; and for the most part "variety of color and shade was the only element which the manufacturers had at command to satisfy the taste for change or caprice of fashion." [1] Before the Civil War, however, the outward appearance of American society, so to speak, had been transformed; indeed, the pendulum of change had swung to the other extreme. From a drabness which to the modern imagination would be depressing, style and production turned to a fancy, and to us an almost fantastic mood. As North puts it so well: "The ten years ending 1860 will always be remembered as a period when the styles and fabrics for men's wear were of greater variety than ever before or since. Vests were made from brilliant patterned cassimeres, velvets, brocades, and silks, but rarely of the same material as the trousers. These last were plaids, checks, stripes, and mixtures, running largely to light and medium colors, and extravagant in pattern." [2] Note, too, the multiplicity of fabrics exhibited in 1869 at the 38th Annual Exhibition of the American Institute at New York: not merely the old broadcloths and cassimeres, — the latter now in much diversity of structure, — but beavers, cashmeres, doeskins, meltons, cloakings, castors, astrakhans, and chinchillas, together with the whole new category of worsted fabrics, from serges, delaines, and lustres, to armures, Italian cloths, poplins, and imperial reps.[3] In fact, practically the whole modern range of woolen goods — excepting only light dress-goods — had been de-

[1] Hayes, *Report on Exhibition of 1876*, p. 40. See also Kittredge in *Dry Goods Economist*, 1896, p. 81.

[2] North, *Bulletin*, 1894, p. 350. Exception to the above statements should undoubtedly be made as far as the more conservative elements of the community are concerned — the professional and more substantial business men — who persisted in the use of broadcloth made up into Prince Albert coats, until the seventies or later. However, already by the close of our present period, 1870, change in the habits of these elements of the population was at least beginning.

[3] *Bulletin*, 1869, pp. 352–370. Cf. also *Report on Wool and Manufactures of Wool*, 1887, p. xlviii; the Jacquard attachment was brought into use to supply the "very ultra styles" made in this period.

veloped by 1870, and in large measure the modern variety of lustrous worsted fabrics. The introduction of light dress-goods of woolen structure, together with the elaboration of the worsted branch, especially in the lines of men's-wear coatings and the soft dress-goods for women's wear, held over until the next decades.

In this matter of increased diversity in output, however, as in size of establishment and in other respects, a distinction must be made between eastern and western mills. The former were the concerns which felt most directly and strongly the effects of the expanding and broadening market; and the latter pursued their way with little change. Fleischmann's descriptions of output in the several western states are indicative of the manufacture there as late as 1845: Ohio, "Kentucky-jeans, satinets, and blankets;" Kentucky, "jeans, kerseys, and negro-cloths;" and Illinois, "satinets, coarse cassimeres, and negro-cloth for the St. Louis market." [1] To a considerable degree, moreover, this coarse manufacture persisted. As the western area developed, there was, to be sure, the attempt at finer production, but throughout this period such fabrics as linseys, satinets, flannels, blankets, and coarse cassimeres formed the predominant output of these mills.[2] In short, the production was modified and directed to satisfy the requirements of the western consumers, who for the most part had no need of, and could not well afford to buy, the finer fabrics demanded by the eastern communities.

But without losing sight of the western situation, one can devote special attention to the more striking changes in the East. Particular note may be made of the introduction of new fabrics into eastern production, and of the conditions, market or technical, which facilitated such action; while incidentally consideration may be given to the less fortunate experience in the eastern trade of fabrics which earlier had played important rôles. The

[1] Fleischmann, p. 43. Similarly, Graham reported for Ohio, Indiana, Illinois, and Michigan:

	Establishments	Sets
Broadcloth and kerseymere	1	2
Kerseymeres, flannels, satinets, and tweeds	42	43
Jeans and negro-cloths	46	61

[2] For a description of the more advanced manufacture, based upon the report of an exhibition in Chicago of 1868, see *Western Monthly*, i, 246.

degree to which conclusions thus reached may be held applicable to the western section of the country will, we know, be modified by the considerations already presented.[1]

1. *Broadcloth.*

Broadcloth is a fabric which passed through various fortunes in the decades which followed 1830. It was declining in relative importance when this period opened, being pressed by cassimeres, satinets, and flannels; but it still maintained a position of much prominence. Mills were not infrequently devoted to the manufacture of this cloth, and for the country as a whole nearly a quarter of the machinery reported by Benton and Barry in 1837 was accredited to this production.[2]

There is evidence, too, of some growth in the subsequent years. It was observed in 1846 that "manufacturers have prospered during the last few years, and the accumulation of capital which results from prosperity, necessarily tends to those alterations and improvements in machinery which enable the manufacturer of woolen fabrics to produce articles of superior style and finish." [3] As late as 1853 the increased use of broadcloth by the "lower classes" was remarked in one account. Formerly this fabric had been the mark of a "gentleman;" but now "every sober mechanic has his one or two suits of broadcloth, and, so far as mere clothes go, can make as good a display, when he chooses, as what are called the upper classes." [4] Records of individual mills go to substantiate this view. The Slater establishment at Webster, after a fling at the newer fabrics, went back to the sole production of broadcloth, and at as high figures as before.[5] The Middlesex Company at Lowell turned out 78,000 yards of broadcloth in

[1] The southern and southwestern sections of the country, obviously, are neglected. We are interested in sections as producing centers or regions, and these particular sections were in this regard too inconsequential for special consideration.

[2] Three hundred and forty-four sets out of a total of 1488; Benton and Barry, p. 124. See Niles, xliv, 267, and xlvi, 413; production at the Somersworth, New Hampshire, and Salmon Falls, New Hampshire, mills.

[3] *New York State Agricultural Society*, vi, 264. This effect of prosperity will be noted again in the later history of the industry.

[4] *Art and Industry at the Crystal Palace, 1853*, p. 231.

[5] Records of S. Slater & Sons Company.

1836, whereas in 1848 this output had risen to 120,000 yards per year and in 1853 to 3000 yards per week.[1]

However, despite some evidence to the contrary, evil days had in reality already come upon this manufacture. Not only was this type of fabric continually losing ground relative to the other portions of the American wool-manufacturing industry, — as will appear in the discussion of the other fabrics, — but after about 1850 there was apparently an absolute decline. The Census of 1845 and that of 1855 for Massachusetts indicated a decline in the broadcloth production from 1,022,000 yards to 760,000 yards. In an enumeration made in 1860, which indicated the employment of machinery in the mills of New England and New York, no mention at all was made of apparatus engaged upon the broadcloth manufacture;[2] and manufacturers writing in 1862 stated that the production of this fabric had practically disappeared.[3] During the Civil War, there was a temporary reaction, to satisfy the military needs; but apparently that movement died away with the coming of peace. A decade later, it could be said that "superfine broadcloths are now used only by a limited class, and by that class rarely, except for dress coats, which last for years."[4] Indeed, since the middle of the century, the men's-wear broadcloth has been really a specialty. Once the aim and hope of all leading American wool manufacturers, it has become a negligible factor in the output of the country, and its production is confined to a few mills.[5]

The forces which brought about this alteration in the status of broadcloth manufacture were in the main the predominant forces

[1] *Handbook for the Visitor to Lowell*, pp. 44–45; Wallis, *Report, British Documents*, 1854 [1717], p. 16; *Census of 1860*, iii, p. xxxii.

[2] *Hunt's Merchants' Magazine*, xlii, 381.

[3] Randall, *Fine Wool Sheep Husbandry*, p. 68. One writer is quoted that "I should not like to assert that there is not a broadcloth manufactory in New England, though I do not know of any machinery, now running, upon that kind of goods;" and a New York State manufacturer, that there were (in 1862) no broadcloths being made in the United States, so far as he knew, except such as were being made for the army and navy, and a few cotton-warp cloths, called "Union."

[4] Hayes, *Report on the Exhibition of 1876*, p. 42.

[5] In the production of lower-grade fabrics adapted to special uses, such as policemen's uniforms, there were evidences, according to Hayes, of much progress both in fabrication and cheapness on the part of American manufacturers (*ibid.*).

in the wool-manufacturing industry during this period. They touch upon the wool supply, technical development, style influence, and the tariff. These forces, moreover, were operating upon a manufacture which had always been under a handicap, — the handicap that the production of this fabric is a particularly difficult affair even among the various lines of wool-cloth fabrication. American mills had never been able to rival foreign producers in the quality and fineness and finish of their goods. Appreciation of the peculiar difficulties involved in the broadcloth manufacture and of the deficiencies in the American fabrics continued to be voiced in these later years. In 1848 the comparative disadvantage of American producers was recognized. "There are some twenty processes in the manufacture of broadcloth," it was said, "and it is difficult to do each and all well." [1] As late as 1870, after decades of trial and effort, the manufacture could be held up as one in which "there is room for indefinite development and improvement at almost every stage of production. The sorting can be made more nice and perfect; the washing and removal of the animal oil can be more thorough; the spinning can be carefully adjusted to the nature of the wool, and the quality or grade of goods in which it is to be wrought. In the fulling, and shearing, and steaming, also, the most careful manufacturer will find that, as perfectly as he may conduct his operations," the West of England goods will surpass his in finish and in freshness of appearance after wear.[2] Yet this fabric had for the most part always been limited in its market to the classes which were especially critical, and which would pay any additional cost for the superior, foreign goods. In short, the broadcloth industry in this country had ever been especially vulnerable.[3]

Let us turn to a consideration of the other factors which unfavorably affected this manufacture, — and first, to that of wool

[1] *Hunt's Merchants' Magazine*, xix, 341.

[2] Greeley, *Great Industries of the United States*, p. 919. See also *Art and Industry at the Crystal Palace, 1853*, p. 232.

[3] The *Census of 1860* (iii, p. xxxiii) could state that "the manufacture of superfine cloths has never obtained a permanent footing in the United States, although upwards of fifty mills, in 1845, made more or less broadcloth, some of it of fair quality."

supply. Despite the injection of better blood by the merino and Saxon "crazes," the fine wool of American growth was generally inferior to that of the Continental flocks. Especially was this true of the wool from the Vermont or American merino, the fine-wool sheep which had been developed from the Spanish stock. This wool was of somewhat longer staple, but of only medium fineness. Though adapted to the manufacture of superior cassimeres or fine flannels, it was not suited to the production of the best broadcloth. Moreover, there had been a decline in the numbers of Saxony sheep in the years after the middle thirties. Randall points out that the Saxony sheep paid best to the farmer during the years 1831–1837; and that thereafter the price conditions favored the American merino with its somewhat heavier but inferior fleece.[1] According to Wright, some sheepmen, like William Jarvis, abandoned their Saxons before 1835, and others after the crisis of 1837; while in the state of Massachusetts, for which alone we have statistics, the number of such animals decreased between 1837 and 1845 from 47,000 to 34,000.[2] During these same years the percentage of all merino sheep in Massachusetts declined from 66 to 56 per cent; and this decline is apparently connected with another phenomenon of the times adverse to the maintenance of a domestic fine-wool supply, i. e., the growing demand for mutton. The fine-wool sheep, whether Saxon or American merino, possessed a poor carcass, and for mutton purposes a crossbred or English-breed sheep is a better animal. Sheep of the latter types increased in numbers in the late thirties and during the forties, curtailing the production of even lower-grade merino wool. To some extent, imported wool, especially from the Argentine, came in to supply the growing deficiency; but this was not a wholly satisfactory substitution, since the greater part of this Argentine wool was distinctly inferior to the representative European qualities.[3] Thus, in short, the situation in the wool

[1] Randall, *Fine Wool Sheep Husbandry*, p. 92.

[2] Wright, *Wool Growing and the Tariff*, pp. 120–121.

[3] Wallis (*Report, British Documents*, 1854 [1717], p. 15) speaks of the La Plata wool as "coarse and cheap." It was cheap, but most writers hold the wool there to have been improved by merino blood, and to have been in considerable measure of medium-fine quality.

supply was becoming increasingly worse for the manufacture of broadcloths. The industry lacked this foundation for fine cloth production.[1]

Contributing to an unsatisfactory condition with respect to the raw material were the tariff arrangements under the act of 1846. Under preceding tariffs it had been customary to provide appreciably higher rates for wool manufactures than for the raw fiber. Thus in the immediately preceding act, that of 1842, while wool valued at less than seven cents per pound — including almost all the wool from the La Plata — was dutiable at only 5 per cent ad valorem, wool manufactures with some exceptions, such as blankets, bore a duty of 40 per cent. This arrangement provided the manufacturing industry with considerable protection. Upon the assumption usually adopted that the cost of the raw material forms half the total cost of the cloth, protection to the industry would work out at 37½ per cent. The tariff of 1846, however, eliminated this gap in rates: both raw wool and wool manufactures were included in the same schedule and taxed at the single rate of 30 per cent. This does not mean that all protection to the manufacturing industry was taken away, but, even on the basis just employed, the net protection would be reduced to 15 per cent. Under preceding tariffs such as those of 1824 and 1828, to be sure, the protection, figured on the same theoretical basis, had not been appreciably greater, but the substantial decrease from the pro-

[1] The *Census of 1860* (iii, p. xxxiii) attributed the decline of the broadcloth manufacture "in part to the quality of American wool, which, though equal in fineness to any in the world, is better adapted by its length of fibre for making soft woolen and worsted goods than fine cloths, which are improved in appearance by a shorter nap than can readily be imparted with native wool."

Yet perhaps a supply of fine wool adequate for the needs of the domestic broadcloth manufacture may have existed in the United States. However, in so far as it could be more profitably used in some other manner, i. e., put to some alternate employment, the broadcloth branch would suffer. Moreover, the trend of fine-wool production may have caused a disparity between the prices of such staple and of other wools, sufficiently great to handicap broadcloth manufacture.

Wright (p. 121) gives the main cause of the downfall of the Saxony sheep as the decline in the broadcloth manufacture. Apparently the big decrease did not come until then. I have tried to point out, however, that the movement of decline began before the broadcloth production had really been threatened. The decline on the industrial side simply accelerated the change on the side of sheep raising.

tection afforded by the act of 1842, coming just when it did, probably contributed to the decadence of this broadcloth manufacture, dependent as that manufacture was in a particular degree upon tariff support. Not only was the actual protection measurably diminished, but the psychological effect of the decrease under the circumstances which surrounded the passage of the Walker tariff was distinctly bad. Hope of subsequent reversal in policy under the existing political situation was bound to be faint; and application of "free trade," it was thought, might be made more thorough.

Yet there were influences more important than tariff or wool supply. Mr. John L. Hayes, an ardent protectionist, remarked in 1876 that while the diminution in the production of broadcloths had "been attributed" to the effects of the tariff of 1846, and while it had also "been materially influenced by the constantly diminishing domestic supply of superfine wools," "the principal cause of the decline" was the popular demand for other fabrics.[1] The growing competition of these other fabrics, especially cassimeres, has been noted with respect to the preceding period; but in these later decades, the movement became more pronounced. The chief competitor of broadcloth in the United States was still the cassimere; but now the form called "fancy cassimere," of which the distinguishing characteristic was the range of possible patterns, came into prominence. This fabric made advantageous use of the medium-fine wools of the country. Moreover, being less difficult to produce than the broadcloth, and being turned out at lower unit cost, it could appeal to a larger market; and its production was especially facilitated by the invention of an improved loom. But particularly important was the fact that this new fabric took the popular fancy, commencing the trend toward extreme or extravagant designs. In brief, the American broadcloth production was chiefly suffering from one of the evils to which the wool manufacture everywhere has been specially subject, — the style influence. England was at this time undergoing a similar experience, when the use of "fancy goods . . . gave

[1] Hayes, *Report on the Exhibition of 1876*, p. 42. See also Kittredge, *Dry Goods Economist*, 1896, p. 82.

a heavy blow to the plain cloth trade," — that trade in which the West of England and the Leeds manufacturers had been principally engaged.[1] Broadcloth had long enjoyed an outstanding popularity, even a renown, while its name had come in the public mind to signify the finest and most desirable wool fabric. But the day of its supremacy had in 1830–1870 passed its noon and was declining steadily toward a long twilight.

2. *Rise of New Woolen Cloths.*

The counterpart of the decline in broadcloth production during the period between 1830 and 1870 is obviously in large measure the rise of manufacture in other lines. The development of such competitors, begun in the earlier period, made extraordinary strides in later years. There was this difference, however: that the earlier increase in diversification, noteworthy as it was, had not been so closely competitive as to depress seriously the broadcloth production. Now the diversification led to direct rivalry, in which the broadcloth manufacture came off second best.

The fancy cassimere, the principal competitor of the broadcloth at this time and a cloth to be distinguished from the plain cassimere of former times, was a fabric of French origin. Credit for the new departure is attributed to M. Bonjean, a prominent wool manufacturer of Sedan, France, who, in 1834, conceived the idea of figured woolen goods in which the smooth surface of previous cloths was sacrificed to the pattern effect. Introduction of the design into the goods was secured by the use of the Jacquard attachment joined to a hand loom. Inasmuch as the possible variety of fabric under these circumstances was as unlimited as fancy, — so the story goes, — he called the new goods "fancy" cassimeres. Foreign fashion seized on this new article with considerable avidity, it appears, and the manufacture of fancy cassimeres spread in European countries; but several years passed before this fabrication found place in the American production, — and then only under methods strikingly different from those used abroad. A gentleman returning from France in 1840 brought an overcoat in which the new fancy cloth was employed as lining.

[1] Baines, *Yorkshire Past and Present*, p. 666.

Mr. Samuel Lawrence, at that time agent of the Middlesex Mills of Lowell, saw the fabric, and was attracted to it. He obtained a sample from inside the coat collar, and set about the manufacture of similar goods in the mills under his charge. It was not feasible to produce fancy cassimeres in the French manner, with the Jacquard attachment and hand labor, — that was obvious; and Mr. Lawrence made a notable contribution to the advance of the American wool manufacture when he brought about their fabrication by power weaving.[1]

The story of this adaptation is the story of the Crompton loom. Prior to the invention of this mechanism, all woolen looms actuated by power had been cam looms, that is, looms in which the harnesses controlling the divisions of the warp had been moved by revolving cams.[2] Such machines put a fairly strict limitation on the number of harnesses that could be employed; and the change from weaving one pattern to weaving another occasioned a laborious rearrangement of cams. Both of these disadvantages were overcome by the Crompton loom. Its inventor, William Crompton, an Englishman who had come to this country only in 1836, had developed his mechanism for use in the cotton manufacture, and indeed it was first used in the weaving of fancy cotton fabrics. In this new apparatus, "the figure or pattern to be produced could be made up on what is known as a chain. This chain is a series of bars, or lags, held together by links, so as to form a chain

[1] For accounts of this episode, see *Report of the Judges at the Exhibition of 1876, Group IX*, p. 43; *Bulletin*, 1877, pp. 109–110; and North, *Bulletin*, 1902, p. 316.

However, it should be stated that the New England Mills of Rockville, Connecticut, have contested with the Middlesex Mills, the honor of first introducing the manufacture of fancy cassimeres into the United States. Whichever deserves the honor of absolute priority, there can be no question that the Middlesex adventure was the one of much the greater significance for the American industry as a whole.

[2] The harnesses of a loom may be described as the frames through which the warp threads are drawn. The warp threads as they come from the loom beam, the large spool which is placed behind the loom, are divided in a preconceived manner, — according to the proposed weave structure of the finished cloth; and each division is drawn through a separate harness, and thence attached to the cloth beam in front of the loom. As the weaving proceeds, the harnesses are automatically moved up and down, raising or depressing given sections of the warp; and thus permitting varied interweavings of filling (or latitudinal) with warp (or longitudinal) yarns. (See Figure 3, p. 121, above.)

of bars, hence the name. On these bars or lags are rollers on pins, placed in such position that as the chain revolves it lifts, at certain predetermined intervals, levers, which in turn cause the harnesses to be raised in such order that the desired design or pattern is produced upon the loom."[1] By this manner the control and operation of a much greater number of harnesses than heretofore were made possible, — modern looms of this type employ as high as thirty harnesses, — while the transition from one pattern to another could be effected with ease, that is, merely by readjusting the lags and bars. Accordingly, the weaving of rather elaborate designs in cloth could be undertaken on power machines, and with at least no more trouble than the production of less complicated patterns on the cam loom.

At Mr. Lawrence's request, Crompton came to Lowell and proceeded upon the adaptation of his fancy cotton loom to the weaving of woolen fabrics. Apparently this was accomplished without peculiar difficulty, and in 1840 production of fancy woolens by power began. This was a notable American achievement. As Mr. Hayes strikingly put it: "Not a yard of fancy woolen fabric had ever been woven by a power-loom in any country till done by Mr. William Crompton, at the Middlesex Mills in Lowell, in 1840."[2] The effects of the invention were immediate. As for the Middlesex Company itself, within three years all the looms in the mill had been altered for use in the new system; and dividend rates which had averaged 11 per cent between 1839 and 1842 jumped to 29 per cent in 1843.[3] The significance of the innovation

[1] Lamb's *Textile Industries*, p. 306. See also Crompton Loom Works, *Catalogue of 1881*, pp. 4–5; Hayes, *American Textile Machinery*, pp. 50–51; and Washburn, "Manufacturing and Mechanical Industries of Worcester," in *History of Worcester County (Massachusetts)*, ii, 1612.

[2] Hayes, *American Textile Machinery*, p. 50.

This statement is something of an exaggeration. Woolen cloths that would come under the category of "fancy" goods have always and still are made upon cam looms. The difference between the cam and dobby looms is rather one of degree: a *greater* diversity of weaves is possibly on the latter.

[3] *Report of the Company, 1857*, p. 19. The dividend record gives rather a good picture of the immediate gain, the differential, secured by a concern through a temporarily exclusive advance in technique. It is as follows: 1839, 15 per cent; 1840, 10; 1841, 10; 1842, 9; 1843, 29; 1844, 20; 1845, 14; and 1846, 13 per cent; but meanwhile the capital of the concern had been increased (through stock divi-

THE ORIGINAL CROMPTON LOOM

Devised by Mr. William Crompton in 1839–1840.

to the wool-manufacturing industry as a whole may be appreciated from the fact that within a generation at least three-quarters of all the woolen cloths then worn had come to be woven on fancy looms;[1] and that the loom was soon introduced abroad and has been employed there in somewhat the same degree. Indeed, it was stated before the Congressional Committee on Patents in 1878 that "upon the Cromptom loom, or looms based upon it, is woven every yard of fancy cloth in the world."[2]

With respect to American production of woolen cloth, the most immediate and striking result was upon the manufacture of fancy cassimeres. The proportion of sets devoted to cassimeres in New England and New York more than doubled between 1837 and 1860: from less than 14 to over 31 per cent of the respective totals; and at the later date the term "cassimeres" signified the fancy type.[3] In Massachusetts alone, the yardage of such fabrics produced rose from a little under 2½ million yards in 1845 to nearly 15½ million in 1865, or, relative to total woolen-cloth production in the state, from a proportion of about a sixth to that of a third. In 1865, too, the proportion of cassimere in the total output of New York factories reached as high as 55 per cent. Meanwhile, not only the broadcloth but other manufactures, notably satinet, were declining relatively in the eastern states; and cassimere became the outstanding feature of American production in the chief manufacturing centers.[4]

dends, it seems) from $300,000 in 1839 to $600,000 in 1841, and to $750,000 in 1844. On the basis of the earlier capitalization, the subsequent dividends would have amounted to over 40 per cent per annum.

[1] Hayes, *op. cit.*, p. 51. This does not mean that three-quarters of the woolen cloths woven are fancy goods. Plainer fabrics are wrought up on "fancy" looms, either because the mills find it profitable so to use their equipment or because such looms make it possible to "mix the fillings," i. e., to use more than one shuttle in the weaving, and thus to reduce irregularities in the fabric arising from lack of uniformity in the weft yarns.

[2] *Ibid.*, p. 50.

[3] Benton and Barry, for the 1837 figures, p. 124; *Hunt's Merchants' Magazine*, xlii, 381, for those of 1860.

[4] The increased production of cassimeres at the Middlesex Company is illustrative: for 1836 and 1839, 328,000 yards are reported; for 1844, 468,000 yards; 1845, 624,000 yards, and 1848, 1,000,000 yards (*Handbook for the Visitor to Lowell*, pp. 44–45; *Census of 1860*, iii, p. xxxii).

The condition of the wool supply was favorable to the production of cassimere; or perhaps better, the new cloths were adapted to the natural change which was taking place in the culture of native wools, — the shift from the growing of very fine to that of medium-fine staple. Of particular importance in this connection, too, was the change in the course of wool imports. The period after 1830 is marked by the rise of wool purchases from the Argentine. The course of these importations was irregular, even under a single tariff, but the quantities on the average were substantial. Indeed, one writer states that "the fancy cassimere manufacture may be said to have been developed by the use" of Argentinian wool.[1] The tariffs of 1832, 1842, and 1857 provided for specially low duties or free importation for wools valued below 8, 7, and 20 cents, respectively. Under these provisions, it was advantageous to bring in the wools from the La Plata, wools of medium-fine staple but heavy condition (much extraneous material such as gravel, wool grease, and vegetable matter). Moreover, not only were these wools loaded down with dirt, wool grease, and the like, but they contained a burr, picked up by the sheep from one of the native plants and tenaciously imbedded in the fleece, which made them less salable. To render such wools usable in the wool-cloth manufacture, it was necessary to remove these burrs. Early this was done by hand, laboriously; but subsequently attempts were made both here and in France and England to accomplish the work by machinery. And at last came a really successful mechanism for eliminating the burrs, a mechanism of American origin. This was "a rapidly revolving guard or blade" by which the burrs were struck from a card or toothed cylinder, — an invention of Mr. Michael H. Simpson of Boston in 1833 or 1834. It proved immediately popular in the American trade, and was widely adopted both here and abroad. Indeed, one indication of its real worth is the sale of the English rights to it for £10,000.[2] Subsequently, not only were improvements

[1] North, *Bulletin*, 1895, p. 42.

[2] Hayes, *American Textile Machinery*, p. 49. Subsequent improvements were made to the burr-picker, such as those by Parkhurst and Sargent, but Simpson's invention is held by Hayes to have supplied the germ of the whole development (*ibid.*, p. 49).

made to this "burr picker" of Simpson's,[1] but other devices looking toward the same end — the removal of vegetable matter from unwrought wool — were developed. Notable among the latter

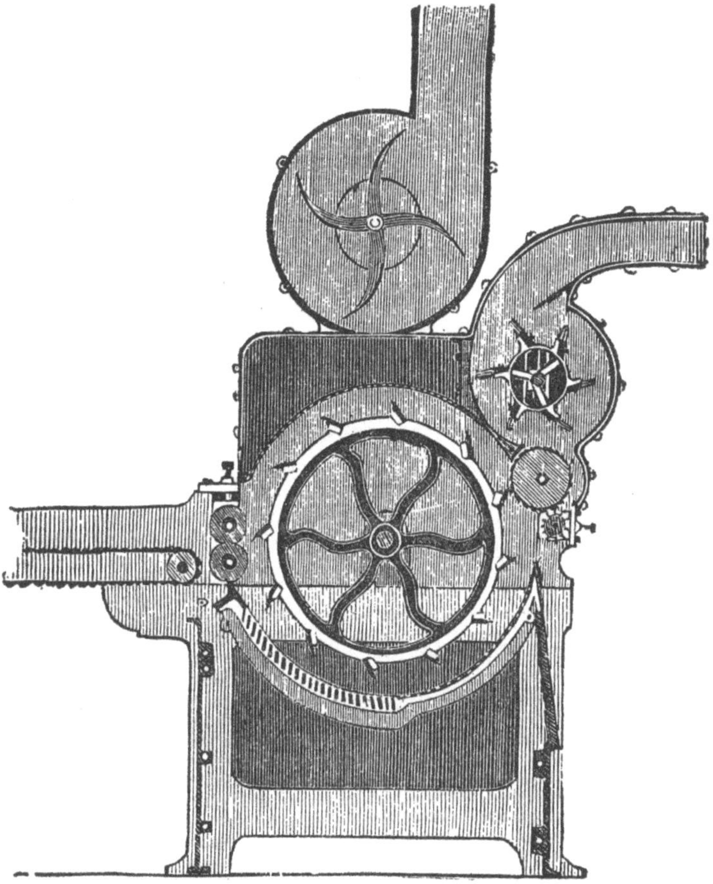

FIG. 8. Working Parts of the Burr Picker as built by Calvert & Sargent, Graniteville, Massachusetts, under a patent of 1861.

was the so-called burr cylinder which about 1846 began to be attached to the carding machines. Placed between the licker-in cylinders and the first working cylinder of the first or breaker

[1] Among such improvements may be mentioned those of Parkhurst and Sargent, and some incorporated in Belgian machines; but Simpson's invention is held by Hayes to have supplied the germ of the whole development (*American Textile Machinery*, p. 49).

section of the woolen card, it served to kick out pieces of burrs that were adhering loosely to the wool fibers.[1]

By virtue of such technical advances, South American wools were made more readily available for American manufacturers, while their importation was facilitated by tariff provisions. Our purchases from Argentine had averaged but 320,000 pounds in the five years 1830–1834. They rose to over 2 million pounds in the years 1835–1838, to nearly 9 million in 1841, and 12 million in 1849; and subsequently they were never less than 5½ million.[2] To this should be added the increasing importations from South Africa, which under the tariff act of 1857 reached an annual total of over 2 million pounds.[3] The years just prior to 1860 were a period when our dependence upon foreign wool reached a point which has never since been equaled.[4] And in large proportion the increased purchases of foreign staple went into the development of cassimere and similar woolen-cloth production, for by their character they were well fitted for manufacture into such goods.

[1] *Bulletin*, 1902, p. 141.

[2] By tariff periods the average annual importation of raw wool from the Argentine was as follows:

1829–1832	435,000 lbs.
1833–1842	2,623,000 "
1843–1846	7,169,000 "
1847–1857	6,952,000 "
1858–1861	9,071,000 "

Moreover, if one divides the long period under the tariff of 1846 into two periods, 1847–1851 and 1852–1857, he finds that importations during the former years averaged approximately 8,000,000 pounds per annum, and in the later years somewhat over 6,000,000 pounds. These facts suggest that here the effects of the tariff of 1846 in imposing equal rates upon wool and wool manufactures were negligible. Not only did the course of importation hold up well as compared with the preceding years under the supposedly more lenient tariff of 1842 (wools valued at seven cents per pound and less were admitted free of duty), but for several years averaged an absolutely larger volume. Apparently the lines of manufacture employing this variety of wool particularly were able to bear up fairly well under the peculiar conditions imposed by the common rate upon raw material and finished product.

[3] The only figures available in this relation are for the whole of Africa; but little seems to have come elsewhere than from the Cape. This wool like the Argentinian has always been heavy wool, but apparently it was of too high a price to be affected by the seven and eight-cent minima of the 1832 and 1842 tariffs.

[4] Wright, pp. 154–155.

The advance in production along these lines was further stimulated by inventions in looms which marked progress rivaling that of the original Crompton contribution. The latter was a narrow loom, only about forty inches wide, was limited in its speed to forty-five picks per minute, and contained provision for but a single shuttle.[1] Soon afterwards, shuttle boxes were added, first upon one and then upon both sides. Thereafter it was possible to "mix the fillings" and to use more than one color of weft yarn, the latter increasing yet further the opportunities for varying the pattern. Of equal importance, if not greater, was the evolution of the Crompton broad fancy loom. This mechanism, developed in 1857, was not merely a broadening of the earlier loom to permit the weaving of fifty-four-inch goods. The operation of twenty-four harnesses and of three boxes in either end was also permitted; and, of yet greater significance, the speed of this loom was markedly increased. Even with the narrow loom, the speed hitherto attained had not been in excess of fifty-five picks per minute. This was now raised to eighty-five picks. Thus both by the greater width of machine and by the enhanced speed of operation, production was much increased.[2] This loom, it may be added, had by 1870 been further improved, not only by virtue of better workmanship but also by the addition of devices through which the machine was rendered more automatic and therefore capable of greater production though operated by less skilled workmen. Some twenty years later, or more specifically

[1] North, *Bulletin*, 1894, p. 338; Lamb's *Textile Industries*, p. 304; *Worcester Columbian Tribute*, 1893, p. 77. In Lamb, the width of these early looms is given as forty-eight inches.

A "pick" is a single transmission of the shuttle across the loom.

[2] The conversion of all weaving machinery in the country to looms of this increased speed, of course, was not immediate. Looms generally possess a long life. Nor apparently were the benefits of the new machine extended at once to all branches of the industry. The weaving of flannels, for example, proceeded at the speed of forty-four picks per minute in the Talbot Mills, of North Billerica, Massachusetts, — a factory built in 1857, — until 1862, when the speed was increased to fifty-six picks (*Textile Manufacturers' Journal*, March 21, 1903, p. 9). This may have been due, however, to the unusual width to which flannels were fabricated, three yards, for which width Hayes reports a speed for flannels of forty-eight to fifty picks in 1860. By 1879 this speed had been quickened to seventy or seventy-five picks (*Bulletin*, 1879, p. 280).

in 1893, it was claimed that fully 75 per cent of the fancy woolen and worsted weaving was being done on looms of this variety.[1]

Under the stimulus afforded by changing and broadening public demand, and facilitated by the peculiarly important technical development just outlined, the woolen manufacture continually took on new lines of production.[2] Special varieties of cassimere arose, such as Harris's famous double and twist cassimere, — a fancy type of cassimere developed by an enterprising Rhode Island manufacturer. Toward the close of the forties, Scotch plaids and tweeds were being fabricated in American mills by power, while the hand loom still prevailed in Scotch homes and small establishments. By the sixties a rich diversity of fabrics was flowing from our woolen factories: not only the broadcloth, cassimere, satinet, and flannel of earlier production, but cheviots, woven shawls, plainer cloths such as castors and beavers, and less important special goods. By the seventies, some mills were said to make not less than fifty distinct classes of fabrics; while a large specialized mill, such as a large cassimere factory, would produce as many as two hundred different designs each season, or four hundred a year.[3] The manufacturing industry by 1870 had taken on quite a modern complexion.

In quality, this new production was of as much significance as in the matter of type of cloth. The decline in broadcloth manufacture might seem to forecast a lowering in the average fineness of the domestic output, but in reality this was not a decisive

[1] *Catalogue of the Crompton Loom Company*, 1881, pp. 5–6; *Worcester Columbian Tribute*, pp. 77–78; North, *Bulletin*, 1901, p. 282; and *Dry Goods Economist*, 1896, p. 44. Hayes wrote in 1876 that he had been assured by his associates from Sweden, Austria, and Germany, in the group of judges on wool and woolens at the Centennial Exhibition of 1876, that the specific Crompton loom, with its recent improvements, was in use in all the principal establishments on the continent of Europe (*Bulletin*, 1879, p. 46), though probably this assertion must contain a considerable measure of exaggeration.

[2] For other improvements in loom construction, see below, pp. 363–364.

[3] Hayes, *Awards and Claims*, p. 450. The extent to which some specialties were produced is illustrated by the experience of the Pontoosuc Manufacturing Company. Between 1860 and 1868, the concern was running upon Balmoral material for skirts, "not only devoting all their machinery to this product, but filling neighboring buildings with hand-looms for the same purpose" (*ibid.*, p. 88).

factor, and one must also consider that some of the fancy cassimeres or doeskins were in fact cloths of very good grade; that the new goods as a whole were largely superior in quality to the satinets or negro-cloths which had been developed in the period before 1830. In general, the tendency was distinctly toward the production of a very fair average grade of cloth, — not the fine quality of some importations, but not a distinctly low quality of output, — and an average at least as high as the output of preceding decades.

Toward the close of the period under discussion, however, came the appearance of a new feature with respect to quality, — the considerable utilization of shoddy or recovered wool fiber. The first mill in the United States to use this substance — fiber recovered by the rending of rags, cloth remnants, wool knit-goods, and the like — seems to have been one located in Quechee, Vermont. This mill is said to have started using shoddy as early as 1836.[1] Another establishment for the use of shoddy was projected in 1842, also in Vermont, although there is no evidence as to what became of the scheme.[2] At any event, the practice of utilizing recovered wool fiber grew apace, and by 1860 concerns for the production of shoddy were reported to number thirty and to contain two hundred and ninety employees. Yet on the whole the expansion through this last date was not significant. The great increase in use occurred during the Civil War. The rise in price of raw wool and the short life of military clothing induced the government to permit large employment of this new material; and thereafter utilization in the industry became more general and widespread. The end of the decade found the shoddy-making industry doubled in size, and this recovered fiber forming 15 to 20 per cent of the wool stock employed in the woolen-cloth manufacture.[3]

[1] Letter to the author.

[2] Hazard's *United States Commercial and Statistical Register*, vi, 189.

[3] Other references to the development of the shoddy manufacture and use: *Art and Industry at the Crystal Palace, 1853*, p. 212; *Census of 1860*, iii, p. xxxv; Kettell, *Eighty Years' Progress*, p. 313.

The proportion of shoddy used in 1870 to the total weight of new and recovered wool fiber is an estimate. It is based on (1) the statistics of shoddy bought by woolen mills in that year, and (2) the scoured equivalent of the raw wool bought,

The more considerable utilization of recovered wool fiber came too late in the period with which we are now concerned to have appreciable effect upon its course. It was rather a prelude to events in the following decades. Neither before nor after 1870, to be sure, did the use of shoddy have any noticeable effect upon the types of wool fabric produced in the American manufacture; but by 1870 the employment of this material was beginning to influence the general quality of output in the woolen branch of the industry.

3. *Other Woolen Fabrics.*

The vicissitudes in the manufacture of other woolen fabrics are partly a reflection of the development in that of cassimeres and similar cloths, and partly an independent history. The manufacture of satinets, for example, shared the disfavor which fell upon the broadcloth production, though for somewhat different reasons and in less degree; whereas the blanket section of the industry experienced a considerable and fairly steady growth. Again, in some instances, as in that of flannels, the phenomenon spoken of above of increasing diversification in production is manifest. An investigation of the experience in each of these important cases is, then, a matter of special interest.

The increasing strength of the flannel manufacture in the period prior to 1830 has been described earlier. The conditions imposed by the tariff of 1828 were perhaps a significant influence in presenting the domestic producer with virtual command of the American market. But the steady decrease in flannel importations before the enactment of that law suggests that this was not the dominant factor, as does also the lack of any reaction toward higher imports when lower tariff rates subsequently came into effect.[1] In fact, such importations became of ever-decreasing importance, as they tended actually to diminish while domestic

secured under the assumption that the ratio of raw to scoured wool was the same in 1870 as appeared in the Census figures of 1880.

It will be noted further that only the woolen branch of the industry is concerned. The worsted branch neither then nor now has used shoddy, except for the production of a few woolen yarns. Fiber as short as shoddy cannot be used in combing.

[1] Importations increased in the prosperous era of the early thirties until they reached a height of 635,000 square yards in 1836. Thereafter they decreased to a

production rose in volume. Indeed, it may be asserted confidently that after 1830 the American fabric was with minor exceptions able to monopolize the domestic market. Such importations as did come in were chiefly the finest qualities, especially the so-called opera flannel, in which the style influence entered.[1]

The success of the flannel manufacture is attributed by some observers to the "peculiar adaptation of American wools to this fabric;"[2] and, to be sure, this factor played an important part. A fine wool was not required and a truly coarse wool was not suitable. The semi-fine to medium-grade wool of our domestic culture with its good staple satisfied peculiarly well the needs of the flannel makers. But equally important, if not more important, was the simplicity of flannel manufacture. All woolen cloth is at one time a flannel, i. e., when it first comes from the loom. Moreover, for the most part, at least in the period under discussion, flannel did not suffer from the effect of style and changing fashion. Flannel shirts, underwear, and petticoats absorbed huge weights of the article. A mill needed to prepare few samples, only those necessary to show the particular shades of the current season, and having secured its orders it could run month after month upon a very limited line of goods. Indeed,

low point of 117,000 square yards per annum in the five years 1842–1846, following which they grew gradually until by 1855–1857 they averaged 361,000 yards. Special demands of the Civil War period brought temporarily higher quantities.

[1] Hayes, *Bulletin*, 1877, p. 118.

In the statistics of machinery or of production, those referring to flannels are mixed with those pertaining to blankets in the later years. Still, a marked increase in the flannel manufacture is apparent, especially when it is recognized, as stated below, that the blanket section of the industry was in a much less satisfactory condition than the flannel section. Benton and Barry reported in 1837 the devotion of 158 sets to flannels and 24 sets to blankets, hats, and yarn, for the whole country. In 1860 New England and New York contained 369 sets devoted to flannels and blankets together. In Massachusetts alone, the production of flannels and blankets rose between 1845 and 1865 from 4,491,000 yards to 20,038,000 yards.

[2] *Ibid.* See also, *Bulletin*, 1874, p. 78; and *Joint Report to the United States Revenue Commission*, 1866, p. 14: "In a class of fabrics, entering perhaps more largely than any other into general consumption — that of flannels — the superiority due principally to the admirable adaptation of the common wools of this country, their strength and spinning qualities, is so marked as almost wholly to exclude foreign flannels."

there were concerns which ran year after year with no substantial changes in weight, construction, or quality of their output. Finally, being a fabric of wide and steady consumption, it relieved manufacturers of much risk that attended, say, broadcloth or cassimere production.

This plain variety of flannel formed an essential part of the output from the increasing number of western mills that grew up during these years. It also continued to be the most important part of flannel production in the eastern states; but here new types began to make their appearance. About 1835 manufacture of the so-called "domett" flannel was started. This fabric, claimed by some to be of American origin, was composed of a cotton warp and woolen filling. Its earlier employment was as a substitute for the linsey-woolsey then largely worn by working-women for petticoats. Later it found other uses in infants' wear, shirting, and the like; and it continued to be a sensible part of American flannel manufacture.[1] Then came other varieties: fine white flannel, plaid flannel, printed flannel, opera flannel, and finally a flannel coating for men's summer wear.[2] Obviously here was increased diversification of product, and, curiously enough, a diversification in the line of higher quality of fabric. The opera flannel, for example, is described as "more highly gigged and finished than the ordinary article, being piece-dyed uniformily, and of many fancy colors, and hot pressed."[3] The production of the fine white flannel at Ballardvale involved double spinning, that is, a repetition of spinning upon a single yarn, in order to

[1] *Report of Judges at Exhibition of 1876, Group IX*, p. 50; *Bulletin*, 1879, p. 211. As to origin of the fabric, see mention of the name by a British manufacturer in testimony in 1828 (Bischoff, *Woolen and Worsted Manufactures*, ii, 178). In more recent decades, it may be added, domett flannel has become an all-cotton fabric.

[2] *Awards and Claims, Exhibition of 1876*, p. 82; *Bulletin*, 1902, p. 136; *Bulletin*, 1877, pp. 120, 122, 119. The first production of fine white flannel is attributed to the Ballardvale Mills in 1836; opera flannels to the Bay State Mills, apparently in the early fifties; and flannel coating to the Middlesex or Washington Mills, both of which claim the honor, about 1859.

Besides the increase in the variety of flannel fabric, there was also an increase in the diversity of its use. Among other employments, there were mentioned in the seventies: under-garments, linings for overcoats, blouses for workmen, fatigue uniforms for soldiers and police, and coats for summer wear (*Bulletin*, 1877, p. 119).

[3] Hayes, *Bulletin*, 1877, p. 119.

secure the fine threads for warp and filling; while the printed flannel was undertaken at a time when it was necessary for the fancier varieties to employ hand block-printing.[1] In short, the flannel manufacture was already beginning to show that token of maturity, the acquisition of finer qualities in production, which the woolen industry as a whole was not to display until some decades later. This feature together with control of the American market is significant in suggesting the relative strength of the flannel manufacture generally. This branch of the wool-manufacturing industry enjoyed no special advantages, tariff or other, over the rest of that industry, except such as were derived from the particular character of flannel making. The situation, then, gives emphasis to the benefit to be derived from large-scale or steady production of such simple, standard goods as were the greater share of the flannels then turned out. Of course, in so far as production tended toward higher qualities, it lost something of the total possible advantage.[2]

Blankets share with ordinary flannels the relative freedom from changes in fashion; and yet in the period before 1830 their production had been far from sufficient for the domestic market. Now one notable obstacle to their domestic manufacture, lack of adequate cheap wool supplies, was eliminated by the increased importations under the tariffs which permitted the introduction of low-priced wools under special rates. The grade of wool utilized in blankets at this time continued to be of the inferior quality employed in the earlier decades, wools for blankets and for carpets being frequently mentioned in the same breath.[3] For the whole period 1832 to 1846, such low staples were available to American blanket manufacturers, and to this fact is attributable, in part,

[1] *Awards and Claims, Exhibition of 1876*, p. 82; Wallis, *Report, British Documents*, 1854 [1717], p. 17. It was said in 1853 that the flannels exhibited by the Ballardvale Company were "unequaled for fineness of texture, and for whiteness, by the best Welch flannels," which were long the superlative in the flannel trade (*Art and Industry at the Crystal Palace, 1853*, p. 215).

[2] There are notes of occasional exportation of flannels in the seventies, both to Canada and to South America (*Bulletin*, 1877, pp. 118, 119).

[3] Randall, *Sheep Husbandry*, p. 87; DeBow's *Review*, 1854, xvi, 468; Bond, "Development of Wool Manufactures in the United States," in *Wool and Manufactures of Wool*, 1887, p. lviii.

the increase in blanket production in this country. Of at least equal importance were two other factors. On the technical side one should note the more general use of power looms in the manufacture, as well as the use of those other mechanical improvements common to the whole wool-manufacturing industry, — improved carding, finishing, and the like. And, secondly, one must take into account the westward movement of the industry, — since blankets formed one of the chief elements in the output of the western mills and since the production there was less sensitive to some of the adverse factors which affected eastern mills.[1]

In fact, the peaceful development of the blanket manufacture was shortly to be harassed by unfavorable conditions, especially as far as the larger eastern mills were concerned. Particularly unfortunate was the experience of this manufacture after 1846. The production did not perhaps "find a grave" in the tariff of that year,[2] but seemingly it was appreciably distressed. That tariff act imposed a duty of only 20 per cent upon blankets, while the wool from which blankets were made bore a rate of 30 per cent. Assuming the price of wool in this country to have been raised by the full amount of the duty, scant net protection remained for the blanket manufacture. Apparently as a result of this situation, imports rose in value from approximately $700,000 per year under the tariff of 1828 to twice that figure in the early fifties; and such figures do not give the whole story, since the value per unit of quantity had fallen. Thus, importations of blankets from the United Kingdom alone rose from slightly over a million yards around 1830 to 4 1/3 million yards in the middle fifties, as the unit value fell from 1s. 8d. to 1s. 2d. per yard. Yet not all was lost. Despite these enhanced importations, the industry seems to have sustained itself in fair shape, though perhaps it did not expand in the degree which one would otherwise have expected. On the other hand, as regards quality, the years

[1] The precise increase in volume of blanket manufacture it is impossible to ascertain. The blanket is usually combined with the flannel production, — and statistics of the combined output have been presented. The frequency with which blankets appear in the reports of mill production in Graham's enumeration of 1845 suggests the widespread manufacture of this fabric.

[2] Cowley, *History of Lowell*, 1868, p. 58.

between 1846 and the Civil War seem to have witnessed a rise in the character of blanket demanded by the domestic market; and the domestic production kept pace with this change in quality. Improved apparatus and new methods were introduced, until by reason of "the excellence of our fabrics" — the result of "the skill previously acquired and the admirable raw material furnished by our domestic wool" — domestic manufacturers were said to supply in the period just before the Civil War "nearly all the grades of blankets which went into American consumption, except those of the lowest sort." [1]

Nor did the improvement in quality cease with 1860. In fact, that movement was probably accelerated in the subsequent decade. By the early seventies, the wool going into the fabrication of blankets is no longer spoken of as cheap foreign wool, but American medium or grade (i. e., part-blood) merino wools. The latter, it was said at that time, composed the material for the great majority of our blankets.[2] Most of the production was of medium quality "for the consumption of the millions;" but there was already a beginning of manufacture in the fine grades.[3] The blanket section of the industry, then, had begun to feel much the same influences and to have in some degree the same experience as had the flannel branch somewhat earlier with its specially fine flannels, its flannel coatings, and the like.

Now let us turn to other fabrics; and here we have largely the reverse of the picture already given of expansion in the production of cassimeres and flannels: namely, the decline in the manufacture of such goods as satinets, linseys, and negro-cloths. To some extent this was an absolute decline, as far as figures upon the industry give evidence. The number of sets within New England and New York, which in 1837 were engaged upon satinets, had

[1] *Bulletin*, 1881, p. 383; an article with protectionist leanings.

Somewhat later there were references to the exportation of blankets. Some produced in Minneapolis were said to have been sent to England "to furnish the new lines of palace sleeping-cars" (*Bulletin*, 1874, p. 78), and horse blankets were also being shipped to England (*Bulletin*, 1879, p. 282). These may well be exceptional cases, although blankets have always played a considerable part in our small, almost negligible export trade in wool fabrics.

[2] *Bulletin*, 1877, p. 121; *ibid.*, 1874, p. 78.

[3] *Bulletin*, 1881, p. 383; *ibid.*, 1879, p. 282.

been 465; by 1860, it had decreased to 374. In the case of linseys and such coarse cloths, the decrease had been from 144 to 95 sets. But relative to all other production, the decline had been even greater. For example, the sets employed on satinets had equaled 37 per cent of the total machinery reported for New England and New York in 1837; whereas in 1860 they amounted only to 17 per cent. The rise of cassimeres in the forties had, indeed, "almost entirely superseded the use of satinets for the best trade;" [1] and in later years the production of satinets was further knocked about by the competition in the lower qualities of its output.[2]

The decline, to be sure, was not immediate after 1830. Indeed, the manufacture of satinets, linseys, and such cloths seems to have benefited as did that of blankets from the relatively low duties on the cheaper types of raw wool during the period of 1832 to 1846. The Hazards of Peacedale, Rhode Island, had commenced the manufacture of negro-cloths in 1830, and they continued that line of production for many years thereafter.[3] In 1845 satinets and Kentucky jeans had formed nearly 40 per cent of the Massachusetts woolen production. Even in the succeeding decade, though a decline had occurred in the relative position of such fabrics, — that is, as compared with other products of Massachusetts mills, — the actual amount of output materially increased.[4] At the same time, production of linseys and negro-cloths was particularly noteworthy around Baltimore and Philadelphia. Most of these goods went south, but considerable quantities were said to be sold in the West, as far as the Missouri River and the Rocky Mountains, "being used there for the cloth-

[1] *Awards and Claims, Exhibition of 1876*, p. 20.

[2] In its last estate, satinet became a markedly low-grade article, composed of cotton warp and shoddy filling. But even with the lower price made possible by such contriving, it could not compete successfully with other fabrics.

[3] Clark, p. 433.

[4] The production figures for Massachusetts for 1845, 1855, and 1865 are as follows for these goods, in thousands of yards:

	1845	1855	1865
Satinets	3559	6736	6472
Kentucky jeans	1652	1949	629
Total of all fabrics	13,877	26,169	46,009

ing of labourers and backwoodsmen."[1] Subsequently, or from the early fifties on, despite improvement in the manufacture of satinets,[2] the production of all such coarser fabrics seems to have decreased steadily in the eastern states. In the western mills, the manufacture of linseys and satinets continued longer, especially in the case of small mills which exchanged their products with the neighboring farmers, but apparently by 1870 this western manufacture of such goods was surely on the decline.

The decrease in the production of satinets, linseys, and the like is especially notable because it fits in with the tendency toward a rising quality among woolen products. The diminution of the broadcloth production was, of course, an element acting in the other direction; but for the rest of the trade, and within most individual sections of the industry, there appears to have been a pronounced movement in the way of improved quality. The coarser fabrics, suitable to frontier conditions, were becoming less and less salable, and in their place came the fancy cassimeres, doeskins, fine flannels, and similar goods. The country was growing richer, the market broader, and the demand more insistent for semi-fine cloths. Beyond the production of this medium-fine quality, the domestic manufacture generally did not go—and by modern standards this quality of fabric might be classified rather as distinctly medium grade. The demand for the finest goods was still supplied by importation, — at least, until the newer conditions imposed as a result of the Civil War and the higher tariff policies made possible a renewed movement toward fine woolen manufacture in this country.[3] Production in the period before 1870, then, began at a relatively low quality, with satinets, linseys, negro-cloths, etc., in special prominence, but the trend dur-

[1] Wallis, *Report, British Documents*, 1854 [1717], p. 18; Freedley, *Philadelphia and its Manufactures in 1857*, p. 238.

[2] In 1853 it was remarked with regard to satinets: "In contrast with articles of this class made in America twenty years ago, they exhibit a true picture of the rapid growth of manufacturing art in this country. The productions of former years were rough, stiff, and coarse, while these are perfectly smooth and pliable. The former harshness of face is entirely removed and they now nearly resemble the French cassimeres" (*Art and Industry at the Crystal Palace, 1853*, p. 233).

[3] See below, vol. II, pp. 174 ff.

ing the decades was unquestionably toward a production steadily rising in quality.

4. *Worsted Fabrics.*

The most extraordinary feature of fabric development in the period now under consideration, more distinctive than the rise of the fancy cassimere production, — which did have substantial roots in the past, — was the introduction of worsted-cloth manufacture. The colonial period, it is true, had seen a small production of worsted fabrics, but it was upon a handicraft basis and limited to a few cloths specially suited to the finer trade. The decades following 1760, while yielding a momentous expansion and consolidation of the woolen branch, witnessed a practical disappearance of the worsted manufacture. Few, indeed, are the references to be found concerning it in the succeeding three-quarters of a century.[1] It may seem strange at first thought that such should have been the case. These decades formed a period of marked growth in the British worsted industry. The methods of the worsted manufacture are not dissimilar to those of the cotton manufacture, more akin than are those of the woolen industry; and these years were notable for the increase of the cotton manufacture in the United States. The typical worsted fabrics of the time, light dress-goods, would have filled a conspicuous gap in domestic output of woolen cloths, since the woolen goods were more suitable for men's than for women's wear. In brief, many factors seemed to favor a growth in the worsted-cloth production.

However, the early worsted manufacture in fact could be operated only under severe handicaps, — handicaps which apparently more than counterbalanced the propitious factors. Three important obstacles may be noted. The supply from domestic sources of long combing wool — that derived from the sheep of English breed — was not great; the American workmen or foremen skilled in the methods of production were few indeed; and

[1] Field (*State of Rhode Island*, iii, 363) reports the formation in 1820 of the Pawtucket Worsted Company for the manufacture of fine vestings, "the first specimen of worsted goods of American make." See also Niles, xxxiii, 211; Bishop, ii, 361; Clark, p. 573.

the processes were as yet not wholly adapted to power machinery. The last was probably the decisive factor, and will bear some special examination. What machinery was employed in the first decades for the spinning process is uncertain, probably the quasi-automatic woolen or the cotton mule, and weaving proceeded on power looms; but for the distinctive worsted process, the wool combing, hand labor was still necessary. In 1835 Mr. Michael H. Simpson of Boston had brought into use a wool-combing machine invented by Samuel Couillard, a Frenchman; but apparently it did not give full satisfaction, and seems to have found employment only in the manufacture of worsted carpet warps. In the worsted-cloth mills, hand-combing prevailed generally as late as 1860.[1] Under the circumstances it is rather remarkable that there should have been any considerable development of a worsted industry before the Civil War.

The original worsted production in this country on a factory basis, barring one or two negligible attempts at fancy worsted vestings, was worsted yarns. The Dedham Worsted Company, of Dedham, Massachusetts, incorporated in 1821, produced "a very superior kind of fine worsted yarns, suitable for coach lace, hosiery, and fringe makers."[2] As late as 1845 the chief worsted product of the New England Worsted Company was worsted yarn, — 350,000 pounds, as compared with 3000 pieces of bunting.[3] The Lowell Manufacturing Company in 1831 set up ma-

[1] Hayes, *American Textile Machinery*, p. 54; North, *Bulletin*, 1902, p. 331; Hayes, *Bulletin*, 1879, p. 280; Clark, p. 424. The Simpson machine is said to have been improved in 1854, and in the seventies to be "in universal use in this country for preparing the wool for carpet worsteds" and to be "indispensable in this manufacture" (Hayes, *American Textile Machinery*, p. 54).

Apparently combing machines began to be introduced from England in the earlier part of the sixties. In fact, Samuel Yewdall of West Philadelphia is reported to have established the first power-combing mill in that region, using Lister combs, in 1860 (*Annual Report of the Pennsylvania Secretary of Internal Affairs, 1888, Official Document No. 14*, p. 1 D).

[2] Kayser, *Commercial Directory*, p. 110.

[3] Fleischmann, p. 42. Mr. George Bond in 1837, opposing a lower duty or free entry of worsted yarn, stated: "The Committee no doubt included this article from the impression that it is not made in this country to any considerable extent. Now, the fact is, that there have been, for some years, small establishments in operation, which, in the aggregate, have produced a good deal for different

chinery for the production of worsted warp yarns.[1] The industry, then, was as yet a subsidiary affair, supplying semi-manufactured goods to the woolen, carpet, and other manufactures. While there was a small production of worsted fabrics, or fabrics in which worsted yarns were considered the important feature, the real expansion of the industry did not occur until the introduction of mousseline-de-laines.

Mousseline-de-laine, as the name implies, was first developed as an imitation in wool of the cotton muslin. It originated in France as an all-wool fabric, made of fine, soft staple; but later it was produced in England with a cotton warp and inferior wool filling. The weave employed brought the wool yarns to the surface, making it superficially a wool fabric. It was finished in plain colors, or more frequently printed, just as muslins are printed. Its cheapness, durability, and sightliness, according to Hayes, made its introduction "an invaluable boon to women of moderate means."[2] For twenty years this fabric, together with cloths derived from and allied with it, dominated the women's-wear section of the wool manufacture.[3]

The first mention of mousseline-de-laine production in the

purposes" (24th Cong., 2nd Sess., *Senate Documents, No. 173*, p. 4).

The Massachusetts Census of 1845 reported ten establishments engaged in the manufacture of worsted goods or goods of which worsted was a component part. They produced 617,000 pounds of worsted yarn and 2,321,000 yards of goods, including seemingly those in which worsted yarn was "a component part."

[1] Clark, p. 573.

[2] *Bulletin*, 1870, p. 257.

The importance of the cotton warp for wool fabrics is well stated by Hayes in this connection: "No event of the century has done more for female comfort and for the industry of wool than the introduction of the cotton warp. Cotton, instead of being the rival, became the most important auxiliary of wool, and has added vastly to its consumption." The utility of the cotton warp in relation to the satinet manufacture has already been noted; and later the importance of cotton-warp dress-goods generally will appear.

[3] The production of this fabric has not wholly died out even yet. For example, the Hamilton Woolen Company, which early made delaines, continued the manufacture "in practically the same construction, as 'Danish cloth' and later as 'Danish Poplar cloth'" (*Brief Record of the Company*, p. 3). This Danish cloth may still be purchased at the dry-goods counter of any large department store, to which the interested reader should apply if he wishes to secure an idea of this early worsted fabric. Danish cloth is now chiefly sold for bathing suits, costumes, and the like.

United States relates to 1840 when a Providence concern is said to have made up such goods in imitation of a piece imported from France.[1] The real commencement of this manufacture, however, seems to have come only when in 1845 the Ballardvale Mills and Hamilton Woolen Company took up the production, and when in 1853 the Pacific Mills were built with the avowed purpose of this manufacture.[2] The Amoskeag Manufacturing Company took on production of the article shortly thereafter; and the Massachusetts Census of 1855 reported three out of seven worsted establishments to be engaged exclusively on this fabric, one of them printing as much as 4½ million yards annually. The first delaines (as the article came to be known) produced by the Amoskeag Company were said to average seven yards to the pound, though subsequently lighter-weight fabrics of similar character were produced.[3] Moreover, new variations of delaines soon appeared, apparently following upon developments in England: reps, coburgs, and the like; until a very substantial group of worsted fabrics — and a group which formed a large part of later worsted dress-goods production — was available for domestic consumption.[4]

The difficulties in turning out the worsted filling yarn were at first so great — wool-combing being of course the chief obstacle — that some mills sought escape by circumvention, i. e., by substituting woolen for worsted yarns. This was not infrequently done, and yet the fabric was still called "delaine." Thus the Manchester and Pacific Mills both resorted in their first production of this article to the use of woolen filling. But soon the requirement of worsted yarns became fixed; and the difficulties had to be met more directly. The Manchester, Ballardvale, and

[1] *Bishop*, ii, 420, note.

[2] Hayes, *Bulletin*, 1877, pp. 134–135; Bagnall, pp. 575–576; Hamilton Woolen Company, *Brief Record of the Company*, p. 2; *The Arlington Mills*, 1891, pp. 94–96; Hayes, *Report on the Exhibition of 1876*, pp. 61–62; Ammidown's *Historical Collections*, ii, 375–378.

[3] Wallis, *Report*, *British Documents*, 1854 [1717], p. 22.

[4] It was stated in 1867 that "in consequence of the domestic manufacture of this fabric (delaines), the importation of printed delaines has almost wholly ceased" (Hayes and Mudge, *Report on the Paris Exposition of 1867*, vi, 25).

other mills seemingly resorted to hand-combing for some years;[1] and then gradually machines were introduced. All types of these machines were of British origin, and many specimens of such apparatus were directly imported from England. The Pacific Mills brought in six Lister machines soon after they commenced the manufacture of delaines. Some "inferior combers of American invention" were employed for a time at the Manchester Mills, ultimately being replaced by Noble combs. In 1860 power-driven combs were in operation at Samuel Yewdall's mill in West Philadelphia; and in two or three years' time John and William Yewdall had introduced the Noble machine at their new Fairmount Mills, Philadelphia. At about the same period a Lister comb was also set up by the Abbot Worsted Company, Graniteville, Massachusetts.[2] Before 1870 the whole worsted manufacture had adopted power combing, employing these machines of English origin, especially the Noble comb.[3]

As for other machinery peculiar to worsted-yarn production, improvement also came in time, and by the same road,—borrowing from England. The British industry had gone through a long experience of trial and experimentation, from the time when, in the latter years of the eighteenth century, Crompton's mule was first adapted to worsted spinning.[4] The first forward step had

[1] The Ballardvale Mills turned out worsted delaines throughout the period 1844–1850, although they apparently had no combing machines.

[2] *The Arlington Mills*, p. 96; Hayes, *Bulletin*, 1877, p. 135; *Annual Report of the Pennsylvania Secretary of Internal Affairs, 1888, Official Document No. 14*, p. 1 D; North, *Bulletin*, 1902, p. 331.

The Lister and Noble combs are the most important machines of this character, both the inventions of Englishmen. The former was patented in 1851, and the latter in 1853. Cartwright had attempted to accomplish combing by machinery in the latter eighteenth century, but his apparatus had not been successful practically. Indeed, until the inventions of Lister, Donisthorpe, Holden, and Noble, all within a decade, hand-combing had been the common practice in England itself.

[3] The *Census of 1870* reported 66 combing machines of foreign manufacture out of a total of 161 in worsted mills. Some of the domestic-made combs may well have been of the Simpson variety, employed in the production of carpet yarns, which was still an important branch of the worsted industry.

[4] The spinning-jenny seems to have been employed previously for a brief time, but probably in household or domestic system for the most part. The first worsted spinning mill in England, erected in 1784, appears to have used the mule.

been the introduction of Arkwright's spinning-frame in a modified form for both the drawing and spinning operations; and, indeed, frames of this general type are still employed universally in the drawing operations under the British method of worsted-yarn manufacture, and to some extent in worsted-spinning proper, as the so-called flyer-frame.[1] But somewhere along 1840–1850 another advance had been made in the British industry. This was the introduction of the cap spindle for worsted frame spinning, — a device invented by an American, Charles Danforth of Paterson, New Jersey, and already taken up and discarded by the cotton manufacture.[2] It was the latter type of improved spinning apparatus that first attracted the attention of American worsted-yarn manufacturers, — perhaps because of its greater productive capacity in comparison with the flyer-frame. The Hamilton Woolen Company, it is said, introduced cap spinning-frames into its factory at Southbridge as early as 1860, and this is claimed as the first use of such frames in the United States. And by the early seventies frame spinning with the

[1] The exact time when drawing-frames of the English model were brought to this country remains uncertain; but probably their introduction came at about the period when the other British apparatus, combs and spinning-frames, were being imported.

In connection with drawing-frames, it is interesting to note that one device "universally adopted in all roving frames or speeders," was of American origin. In 1822 Aza Arnold of Rhode Island invented the so-called "compound gear," "differential box," or "equation box," which was patented the next year, and, subsequently, patented in England by one Houldsworth. Its function was to regulate "the different velocities of spindle and bobbin, so that the surface of the bobbin, while increasing constantly in size (as the spinning proceeds), still preserves the same relation to the speed of the rollers" which are delivering the roving. See Webber, *Manual of Power*, p. 44; and Hayes, *American Textile Machinery*, p. 37.

[2] The ring spindle had displaced the cap apparatus in the cotton manufacture, at least for most types of cotton spinning.

As regards the development in British worsted-spinning technique, see Forbes, *Lectures on the Great Exhibition*, 1851, pp. 310, 319; James, *History of the Worsted Manufacture in England*, pp. 346–347; James, *Continuation and Additions to the History of Bradford*, 1866, pp. 222–223; Ure, *Dictionary of Arts, Manufactures, etc.* (ed. 1878), p. 989; Cudworth, *Worstedopolis*, p. 66; Baines, in *Journal of the Royal Statistical Society*, 1859, p. 7. According to Baines, who gives the best approximate dates, "the old spinning frame, called the fly frame, generally used ten years ago," had been by 1859 largely pressed out by "the new frame, called the bell frame" (or cap frame).

cap spindle was said to be spreading rapidly in the domestic manufacture.[1]

Finally, there was advance in the finishing end of the industry, in the printing operation, — a process which had a special importance for the delaine production. The printing of the woven fabric had at first been accomplished by hand, i. e., by the old block method. The Ballardvale Mills sent their goods to North Andover where they were printed by hand, and the Manchester Mill used the same method in its own shop. Soon, however, and again under the lead, it seems, of the Hamilton Woolen Company, the printing came to be done with cylindrical printing machines, — machines similar to those which the cotton-manufacturing industry had been using for some time.[2]

By 1860, then, the technical difficulties of the young industry were overcome, or in the way of solution; and the road was being cleared for future development and industrial expansion. And the first indication of this advance was the introduction of a number of new fabrics.

An increased supply of long English wool was made available for a decade after 1856 through the operation of the Canadian reciprocity treaty; and for the manipulation of this type of wool the Lister combing machines were specially adapted. By reason of these circumstances, as well as through mere imitation of British fabrics, the trend was toward the production of smooth, shiny, rather stiff cloths, — what were then generally called, and in England are still called, worsted "stuffs." The fabrics were made upon cotton warps, were generally piece-dyed in blacks or dark blues, and like the delaines were distinctly of the light-weight, dress-goods character. Modern cloths of nearest equivalence would be mohair summer suitings or alpaca coat-linings, the manufacture and use of the original goods having largely disappeared in the United States. However, for a number of years in the sixties and seventies — the time when the yet stiffer and shinier crinoline cloth had some vogue — worsted stuff-

[1] *Brief Record of the Hamilton Woolen Company*, p. 2; Webber, *Manual of Power*, p. 46.

[2] Hayes, *Report on the Exhibition of 1876*, pp. 61–62; *Art and Industry at the Crystal Palace, 1853*, p. 237.

goods formed a prominent part of the domestic worsted-cloth manufacture.

In addition to such fabrics, new goods were constantly being introduced, some of British and some of American origin. After the American industry had taken up the production of delaines, the British are said to have turned to stripes and plaids, and to a cloth called coburg which had quite a fashion. This latter was a piece-dyed, twilled fabric, also with a cotton warp, which the British made up in imitation of the all-wool French worsted cashmere. And the American manufacturers were impelled to follow such leads.[1] On the other hand, the American manufacture had made independent progress through the refinement of the earlier types of goods. For example, whereas the first delaines were spoken of as an indifferent quality of cloth, reference in later years is not infrequent to delaines made of relatively fine wool. In time progress in this direction was so great, and the convenience of differentiating such wools from the longer, lustrous wools of the later worsted manufacture became so important, that domestic wools suitable for the finer delaine production came to be denominated as "delaine" wools.[2]

As a result of these several factors, a considerable diversity of worsted goods was being turned out in American mills by 1870. At an exhibition in 1869 the goods displayed were reported as follows: "Besides the beautiful delaines, armures, and coburgs of the older manufacture, — the fabrics originated since the war, — the worsted plaid poplins, the Caledonian cloakings, serges, printed cashmeres, alpaca and mohair lustres, Roubaix poplins,

[1] *Brief Outline of the Business of William Whitman & Company*, p. 77.

[2] A writer in 1872 described the respective qualities of combing and delaine wools. The former "should have a staple from five to nine inches in length" and "is more valuable if lustrous." They were derived from Leicester and Cotswold sheep and cross-bloods from these stocks. Delaine wools, on the other hand, "should have a length of staple say from three to five inches long. . . . . Lustre is not expected of delaine wools, but strength, soundness, and softness to the touch are necessary." The half-blood merino is given as typical of this variety (*Bulletin*, 1872, p. 265). In modern parlance, delaine wools are fine combing wools from Ohio and the vicinity.

On the adaptability of native wools to the delaine manufacture, see Hayes and Mudge, *Report on the Exposition of 1867*, vi, 25.

black mohair lustres, mohair poplins of all shades" together with lastings or prunellas, for ladies' shoes, "for the first time successfully manufactured here within the last two years." [1] Other fabrics of the period included reps, barèges, grenadines, and bunting. Yet from another, more modern point of view the range of these worsted cloths is rather narrow. Almost all of them were composed of cotton warp and wool filling. Indeed, with the exception of bunting, webbings, and braids, — of which the first alone would be classified as a cloth, — no all-wool worsteds were made in this country at that time.[2] Moreover, not only were the soft, drapy dress-goods missing from the list, — the sort of fabric which is now produced from short, fine merino wool spun in the Continental method, — but also men's-wear worsteds and white worsted goods were conspicuously absent. The production consisted, then, of a considerable number — described by contemporaries as "an infinite variety" — of fabrics for female wear, running from the semi-soft delaines made from "delaine" wool to linings, lastings, and upholstery goods chiefly of the lustrous, stiff type. In 1870 the latter sort, the characteristic "stuff" goods, apparently predominated in the domestic output.

The worsted manufacture, then, though of negligible proportions in 1830, had risen by 1870 to fill a substantial place in the American wool-manufacturing industry. At the latter date, judged by the value added by manufacture or by the number of employees, the worsted branch had come to constitute between 10 and 15 per cent of the total industry. While no official data are available upon the constituent elements of the production at that time, a trade account of the period stated that ten or twelve mills were engaged upon worsted yarns, five or six on worsted reps, terry, and like goods, while apparently the bulk of the industry, including "ten or twelve of the largest mills of the country" were turning out delaines, alpacas, mohairs, Italian

[1] *Bulletin*, 1869, pp. 387, 386.

[2] *Bulletin*, 1884, p. 305.

At this period, the British manufacturers were also chiefly engaged on cotton-warp fabrics. A writer in 1873 stated that "probably seven-eighths of the pieces now produced (in the Bradford district) are made with cotton warps" (*Bulletin*, 1873, p. 429).

cloths, and similar women's-wear fabrics, indeed, "everything known in dress goods of worsted, mohair, etc."![1] The manufacture had been well launched. Its permanence seemed assured, and its promise for the future bright.

But why was the launching of the American worsted manufacture so long delayed? As late as 1879 — when the first American figures on machinery are available — there were only 337,000 worsted spindles in the United States, whereas England contained over 2 million. And no discrepancy of such considerable magnitude existed on the woolen side. At the date just mentioned, 1879, the woolen spindleage was 1,770,000 and 2,740,000, respectively. Why such a difference in the time of development in the two cases?

In search of explanation for such a difference, one would perhaps turn first to an inspection of tariff conditions. And here he would find what at first sight looks like a good case for the effectiveness of protection. In the earliest tariffs, to be sure, those through 1812, worsted goods and woolen cloths came under the same rates. They were taxed at rates which rose steadily under successive laws until imports bore a duty of 25 per cent under the act of 1812. Then came differentiation between the duties on worsted stuffs and on woolen fabrics. In the act of 1816 the rate on worsted goods was 15 per cent, as compared with one of 25 per cent upon woolen cloths. And such discriminatory treatment was continued in the period 1824–1832, while under the "Compromise Tariff" worsted stuff goods were allowed free entry, though woolen fabrics were still substantially taxed. On the other hand, a substantial change of policy came in the acts of 1842 and 1846. Duties of 30 and 25 per cent, respectively, were imposed upon worsted goods — duties which were still lower than those upon the kindred woolen manufactures, but yet were appreciable.[2] Now comes the interesting part. Under the

[1] *Bulletin*, 1870, pp. 145–146. Among the important mills mentioned in the dress-goods end were: the Pacific, Atlantic Delaine, Lowell, Manchester, and Hamilton.

The *Census of 1870*, it will be recalled, reported 102 mills in the worsted industry.

[2] Under the act of 1857 the rate on worsted stuffs was reduced to 19 per cent, and in that of 1860 increased again to 30 per cent. In both cases, the rates were

regime of free importation for worsted fabrics, one hears exceedingly little of domestic production. After the imposition of the 30 per cent rate in 1842, one finds the real commencement of such manufacture, the true initiation of mousseline-de-laine production. Seemingly, as I indicated above, the case argues strongly in favor of the effectiveness of protection.

I am not disposed to argue that the increased protection after 1842 was not without effect. Unquestionably it would have a steadying influence upon the young industry. But in the early period when rates on woolen and on worsted fabrics were similar, there was growth in the one and not in the other manufacture. Moreover, even under the higher duties after 1842 the expansion of the domestic worsted industry was not great until the decade of the sixties. To explain adequately the difference of development in the two manufactures one must take other factors into consideration. The nature of the domestic wool supply in the early decades of the century was not conducive to the launching or expansion of the American worsted manufacture. The worsted manufacture and the merino cultivation had as yet nothing in common. Apparently, too, the character of the products prior to the invention of mousseline-de-laines did not support the development of domestic worsted production. Stuff-goods were fabrics too elegant for common consumption in the American homes, though probably in the larger towns such goods of foreign origin had some sale. But I would be inclined to put most emphasis upon the state of technical equipment for worsted manufacture. While the chief operations of the woolen branch were early transformed into machine or quasi-machine processes — at least in so far as they are so constituted today — one of the primary and most important operations of the worsted manufacture, combing, remained long under the cramping control of hand work.

lower than those imposed upon woolen cloths. In 1862 and thereafter, however, worsted goods were included under the same duties as woolen fabrics, and with the latter came to be subject to increasingly heavy rates. (For the purposes of accuracy, note should be made that during practically the whole period of the 1883 tariff worsted cloths, the heavier men's-wear fabrics, were through interpretation of the courts made dutiable as "manufactures not specially provided for" at rates which for goods of low value were less than upon similarly valued woolen cloths.)

Until combing machines had been invented and had been introduced into the United States, in short, until the automatic combing process was thus secured, the worsted manufacture could have relatively small development in this country. With the general utilization of machine-combing in the sixties, and with other conditions favorable, — including a propitious tariff policy, — the manufacture was stabilized.

CHAPTER XVII

IMPORTATIONS

THE importations of wool fabrics from abroad played a more important rôle in the period 1830–1870 than in any other period in our history, barring perhaps the few years immediately following the Peace of Ghent. In both volume and quality this movement has much significance. The period 1830–1870 embraced the decade or more of the first real reaction from protection since the upward trend of import duties began, — the years under the low tariffs of 1846 and 1857. It was the first period, too, when the domestic industry could make appreciable resistance to the inflow of foreign goods. And, finally, this was the first period when the domestic manufacture had to face competition other than that of British origin. For such reasons particular weight may be given the history of importation. Incident to a general discussion of the import movement, certain aspects of the import trade deserve special emphasis, — particularly the fluctuation in the total movement during the several decades and under the several tariffs, changes in the composition of the incoming flow, and changes in the sources of that movement.

The course of importation during the period 1830 to 1870 with respect to woolen cloths and dress-goods, the two most important items, tells an interesting story. Moreover, since importations of wool cloths and dress-goods composed in terms of value 80 to 90 per cent of all the wool-goods importations with which we are concerned (i. e., exclusive of carpets, knit-goods, and the like), and since the movement of such smaller factors as blankets and yarns was generally similar to that of the two major items, this story regarding cloths and dress-goods may be taken as indicative of the whole import movement in wool manufactures.

1. The general trend of cloth and of dress-goods importations during these decades, at least until war conditions supervened, is evident in the accompanying graph (Figure 9); but certain features deserve special attention. First, the effects of the two

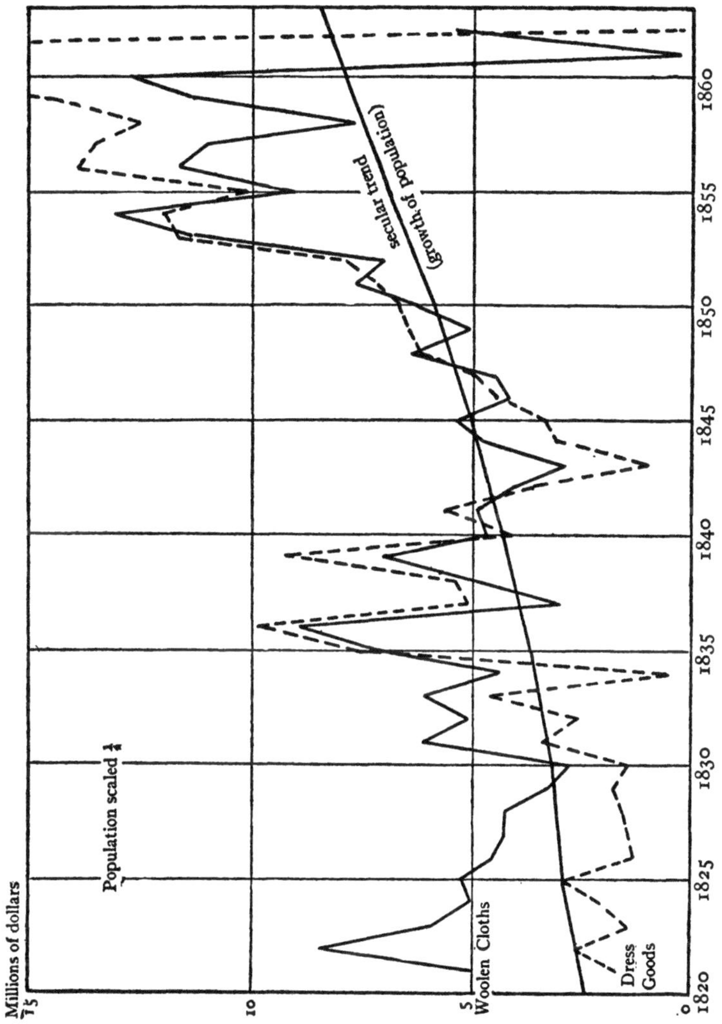

FIG. 9. Importation of Cloths and Dress-goods (in terms of value), 1820–1862.

chief speculative movements culminating in 1837–1839 and in 1857 are evident. In the earlier period the volume of imports showed an upward trend beginning in 1831, reached peaks in 1836 and 1839, and subsided to more normal figures in 1841–1842. In the later period, action may be considered to have started by 1850, when both cloths and dress-goods began to be purchased in particularly great volume; and imports of both increased rapidly for a few years. Then came forces which in some measure broke up the simple cyclical course, especially in the case of dress-goods. The importation of cloths attained its highest point in 1854, and thereafter generally declined except for a reaction in 1859–1860, which may well have been merely in anticipation of the coming change in tariff rates. While there are irregularities in this movement, on the whole it does not depart widely from the normal course of speculative up-and-down swing. Not so with dress-goods, however. With only momentary hesitations in 1855 and 1858, imports of these fabrics rose steadily to 1860. There was indeed a persistent upward trend after 1843, barring the two years just mentioned, until in 1860 the total value of such importations reached a point seven times the average value of 1843–1845.

These deviations of cloth and dress-goods import movements from what I have called the simple cyclical course may really be set apart with other irregular trends as giving a second peculiarity to the decades under consideration. One should note, for example, that just prior to the beginning of the period, that is, in the twenties, dress-goods importations were much less than those of cloths; whereas by the thirties and forties they had come at least to equal, and by the fifties far to exceed, the latter. Again, for the later decades — from 1843–1845 to 1860 — curves representing both types of importations indicate an extraordinary advance in that movement. In some measure, to be sure, the figures reflect only the enhancement of world prices which began with the gold discoveries of 1849, in so far as they do not manifest merely the influence of the speculative up-swing of prices which preceded 1857. However, this is not sufficient explanation. The quantity of importations in terms of yardage also rose substantially. The country was demanding more foreign wares, and various factors made possible increased foreign contribution to American supplies. Of these factors the most obvious are the tariff conditions, the relatively low tariff rates under the acts of 1846 and 1857, whereby the competitive power of European industries was increased. Thus, it is apparent that the years under the higher duties of the 1842 tariff formed a period of comparatively low importations. Yet the tariff is by no means the whole affair. The downward movement of imports after 1837 had occurred despite declining tariff rates, and in the forties and fifties the upward trend continued though import duties were stable. Finally, as we shall see, there was a rise in importations during the sixties which accompanied markedly increased tariff rates; and, with respect to dress-goods, even the act of 1867 could not check the inward movement. Conditions more fundamental than the tariff duties were responsible for the more persistent and more pronounced trends, — including the relative movement of cloth and dress-goods imports above noted; and among these one may note the introduction of new fabrics, especially new worsted dress-goods, of which no sufficient domestic production as yet existed; the enhanced domestic demands for finer fabrics with the rising level of wealth in the United States; the advent of new competition through the incursion of French and German goods into the American market; and the increasing force of all foreign competition by virtue of specially quickened technical improvements abroad. More will be said of these features later.

The war years, too, exhibited certain peculiar developments in the course of importations (see Figure 11).[1] Both cloths and dress-goods took prodigious slumps after 1860 and 1861, respectively, and recovery to more normal figures was slow. How shall one explain these vicissitudes? Surely the most obvious change in competitive conditions, the readjustments of the tariff, is not adequate. The first drop in importations was too great to be attributed to this single cause, and, as just suggested, the succeeding years brought increased flow of foreign goods despite rising tariff rates. The proper explanation lies, I think, rather in

[1] See below, p. 383.

the dislocation of commercial arrangements which accompanied the war, the effective closing of the southern markets, and the like.

Finally, the period closes with the inward movement in general still proceeding at a high level. The import of cloths, to be sure, had reacted after touching a high point for all time in 1866, — a high point occasioned apparently by the speculative movement that culminated in that year, and by anticipation of yet higher tariff duties.[1] But the importation of dress-goods attained an average for the latter years of the sixties greater than for any earlier period of similar length. The height attained was in fact so great that, including dress-goods with the other wool goods imported, the general average of importations was still running high and still showed a particularly marked advance over the volume of imports at the beginning of the interval now under discussion, i. e., the early years of the thirties. Absolutely the increase was well over three-fold. But perhaps more interesting and important was the share contributed by imports to the total domestic supply of wool manufactures at the two periods. Around 1830 importations formed something like a fifth of the total wool-cloth supply of the United States, that is, if we include in the latter the output of household looms.[2] On the other hand, at the time when we get the first adequate census figures of domestic factory production, 1849 and 1859, and when household operations had ceased to form so significant a proportion of total American cloth supply, the ratios of importations to the latter on the basis of values were 29 and 34 per cent, respectively. Even in 1869, after some decline in the import of cloths, foreign goods still formed about 25 per cent of the total domestic consumption.[3]

[1] The diversion of domestic manufacturing capacity in considerable measure to the satisfying of military demands was another significant factor.

[2] See above, p. 261.

[3] These ratios are based on the production and average annual importation (covering the three years around the census date) of cloths, dress-goods, blankets, flannels, and yarns. The detailed figures are as follows (in thousands of dollars):

Census year	Production	Importation (duty paid)	Total	Ratio of Imports to Total
1849	$43,207	$17,470	$60,677	28.7
1859	65,596	33,544	99,140	33.8
1869	177,496	41,136	218,632	18.9

Consideration of the import movement from the viewpoint of consumption per head of population leads to somewhat the same conclusions. Importations per capita, whether on the basis of value or of quantity, move in sympathy with the fluctuations in general business conditions; and they manifest the same increase from about 1845 to 1860. The most striking feature of these figures, however, is the height to which they attained in the latter fifties. Though imports per capita had touched a similar height momentarily at the climax of the speculative movement before 1837, they maintained a position in the later period — from 1854 on — which was never before and has never since been reached.[1] By 1870 there had been some recession, but goods were still com-

Since the value of domestic production in 1870 is inflated by the depreciation of the Greenbacks, whereas the value of importations (since these were based on foreign specie valuations and paid in gold) was not so affected, the ratio of imports to total consumption as above presented gives an erroneous picture. With best allowance for all the circumstances, a figure of 25 per cent would be more nearly correct.

[1] The per capita value of the importations of wool cloths and dress-goods by five-year intervals was as follows, the figures presented being averages for the three years around the date quoted:

1825	$.63	1850	$.56
1830	.49	1855	.85
1835	.85	1860	.83
1840	.69	1865	.70
1845	.42	1870	.68

With as close an approximation as possible, the average per capita importations of cloths and dress-goods in terms of quantity were: for 1827–1830, 1.93 yards, and for 1860, 3.22 yards. (The method used was to ascertain the British exportation of such goods in terms of yards, and increase this figure by the ratio between British and total imports of wool manufactures into the United States, stated in terms of value.)

Dr. Clark (*History of Manufactures*, p. 248) gives an estimated increase over the same period of much greater magnitude: from one-quarter of a yard in 1827–1830 to 1.50 yards (from England alone) in 1860. Such data, I believe, gives an erroneous impression. I differ particularly as to the figure proper for the earlier period, 1827–1830. Dr. Clark used Pitkin's figures, but comparison of the latter with statistics from the British documents indicates that Pitkin erred. Again, and by reason of the same mistake on Pitkin's part, Dr. Clark gives what seems to me an erroneous picture of the decrease in the value per yard of wool-cloth imports, — from $2.12 per yard in 1827–1830 to 18.8 cents a yard in 1860. The British export statistics show a decline from 1s. 5d. per yard in the former period to 10d. a yard at the latter date.

ing in at a rate per inhabitant substantially higher than had prevailed in 1830.

Roughly speaking, then, the period under discussion stretches from the close of one movement in importation to the commencement of a new phase in the general development. The years around 1830 covered the culmination of a downward trend in imports extending through the twenties. Then came the rise and fall through the speculative boom and collapse which reached over rather more than a decade. And this was followed by a movement even more pronounced, partly speculative, but partly not, — a movement that brought the volume of importations in the latter fifties to a point of particularly great height. Finally, in the last years before 1870 the volume again rises to a level which really forms the starting point for the modern period, — a period when the quantity of the goods brought in tended to decline. Accordingly, the decades 1830 to 1870 embrace the years of most serious threat to the domestic manufacture from the assaults of foreign competition.

2. Equally important, however, with the marked changes in the quantities of importations into the United States were the changes in the sources of those importations. During the greater part of our foregoing period, England had been practically the sole purveyor of goods for the American market. This was a situation to be expected. England had the most advanced wool manufacture of the times, and she still held us by economic interests despite political separation. Moreover, for many years in that period England alone of European wool-manufacturing nations had command of the seas. Even in the early twenties, according to a comparison in terms of value between English exports and American imports of wool fabrics, that nation still supplied all but 5 per cent of the total. But later years in the same decade ushered in a change. By 1830, on the basis of a similar comparison, England was shipping only 80 to 85 per cent of the total.[1]

As the years passed, competition with England on the part of

[1] Allowance has been made for commissions and handling charges, but this must of course be largely pure estimate.

the other European nations became more and more successful, at least in divers lines. Germany was coming to the fore in the shipment of "cloths" and yarns. In 1850 she sent cloths which in value equaled 15 per cent of the total import of such goods; by 1860, 24 per cent; and in 1870, 38 per cent, — the last being a ratio not subsequently attained with respect to such goods.[1] Of the less important item of woolen and worsted yarns, Germany in 1860 and 1865 supplied over 70 per cent (in value). For a few years, too, France threatened severe competition. The French government in the years immediately following the Revolution of 1848 distributed a "prime" or bounty on the exportation of wool manufactures; and by 1850 that country was sending over a fourth (in value) of American imports of wool "cloths." In later years, apparently after the cessation of the bounty, these imports from France rapidly dwindled, until in 1865 and 1870 they did not amount to 5 per cent of the total. However, in certain lines, notably in stuffs or dress-goods and in blankets (in so far as the latter were imported), England still retained a dominant position. In worsted stuffs, she was sending 70 per cent in the fifties. After 1865 we were receiving from England 85 per cent of all "dress-goods" imported, — "dress-goods" being the title under which now were included all light-weight fabrics imported. While by 1870 this ratio had declined to 80 per cent, the competition of other European countries in this line became really severe only in the later decades. Of blankets, no country other than Great Britain has ever supplied any considerable proportion. Finally, with respect to all wool manufactures even, the ratio of England's shipment as late as 1869–1871, 77½ per cent, indicates that that country was still the dominant factor in the import trade into this country. Her position was not secure, for it was being assaulted by the rising industries of the Conti-

[1] The prominence of Forstmann & Huffman, a leading dress-goods manufacturing concern located in Passaic, New Jersey — it was erected as a branch of a German house in 1903 — lends interest to a passage to be found in the *Tribune's* account of the Exposition of 1853–1854: "Messrs. Foistmann & Huffman (*sic*), Werden-on-Ruhr, Prussia, are large manufacturers for the American market. So well known are their goods, that they are commonly called F & H goods, and are considered to be among the best of the foreign goods brought to America" (*Art and Industry at the Crystal Palace, 1853*, p. 236).

nent, but as yet it had given way only in part. The growing diversity of origin for our imports merely foreshadows the developments of the subsequent period, and in this movement the changing character of our importations played an important part.

3. In some respects, the changes in the constituent elements of the import trade during the period 1830–1870 are wholly consistent with the promises held forth in the earlier decades. Thus, the decline in flannel imports had been specially marked in the middle and later twenties. To be sure, that was a novel situation as regards flannel imports, and there might have been question as to the permanence in these conditions. However, though the business expansion culminating in 1837 was strong enough to bring a small reaction, thereafter such imports again became negligible; and they remained negligible through the thirty years 1840–1870, except for the brief period of the Civil War. In the latter sixties, the only flannel reported as largely imported was the so-called "opera" flannel, — a highly gigged and finished fabric, and, relatively speaking, a luxury article.[1] The domestic flannel manufacture was for the most part solidly entrenched. Again, importation of broadcloths proceeded in about the fashion that one would expect from a knowledge of the domestic situation with respect to this fabric. The American industry had turned aside from broadcloth production, and the popular demand for this sort of fabric was declining. What goods of this nature were required, therefore, came principally from abroad, but the importation was on a much lower level than it had been prior to 1830. A report in 1854 summed up the case well, when, admitting "the comparatively low position of the United States in the manufacture of fine broadcloths," it enumerated these fabrics — "fine broadcloths" and "cloths of the finer sorts" — as chiefly drawn from foreign sources.[2]

[1] Hayes, *Report on Group IX at Exhibition of 1876*, p. 51. See also Niles, xlviii, 399; *Joint Report of National Association of Wool Manufacturers and of Wool Growers to the United States Revenue Commission*, 1866, p. 14; Hayes, *Bulletin*, 1877, p. 118.

[2] Hayes, *Report on Exhibition of 1876*, p. 41. See also Fleischmann, p. 37; North, *Bulletin*, 1895, p. 44.

The *Census of 1860* (iii, p. xxxiii) has the following to say of foreign broadcloths:

In other lines importation was subject to new forces during the period under consideration. With the increased proficiency of the American industry, a higher quality of fabric could advantageously be produced in domestic mills. Thus, cassimeres of American manufacture came to dominate the domestic market, even the so-called fancy cassimere, whereas in the period before 1830 the only type of wool fabric in which we were practically independent was the satinet, a substantially inferior grade of cloth. One hears of foreign types and designs in cassimeres, but chiefly in connection with their adoption and manufacture in this country.[1] The development of the Crompton loom and the adaptability of American wools to this variety of fabric rendered such production relatively secure even in periods of heavy general imports from abroad. In the production of delaines, also, the domestic manufacture acquired special strength. The first cloths of this type had come from abroad, but they soon began to cut a considerable figure in American production, perhaps because, as one writer stated, "they had much of the flannel character."[2] Commenced during the relatively high-tariff period of 1842–1846, the manufacture apparently did not suffer severely even in the later years of high general importation. Indeed, the Pacific Mills, organized particularly for the manufacture of this fabric, were launched in 1853, in the middle of the low-tariff era.[3] It is improbable that importations of this and similar cloths ceased entirely, but apparently the domestic mills had been

"The great and deserved popularity of the West of England superfine cloths, and the cheapness of all English broadcloths, produced by the cheap labor and perfect machinery now in use, the elegant finish of the French, and the lightness of the French and German cloths, which adapt them to our summer use, have (with the nature of the domestic wool) prevented our manufacturers from obtaining possession of the home market under the low tariffs which have generally prevailed."

[1] North, *Bulletin*, 1894, pp. 338, 350; Kittredge, *Dry Goods Economist*, 1896, p. 81.

[2] Hayes, *Bulletin*, 1877, p. 134.

[3] Whitman, *Bulletin*, 1911, p. 222.

On course of delaine importation: see *Brief Outline of the Business of William Whitman & Company*, p. 77; Hayes and Mudge, *Report on the Paris Exposition of 1867*, vi, 25.

able to consolidate their position and to maintain a satisfactory output.[1]

In the case of blankets the rôle of imports was more significant. The domestic manufacture, it appears, had been stimulated by the cheap wool made available in a special degree by the tariffs of 1833 and 1842, and during these years, except for the up-swing of importations in the middle thirties, the quantity of blankets brought in was relatively low. Under the tariff of 1842, indeed, "nearly all the medium (grade) blankets consumed here were of domestic fabrication."[2] Then came a substantial increase in importations from 1846 to 1860, under the low duties of that period. In value importations nearly doubled between 1844–1846 and 1858–1860 (the former by no means a specially low point), while quantities seem to have increased in even greater measure. British exports of blankets to the United States rose from an average of something less than 1½ million yards in 1843–1845 to one of over 5⅓ million yards in 1858–1860. While the domestic blanket manufacture continued to operate in moderate scope throughout these years, enhanced importations must indeed have proved a check upon any considerable movement of expansion. Such domestic production as persisted was apparently of the medium-quality goods above mentioned, while imports were either of the cheap grades suitable for southern consumption or of the better varieties to which domestic goods were admitted to be inferior.[3] The domestic producers were able to secure dominance of the American market only when tariff rates began to rise with the Morrill act of 1861. By the end of the sixties, English exports of blankets to the United States hardly exceeded 100,000 yards. The tariff duties were peculiarly effective.

Experience different from any of the foregoing occurred in the case of dress-goods. This was the importation which responded

[1] During the Civil War period other additions were made to the list of fabrics in the production of which we were largely self-sufficient. Apparently among these were "the Esquimaux and Moscow beavers, which we have imitated from the Germans" (Hayes and Mudge, *Report on the Paris Exposition of 1867*, vi, 21).

[2] *Bulletin*, 1881, p. 383.

[3] *Art and Industry at the Crystal Palace, 1853*, p. 215.

least to variations in import duties, or perhaps better, it was an importation which showed the influence of other factors to be fully as important as that of the tariff. It will be noted, for example, that between 1830 and 1870 a marked change had come in the relative positions of cloth and dress-goods importations (see chart above). Whereas around the earlier date imports of cloths had averaged something like two and a half times those of the lighter fabrics in terms of value, by the close of the period the relations were reversed. Indeed, each decade manifested with respect to dress goods a higher level of importation than the preceding, — the level under the relatively high tariff of 1842 being substantially higher than it was a decade earlier, — until in 1859–1861 the value of such imports was over ten times the corresponding figure for 1828–1830.

In terms of quantity the increase was even greater. Not only was there a decrease in the unit price of such goods, but in the interim dress-goods of cotton warp had been introduced, — a feature which, appearing in the manufacture of the Bradford (England) district first in 1834, changed the whole face of this light-weight trade. In the latter fifties, these cotton-warp fabrics, or "mixed stuff goods," were exported to this country from England alone in quantities as great as 40 million yards a year. Adding the relatively small volume of all-wool goods, the exportations of "stuffs" from England to the United States averaged nearly 43 million yards, as compared with some 700,000 yards in 1828–1830. Nor is this all; for at the earlier dates England was practically our only source of such goods, and by 1860 she was supplying us with only 70 per cent of our dress-goods purchases, measured in terms of value.

Finally, it may be noted that after a precipitate and extraordinary decline in such importation during the first years of the war, — falling from an average value of 19 million dollars in 1859–1861 to one of a few hundred thousand dollars in 1861–1862, — a revival soon appeared. By 1870, even despite the high tariff of 1867, this trade, measured in terms either of value or of quantity, was on the road to new heights, astounding even compared with those reached in 1859–1861.

An increase of importation so long continued demands explanation; nor is the explanation difficult, at least in part. The manufacture of light-weight fabrics of the dress-goods type was slow in developing in the United States. Linsey-woolsey, flannel, and homespun were the fabrics for women's wear, offered by earlier domestic production, with perhaps some of the lighter satinets; and none of these could compare in sightliness with "stuff" goods. As domestic wealth increased and the style influence extended its domain, worsted fabrics came into ever greater demand, — and as yet the United States boasted scarce a single worsted spindle. With the rise of delaine and similar manufacture in the forties and fifties, a small supply of dress-goods from domestic sources became available; but in volume, and particularly in range of variety and quality, the American industry at that time was deficient, as, for example, in mohairs, lustres, all-wool merinos and cashmeres, and the like.[1] And something of this situation persisted, even after the Civil War. The late start continued to handicap the domestic production of dress-goods for many years; the stimulus given that production by free entry of Canadian long wools came to an end in 1866; foreign industries ever devised new fabrics; and shortly thereafter soft fabrics of the Continental type began to find favor in the American market. These several factors conspired to prolong the period during which foreign light-weight fabrics should play an important part in the supply of the domestic market. In fact, not until after the tariff of 1897 did a marked decrease in such importations occur.

The period 1830–1870 closes, then, with a peculiarly divided prospect. In the woolen branch, there was calm as after a storm. The domestic production had weathered the heavy importations of the fifties and now could ride at ease behind the protecting wall which had been gradually built up since 1861. Imports, though still considerable, did not threaten to increase, and the domestic industry by increasing effectiveness in its operations

[1] See above, pp. 324–332, for additions from time to time to domestic production; also, *Bulletin*, 1874, p. 11; and Hayes, in *Awards and Claims. Exhibition of 1876*, p. 455.

could indeed look forward to curtailing sooner or later the field supplied from abroad. On the other hand, the worsted manufacture, as yet of a restricted scope as far as character of production was concerned, was still suffering from heavy foreign shipments. The industry itself was young and of questionable strength. The future was uncertain. This difference in the position of the two branches is striking; and of course, reflects chiefly the difference in historical development. It is the more noteworthy because the following decades were to make such a change, as the worsted manufacture rushed to the front as the conspicuously capable and sturdy section of the wool-manufacturing industry.

CHAPTER XVIII

TECHNICAL ADVANCE

ALTHOUGH the period before 1830 had been one of extraordinary technical progress, improvement of machinery and processes is not the monopoly of any era. In some ways the headway made during the decades 1830 to 1870 was even more interesting than that of the earlier period. Many of the changes of the earlier times were borrowings from abroad; many were the initial steps in the attainment of real machine operation after the basis of modern machine fabrication had been laid through the contributions of foreign and of domestic invention; and all took place under general economic conditions which, like the specific conditions of the tariff, were on the whole favorable to the domestic manufacture. In the years after 1830, and especially those after 1840, conditions were not so comfortable for the domestic cloth production, particularly with the increasing influx of importations. Yet improvement continued; and in certain portions of the manufacture important gains were registered. To appreciate the situation of the American manufacture in all its aspects, a review of the particular advances made during these decades is peculiarly valuable.

In connection with the discussion of other matters, some of the major developments in the period 1830–1870 have already been described: the introduction of burring apparatus for use in conjunction with carding machines, the improvement in character and increase in speed of looms, and the importation of worsted preparing and spinning machinery.[1] These advances were of special influence in facilitating changes in the types or qualities of domestic cloth production. But there were other advances less intimately related to this particular phase of our history which deserve consideration here. It will be convenient to

[1] See above, pp. 307–309, 310–312, 313–314, 327–330.

THE FINISHER SECTION OF A CARDING MACHINE OF THE SIXTIES

Showing the roller condensers of that period

THE FOREPART OF A DOUBLE BREAKER CARD OF THE SIXTIES

Showing the hand-feeding apparatus

examine the chief operations of the manufacture to ascertain the conditions which prevailed in 1870, and the source and character of new apparatus; and to these features may be added some comparison with foreign developments.

The year 1870 found methods and mechanisms for cleaning the wool fiber much changed or in process of modification, as compared with earlier practice. This operation covers the removal from the wool of the dirt, grease, and suint with which the fleece is impregnated when first clipped from the sheep's back; and, in 1830, it was still conducted in a crude fashion, both chemically and mechanically. Of the chemical changes that brought the industry to modern practices, little is known; but apparently by 1870 the use of more scientific means, involving treatment by potash and soda soaps, had become fairly general. Cleansing could be prosecuted with greater care and accuracy, diminishing the danger of damage to the wool fibers, and yet assuring a wholly clean product. By reason of the influence of such improved conditions upon the whole series of subsequent manufacturing processes, this change in method may be regarded as of a particularly fundamental type.

But modifications of apparatus were equally important. The early equipment consisted of large troughs or bowls in which the wool was immersed. There the wool was soaked, and stirred more or less continually by men armed with long poles. When the cleansing was deemed to have progressed sufficiently, the wool had to be laboriously fished out and spread to dry in a room specially devoted to that purpose. Such arrangements were obviously labor-consuming in a high degree. Efforts to reduce the labor element probably occurred in the American industry, though we have no definite information. Surely the successful advances were made elsewhere, and subsequently introduced into the United States. A machine invented in 1835 by one Garcel, seemingly of France, is regarded by Grothe as the basis of all subsequent developments.[1] Improved by divers contributions, — French, Belgian, English, and German, — the apparatus may be said to have reached its modern form when John Petrie

[1] Grothe, *Technologie der Gespinnstfasern*, p. 84.

of Rochdale, England, and Eugene Melen of Verviers, Belgium, brought out their machines, around 1860.[1] American mechanisms have followed the lines laid down in these foreign devices. However, whatever the origin, the American manufacturing in-

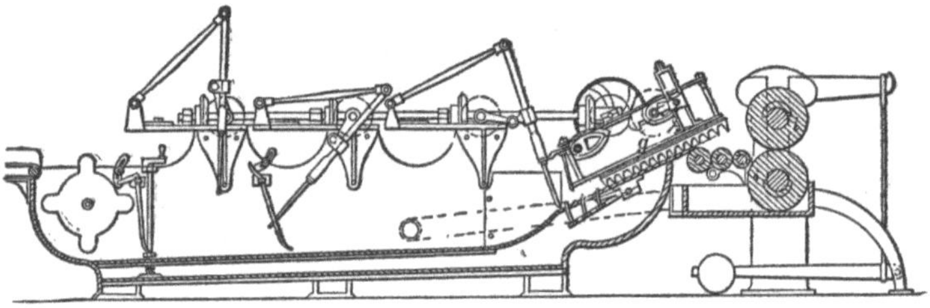

FIG. 10. Working Parts of a Scouring Bowl (a McNaught model of about 1860).

dustry was by 1870 in the way of securing a material addition to its effectiveness through the adoption of this new labor-saving apparatus. Thereafter the raw wool was thrown into one end of a series of long bowls or troughs which were each supplied separately with water and chemicals and which could be separately drained. The wool was acted upon and pushed forward by mechanical rakes, and was squeezed by sets of rollers both between bowls and at the final delivery end. As one may easily see from this description, hand-labor was almost wholly eliminated. But the further facts are noteworthy: that the work was more effectively done than it could ever have been accomplished under the older method; and that the new apparatus was particularly adaptable to the handling of large weights of wool. It was apparatus, indeed, which fitted in exceptionally well with American requirements.

The equipment of the carding process had also undergone appreciable modification in the years after 1830. First, there was a widening of the carding machines. The original Scholfield card had been 24 inches wide, but by 1830, 36-inch machines were coming in. The latter remained for many years the standard equipment of American mills. Even in the latter fifties the

[1] The exact dates of the respective patents are 1859 for Petrie and 1863 for Melen.

Stevens mills at North Andover retained that type. During this period, however, came the introduction of 40 and 48-inch apparatus, the first Census figures on the matter, those for 1890 showing half the machines in American factories to be of the last, 48-inch variety.[1] Again, alteration had meanwhile come in the intermediate feeds and in condensing. In the early, three-part carding machines, the wool had been doffed from the final cylinder of the breaker card, and from that of the intermediate or second card, in the form of a broad sheet of fibers. This sheet was wrapped upon a roller, and from that fed into the succeeding portion of the apparatus. Such a method did not permit mixing of the wool in the thorough degree desirable: the various sections in the web of wool retained the same position relative to the other sections of the web in each successive machine. This hindered the manufacture of uniform, even yarn. Then, at some time soon after 1830, if not before, came an improvement: the introduction of so-called "side-drawing" from the first and second (or intermediate) breakers.[2] The wool fibers loosed from the final cylinder of the breaker were drawn to one side of the carding machine and passed through a revolving cylinder which smoothed the strand, imparting what was known as a false twist. The strand was wound upon spools, this part of the operation being known as "balling." A frame containing a number of these spools, sometimes as many as forty, was set up before the

[1] North, *Bulletin*, 1894, p. 345; *American Wool and Cotton Reporter*, 1909, p. 879; Interview with William H. Jowett, for sixty years employed by M. T. Stevens & Sons Company.

[2] Mr. Davis of Davis & Furber, machine builders, testifying at the Goulding trial in 1865; quoted by North, *Bulletin*, 1901, pp. 267, 269; D. C. Fisher, in *American Wool and Cotton Reporter*, 1909, p. 879.

The carding operation is in reality carried through upon two or three separate machines, sometimes lumped together and called a "carding machine." Each of these separate machines has a main cylinder or "breast," or two large cylinders of equal size. In England the general practice is to employ two machines, one single and one double breasted, for the carding operation; while in the United States, both the English practice and that of three single breasted machines are employed, though the three-part apparatus is the more common. In the latter case, the first machine is called the "breaker;" the second, the "second" or "intermediate breaker;" and the third, the "finisher." The description in the text proceeds on the basis of this three-part machinery.

feed end of the succeeding part of the card, the second breaker or the finisher. Subsequently, apparently around 1860, the contents of several short spools were wound upon one long one to be placed as was the rack of small ones.

The side-drawing and balling attachment is noteworthy as the first attempt to provide for a mixture of the fibers in the carding batch by means of a labor-saving device at the stage of transfer between parts of the carding machinery, — a practice now almost universal. If the wool fell loose from the last cylinder of the breaker or intermediate card, as in the earliest carding arrangements, it would be mixed, to be sure, in the process of hand-feeding at the succeeding engine; but obviously that involved much labor. The lap system just mentioned, in which the sheet of wool was wound upon a cylinder and fed therefrom into the next machine, was economical of labor, but no general mixing of the fibers was possible.[1] By the balling or side-drawing system, however, batches of fibers which had followed one another in the first machine were fed in together in the second, and fibers from one section of the web were mixed with those from other sections. This tended to produce a more homogeneous series of rovings at the delivery from the finisher card. Such rovings, in turn, would be less liable to breakage in the spinning operation, and would yield superior yarn. Moreover, this mixture could be secured, if the balling system were used, without the employment of much labor.

The idea of side-drawing was unquestionably English, said to have been invented by one Robert Peele as early as 1779; but apparently it was then applied only to cotton carding.[2] Its adaptation to woolen carding may also have come in England, — I can find no evidence bearing either way, — but surely wide utilization of the apparatus came first in the United States. While it was spreading in this country in the thirties, the first reference to its use in England is under date of 1853, and that

[1] Considerable mixing of the fibers would, indeed, take place if several laps were fed together into the succeeding portion of the carding machine; though even a greater intermixture would be possible through the side-drawing method.

[2] Bramwell, *The Wool-Carders' Vade Mecum*, p. 133.

reference does not imply a general knowledge of the mechanism.[1] Toward the end of the period 1830–1870, however, the English manufacturers were not only catching up through the wider adoption of the balling system, but were stealing a march on the American. In or about 1850 the Apperley "feed" was invented in England and its construction and sale begun.[2] This, like the balling arrangement, was in essence merely a means of transferring the wool from the delivery end of one machine to the feed end of the next. Similar to it in some respects was the so-called Scotch feed, which seems to have been introduced not long after the Apperley.[3] At least both are spoken of by 1870 as rather common features of English woolen mills. Apparently, too, these varieties of apparatus were by that time far from unknown

[1] Ibberson, *The Woolen Manufacturers' Guide*, 1853, p. 13: "The downy wool or sliver should be doffed from the scribbler in the ordinary way, but the sliver must run through a revolving tube, and between two iron rollers on to a large bobbin, as a necessary preparation for the self-acting feeder" of the carding engine.

Bischoff (*A Comprehensive History of the Woolen and Worsted Manufactures*, 1842, ii. 392), quoting from a description which "was published in September last," — so evidently a recent account, — speaks of the wool being delivered from the scribbler: "The wool is wound around a revolving roller in an endless fleece, having the appearance of a fine blanket." Obviously, this was the lap system already being discarded in the United States. Again, Dodd (*The Textile Manufactures of Great Britain*, 1851, p. 99), a less accurate writer, states that "the wool falls from the last cylinder (of the scribbler) in a state of a light, flocculent, downy layer," — a still less advanced method.

[2] Bramwell, p. 228. By the Apperley "feed," the wool stripped from the doffer cylinder by the vibrating doffer comb is formed into a large, rounded strand. Then it is carried to the feeding apron of the next machine by an automatic device, and laid upon that apron in diagonal lines.

[3] In the Scotch "feed" or intermediate transfer apparatus, the wool stripped from the doffer is removed in a continuous ribbon of fibers six or eight inches broad. This ribbon is carried mechanically to the feed-apron of the succeeding machine, and deposited in a line parallel to the licker-in cylinders, but in such manner that each successive line or layer overlaps somewhat on the preceding one.

This apparatus was never popular in the United States. In fact, it is not much employed in American mills, although latterly it has been coming into greater use. Probably this disregard is accounted for by its close sequence upon the Apperley "feed," which was widely adopted in American mills and is now almost universally employed here. In England, however, while the balling system is still occasionally used, and while, indeed, an improved type of lap arrangement (the Blamire) is not infrequently to be found, the Scotch feed apparatus is perhaps the most usual variety, even more usual than the Apperley so popular here.

on the Continent.[1] The advance of such devices over the balling method was two-fold: the transfer was accomplished without the employment of labor, once the proper adjustments were made and the machine started; and, again, they gave a more efficient mixture of the wool fibers than did the balling system, a feature preferable for most purposes.[2] Though probably it was not until the latter years of the period 1830–1870 that these devices came into general employment even in English mills, it was even later that they played any considerable part in American practice. Indeed, I have found no reference to any utilization whatsoever of either mechanism in our mills prior to the close of that era.[3]

With respect to the final removal of the wool from the last or finisher card, advances had also been made in the American industry. Not only did the Goulding condenser complete its conquest of the domestic field,[4] but improvements were made in its construction. Chief among these was the substitution of rubbers for the older revolving tubes. Both devices, it may be suggested, aimed at giving a smoothness and a moderate consistency to the roping which was being drawn from the ring doffer. The first type of rubbing device was, seemingly, the so-called "three-roll rub," introduced sometime in the thirties. This variety contained three pair of rollers as wide as the carding machine,

[1] For example, Alcan places the adoption of the Apperley attachment in France in 1862–1867 (*Bulletin*, 1870, p. 427).

[2] As will appear later, the Apperley feed sacrificed parallelization of the wool fibers, one of the aims in the carding operation, to the mixing of these fibers, another chief purpose of that operation. The increased use of the Scotch feed in the United States during the last decade or so may perhaps be interpreted as a late appreciation of this fact.

[3] On the Continent there were the beginnings of another interesting and important development, though it came so near the close of the period under discussion that it probably had little effect until after 1870. In 1864, a Belgian, one Jean Sebastian Bolette, had invented a mechanism for feeding automatically the loose wool into the first or breaker card. This device, probably not the original one looking in the same direction, was the forerunner of Bramwell's "automatic feed" which has come to be the standard mechanism in both the British and American industries. It is of special importance in that it eliminated the hand labor theretofore necessary in the weighing of the wool and its even distribution on the feeding apron, at the feed end of the breaker card (Bramwell, p. 212).

[4] See above, pp. 102–105, for introduction of Goulding condenser.

covered with rubber, between which the ropings passed. These rollers were made not only to revolve but also to oscillate sidewise at the same time. Revolving with a surface speed in predetermined proportions to the forward movement of the line of ropings, — there being some incidental draft introduced into the woolen strands, — these rollers by their oscillation imparted a smoothness and a compactness, or "false twist," to the ropings, which could not be secured by the use of revolving tubes.

In the thirties, carding machines with rubbing attachments were not being turned out in any considerable volume. According to a representative of the principal woolen-machine manufacturers, his concern was then making "one machine with rubbers to twenty machines with tubes." But gradually the demand for such devices spread. By the middle sixties, these same builders were turning out an equal number of rubber and tube machines; and "the seven-roll rubber," which had come into use within the last three or four years, and which was considered "a very good thing," had been "gradually driving out the tubes." [1] Again, as indicated by this last quotation, the rubbing device was being improved during the same interval. This builder was in 1865 making "three, five, seven, and nine-roll rubbers." [2] By multiplication in the number of rubbing rollers, the line of ropings drawn from the card could be divided and each half or each third treated separately, and so with somewhat better results.[3] Such American improvements as these, it may be added, were fully abreast of foreign practice, except for the fact that at the very close of the period 1830–1870 the so-called tape condenser was beginning to be introduced abroad. This device, invented by Celestin Martin of Verviers, permitted a more minute division of the wool-web drawn off the final card cylinder; and accordingly was specially adapted to the manufacture of fine yarns. In

[1] Mr. Davis of the Davis & Furber Machine Company, at the Goulding trial; quoted by North, *Bulletin*, 1901, p. 270.

[2] *Bulletin*, 1901, p. 269.

[3] Ultimately, to secure greater rubbing power, machines with as many as fifteen rubbing rollers were employed. But in the seventies and eighties came a simplification of the mechanism through the introduction of rubbing aprons — of which more later.

later years it became of greater significance to the domestic wool-manufacturing industry. In 1870, however, the older method as now improved was of sufficient fineness for the quality of fabric turned out by American mills at the time.[1]

On the whole, the carding process had been much bettered in nicety and effectiveness of performance in the decades preceding 1870. While not fully in line with the European developments, it was nevertheless in far different shape than it had been forty years earlier. Particularly significant had been the changes which meant increased productivity through large-scale operations and the attainment of better quality of product.

Let us turn to a consideration of woolen spinning. Here a situation existed in the period 1830–1870 quite different from that with respect to wool-cleansing or wool-carding. It was a period of relative stagnation. The course of development in the United States during these decades consisted, with negligible exceptions, solely in the extension of the semi-automatic jack devised in the earlier period. By the latter sixties, despite the difficulties, frequently voiced, which the employment of jack-spinners involved, and despite the example of the cotton manufacture,[2] little progress had been made in the institution in woolen spinning of equipment other than jacks. There are isolated cases such as that at Manchester, New Hampshire, where mules, imported from England, were utilized;[3] but an author writing in 1869 of twenty-five years' experience in woolen spinning speaks only of the old jacks.[4] In short, the earlier technique remained.

To secure a basis for assessing the possible fault of the domestic industry, contrast may be made with the advance in foreign coun-

[1] As to introduction of tube condensers into the United States, see above, p. 103.

[2] Hayes, *American Textile Machinery*, p. 41. Besides the invention of Richard Roberts, a self-actor for use in the cotton industry was independently evolved by Ira Gay of the Nashua Machine Shop, — a machine which was employed in a few cases, — and another self-acting mule was constructed by Mr. Mason of Taunton, Massachusetts, in 1837, and used rather widely in the cotton manufacture.

[3] Wallis's *Report*, *British Documents*, 1854 [1717], p. 22; Webber, *Manual of Power*, p. 54. For other cases, see below, Vol. II, p. 90, note 2.

[4] Demond, *Twenty-five Years' Experience in Wool-Carding and Spinning*, 1869.

THE SPINNING JACK OF THE FIFTIES

Photograph of a machine bought by the Ebenezer Society of Ebenezer, New York, from Davis & Furber of North Andover, Massachusetts, in 1854

tries. In England, Richard Roberts, who in 1825 had devised the automatic mule for use in the cotton industry, in 1832 patented his so-called radial arm, or sector. This latter device made the self-acting mule applicable to woolen spinning.[1] Then followed a gradual adoption of the new mechanism, as for example in Huddersfield by 1839. By 1870 it could be said that "self-acting mules have become common, and as existing mules require replacing, self-acting mules will soon become universal."[2] In France progress was less rapid. In spinning equipment the wool-manufacturing industry at the middle of the century found itself then "much less advanced" than did the cotton manufacture.[3] Still, toward the close of the sixties, the "mule-jenny automatique" had been adopted "in the majority of the large establishments that manufacture woolens or worsteds;"[4] or, according to another writer, this machine "was coming into general use" in the spinning of wool.[5] Only a few years later, in 1878, an official reporter on the international exhibition of that year pointed a period to the story regarding the adoption of the "self-acting:" "La transformation est complète. . . . Le dernier mule-jenny doit avoir vécu."[6] Even in Germany, where one would of course expect rather tardy development on account of the late appearance of the industrial revolution, some advance in this line had occurred. Quandt indicates that the adoption of the "Selfactor" had commenced in the sixties, and that

[1] Bramwell, *op. cit.*, p. 381.

[2] Baines, *Yorkshire Past and Present*, 1870, p. 665. See also Bowley, *Journal of the Royal Statistical Society*, 1902, p. 120.

[3] Picard, *op. cit.*, iv, pp. 202–203. Picard narrates that manufacturers of the period relied on fulling and finishing to cover up the defects in spinning; and that they even contemplated the supersession of weaving by felting.

[4] *Ibid.*, p. 209.

[5] Chevalier, *Introduction to Rapports du Jury International at the Exposition of 1867*, p. 162. Alcan speaks of both the self-acting mule jenny and of the "demi self-acting" ("où le renvidage a lieu à la main") in his treatise written in 1867 (*Traité du Travail des Laines*, i, 465). See also *American Consular Reports, No. 23*, 1882, p. 124.

[6] Levasseur, *Questions Ouvrières et Industrielles*, p. 105. According to Levasseur, the older mule-jenny had around 200 spindles, while the "self-acting" held 500 or more. Yet for the superintendence of either, only a spinner and two piecers were necessary (*ibid.*, note 1). See also Levasseur, *Histoire des Classes Ouvrières*, ii, p. 563; and *American Consular Reports, No. 23*, 1882, pp. 124–125.

this movement reached the distant Niederlausitz in the early seventies.[1]

Obviously, then, the American industry had failed to keep pace with foreign developments as far as machinery for wool spinning is concerned, especially compared with developments in England and France. But the question why this should have been the case is difficult to answer. The great value of such an automatic machine was well recognized. As one writer put the technical aspect: "It is well known that the quality of woolen yarn, especially as regards strength and smoothness, depends much on proper and judicious draft. The draft of the common spinning jack is lateral, and under the control of the person operating the same. No two spinners control this draft or draw alike, and consequently we get good and indifferent yarn from the same lot of roping." [2] Again, the character of the men employed to operate these machines was a subject of unanimous complaint. Manufacturers claimed that one of the greatest evils with which they had to contend was the circumstance "that they were subject to men employed as jack-spinners, who were generally foreigners, and had brought with them the disorderly habits of English workmen." [3] Drunkenness and consequent irregularity of their work were specially complained of, as well as their insolent bearing. But the reasons advanced then and subsequently to explain the failure of American mills to follow the lead of both the domestic cotton manufacture and foreign woolen manufactures seem of no considerable weight. The opposition of the jack-spinners is sometimes spoken of; but as yet there existed no organization of such workers to make their opposition effective on any appreciable scale. It is also alleged that the mules were too heavy and not well adapted to American conditions. Thus: "Spinning in large establishments abroad is

[1] Quandt, *Die Niederlausitzer Schafwollindustrie*, p. 177. See also Grothe, *op. cit.*, p. 568; Wachs, *op. cit.*, p. 38.

[2] Advertisement of a spinning machine invented by Goulding: *Worcester Spy*, April 1, 1865.

[3] Hayes, *American Textile Machinery*, p. 31. Hayes was obviously in error when he stated (p. 32) that self-actors "have been tried in England with but little success."

usually performed by mules, while jack spinning is more generally adopted in New England as better suited to the different qualities and quantities of yarns demanded by the variety of fabrics usually produced in our mills." [1] Such explanation, however, is not wholly acceptable, since it is improbable that the diversity of production in American mills was any greater than that of most foreign establishments, e. g., in the fancy-goods industry about Huddersfield, where the introduction of self-acting mules began early. The true explanation seems to lie in the force of inertia. Given a body of skilled operatives such as the jack-spinners, the spinning operation could be carried out with less attention from the manufacturer himself if jacks were used than if self-operating mules were employed. For example, changes necessary for shifting production from one count or quality of yarn to another were much simpler, since much of the responsibility fell directly on the jack-spinner. Accordingly the mill-owners were not inclined to make a change. To be sure, the growth of the wholesale clothing industry, with the effects of that development in increasing the average size of order for cloth, may have added to the advantages which could be secured from the employment of the self-acting mule; but the influence of that industry had not become sufficiently great by the decade of the seventies to be a determining factor. The American woolen manufacture, in truth, cannot be relieved of serious criticism in this regard. What ultimately occurred in the seventies might well have been brought about many years earlier.

Of technical changes in the younger branch of the domestic wool manufacture, the worsted industry, little need here be added with respect to yarn preparation beyond what has already been said.[2] In origin, worsted machinery was altogether foreign. To be sure, specific devices employed in worsted-yarn production had first come from the United States, but the essential step of adaptation had been made abroad. When American manufacturers sought to establish the industry in the United States, they

[1] Hayes and Mudge, *Report on the Paris Exposition of 1867*, vi, 29; and interview with Mr. Archer of the Blackinton Woolen Company, North Adams, Massachusetts, who in 1915 had been working fifty-eight years for that concern.

[2] See above, pp. 327–330.

went to England for mechanisms to cover the whole production, — and in view of the age and advanced development of the worsted manufacture in England, such a course was one which might well be expected. Similarly, in consideration of the relative youth of the American industry prior to 1870, especially the recent acquisition of any considerable production, probably we should not be surprised that no independent advance in technology had been registered in the United States before that date. Surely, there was no such advance. "In this department of the textile industry," wrote Hayes in 1879, "we have exhibited less originality of invention or construction (than in the cotton and woolen branches), and have contented ourselves with copying or importing English and French machinery."[1]

However, the enhancement of productive capacity in the American worsted manufacture had been large before 1870. In place of combing by hand and of mule-spinning apparatus, which had characterized the yarn production in the thirties, now there had been substituted the machine combs and the drawing and spinning machinery of the modern type. Specially important was the introduction of mechanical combs, — the Simpson and Lister, and particularly the Noble machines. Hand-combing would have proved a decisive constraint upon any considerable expansion of the domestic manufacture. Appreciably important, too, from the viewpoint of economy in labor, was the adoption of frame drawing and spinning. In all lines the advance made for mass production upon quasi-automatic processes. Thus, impediments which had stood in the way of extensive domestic manufacture of worsted yarn, and so of worsted cloth, were removed; and the course was already laid for that tremendous growth of the worsted industry which came about in succeeding decades.[2]

[1] *American Textile Machinery*, p. 53. Hayes attributes the failure of the American industry to furnish independent advances to the fact that British prohibitions upon the exportation of machinery had been removed before the American worsted manufacture commenced on any appreciable scale. In the light of numerous importations from foreign development prior to the removal of these prohibitions (1845), — the woolen card, billy, mule, and the like, — the validity of this contention is open to serious question.

[2] As to the later advance in worsted spinning technique abroad, we need not go into detail. It suffices to note that no important innovation came from do-

In the most important section of wool-cloth production common to both branches of the manufacture, that of cloth weaving, the developments in the domestic industry prior to 1870 placed the American manufacturer in a particularly advantageous position as compared with his situation forty years earlier. Improvements had made possible more diversified output from mechanical weaving, and had also increased the productivity of the weaving operation. In this regard, attention has already been given to the inventions of William Crompton, — machines which aided particularly in the growth of the fancy cassimere and other fancy woolen-cloth production.[1] Note should now be made of another important development.

While the introduction of Crompton's machines was proceeding, another inventor was coming to the front as a maker of looms, one Lucius J. Knowles. In his machines a new variation in loom construction was involved.[2] The Crompton looms had been built upon what is known as the "closed shed" principle. This meant that with each pick of the shuttle all the harnesses, and

mestic sources. However, it may be mentioned that apparently by the close of the period 1830–1870, perhaps sometime earlier, the machinery of the modern types had been elaborated and brought into quite common use abroad. For example, in Ure's *Dictionary of Arts, Manufactures, etc.* (1878), gill-boxes, drawing boxes, and roving frames are noted, and the descriptions there given indicate that they had already assumed quite the modern form (iv, 984, 988). These machines, however, were but improvements on the somewhat similar equipment described by Ure in his *Philosophy of Manufactures* (1835, pp. 151–159) and in Bischoff (ii, 403–404).

Machine combing was being adopted in England at about the time that the worsted industry was making its early strides in the United States. In 1851 there were said to have been 12,000 to 14,000 hand-combers in the Bradford district alone, and there was a distinct prejudice among manufacturers for hand-combed tops. See Dodd, *Textile Manufactures*, 1851, p. 129; Forbes, *Lectures upon the Great Exhibition*, 1851, p. 316; Killick, *Bulletin*, 1907, pp. 366–367. However, between 1851 and 1870 the use of the power-driven combs steadily increased, although, according to Radcliffe, hand-combing continued to be practiced by many until about 1870 (*Woollen and Worsted Yarns*, p. 63). See, however, Bowley, *Journal of the Royal Statistical Society*, 1902, p. 109.

[1] See above, pp. 307–309, 313–314.

[2] The Crompton Loom Company always contested the novelty of the Knowles contribution, insisting that they had tried out the device and discarded it as unsatisfactory. However, Knowles apparently came by his particular idea independently, and was able to embody it in apparatus which has since been of much importance in the whole world manufacture of wool.

so all the threads of the warp, were either raised or depressed; and subsequently, after the passage of the shuttle, the "shed" or division of the warp threads was closed, to be reopened in a different shed for the succeeding pick. This method of securing the shed not only required a large amount of power, but also put a considerable strain and wear on the warps through the repeated elevations and depressions. The "open shed" loom patented by Knowles in 1863 aimed at the reduction of these disadvantages. Under the "open shed" system, a harness once raised was maintained in that position perhaps during two or three picks, until the demands of the pattern chain occasioned its depression.[1] This machine, called by Hayes "a marvel of ingenuity and mechanical skill," was a loom specially adapted to the wool manufacture. Woolen yarns are weak as compared with most other textile yarns, and the open shed relieved the warp strands of an appreciable amount of strain. It is significant that, after some years, arrangements were made with an important British loom-building concern for the manufacture of this loom under lease from the Knowles Loom Works; and that by 1893, 10,000 Knowles looms had been placed in the United Kingdom and on the Continent.[2] At the present time, looms of the general Knowles type, with modifications of British origin, are the chief type of machine employed in England for the weaving of woolen fabrics.

Now, one final point. Besides the important improvements above considered in cleansing, carding, spinning, and weaving, — to which might be added a few advances in the complex finishing operations,[3] — the technical side of the industry has another significant aspect in the period before 1870. Then for the first time can there be said to have arisen a specialized machine-

[1] *Awards and Claims, Exhibition of 1876*, p. 201. Mr. Knowles had in 1857 developed a special drop-box mechanism, later incorporated in the Knowles loom, which was an important contribution.

[2] *Worcester Columbian Tribute*, 1893, p. 73.

[3] Reference has already been made to the improvement in printing through the change from block to roller method (see above, p. 330). There also were improvements in the technique of dyeing, and increase in the size of various finishing machines (Bishop, ii, 372, note; Mudge and Hayes, *Report on the Paris Exposition of 1867*, pp. 39–44).

BROAD CAM LOOM WITH DROP BOXES

As constructed by Mr. George Crompton in the fifties

NARROW CROMPTON LOOM OF THE FIFTIES

Showing pattern chain for controlling the harnesses

building industry of the modern sort. Theretofore it had been customary for the person or persons responsible for the introduction or invention of a specific device to undertake its construction. One will recall that Arthur Scholfield had set up the manufacture of carding machines and billies. So, too, the inventors of the napping and shearing machines, brought out in the early years of the century, not infrequently had set up the manufacture of their own inventions. And even in later decades men like Goulding and Lucius Knowles organized concerns for the construction of their respective innovations. Exceptions to this practice with respect to new apparatus were chiefly cases where a given small machinist was licensed to build and sell a specific piece of machinery, as when Phelps & Bickford of Worcester, Massachusetts, were licensed to build the Crompton loom. For the manufacture of older machinery, — that which had never been patented or for which the patent rights had expired, — a multitude of small shops had sprung up. Worcester had early become an important center for such small enterprises, but they were common in many places where woolen-cloth manufacture was largely pursued.[1]

These establishments, however, had not been able wholly to supply the domestic mills. The latter had been accustomed in the early days to build a substantial portion of their necessary apparatus, even as the Scholfields had been compelled to do when they began. Looms were commonly put together by the mechanics employed directly by the mills, or perhaps by the village carpenters and blacksmiths. Thus a woolen and cotton mill of East Haddam, Connecticut, in 1819 is reported as having "a machine room, where all the wood, brass, and iron machinery are made and repaired for the establishment." [2] Such individual construction was made possible by the relatively simple and light character of the early apparatus. Wood was the chief component of early machinery, from cards to looms. Wherever special skill or the use of steel and heavy iron construction was necessary, a

[1] See files of the *Worcester Spy;* or Washburn, in *History of Worcester County*, ii, 1605–1617.

[2] Field, *History of Middlesex County*, 1819, p. 78.

specialized production tended to spring up, as in the manufacture of card-clothing, shuttles, the enlarged carding machines, and the like. Such production accounts in an important measure for the numerous small machine shops of the early thirties.

The period between 1830 and 1870 witnessed a distinct change. With the increased complexity of apparatus, such as the condensers or the new looms, and with the enhanced size of the various machines, which required a greater use of metal structure, came the substantially complete divorce of wool and machine manufacture: wool-working mills gave up their machine construction and became dependent upon the specialized builders of textile apparatus. Moreover, the small localized machine shops ceased to play so important a rôle. As they decreased in number, there rose a few large enterprises. The Crompton and the Knowles loom-building concerns stood out among the producers of that type of machinery. The C. G. Sargent enterprise rose to first rank in the manufacture of scouring machines and similar preparatory apparatus. And in the New England and Philadelphia areas, the concern of Davis & Furber and the Smith Woolen Machinery Company grew in domination among the producers of carding and spinning machines in their respective districts.[1]

As always with specialization, the development of these larger machine-builders spelled increased effectiveness. They stood ready to take advantage of suggestions from users of their machinery; they maintained a corps of investigators seeking the improvement of their own devices; and they served to store up the fruits of past experiment and past experience. The place of the individual inventor became less important as invention was organized, so to speak; but many notable innovations, as the

[1] Hayes, *American Textile Machinery*, pp. 30–31; publication of the Davis & Furber Machine Company entitled "The Davis & Furber Machine Company and the Men who made it" (1908). The latter concern was first brought together in 1832, and the Smith Woolen Machinery Company (now Smith & Furbush) claims a century of continuous existence.

Another important enterprise in this field was Alfred Jenks & Son of Philadelphia, but like many producers of textile machinery in that region it covers cotton-manufacturing apparatus as well as woolen.

automatic looms of the subsequent period, came from their workshops. In short, this development presaged continuing advance in technical lines, while also suggesting the growing maturity of the wool-manufacturing industry.

Summary. Despite the backwardness in certain portions of the field, especially in woolen spinning, technical advance in the period 1830–1870 had contributed a material forward impulse to the domestic wool manufacture. Domestic invention and borrowings from abroad, both of great significance, had brought that manufacture to a much higher level of productivity and effectiveness than it had boasted forty years earlier. These improvements had facilitated the introduction of diversified production in woolen fabrics, had made feasible the wider expansion of the worsted manufacture, and in both the woolen and worsted branches of the industry had brought substantial savings in labor and in the skill necessary for good quality in output. The foundations were being laid for the further extension of large-scale production which was to be the conspicuous feature of the period subsequent to 1870.

CHAPTER XIX

LABOR AND LABOR CONDITIONS

During the period between 1830 and 1870 many changes had come to the industry and to the country which changed the conditions of labor within the manufacture. At the earlier date the industry shared in that homeliness which has elsewhere been pictured for the cotton manufacture with its dormitories, its publications, and its relatively high moral tone.[1] The woolen mills, to a degree greater than cotton-manufacturing establishments, were scattered over the country in consequence of their search for water power and of their partial dependence upon local markets; and small communities centered around the local mill were the normal result. Boarding houses were frequently, if not commonly, provided for the operatives; and the company's store was a usual feature. Except for a sprinkling of English and Irish people, the workers were wholly native. Add to these characteristics the small size of the typical mill, — ensuring close relationship between employer and employee, — and the wage scales sufficient to attract workers into industrial activity, and one has a situation smacking of the ideal, at least as compared with the grimy, overcrowded, and complex mill towns of the present day.[2]

By 1870 the change to the modern conditions was under way. While the industry still showed a rather wide geographical distribution, forces were already in action to bring somewhat greater

[1] Abbott, *Women in Industry*, pp. 113–120; Robinson, *Loom and Spindle*, pp. 71 ff.; *United States Industrial Commission*, vii, 221–223.

[2] Of course, one should not forget the long factory hours. And probably there were other equally bad features. The Company store and the truck system were sometimes likely to work hardships. The food at the Company boarding houses was poor, presumably. Sanitary conditions in the mills unquestionably were bad. And the life in such a town doubtless was terribly humdrum. Still I am inclined to believe that, taking social as well as economic factors into account, the advantage lay on the side of the old mill village.

concentration. The fact that already nearly 40 per cent of the horse power generated for the mills was from steam boilers is indicative of the fact that mills had been emancipated from the restraint on location theretofore exercised by water power. Plants were now free to localize.[1] Modern conditions were appearing in another line, — the beginning in the employment of foreign "hands" upon any considerable scale. The existence of an old and extensive wool manufacture in England had been responsible for the attraction to American mills of some English immigrants. Such workers seemingly continued to command a premium, especially as long as manual skill played an important part in certain operations, e. g., jack-spinning and weaving. But the proportion of such workers was never large, although as foremen and as operatives in the more skilled occupations they played a part in the manufacture which their numbers would fail to indicate. In the field of woman labor, the admixture of foreign-born was probably less even than in the case of men. In the cotton mills of Lowell as late as 1845, there were only 48 Canadian and 116 Irish women out of a total of 1527 women employed in eight establishments; and there is no peculiar reason why a somewhat similar proportion should not hold for the larger wool manufactories of that period.[2] With the Irish famine, however, came a substantial increase in the flow of immigrants from that island, and a considerable share of the new arrivals sought the mill towns. Mr. Harriss-Gastrell in his report of 1873 upon the American textile industries speaks of the labor force in our cotton mills as chiefly Irish and makes no differentiation between the cotton and wool manufactures.[3] In the Philadelphia area surely the establishments contained a goodly proportion of these

[1] By the *Census of 1870*, the amount of horse power generated in the woolen and in the worsted branches was as follows:

	Woolen Mills	Worsted Mills
Water Wheels	59,332	4634
Steam Engines	35,900	3382

[2] *Lowell as it Was and as it Is*, 1845, pp. 165–185.

[3] *Report on the Hours of Labour, the Rates of Wage and the progressive Production of Cotton and Woolen and other Textile Manufactures in the United States: British Documents*, 1873 (826). Mr. Harriss-Gastrell also speaks of a sprinkling of French-Canadians.

new immigrants, — a proportion, however, which was larger in the case of men than in that of women.[1] This influx, too, was of more significance than appears on its face. Unlike the small infiltration of immigrants that had preceded, this movement brought a marked break in textile labor conditions. Whereas earlier the proprietors had been "almost patriarchal" in their "constant oversight of their native operatives," now came certain changes in American mill towns, dating from these days of Irish immigration. Employers had a different feeling, and took a different attitude toward all their employees.[2] Yet it is not necessary here to trace this alteration further. One need note merely that when the influx of French-Canadians followed upon that of Irish, American mill towns were on their way to more modern character. Whatever the social effects, this movement of immigration meant to the domestic industry some enhancement of competitive power, in so far as these additions formed a more permanent factory class and tended to lower wages, or to keep wages from rising, relative to wage levels of the country as a whole.[3]

Other important changes on the labor side of the industry are the increase in the employment of women and children and the curtailment of working hours. The point has already been made that the early woolen mill called for a particularly large proportion of men.[4] The earliest satisfactory statistics upon the wool manufacture pertain to the mills of Massachusetts in 1837.

[1] Statement of Mr. John P. Wood. English and Scotch male workers also made up a sizable contingent in Philadelphia mills.

[2] *Industrial Commission Report*, vii, 221. See also Abbott, *Women in Industry*, pp. 143–144.

[3] Two odd cases in the type of mill operatives deserve a brief note. In Adams County, Mississippi, there was in 1845 a sizable wool and cotton factory — thirty hands — employing negro labor alone (29th Cong., 1st Sess., *Executive Documents*, *No. 6*, p. 676); while the Mission Woolen Mills of San Francisco in the middle sixties apparently employed Chinese labor largely (*Report on the Paris Exposition of 1867*, *General Survey of the Exposition*, p. 103).

As to the turn-over in the early textile mills, see Batchelder, *Early Progress of the Cotton Manufacture*: "The greater part of those at work in the mills were only a succession of learners, who left the business as soon as they began to acquire some skill and experience."

[4] See above, pp. 237–238.

A MILL-TOWN SCENE OF THE FIFTIES

Photograph taken in the yard of a company house at Stevens Village, North Andover, Massachusetts, some time in the middle fifties

Divided only between males and females, — no separate figures being presented for children, — the proportions were practically even: 51 per cent of the former and 49 per cent of the latter. Subsequent to that time there was a distinct tendency for the proportion of women to decline. In Massachusetts the ratio of females had fallen to 41 per cent by 1855, and except in the war period did not rise above that point. For the wool industry as a whole, the first statistics relate to 1849. At that time females composed 42 per cent. Twenty years later, when separate enumeration of children was first made, the ratios among the three groups in woolen mills were: men, 53.4 per cent; women, 34.6 per cent; and children, 12.0 per cent.[1] The change in proportions of men and women thus manifested was a result chiefly of the technical improvements and of the change in quality of product that occurred during these years, though also affected by the immigrant movement just noted. Advances in technique, such as those in carding and in the processes intermediate between carding and spinning, or between spinning and weaving, involved the substitution of heavier machines, more highly skilled work, or work requiring heavy lifting. The need of woman labor tended to decrease. Thus, the burr-cylinder dispensed with the burr-pickers who had been women and children; and the use of lap or balling intermediate "feeds" meant the lifting and moving of heavy spools. The improvement in type of output, moreover, together with the introduction of superior looms, made a demand for adult male labor: the work required more skill and was also more exacting. The substitution of fancy cassimere for satinet production is a case in point. Finally, the influx of immigrant labor was a factor. Through that means Irish or French-Canadian men could be substituted with little or no advance in cost for native American women.[2]

[1] These figures exclude the carpet and rug mills.

[2] Not all improvements, however, were in the direction of increasing the use of adult male labor. For example, in the processes intermediate between spinning and weaving, there was sometimes a simplification of processes which induced the larger employment of women. Such was the effect of the warping machine, described as "an American invention" and as "far superior to those used in Great Britain." It signified the substitution of machine work in a process which had pre-

In the worsted branch, the proportion of female labor was even greater than that in the woolen branch. The earliest satisfactory figures relate to the Massachusetts worsted mills in 1855 where the percentage of female employees was 57 per cent. In later state censuses of Massachusetts the ratios showed some tendency to increase: 68.7 per cent in 1865 and 61.3 per cent in 1875; although in the 1865 ratio allowance must be made for war conditions. For the country as a whole the proportion of women was given as about 55 per cent in 1869, and of children nearly 15 per cent. Thus at the close of the period now under consideration, adult female labor in the worsted branch comprised a substantially higher proportion of the total working forces than in the woolen section: 55 per cent as against less than 35 per cent; and this difference is of particular importance in relation to the comparative advantage of the two branches of the industry. The reasons for the variation are not hard to ascertain. The processes in the manufacture of worsted yarns were much better suited for female and child labor. In the combing operation women could be employed in some measure; in the spinning process, the employment of frames instead of mules made possible the utilization of women as spinners and children as doffers, whereas men and youths were required for supervision over woolen mules; while in the finishing operations the elimination of fulling, napping, and shearing, where men in the woolen mills were chiefly employed, tended in the worsted establishments to enhance the proportion of women. Being able, then, to dispense with a considerable percentage of adult male labor, the worsted industry, in 1870 still unsure of its powers, promised to attain greater competitive power than the older branch of the industry. Under American conditions, the utilization of quasi-automatic machinery suitable to the guiding hand of relatively less expensive female labor meant a strengthening of the manufacture against the assaults of competitive domestic goods as well as those of competing foreign goods.

viously been substantially a hand process, and likewise the substitution of female for male labor. See Gilroy, *Art of Weaving*, 1844, p. 332; North, *Bulletin*, 1902, pp. 116–117, 133.

Beyond changes in the composition of the working forces, there was also an important change in duration of the working day at wool manufactories. Accounts of mill hours even in the middle of the century have a strange ring nowadays. For example, at the Bay State Mills, Lowell, Massachusetts, in 1850, "labor begins, or the gate closes, at 5 A.M. from May 1 to September 1, and at ten minutes before sunrise the remainder of the year. A first bell is rung forty minutes before, to allow time to prepare for work. Labor ends 7.30 P.M. from September 20 to March 20; and 7 from May 1 to September 1; and fifteen minutes after sunset for the remainder of the year. During the whole year dinner is at 12.30 P.M. Forty-five minutes are allowed for each meal."[1] Of the smaller mills it was said that "prior to 1850 it was customary to begin work as soon as there was sufficient light, even in the long summer days, and to work as late as the light would permit, with no fixed regular hours. . . . In the short days, or for about six months of the year, it was customary to work until 9 o'clock in the evening, beginning early in the morning and taking about a half-hour each for breakfast, dinner, and supper."[2] Working days, however, began to shorten soon after 1850, if in fact the movement had not commenced before. A tabulation presented in the *Census of 1880* shows a decided drift in that direction.[3] Ten-hour laws had been enacted in

[1] *Report of Massachusetts Sanitary Commission*, 1850, p. 444.

[2] Mr. William H. Vose of the Fitchburg Woolen Mill Company, in *Census of 1880*, xx, p. 391.

[3] The tabulation in the *Census of 1880* (xx, 375) is of special interest, covering the period 1830 to 1880 and mills in various parts of the country:

	10 hrs.	10½ hrs.	11 hrs.	11½ hrs.	12 hrs.	12½ hrs.	13 hrs.	Sun to sun
1830	..	..	..	..	..	1	2	..
1835	..	..	..	..	..	2	2	..
1840	..	..	..	..	..	2	2	..
1845	..	..	1	..	1	1	2	..
1850	..	..	2	1	2	1	2	..
1855	..	..	7	..	2	1	1	..
1860	2	..	6	1	2	..	1	..
1865	7	1	13	3	2	..	..	..
1870	8	2	16	4	1	..	..	2
1875	13	2	15	3	..	..	..	2
1880	12	2	17	2	..	..	..	2

See also Aldrich, *Report on Wholesale Prices, Wages, and Transportation* (52nd Cong., 2nd Sess., *Senate Report, No. 1394*), i, 178–179; *Report on Woman and Child Wage Earners*, ix, 69–72.

several important industrial states prior to 1855, — New Hampshire, Maine, Pennsylvania, New Jersey, and Rhode Island, — and though these early laws were not efficiently administered, they undoubtedly had an influence upon mill practice. By 1870 the typical factory was running from 7 A.M. to 7 P.M. with an hour out for dinner, or really an eleven-hour working day.

Finally, it is possible here to secure some general view of the improving condition of the wage-earners apart from the reduction in number of working hours. In actual wages, to be sure, such data as are available do not indicate any appreciable improvement that was not shared by workers in other branches of the textile industry and by workers in all other industries. Indeed, the advance in wages over the decade of the fifties seems to have been rather greater in these other lines than in the wool manufacture; and after the close of the Civil War the reaction appears to have been less considerable. However, the progress in the woolen industry was never much out of line with that elsewhere, — the industry felt general conditions acutely.[1] Yet from another angle the progress of the operatives in the wool manufacture is more evident. Wages paid in the woolen industry increased approximately 180 per cent between 1859 and 1869; whereas the "value added by manufacture" within the industry (value of products minus value of raw materials) increased only 133 per cent. In the younger worsted manufacture much the same change occurred: wages paid rose to eight-fold their earlier figure, while value added by manufacture rose but little over six-fold. To some degree these diversities of movement reflect merely the peculiar position of the wool-manufacturing industry in the years following the Civil War, — the severe competition in an overextended manufacture, continued higher importations, and the like. At least, there is a *prima facie* case that profits rather than wages were bearing the brunt of the difficulties.[2]

On the whole, the conditions of labor from the viewpoint of the worker himself had substantially improved in the decades

[1] See indices of wage changes in *Aldrich Report*, Pt. I, 173–174.

[2] In this period there was a beginning of welfare work by the better managed and more prosperous mills. See *Awards and Claims, Exhibition of 1876*, p. 202; and Hayes, *Report on the Exhibition of 1876*, p. 64.

before 1870, with the shorter hours and higher wages. The curtailment in working hours has a particularly modern aspect, as also has the beginning of the flow of immigrants into the mills. In these factors as well as in the proportions of men and women in the manufacture, the industry was moving toward the conditions of the present time. The picture of the years around 1870 shows the industry in transition.

CHAPTER XX

THE CIVIL WAR PERIOD

THE period of the Civil War, like that of the War of 1812, forms an important episode in the history of the American wool manufacture. In both cases there was a marked expansion of the industry due in greater or less degree to interrupted commerce; in both, there came an increase in the diversity of domestic production; and in both, there followed a difficult period of enforced readjustment within the industry, incidental to which arose a demand for, and ultimately the enactment of, a more "adequate" protective tariff on wool manufactures. The character of the American industry and the circumstances surrounding it were substantially changed as a result of war-time experience.

However, striking as are the similarities in the two cases, the differences are equally notable. With respect to causation: one may observe that the weight to be assigned the interruption of preëxisting commercial relations as a cause of industrial change differs in the two instances: in the one case, chief interest attaches to this factor, but in the other only that of one among several important influences.[1] The military demands in 1861–1865 played a more considerable part than they had in 1812–1815. Inflation of the currency through the issuance of the Greenbacks gave a special impetus to industrial activity in the Civil War period. And, then, the peculiar conditions in the cotton industry at that time, — the force of the "cotton famine," — drew particular attention of the whole textile industry to the manufacture of wool. Secondly, as far as results are concerned: the influence of the two episodes on the subsequent tariff changes was materially different. In the one case, protection was resorted to with some hesitation and imposed in only a very

[1] Interruption of commerce in the Civil War period came chiefly as the result of deliberate legislative action, the increase of tariff duties enacted mainly for fiscal purposes.

moderate measure; whereas at the later date protection was confidently demanded by the domestic industry, was developed in all the modern formulæ of "compensatory duties," "protective duties," and the like, and was elevated to a plane of effective power which had not been dreamed of in the pre-war period. On account of these peculiarities of the Civil War experience, the events of that troubled decade deserves special consideration.

The enlarged requirements of the war came upon the woolen branch of the industry — which alone was seriously affected — after this branch had just passed through a decade of restricted growth, only partly relieved by the modification in tariff matters effected through the act of 1857.[1] For a time the War Department experienced difficulty in securing adequate supplies of uniform cloth, blankets, flannels, and the like, being compelled to resort to appreciable purchases in England and France.[2] Soon, however, domestic mills got into war production, until by 1864 the consumption of wool exceeded 60 million pounds for the army goods alone, that is, exclusive of requirements for the navy, cartridges, and the like.[3] At that time, consumption for military demands equaled something like a third of the total domestic consumption of wool fiber.

Expansion in the industry as a whole, however, proceeded at great rapidity and quite independently of the direct war needs. Measured in wool consumption, the number of establishments, or number of employees, the increase in productive capacity was proportionately greater than in subsequent decades, and particularly great as compared with the advance in the decade just preceding. In terms of quantities, such as those already sug-

[1] That is, by the readjustment of the relation between duties on raw material and finished goods.

[2] *Census of 1860*, iii, p. xxxiv; Fite, *Social and Industrial Conditions during the Civil War*, p. 83. Fite narrates that complaint arose in consequence of the foreign purchases: that the government should patronize home industries; but when it bought any cloth obtainable, of any color, Union soldiers shot one another in the woods of the battlefields.

[3] Hayes, *Fleece and the Loom*, 1865, pp. 46–47; Fite, *op. cit.*, p. 84. Fite puts the annual military consumption of wool at the height of the war, at 75 million pounds.

gested, the industry doubled in size — indeed, rather more than doubled — between 1859 and 1869.[1] At the peak of production during the war, total domestic consumption of wool probably ran as high as 200 million pounds, as compared with 71 million pounds in 1849 and 86 million in 1859, or with 189 million in 1869.[2] Apparently, after a particularly rapid expansion during the first half of the decade 1859–1869, there was some recession before its close.

Typical of the experience of individual firms under the forces making for expansion was that of the Sawyer Woolen Mills of Dover, New Hampshire. Before 1860 the property consisted of two small establishments, operating on flannels, each of two-set capacity. In that year one of the mills was increased to four sets; and again in 1863 enlarged to eight sets; while in these years the old machinery had been replaced by new and improved apparatus. The mills ran on flannels until 1866, when they changed over to fancy cassimeres and similar cloths.[3] The Pacific Mills started with 1000 looms in 1853, but by the close of the Civil War had grown to a weaving capacity of 3500 looms.[4] Between July, 1862, and December 31, 1863, according to estimates by the Boston Board of Trade, 1000 sets of woolen machinery had been added to the previous power of the North.[5] The effects were still visible as late as 1869 when the Census of that year reported marked increases in the number of establishments as compared with 1859: in the woolen branch, an increase from 1260 to 2891,

[1] The actual statistics, some of which have been already produced, are as follows:

	Woolen Mills			Worsted Mills		
Year	No. of Estabs.	No. of Employees	Lbs. of Wool Consumed (*millions*)	No. of Estabs.	No. of Employees	Lbs. of Wool Consumed (*millions*)
1849	1559	39,352	70.9	. .	. . .	. . .
1859	1260	41,350	83.6	3	2,378	3.0
1869	2891	80,053	172.1	102	12,920	17.1

Figures based on value are, of course, vitiated by the decrease in the value of the immediate monetary standard, Greenbacks; and, accordingly, I have not attempted to use them.

[2] Hayes, *Fleece and the Loom*, p. 47; Fite, *op. cit.*, p. 84.

[3] *Awards and Claims, Exhibition of 1876*, p. 209.

[4] Clark, p. 453.

[5] *Report of the Board*, 1864, p. 115.

and in the worsted branch from a dozen (the Census gives three) to 102.

Among the accessions to the growing list of wool-manufacturing ventures was an astonishingly large group of concerns erstwhile engaged in the working of cotton. The cotton mills of the country were much perplexed when war supervened and market supplies of cotton vanished overnight. Partly influenced by the sentiment that there would be "peace in sixty days," several of the mills closed their doors, dismissed their operatives, and sold their stocks of cotton. But thereafter their troubles were manifold. Finding it impossible to get back to profitable cotton manufacture, or attracted by the high profits expected in the manufacture of wool under the abnormal war demands, a number of such concerns, including the Suffolk, Hamilton, and Tremont Companies, changed all or part of their equipment to the production of woolen goods.[1] The Wanskuck Mills at Providence, and the Lippitt Woolen Company at Woonsocket, Rhode Island, also came into the wool manufacture at this time. In both instances, cotton mills were purchased by new adventurers and converted to the production of wool goods.[2] Never before nor since were there so many shifts from one branch to another of the textile industry in so limited a time. For the present pur-

[1] Cowley, *History of Lowell*, 1868, pp. 48–61, who voices severe criticism of the action of the cotton mills, especially of the Lowell concerns. Speaking of the Merrimack Company, which had been started in 1822 by Nathan Appleton, he says: During the war, this concern "showed great 'lack of sagacity and forethought' (*Report of the Committee of the Proprietors*, 1863) — in stopping their mills — in dismissing their employees — in discontinuing the purchase of cotton — and in selling their fabrics at a slight advance on their peace prices, and at less than the actual cost of similar fabrics at the time of sale. . . . Instead of boldly running, as companies elsewhere did, they took counsel of their fears. . . .

"The blunders of this company were naturally copied by others — the younger companies being accustomed to 'dress' on the Merrimack. In this instance, the blunders of the older company were not only copied, but exaggerated and intensified to a fatal degree. The other cotton companies actually sold out their cotton, and several of them made abortive experiments in other branches of manufacture, by which they incurred losses, direct and indirect, exceeding the amount of their entire capital" (p. 48).

See also Webber, *Manual of Power*, p. 64.

[2] Letter from Wanskuck Company; Richardson, *History of Woonsocket*, p. 141; and *Bulletin*, 1891, p. 264.

pose, however, the most important feature was the added productive capacity in the wool manufacture which came about in this manner.

Another factor which induced this marked expansion in number of establishments and in total manufacturing capacity, and one of the most influential, was the high level of profits secured by the preëxisting enterprises. "Profits were enormous," says Fite, and in fact they attained proportions which not only contrasted sharply with the low range during the preceding decade but set a high-water mark, at least until the period of the World War. One manufacturer was reported a few months after the outbreak of the war to have made $200,000; and another was making $2000 a day.[1] The Pontoosuc Manufacturing Company, whose net profits had averaged a little over $20,000 in the ten years 1851–1860, reaped gains of $107,000 in the three years 1863–1865.[2] The stockholders in the Pacific Mills, Lawrence, Massachusetts, who in 1853 had invested $2,500,000 in the concern, drew out in dividends before 1867 — and almost wholly in the war period — $3,000,000; in addition to which a considerable quantity of earnings had been put back into the business, and the treasurer in 1867 had on hand "a very large amount" of undivided profits.[3] A composite schedule of dividend payments from those companies whose records are available shows an increase from approximately an average of 9 per cent, during the eight years preceding the war, to one of 27⅕ per cent in 1865.

To a considerable degree, these returns were in a special meaning "paper" profits, inasmuch as the rise of prices consequent on the issue of the Greenbacks gave special facility to the registering of nominal gains. The price of wool was steadily rising for several years: domestic fleece wool for example increasing from 35–48 cents per pound in April, 1861 to 90–117 cents per pound in August, 1864. The case of Mr. Blackinton, proprietor of the Blackinton Woolen Company, North Adams, Massachusetts, is illustrative of the gains that arose through the appreciation of

[1] *London Economist*, December 14, 1861; quoted in Fite, p. 84.

[2] Records of the Company. Dividends which had averaged $17,400 in the decade of the fifties, reached an average of $88,000 in the three years 1864–1866.

[3] *Report on the Exposition of 1867*, vi, 130.

raw-material values. At about the time when war seemed inevitable, he heard of a big block of wool in central New York State, some 23,000 pounds. He bought it at once, paying 50 cents a pound. Before it was worked up, its value had doubled.[1] "In a majority of instances," said the Special Commissioner of the Revenue in 1869, "the large profits realized by the woolen manufacturers from 1863 to 1866 were due rather to the rise in the price of their raw material than to any legitimate profits derived from the manufacture and sale of their productions."[2] However, whether the source of profits was merely inflated wool prices or not, their realization unquestionably provided a direct stimulus to the enlargement of old plants and to the establishment of new enterprises in this field.

A third important factor, which was instrumental in attracting capital to that field, was the increasing import duties on wool fabrics. The Morrill act of 1861 had made a substantial advance over the tariffs of 1846 and 1857; but the rates were destined to go yet higher. Moreover, the frame-work of the duties carried in the war-time laws is significant as foreshadowing the modern type of duties on wool goods. The decade began with the Morrill act, which imposed a tax of 12 cents a pound plus 25 per cent ad valorem upon all cloths and dress-goods. By 1864 the duty upon goods coming in as "cloths" had been advanced to 24 cents per pound and either 40 or 45 per cent ad valorem, according to the value of the fabric, while for dress-goods a more complicated schedule provided rates running from 4 cents per square yard and 25 per cent ad valorem to 6 cents per square yard and 35 per cent ad valorem. The ad valorem rates were intended as the only true protective duties. The specific rates were conceived as mere compensation to domestic manufacturers for the enhancement in the price of their raw material due to the duties levied on wool. As will appear in the discussion of the Woolens act of 1867, these compensatory duties to be sure carried a substantial amount of incidental or concealed protection. Yet, apart from

[1] Interview with Mr. Archer, who in 1915 had been connected fifty-eight years with the Blackinton Woolen Company.

[2] *Bulletin*, 1870–1871, p. 3.

such protection, the assistance extended by the ad valorem rates alone was obviously much increased during these war years.[1] The action of this rising protection is evident in the course of importations. For example, wool "cloths" which had been brought in to the value of 10.9 million dollars per year during the period 1856–1860 were imported in the next five years to less than half that amount per annum; and imports of blankets showed a similar movement. Even the course of dress-goods importations was affected temporarily. Their value per year fell in the corresponding periods from 14.5 millions to 8.6 millions. An opportunity in the American market was thus offered domestic producers, which they were not slow to take.

The era of abnormally high profits and of increasingly high protection which the war induced had two striking effects, — two effects, it may be remarked, which appeared again during the somewhat similar period of the World War.[2] First, there was a distinct tendency toward the production of fine-quality goods. In the woolen branch, superior beavers, coatings, chinchilla cloakings, and fine French and Scotch cassimeres are spoken of as among the new departments essayed in these years. Opera flannels and flannel suitings whose production was initiated just prior to 1860 secured an appreciable manufacture only during the Civil War era. Similarly the line of finer worsted fabrics — Italian cloths, poplins of worsted and mohair, cashmeres, and the like — was a by-product of the abnormal war conditions. Mr. Erastus B. Bigelow, speaking in 1869, said with some exaggeration, "Ten years ago our manufacturers had attempted scarcely anything beyond common goods of the coarser kinds. Now they produce almost every variety of wool fabric in general use." Of that specially important cloth so largely produced in

[1] A part of this additional "protective" rate was imposed to compensate domestic manufacturers for the 10 per cent excise tax payable on their productions. However, here too was some concealed or incidental protection, since the latter could be paid in the depreciated Greenbacks, while import duties had to be paid in gold.

[2] The results in neither case were clear during the period of conflict itself. The early post-war years should be embraced in the same general intervals, as they revealed in both cases the forces which were striving for assertion during the actual war periods.

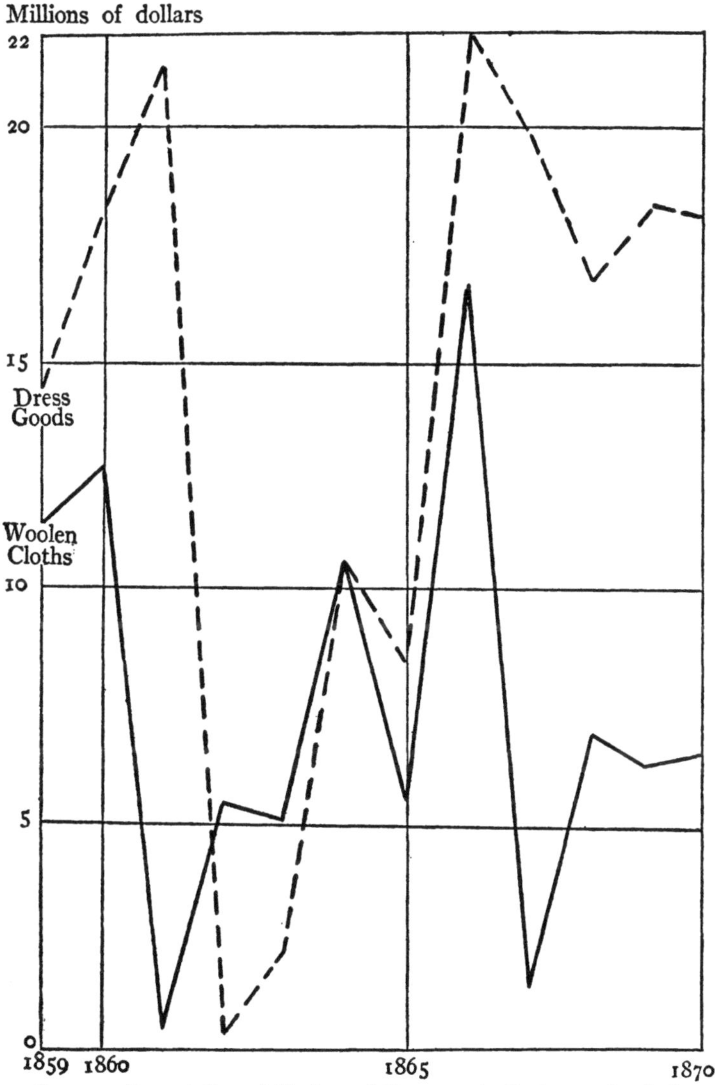

FIG. 11. Importation of Cloths and Dress-goods (in terms of value), 1859–1870.

the United States, cassimere, he stated that "in no market of the world could better cassimeres be found than some of those" turned out in American mills.[1] Again, the report of the House

[1] *Address at the Exhibition of the American Institute in New York*, 1869, pp. 5–6.

Committee on Manufactures asserted in 1870: "The distinctly fine goods (both woolen and worsted) are almost all the growth under the tariffs since 1861." [1] While such a development was perhaps a normal one under the circumstances, it did bequeath a problem to the legislators in the post-war period. In the technical, labor, and market conditions surrounding the wool manufacture of that time, manufacture along such lines was not so well fitted to the American industry as the production of more common fabrics. Domestic producers were likely to seek protection from foreign competitors at least as great as that under which the newer departments of manufacture had developed; and the measure of protection necessary for support of these newer ventures would probably be taken as the minimum for the whole industry.

Again, the abnormal period through which the industry had passed left the manufacture with a substantially overexpanded equipment. The statistics of growth already presented indicate a much more rapid expansion than the increase of population, while the course of importations does not indicate a change in the sharing of the domestic market between American and foreign producers sufficient to take care of the increased domestic capacity. There was, to be sure, some small increase in the size of the domestic market beyond that supplied by the advance of population, derived from the continued encroachment of the factory upon the household system; but on the other hand that market was for a time contracted by the impoverishment of the southern states. Even the northern market was adversely affected by post-war conditions, e. g., by the sale of the government's surplus army supplies. The quartermaster of the army, it is reported,

[1] *Bulletin*, 1870, p. 145.

Another interesting and perhaps inevitable development during the peculiar period of the war was the decline in efficiency of production, — a phenomenon remarked in England and the United States during the years of the World War. In 1867 it was noted as regards the United States that "during the war, the standard of excellence in our goods was undoubtedly far too low, and discredit was thrown upon our national production." This was, however, only a temporary condition, remedied by the forces of keener competition in the subsequent years. See Hayes and Mudge, *Report on the Exposition of 1867*, vi, 22; North, in *Bulletin*, 1895, p. 42.

disposed of "an immense amount of military clothing," including over 2 million overcoats, nearly a million blankets, and more than 2½ million articles of clothing. Horace Greeley wore the uniform of blue cloth and brass buttons for many years thereafter; and the old army overcoats became the customary garb of city cabmen. Even today an overcoat of similar design is still to be seen upon the fast-disappearing race of cabmen in some sections of the country.[1] At least, it is sure that no enlargement in the domestic consuming power for new goods had occurred which would accommodate the marked enhancement of productive facilities. Bigelow put the case briefly in an address delivered in 1869: having noted the war-time scarcity of cotton and the effects of the military demand, he found the effect was "greatly to stimulate the growing and manufacturing of wool. . . . The wool-manufacturing ability of this country was increased with a rapidity and to an extent wholly unknown before. Cotton mills were converted into woolen mills, and new establishments sprang up as if by magic in many parts of the United States. And now we behold the natural — I think I may say the inevitable — result, namely, the amount of production which is largely ahead of the demand. Though the machinery in operation was no more than the imperative needs of the war required, it far exceeds the normal demand in time of peace." [2] Indeed, in that year a depression in the wool manufacture occurred which was attributed to overproduction within the industry.[3] Nor, apparently, was readjustment attained in all lines for a considerable period. Overproduction in the blanket section of the industry, caused by the war-time entry of many small producers

[1] On amount of clothing sold, see Stanwood, *American Tariff Controversies*, ii, 169.

[2] Bigelow, E. B., *Address at the Exhibition of the American Institute at New York*, pp. 10–12. See also *Bulletin*, 1869, p. 293. North (*Bulletin*, 1895, p. 44) says that "for several years (after the war) the wool manufacture suffered the usual consequences of over-production," though in his opinion less seriously than after the War of 1812, both because the country grew rapidly and because the tariff checked imports.

[3] *Bulletin*, 1870, p. 24. Here it is stated: "We have authority for the assertion that in eight years our production of woolen manufactures has increased 150 per cent, while our population has advanced only 30 per cent."

upon that manufacture and by their continued operation subsequently, is said to have led to a "glut" in the market and to a large auction sale in New York City as late as 1878.[1]

The influence of these two war-time developments in the wool manufacture was manifested in several ways. We may note first the diminution of profits which oppressed the industry for a number of years. The Pontoosuc Manufacturing Company which had enjoyed a profit of $225,000 in 1865 found its net earnings reduced the succeeding year to $13,000, while in 1867 and 1868 the balance sheet indicated losses averaging over $5,000 each year.[2] The Arlington Mills after a series of prosperous war years underwent a reorganization in 1869.[3] Five relatively large and strong companies were compelled to decrease their dividend payments on the average by half from the high level of 1864–1866, and probably these were in part paid out of the war profits. It is likely, too, that the general run of concerns through the country suffered much more severe reverses. Furthermore, the reaction after the war went to strengthen the forces of concentration and localization within the industry, as will appear in consideration of the subsequent period; while seemingly it also went to stimulate the introduction of improved technical equipment, some of which was already known in the manufacture, e. g., the Knowles and Crompton looms.[4] Finally, the situation engendered "the natural — I think I may say the inevitable — result," a demand for higher protection. Probably the whole manufacturing industry was interested and involved in greater or less degree as a consequence of general overproduction; and surely the recently acquired portions of the manufacture, as I have already suggested, were particularly concerned, because of their special weaknesses. A "National Association of Wool Manufacturers" had been organized in 1864. By its initiative a convention of wool growers and wool manufacturers was held at Syracuse, New York, in December, 1865, "for the

[1] *Bulletin*, 1881, p. 386. See also auction of flannels, Hayes, *Awards and Claims at the International Exhibition of 1876*, p. 338.

[2] Records of the Company.

[3] *The Arlington Mills: An Historical and Descriptive Sketch*, 1891, p. 35.

[4] See above, pp. 307–309, 313–314, 363–365.

purpose of consultation in relation to their mutual interests, especially as to the representations to be given respecting the wool-producing and wool-manufacturing interests before the United States Tariff and Revenue Commission."[1] Little or nothing was said at that time regarding the condition of the manufacturing industry, but when in the spring of 1867 the project of a general tariff revision was lost, complaint of the "depressed condition" in the manufacture was frequent. The worsted branch was alleged to be "prostrated," because the Canadian reciprocity treaty had been allowed to run out (thereby closing the door to the free entry of combing wools), and yet nothing else had been done for the new industry.[2] As to the wool manufacture generally, it was stated that "many small mills have stopped running," and that "the larger ones have been run on as short time as they could be without breaking-up, scattering, and driving into other pursuits that skilled operative labor which will be necessary when they can find remunerative markets."[3] As a result of such argument and of the persistent representation of their needs by the delegates of the two interests, a special act was formulated and passed, the Wool and Woolens act of 1867. The only manufacture which took precedence over that of wool was the production of cigars and tobacco, increased rates upon these articles having been granted by Congress in the summer of 1866. Referring to the special consideration given these two manufactures, tobacco and wool, Mr. Hayes, secretary of the new National Association of Wool Manufacturers, in 1867 made the striking comment: "The outposts of protection have been won by provision for the most suffering industries."[4] Indeed, as far as wool is concerned the act of 1867 marks the definite extension of wool and wool-fabric protection to new areas. It consolidated the rising level of rates secured during the Civil War

[1] See the letter calling the convention: *Report of the Proceedings of the Convention*, p. 6.

[2] *Third Annual Report of the National Association of Wool Manufacturers*, 1867, p. 15.

[3] *Ibid.*, p. 23; quoting from an article by Mr. Henry S. Randall in the *Rural New-Yorker*, an agricultural paper.

[4] *Ibid.*, p. 14.

period. More than that, it denotes the beginning of a new era in the wool manufacture, a new basis of international relations, since reductions in subsequent tariffs from the level attained in 1867 have been but temporary and partial. We have never returned to the relatively low tariff duties which characterized the period before the Civil War. In short, this heritage of the war forms a turning point in the history of the American wool manufacture. On the side of tariff policy, as in character of production, geographical distribution, or other features connected with the wool-manufacturing industry, the decades after 1870 form a distinct period.

CHAPTER XXI

CONCLUSION — THE INDUSTRY IN 1870

THE foregoing discussion has traced the development of the American wool manufacture during the period 1830–1870 in various aspects. To some extent the argument in the several chapters has perforce been individually distinct, despite efforts to tie the story together. Accordingly, there is reason to pause before entering upon an analysis of the more recent decades, in order to survey the advances which were made in the forty-year period before 1870, and to ascertain more generally the real situation in the latter year. In what chief features did the American wool manufacture of 1870 differ from that of 1830, and what were the tendencies of the development?

As the title of this Part suggests, the factory, in my opinion, had reached maturity by 1870. As an industrial form, the wool factory in 1830 had been a new phenomenon, and in many ways had showed this status. Frequently the new-sprung mills had relied upon outside aid of various sorts to help sustain their positions. If they did not commonly employ labor outside their walls, they often supplemented their own manufacture by taking in carding, spinning, and other work from quasi-household producers. Nor were cases rare in which the mills depended largely upon the strictly local markets, sometimes even exchanging finished cloth for wool or other supplies. Now by 1870 this situation had changed. For a large and growing section of the industry — that is, barring the western mills — establishments were as self-dependent as they are today. The transformation of dirty and greasy wool into finished fabrics was carried through wholly inside the factory walls; and the disposal of the production was achieved through a broad and well-organized marketing system.

The factory had also gained a very considerable improvement in manufacturing technique. Except for the apparatus of the spinning process, the machinery and methods had become extraordinarily like those of the present time. Advance in scouring and in weaving was perhaps most striking in this period. In the one case, hand work with crude and inaccurate methods was being replaced by practices and apparatus which allowed for more satisfactory and quasi-automatic treatment of the raw wool. In the case of weaving, the period opened with the plain loom alone in operation, — and a slow and confining mechanism it was. A very limited range of weave-designs was possible; and its speed would today be considered a snail's pace. By 1870 the industry possessed several notable types of apparatus, — looms equipped with closed-shed and open-shed warp control, with drop boxes, and the like, — and this apparatus could be driven at particularly increased rapidity.

Such improvements not only made for more effective domestic manufacture, but they tended toward production on a larger unit scale of operations. Even before the Civil War this movement toward larger scale of operation had begun; and one could say — having in mind a certain range of establishments in the East — that "the largest textile factories in America before 1860 made woolen goods."[1] The existence of many small woolen concerns in the West and South, as well as some small mills scattered in the East, would prevent the conclusion that woolen mills in 1860 generally were large affairs. But some establishments, such as that of the Middlesex Mills, were leading the way; and the course seemed set for the further growth of similar plants in the eastern regions, with the gradual undercutting and elimination of the country's small concerns. Increased concentration of the trade in raw wool, development of subsidiary industries, greater attention to medium qualities of manufacture, and improved systems of cloth distribution, — these all tended to stimulate the movement toward large-scale enterprise.

But if the self-dependence of the mill operation, the improvements in technique, and the development of production by certain concerns to a substantially large-scale basis spelled a real maturity in the producing factory, the industry itself was still

[1] Clark, p. 453.

showing signs of the gauchy youth. It lacked much of the maturity and stability which one may find in it at the present time. Assuredly, the rapid disappearance of the household manufacture and diversification in type of production which came about in the decades between 1830 and 1870 were important steps in this direction. So also were the moderate development of the wholesale clothing industry and the full bloom of the "regular" cloth-distributing system. But the end was still far off.

As yet the industry was scattered widely through the country, local conditions of water power and the like impeding the tendency toward concentration within a particular area. Again, the representative establishment was still an affair of moderate size, at least as compared with more modern standards; and it was still chiefly an isolated concern, — except in so far as common connection with other establishments through a common selling agency gave such an establishment membership in a larger group of producers. No tendency toward combination or consolidation obtained in appreciable degree. Furthermore, the character of the labor force in the industry was in process of change. Immigrant help was increasing in proportion, but the conditions of recent years were still unknown. The old situation with a working force virtually complete of native Americans was gone; but the situation with such a force made up largely and consistently of foreign workmen had not yet appeared. Finally the character of the industry's output was by no means fully modernized. Some diversification of factory production, to be sure, had occurred, but in various respects maturity was lacking. For instance, a part of the newer manufacture — that of worsted fabrics — had not as yet become well rooted. Here the real multiplication in type of production had not come by 1870; the industry was still too widely scattered; and it was carried on in too small establishments. Again, neither in the woolen nor worsted manufactures had any notable standardization of products arisen, — barring perhaps standardization in the flannel and blanket ends of the industry. Yet standardization of production is one of the chief features of the modern manufacture. The expansion of the wholesale clothing industry had been a development which before 1870 had exerted a stimulus in this direction; but by that date the wholesale manufacture of men's clothing was in no such position as today, and work in the production of women's wool garments had hardly begun.

In closing, we may note that some of the features met with in the study of conditions around 1870 were the result of peculiar circumstances affecting that year or the years immediately preceding. For example, there was an excessive manufacturing capacity in the industry and a particularly high quality of output, resulting from the abnormal war situation. And closely tied with this consideration are the tariff position and the existing trend of importations. The tariff had lately been fixed at a level that was distinctly elevated compared with any legislation which had preceded it, and especially compared with the laws enforced in the latter forties and the fifties. This new height was the effect partly of the war conditions and partly of the circumstances in the industry which were themselves due to the war. On the other hand, the import movement was entering upon a new phase. The entrance of foreign cloths had been notably great in the period of the fifties, both in absolute volume and in terms of consumption per capita; but the rise of importation in the later sixties, particularly with respect to dress-goods, had been a new movement, and by 1870 the top was reached. One awaited intimation as to the exact course that importations, affected in greater or less degree by the height of the tariff wall, would take in the subsequent decades.

The period 1830–1870 was an era of real growth, — a growth perhaps not so striking as in the decades before or afterwards, yet very substantial. In view of certain difficulties which hedged the industry about through part or the whole of this period, — lack of standardized output, tariff conditions, and the like, — the advance is all the more significant of the industry's vigor.

Bei Fragen zur Produktsicherheit wenden Sie sich bitte an:
If you have any questions regarding product safety,
please contact:

Walter de Gruyter GmbH
Genthiner Straße 13
10785 Berlin
productsafety@degruyterbrill.com